THE SCHOOL
OF
ST. MATTHEW

KRISTER STENDAHL

THE SCHOOL

OF

ST. MATTHEW

AND ITS USE OF THE OLD TESTAMENT

With a New Introduction
by the Author

FORTRESS PRESS · PHILADELPHIA

First published in 1954 as Volume XX of
Acta Seminarii Neotestamentici Upsaliensis
by C.W.K. Gleerup, Lund, and Ejnar Munksgaard, Copenhagen.

First American Edition © 1968 by Fortress Press.

Library of Congress Catalog Card Number 68-19899.

Printed in Denmark
by Villadsen & Christensen,
Copenhagen

Preface to Second Edition

It is with rather mixed feelings that I write this Preface to a second printing of The School of Matthew. The book has been out of print for some time, and I think that it has served as a useful tool for the complex and significant study of Old Testament quotations in the synoptic tradition and particularly in the Matthean gospel. For that reason, a re-print seems justified. But there is cause for some hesitation — and consequently for some caution in the use in the late 60's of this study from the early 50's. Any writer gets second thoughts which call for revision. Some of these come from the reading of his careful and perceptive critics,[1] some from further work of his own and some from the availability of new data and texts.

In spite of the title with its reference to a School and of the introductory chapter with its discussion about the creative milieu (Sitz im Leben) of the gospel, it must be stressed at this point that the primary justification for this study was — and is even more now — its analysis of the O. T. text in the gospel.

The original study grew out of the happy circumstance that I became involved at an early stage in the study of the Qumran texts. Since those early years much has happened which drastically changes our image of both the Hebrew and Greek Old Testament texts.[2] There is little doubt that many of my notations and some of my evaluations concerning the readings available in New Testament times will need revision. On the other hand, such revisions should await further publications, especially of the biblical material from Qumran Cave IV, but also of careful monographs on the text of the pertinent books, i.e. those most quoted in the New Testament.

---

[1] For a list of reviews, see below, p. xv. Special attention should be drawn to that by B. Gärtner, *Studia Theol.* 8 (1954), 1–24, which constituted his critique of my dissertation at its public defense at Uppsala University, May 1954.

[2] Note also the comprehensive article by J. W. Wevers, Septuaginta-Forschungen, *Theol. Rundsch.* 22 (1954), 85–138, and 171–90.

For these reasons I have decided to leave my study from 1954 in its dated form, and furnish it with some references to areas which call for special further attention. Without such a supplement this reprint will not foster the study which it set out to encourage.

It so happened that the first more extensive biblical manuscript from Qumran to be published was the complete Isaiah scroll from Cave I (1QIs^a). This text appeared to be a stunning witness to the antiquity and stability of the proto-Massoretic textual tradition.[1] I must confess that this fact influenced me in the direction of more confidence in the M. T. than now can be defended.[2] The work by BARTHÉLEMY,[3] and especially by my colleague FRANK M. CROSS, JR. has re-opened the textual question both as to the Hebrew and the Greek Old Testament, and there is little doubt that the manuscript evidence points to "a series of attempts to bring the Greek Bible into conformity with a *changing* Hebrew textual tradition".[4]

---

[1] The agreement with the M.T. is even more striking in 1QIs^b, see, e.g., B. J. ROBERTS, The Second Isaiah Scroll from Qumran (1QIs^b), *Bull. of J. Ryl. Libr.* 42 (1959), 132–44. The fragments of this Isaiah scroll contain perhaps not more than one variant of major significance. In 53₁₁ it agrees with 1QIs^a (and the LXX) in reading "he shall see *light*".

[2] On closer scrutiny 1QIs^a contains substantial and significant variants. J. ZIEGLER, Die Vorlage der Isaias-Septuaginta (LXX) und die erste Isaias-Rolle von Qumran, *Journ. of Bibl. Lit.* 78 (1959), 34–59. Some corrections of the text published by M. BURROWS (1950), see M. H. GOSHEN-GOTTSTEIN, *The Book of Isaiah* (Jerusalem, 1965), p. 34. For the later discussion, see E. Y. KUTSCHER, *The Language and Linguistic Background of the Isaiah Scroll* [Hebrew] (1959) and W. H. BROWNLEE, *The Meaning of the Qumran Scrolls for the Bible, With Special Attention to the Book of Isaiah* (1964). See also F. M. CROSS, JR., *The Ancient Library of Qumran* (1961²), 177 f., and the literature there listed. SH. TALMON, Aspects of the Textual Transmission of the Bible in the Light of Qumran Manuscripts, *Textus* IV (1964), 95–132, demonstrates his thesis greatly on the basis of 1QIs^a. For 1QIs^a and the N.T., see also J. DE WAARD, *A Comparative Study* ... (below, p. iii, note 2), pp. 6–13, especially the reading השם for M.T. השמן in Isa. 6₁₀ (see below, p. 130), and וקרא for M.T. וקראת in Isa. 7₁₄ (see below, p. 98).

[3] In addition to his article in *Rev. Bibl.* (1953; see below, p. 177), which I depended on in 1954, see now especially his work pertaining to the *kaige* recension, *Les devanciers d'Aquila.* Première publication intégrale du texte des fragments du 'Dodécaprophéton' trouvés dans le désert de Juda, précédée d'une étude sur les traductions et recensions grecques de la Bible réalisées au premier siècle de notre ère sous l'influence du rabbinat palestinien (Suppl. to Vetus Test. 10; 1963). See also the detailed review by R. A. KRAFT, *Gnomon* 37 (1965), 474–83.

[4] F. M. CROSS, JR., The History of the Biblical Text in the Light of Dis-

The results of Barthélemy and Cross do, however, give us less direct help than we could expect, since we have no firm textual basis for similar precision in the textual studies of those O.T. books which are most quoted in the N.T. or especially in the Matthean gospel. Thus we must await either further finds, or such an advanced stage of these studies as to allow us to project the results into books like Isaiah and Psalms and those parts of the Minor Prophets as are not extant in the find from the Cave of Horror.[1]

In any case, it is now clear that little progress can be made in this area until the reference to the readings in the Greek O.T. are more carefully assessed as to text types and Vorlage. Atomistic references to variant manuscripts do not help.[2] It will be impossible to proceed without more synthetic hypotheses concerning the O.T. text. Hebrew and Greek, as well as Syriac and Latin evidence, and references to Aramaic Targums[3] must become controlled by such hypotheses.

The same applies no doubt to the discussion about possible *testimonia* collections, their role and nature in Judaism and Christianity. I have argued that such collections do not solve the problem of the formula quotations in Matthew. For that reason, the find of actual *testimonia* and *florilegia* at Qumran[4] does not necessarily alter the data

coveries in the Judaean Desert, *Harv. Theol. Rev.* 57 (1964), 283; see also IDEM, The Contribution of the Qumran Discoveries to the Study of the Biblical Text, *Israel Exploration Journ.* 16 (1966), 81–95.

[1] The text to the Minor Prophets, partially published by BARTHÉLEMY in 1953 (see p. ii, note 3), has now been identified as coming from the so-called Cave of Horror in the Naḥal Ḥever, see B. LIFSHITZ, The Greek Documents from the Cave of Horror, *Israel Exploration Journ.* 12 (1962), 201–07, with additional fragments from the same scroll.

[2] On the whole, this limitation — to which I plead guilty in this study — still plagues the otherwise careful and significant study by J. DE WAARD, *A Comparative Study of the Old Testament Text in the Dead Sea Scrolls and in the New Testament.* (Studies on the Texts of the Desert of Judah 4; 1965).

[3] A. SPERBER's edition of Onkelos and Jonathan is now available, *The Bible in Aramaic*, vols. 1–3 (Leiden, Brill, 1959–62). On the Targum Neofiti, identified in the Vatican Library in 1956, see now M. MCNAMARA, *The New Testament and the Palestinian Targum to the Pentateuch* (1966), and IDEM, Targumic Studies, *Cathol. Bibl. Quart.* 28 (1966), 1–19. See also G. VERMES, *Scripture and Tradition in Judaism* (Studia Post-Biblica 4; 1961).

[4] See J. M. ALLEGRO, Further Messianic References in Qumran Literature, *Journ. of Bibl. Lit.* 75 (1956), 182–87 (4Q test.) and IDEM, Fragments of a Qumran Scroll of Eschatological Midrashim, *ibid.*, 77 (1958), 350–54 (4Q flor.). For a good assessment of how these texts bear on my arguments, see J. A. FITZMYER, 4Q Testimonia and the New Testament, *Theol. St.* 18 (1957), 513–37; cf. also IDEM, The Use of Explicit O.T. Quotations in Qumran Literature and in

as here presented. The question still remains rather one of analysis as to the relationship between these Matthean quotations and their context.[1]

While I took some notice of O.T. quotations in the extra-canonical literature of Early Christianity, it is obvious to me now, that closer attention must be paid to it. Much good work has been done in this area during the last decades.[2]

Such material is of the more significance since it has become increasingly clear that traditional material reached into the second century in forms independent from the one represented by what is preserved as the canonical books of the New Testament.[3] Thus the present state of O.T. textual criticism is one of greater flux than I surmised in this study. New data are about to allow new and better founded hypotheses about text forms available in the first century A.D. Such a promising yet unfinished state of affairs both hinders and helps further progress in the study of the Matthean quotations. It makes it more probable that readings found in Matthew could witness to text forms actually available in Greek, prior to Matthew. It makes the recourse to testimonies less compelling as an explanation of textual peculiarities. It strengthens the suggestion that Hebrew texts continued to cause revision of Greek texts. And we are increasingly informed that the O.T. text — Greek and Hebrew — was not yet standardized. In manuscripts like 1QIs[a] we have examples of alternative readings given in the manuscript itself. When such and similar alternatives appear as the basis for later midrashic exegesis, we can be rea-

---

the New Testament, *N.T. St.* 7 (1960/61), 297–333, and Further light on Melchizedek from Qumran Cave 11, *Journ. of Bibl. Lit.* 86 (1967), 25–41.

[1] For further discussion, see below, p. vii.

[2] See, e.g., P. PRIGENT, *Les Testimonia dans le christianisme primitif: L'Épitre de Barnabé i-xii et ses sources* (1961); R. A. KRAFT, *The Apostolic Fathers, vol. 3: Barnabas and the Didache* (1965), cf. IDEM, *Journ. Theol. St.* 13 (1962), 318–20, 401–08, *Journ. of Bibl. St.* 80 (1961), 371–73, 81 (1962), 316 f.; J. P. AUDET, L'hypothèse des testimonia, *Rev. Bibl.* 70 (1963), 381–405. J. S. SIBINGA, *The Old Testament Text of Justin Martyr, vol. 1: The Pentateuch* (1963), cf. KRAFT, *Gnomon* 36 (1964), 572–77.

[3] See H. KOESTER, *Synoptische Überlieferung bei den apostolischen Vätern* (1957), and now demonstrated also in the texts from Nag-Hamadi, cf. KOESTER's blueprint of the History of Early Christianity in the light of such data, GNOMAI DIAPHOROI: The Origin and Nature of Diversification in the History of Early Christianity, *Harv. Theol. Rev.* 58 (1965), 279–318. See also A. J. BELLINZONI, *The Sayings of Jesus in the Writings of Justin Martyr* (Suppl. to Nov. Test. 17; 1967).

sonably sure that they have often existed as actual readings — actual texts.[1]

Much work has been done on the biblical exegesis as carried on at Qumran, a field so wide that, in addition to studies already mentioned, reference can only be made to a few.[2] Especially in this area I must resort to refer to the standard bibliographies for Qumran studies.[3]

The broader spectrum of the Jewish use and interpretation of Scripture in relation to New Testament studies has also received substantial attention. Simultaneously with my own work there appeared a careful study of the possibilities and limitations of the rabbinic material to be used for such purposes.[4] Three years later a Swedish scholar published a similar study, in which also the Qumran material was taken into account.[5]

A good study of Paul's O.T. quotations with attention to the Qumran material is available,[6] and in his study of the Johannine quotations, E. D. FREED argues carefully in favor of ἡ γραφή as sometimes referring to synoptic or intra-Johannine sayings.[7]

The relation between Philo and Hebrews was studied[8] as well as the Psalm quotations in that letter.[9] A Dutch four-volume work

---

[1] See SH. TALMON, *Aspects* ..., p. 125–32.

[2] O. BETZ, *Offenbarung und Schriftforschung in der Qumransekte* (Wiss. Untersuch. z. N.T. 6; 1960), and F. F. BRUCE, *Biblical Exegesis in the Qumran Texts* (1960).

[3] CHR. BURCHARD, *Bibliographie zu den Handschriften vom Toten Meer*, (Beihefte 76 und 89 zur Zeitschr. f.d. alttest. Wiss., 1957 und 1965). Note especially the Index of Biblical Texts, etc. in vol. 89, pp. 321–59. M. YIZHAR, *Bibliography of Hebrew Publications on the Dead Sea Scrolls, 1948–1964* (Harv. Theol. St. 23; 1967); and the continuous bibliography in *Rev. de Qumran* (1958–). For a survey and evaluations organized by N.T. passages, see the review articles by H. BRAUN, *Theol. Rundsch.* 28 (1962), 97–234; 29 (1963), 142–76, 189–260; 30 (1964) 1–38, 89–137. Also published in book form, *Qumran und das Neue Testament*, vol. 1 (1966); vol. 2 (1966) covers the material topically.

[4] J. W. DOEVE, *Jewish Hermeneutics in the Synoptic Gospels and Acts* (1954).

[5] ERIC STARFELT, *Studier i rabbinsk och nytestamentlig skrifttolkning.* (Studia Theologica Lundensia 17; 1959); with an English Summary, pp. 260–88. N.T. texts studied in detail are: Acts 1₁₆–₂₀, 2₁₇–₂₁, 2₂₅–₂₈, 3₂₂ f. and 13₃₄ f.

[6] E. E. ELLIS, *Paul's Use of the Old Testament* (1957).

[7] *Old Testament Quotations in the Gospel of John* (Suppl. to Nov. Test. 11; 1965). The passages are 7₄₂, 20₉ and 17₁₂, pp. 51–59, and 97.

[8] S. G. SOWERS, *The Hermeneutics of Philo and Hebrews* (Basel Studies of Theology 1; 1965).

[9] S. KISTEMAKER, *The Psalm Citations in the Epistle to the Hebrews* (1961).

(with a French summary to each volume) covers the whole N.T. as to both explicit and implicit O.T. quotations.[1] A new exchange about whether quotations imply the context from which they are taken occurred.[2] For Matthew I note in addition to what follows three articles of interest.[3]

Finally, attention should be drawn to a recent study in which the study of O. T. quotations is utilized for tracing the development of early theologies. BARNABAS LINDARS[4] achieves this by observing shifts of application as well as modification of texts. While the method is not new, the broad front on which he moves proves the significance of the approach. More recently NORMAN PERRIN has put this method to work at a crucial point in his analysis of the Son of Man christology as he studies how Ps. 110 and Dan. 713 were combined.[5]

But we must now return to the primary concern for any study of O.T. quotations, i.e., the assessment of the available textual evidence, and how it affects our views of the Matthean formula quotations. It is clear that a wider variety — actually demonstrated and reasonably projected — minimizes to some extent the degree the textual creativity which this study assigns to "the School of St. Matthew". Nevertheless, the Matthean formula quotations stand out as peculiar in their text form, and this fact calls for an explanation. GEORG STRECKER has built up a case[6] for considering the formula quotations as constituting a distinct source which Matthew has made use of, "a collection of prophecies, which had reached Mt. in written form" (p. 83). In addition to Mk. and Q, this is, according to Strecker, the only written source which can be defined; other material comes primarily from oral tradition (p. 13 f.).

---

[1] C. SMITS, *Oud-testamentische Citaten in het Nieuwe Testament*, vols. 1–4 (1952–63).

[2] S. L. EDGAR, Respect for Context in Quotations from the Old Testament, *N. T. St.* 9 (1962/63), 55–62, and the answer by R. T. MEAD, *ibid.*, 10 (1963/64), 279–89. Cf. C. H. DODD, *According to the Scriptures* (1952).

[3] A. BAUMSTARK, Die Zitate des Matthäusevangeliums aus dem Zwölfprophetenbuch, *Biblica* 37 (1956), 296–313; J. J. O'ROURKE, The Fulfilment Texts in Matthew, *Cath. Bibl. Qu.* 24 (1962), 394–403; and CH. DE BEUS, Een onderzoek naar formulecitaten bij Mattheus met het oog op het vroegste christologische Denken volgens het N. Testament, *Nederl. Theol. Tijdschr.* 14 (1959/60), 401–19.

[4] *New Testament Apologetic. The Doctrinal Significance of the Old Testament* (1961).

[5] *Rediscovering the Teaching of Jesus* (1967), 172–85.

[6] G. STRECKER, *Der Weg der Gerechtigkeit. Untersuchung zur Theologie des Matthäus.* (Forsch. z. Rel. u. Lit. des A. u. N.T. 82; 1962), 49–85.

Strecker stresses the lack of organic relation between quotations and context, (e.g. 13₃₅) and argues that the quotations like those in 4₁₅–₁₆, 2₁₅ and 279 f. have influenced the context rather than the other way around.

The question raised by Strecker at this point is of great significance for the way in which the formula quotations can be used as a means to determine the nature and origin of the Matthean gospel. I argued — more tentatively than most of my critics seem to recognize — that these very quotations could constitute a key to that question. According to Strecker the formula quotations cannot give us information as to the creative milieu of the gospel as a whole. To that matter we shall return. First, let us limit our discussion to the quotations themselves. It does not strike me as strange that these quotations show a certain tension with the context at the points where they are added to the Markan material. Outside of Mt. 1–2 all formula quotations are triggered by the Markan material (for Mt. 279–10, see Mt. 2615/Mk. 1411). In their application they sometimes cause some adjustment of the context, as would be expected. This could be the case also in 211–9, although I still am inclined to think that Mt. is familiar with the two animals (implied in Mk. 112) and thus applies his quotation and changes the context accordingly (see below, pp. 119 and 200). Strecker is certainly right in pointing out that the quotation in 1218–21 is "oversized" for the point it makes in the Matthean context (Strecker, pp. 69, 83). It is, however, not triggered by the request for silence as such, but by the very phrase "that they were not to make him φανερόν". I have not argued that this passage — or any of the other passages in question — had never been used by a Christian prior to Matthew. The question is rather whether the actual text-form here to be found can be seen as shaped and tailored to fit the context. In that respect I still find the ἐν πλατείαις striking, even if it does occur elsewhere in the LXX (Strecker, p. 69, see below, pp. 113 and 204). To 13₃₅, I would note that the place of this quotation is less strange if it is seen as a transition to the interpretation which follows in 13₃₆–₄₃. Thus there is not only the Stichwort παραβολαί in 13₃₄–₃₅ (so Strecker, p. 71), but also the possibility of understanding ἐρεύξομαι as pointing to the interpretation for the insiders, which follows; cf. the similar function of a Q saying in Mt. 1316–17 prior to the interpretation of the parable about the Sower.

Of more importance, however, is the interplay between quotations and context in Mt. 2. The quotations in this chapter are all related to geographical names and they function within the argument of Mt. 2,

an argument which is intended to explain how the one born in Bethlehem was known as coming from Nazareth in Galilee.[1] But the traditions which Matthew draws upon in this chapter have clearly had
quite different foci. Apart from the independent story about the Magi,
the material seems to be held together by a concern with Herod.[2]
Such observations do, however, not strengthen the case for these
quotations as taken from a written source. On the contrary, once we
ask the question about Matthew's editorial activity we note that these
quotations are the very means by which Matthew transforms otherwise
oriented material into his apologetic argument. Especially "the prophetic alibi" with its striking and somewhat farfetched reference to
Rama (rather than "in the highest") is hard indeed to imagine as
meaningful outside of the precise function which it now has in Mt 2.

Thus I find it difficult to separate the author of Mt. 2 and the
originator of the formula quotations in that chapter (i.e. 4 out of the
11 formula quotations in Matthew), and I would extend these observations to Mt. 1₂₃ and to the Matthean introduction to the Galilean
ministry, which again is anxious to tie the Galilean ministry to the
Scriptures (4₁₅–₁₆). Thus 6 of the 11 formula quotations are integral
to a specific type of presenting the gospel material, and that in a
fashion which sets the tone of the gospel.[3] On any analysis, one should
rather ask why there are so relatively few of these quotations, once
this stage has been set. It should also be noted that the most elaborate
of these occur where Mt. has the slightest base in the Markan material,

---

[1] See STENDAHL, Quis et Unde? An Analysis of Mt. 1–2, in *Festschr. Joach.
Jeremias* (Beih. 26 zur Zeitschr. f.d. neutest. Wiss. [1960]), 94–105, esp. p. 97.

[2] In addition to the suggestions made by STRECKER, *op. cit.*, p. 51–63, see
also D. DAUBE, The Earliest Structure of the Gospels, *N.T. St.* 5 (1958/59),
184–86, with its reference to the role of Laban the Idumean in the Passover
Haggada; cf. IDEM, *The New Testament and Rabbinic Judaism* (1956), 189 ff.
See also my *Quis et Unde*, p. 99.

[3] My answer to P. NEPPER-CHRISTENSEN, *Das Matthäusevangelium: Ein
judenchristliches Evangelium?* (1958) applies also to Strecker's critique, see my
Quis et Unde, p. 104, note 44. Observe also the absence of the Star-quotation,
Num 24₁₇. Its absence is strange indeed if the point was to show just "eine
Historie die unter der alttestamentlichen Weissagung steht, eine 'erfüllte',
'heilige' Vergangenheit" (STRECKER, p. 63). The tendency to bring Mt. 1–2 and
Lk. 1–2 too close to one another is part of Strecker's larger hypothesis concerning Mt.'s understanding of history. See now also his article, Das Geschichts-
verständnis des Matthäus, *Evang. Theol.* 26 (1966), 57–74. R. HUMMEL, *Die
Auseinandersetzung zwischen Kirche und Judentum im Matthäusevangelium*
(1966), asks the valid question: "An die Strecker'sche Matthäusdeutung ist
die Frage zu stellen, ob sie Matthäus nicht lukanisch interpretiert" (p. 168).

i.e. in the Judas pericope. Here again the interest is not really in the *life* of Jesus, but in the answer to the question of how such an act like Judas' could be according to the will of God. Thus the formula quotations seem to grow best where Mark was supplemented rather than edited. This would, again, point to a closer tie between these quotations and the properly Matthean stage of production.

Once this has been said, I would like to stress the proper limitation of my intentions when I spoke of a "School of St. Matthew," a limitation in two directions.

The type of scriptural activity here described, and the degree of education here presupposed applies to the Matthean church, or to a few of its officers. I find it increasingly difficult to project such phenomena back into the ministry of Jesus, along the lines argued by RIESENFELD[1] and, with more caution, by GERHARDSSON.[2] Here both Jesus[3] and his early followers are placed in a setting similar to that of the Rabbinic schools. "The traditionist/teacher passed on the tractate, passage or saying to his pupil or pupils by means of continued repetition; he taught the pupil to repeat it, after which he gave the required interpretation. We catch glimpses in the synoptic material — particularly in Matt., 'the rabbinic Gospel' [note: See Stendahl, The School.] — of certain teaching situations which are worthy of our attention in this context, since they certainly reflect teaching practice in the church in which the tradition in question was formed."[4]

Apart from the anachronistic element in applying the rather developed methods of transmission in post 70 Judaism to Jesus and his disciples,[5] there are serious questions whether this "Matthean" view of Jesus can be equated with the historical Jesus. Matthew achieves his picture of Jesus the Teacher by his editorial arrangement of the fa-

---

[1] H. RIESENFELD, *The Gospel Tradition and Its Beginnings* (1957), also in *Studia Evangelica* (Texte und Untersuchungen 73; 1959), pp. 43–65.

[2] B. GERHARDSSON, *Memory and Manuscript* (1961), cf. IDEM, *Tradition and Transmission in Early Christianity* (Coniectanea Neotestamentica 20; 1964) in which he answers a series of critics and criticisms.

[3] GERHARDSSON, *Memory*, p. 334: "Jesus' teaching methods were certainly imitated by his disciples. It ought therefore to be possible on the basis of the practice of these disciples, to draw certain conclusions as to the methods applied by their Master."

[4] *ibid.*

[5] See M. SMITH, A Comparison of Early Christianity and Early Rabbinic Tradition, *Journ. of Bibl. Lit.* 82 (1963), pp. 169–76; and GERHARDSSON's answer in *Tradition and Transmission*, p. 13–16.

mous five discourses, partly by the use of Q-material.[1] His concern for all that Jesus had commanded (28₂₀) is peculiar to him.[2] When GERHARDSSON, in the passage just quoted, makes my "School" a datum in favor of his theory, I must confess that I played carelessly with that idea in one passage in this book (see below, p. 34). But it should be remembered that the kind of scriptural interpretation I detected in the formula quotations, and which caused me to speak of the School of St. Matthew, is of a kind not found in the teachings of Jesus, nor placed in his mouth. This, together with the structure of the gospel, gave me some reason to speak of a School of St. Matthew,[3] not the School of Jesus. At the present time, this limitation stands, as far as my evidence is concerned.[4]

The other note of limitation is of greater significance, although it would lead much too far if I were to elaborate its consequences. Neither this book nor my short commentary on the Matthean gospel[5] come to grips with the great problem of finding the place of Matthew within the spectrum of early Christianity. In this study I present the evidence for an advanced form of Jewish exegesis, based on access to both Hebrew and Greek O. T. texts. But that says little or nothing about the theology of its "author". And even less about the church in which and for which it was produced as a Greek original, dependent on the Greek Mark and a Greek Q (cf. below, p. 155 f.).

Three of the major studies in Matthew since 1954 have in different

---

[1] For the nature and implicit theology of such sayings, see J. M. ROBINSON, LOGOI SOPHON. Zur Gattung der Spruchquelle Q, in *Zeit und Geschichte* (Festschrift Bultmann; 1964), 77–96.

[2] See G. BORNKAMM, Der Auferstandene und der Irdische. Mt. 28₁₆–₂₀, *ibid.*, p. 186 f.

[3] See now G. SCHILLE, Bemerkungen zur Formgeschichte des Evangeliums, II. Das Evangelium des Matthäus als Katechismus, *N.T. St.* 4 (1957/58), 101–114.

[4] It is most interesting to note how differently GERHARDSSON deals with material which he does not consider grounded in the firm transmission from the Lord, see his *The Testing of God's Son. Mt. 4₁–₁₁ and par. An Analysis of an Early Christian Midrash* (Coniectanea Biblica. N.T. Series 2:1; 1966). It leaves the reader with the question whether the texts themselves call for such a drastic distinction between a narrative with "very slight connection with history" (p. 7), and, say, the synoptic apocalypse. On the latter, see the careful study by L. HARTMAN, *Prophecy Interpreted. The Formation of Some Jewish Apocalyptic Texts and of the Eschatological Discourse, Mark 13 par.* (Coniectanea Biblica. N.T. Series 1; 1966).

[5] In the *Peake's Commentary on the Bible*, M. Black and H. H. Rowley, eds., (1962), pp. 769–98.

ways argued for a "gentile" origin of the gospel. NEPPER-CHRISTENSEN gathers his analyses around the question "Who were the readers" of this gospel?[1] In so doing he finds both philological and theological reasons to refute the ancient and modern claims for a Jewish Christian setting. He gives, however, little attention to the positive side of his claim or to the ambiguity of the term "Jewish".

Both WOLFGANG TRILLING[2] and GEORG STRECKER[3] see the final Editor of the gospel in clearly gentile terms. Especially in Strecker's work, this is achieved by minute and sharp distinctions between Matthew and his sources, written or oral, cf. our earlier discussion with Strecker concerning the formula quotations. A more balanced view is that represented by BORNKAMM,[4] G. BARTH,[5] and R. HUMMEL.[6] Here Matthew is seen as carrying on a double polemic, against pharisaic Judaism and against antinomian Hellenists. Thus the work of Matthew does not follow a one-way street, away from the Jewish Christian sources toward gentile Christianity. In his critique of antinomian tendencies, Matthew makes positive use of material of Jewish Christian provenience.[7]

Let me limit myself to a few observations which, I think, should guide our assessment of the gospels' place in early Christianity. In so doing I hope to give a tentative framework to the quotation phenomena, which are the center of this book.

It is clear that the most obvious polemic in this gospel is directed against "the scribes and the pharisees". In Matthew these are neither the actual opponents of Jesus, nor are they general examples of haughty behaviour, as in Luke. They are the representatives of the synagogue "across the street" in Matthew's community. The line between church and synagogue is drawn definitely.[8] And Christianity is

---

[1] *Op. cit.*, p. 202 et passim.

[2] *Das wahre Israel.* 3. Aufl. (St. z. A. u. N.T. 10; 1964).

[3] *Der Weg der Gerechtigkeit.*

[4] *Op. cit.*, above, p. x, note 2.

[5] Das Gesetzesverständnis des Evangelisten Matthäus, in G. BORNKAMM et al., *Überlieferung und Auslegung im Matthäusevangelium* (Wiss. Monogr. z. A. u. N.T. 1; 1960, 1965²). The volume is translated into English, *Tradition and Interpretation in Matthew* (1963).

[6] *Op. cit.* above, p. viii, note 3.

[7] See, e.g., BORNKAMM, Der Auferstandene ..., p. 180, and HUMMEL, *op. cit.*, "... ein universal ausgerichtetes, mit hellenistischen Vorstellungen durchsetztes Judenchristentum ...," p. 166.

[8] Cf. W. SCHRAGE, Ekklesia und Synagoge, *Zeitschr. f. Theol. u. Kirche* 60 (1963), 178 ff.

in all respects superior to Judaism. Its righteousness is better than that of the synagogue's (5₂₀). Now it is important to note, that Matthew chooses to demonstrate this better righteousness and the fulfilment of the Law by a collection of antitheses which in no way deal with the problems which vexed the relations between Jewish and Gentile Christians, according to Acts 15 or Paul's letter to the Galatians (such as circumcision, food laws, etc.). Instead he gives shining examples of the ethical superiority of Christianity (5₂₁₋₄₈).[1] For this reason I find it difficult to see such material as directed against antinomian tendencies within the church.[2] The commandments about murder, oaths, retaliation, etc. were not under questioning by any antinomians, and as to divorce, the Jewish and gentile laxity fits the case better than any antinomian attitude (cf. Paul's argument against rigorists in 1 Cor. 7).

A better case can be made for the striking denunciation of false prophets and wonderworkers (7₁₅₋₂₃),[3] especially since Matthew lacks the positive statement about the strange exorcist (Mk. 9₃₈₋₄₁, Lk. 9₄₉₋₅₀). But when Matthew accuses them of "not doing the will of the heavenly father", there is little reason to think that he sees them as antinomians, since this expression elsewhere has no reference to the Law, but rather to the response in faith and repentence (12₅₀, 21₃₁).

Thus we find little evidence of intra-Christian polemic. The emphasis on the superior obedience to the Law is positive and is achieved by presenting Christian ethics as superior to that of Judaism. The term ὑποκριταί in 24₅₁ is used similar to Did. 8₁, i.e.=Jews. There is hardly any attempt to convert Jews in "their synagogues" (4₂₃, 9₃₅, 10₁₇, 12₉, 13₅₄), with "their scribes" (7₂₉). There is little attention to questions of contention between Jewish and gentile Christians, and the treatment of clean and unclean in Mt. 15₁₋₂₀ lacks the programmatic statement in Mk. 7₁₉. The gentiles have their place in the church, pre-

---

[1] W. D. DAVIES, in his monumental study, *The Setting of the Sermon on the Mount* (1964), has suggested that the Sermon on the Mount can be regarded "as the Christian answer to Jamnia" (p. 315). If so, it is an answer in completely different key, one of ethics and exhortation rather than *halaka*. On the other hand, the new consolidation of Judaism at Jamnia under the total hegemony of the pharisees is a natural background for Matthew's way to picture Judaism as equal to the pharisees. But the influence of Palestinian Judaism on the gospel of Matthew can hardly be as direct as Davies' study presupposes. For Matthew works in Greek with primarily Greek traditions, Mk., Q, and others.

[2] So also STRECKER, *op. cit.*, p. 137, TRILLING, *op. cit.* 211.

[3] See BARTH, *op. cit.*, p. 149–154; BORNKAMM, Der Auferstandene, p. 181.

figured by the Centurion (8₅–₁₃) and the Canaanite woman (15₂₁–₂₈), and is according to the command of the Risen Lord 28₁₈–₂₀.

It is in such a gospel we find our formula quotations, which presuppose a rather advanced form of Hebrew exegesis, and we have given reasons for the view that these are not just lifted from a Jewish Christian source. And there are all the other elements which strike us as Jewish, even "rabbinic". How can this be held together?[1] Could there not have been Christian communities which had not been plagued or blessed by the issues which dominate much of Paul's correspondence, issues which then caused the irenic Luke to write his Acts as an attempt at ecumenism? The Hellenistic setting of the gospel is clear from its language, its interest in ethics rather than *halaka*, its positive familiarity with Hellenistic christology.[2] The Jewish setting is equally clear, from our quotations, from stylistic peculiarities, and perhaps also from the intense preoccupation with those Jews, who had not accepted Jesus as the Messiah of whom the Scriptures spoke. These two sets of data add up to a church which grew out of Hellenistic Judaism, but which had still its contact with Jewish learning in the person of at least one of its members; a church which had learned to make the transition to an increasing gentile constituency without suffering much tension or problem in that process. And now it existed in sharp contrast to the Jewish community in town. For in this church things Jewish meant Jewish and not Jewish Christian versus gentile Christian. In such a setting traditions could be preserved and elaborated in a style which in other communities had become suspect or outdated. On the basis of such traditions and in such a milieu Matthew brings his gospel to completion. That he once was a Jew cannot be doubted. That he had had Jewish training in Palestine prior to the War is probable. That he belongs to a Hellenistic community is obvious. That this community includes gentiles is sure. What does this make the gospel? A witness to a far smoother

---

[1] E. P. BLAIR, *Jesus in the Gospel of Matthew* (1960), p. 156 ff., also stresses the Hellenistic nature of Matthew. He then combines these observations with CULLMANN's suggestion (The Significance of the Qumran Texts for Research into the Beginnings of Christianity, in K. Stendahl, ed., *The Scrolls and the N.T.* [1957], pp. 18–32; also *Journ. of Bibl. Lit.* 74 [1955], 213–26) that the Hellenists in Acts constitute the link between Qumran and Christianity. This would fit my problem well, but the evidence for such a connection is not strong enough to fall for the temptation.

[2] See BORNKAMM, *op. cit.*, 176 ff.

transition from Judaism to Christianity than we usually suppose. Luke is irenic by effort, as his Acts show. Matthew is comprehensive by circumstance, and that makes it a rich and wise book.

Harvard Divinity School, October 1967.

Krister Stendahl

Addendum to p. vi: ROBERT H. GUNDRY, *The Use of the Old Testament in St. Matthew's Gospel* (Suppl. to Nov. Test. 18; 1967) includes allusions in his study and this leads him, of course, to a minimizing of the peculiar features of the formula quotations. I hope to give a detailed evaluation of his thesis in a future issue of *Biblica*. — Cf. also a Harvard Ph. D. dissertation (June 1968) by CARL H. MARBURY, in which the *Vorlage* studies of F. M. Cross and his students are brought into the discussion of Matthean and other N. T. quotations.

Reviews

Sv. Morgonbl. 14 juni 1954 (Ivar Wennfors)

(Finsk) Teol. Tidskr. 59 (1954), 211–15 (Esko Haapa)

N.T. St. 1 (1954), 155–57 (T. W. Manson)

Ephem. Theol. Lov. 30 (1954), 48–83 (E. Massaux)

Theol. St. 15 (1954), 644–46 (Herbert A. Musurillo, S. J.)

Studia Theol. 8 (1954), 1–24 (B. Gärtner)

Journ. Bibl. Lit. 74 (1955), 54 (F. V. Filson)

Rev. Bibl. 62 (1955), 297 f. (Milik)

Rev. Bibl. 62 (1955), 454 f. (M.-E. Boismard)

Augustana Seminary Review 7 (1955), 27–28 (E. Wahlstrom)

Exp. T. 66 (1955/56), 380 (H. H. Rowley)

Rev. of Rel. 19 (1955), 211 f. (Paul Minear)

Rev. Sc. Phil. et Théol. 39 (1955), 276 (A. Viard)

Ny Kyrkl. Tidskr. 23 (1954), 149–52 (Å. V. Ström)

The Princeton Seminary Bulletin 49 (1956), 50–51 (Bruce M. Metzger)

Biblica 36 (1955), 527–29 (Zerwick)

Theol. Lit. Zeit. 81 (1956), 40–42 (P. Vielhauer)

Cahiers Sioniens 9 (1955), 120–22 (G. Vermes)

Journ. of Rel. 36 (1956), 58 f. (H. M. Teeple)

Journ. of Theol. St. 7 (1956), 103–05 (H. F. D. Sparks)

Gnomon 29 (1957), 330–32 (P. Katz)

Vigiliae Christ. 11 (1957), 113 f. (G. Sevenster)

Theol. Zeitschr. 13 (1957), 68 f. (Mathias Rissi)

Scholastik II/1958, 299 f. (Brinkmann)

Rev. d'Hist. et de Phil. Rel. 38 (1958), 291–93 (P. Prigent)

Corrections

p. 15, line 16: worldly (not: wordly).

p. 23, line 5 from bottom: by noting (not: through the).

p. 34, note 2: Judaïsme; also in Bibliography p. 223.

p. 40, line 5: sperabunt (not: sperabit).

p. 54, note 2: Rahlfs' (not: Rahlf's).

p. 60, line 1 of Greek: [twice] προσκολληθήσεται (not: τ).

p. 61, Ex. 20 line 3 of Greek: φονεύσεις (not: ψ).

p. 62, line 4: that different (not: the different).

p. 73, note 1, line 6. The whole line should read:
> Cf. the phylactery from Murabaat, F.M. Cross, *Bibl. Archeol,* 17 (1954), p.7. Verse

p. 75, note 4: "l'esprit" (no accent).

p. 81, note 1, line 2: stylistic (not: stilistic).

p. 84, note 1, line 4: the שכחתני of Ps. 42₁₀, (i.e. כ, not ב; and ח, not ה).

p. 86, last line, should read: is an Attic phenomenon (only here in the N.T. and rarely in the LXX[3]),

p. 86, add to note 3: Katz's "outer margin" refers to "marginal use", not to margins in manuscripts.

p. 92, note 2, line 3: apart from (not: except in).

p. 98, note 3, line 4: M.T.'s (not: T.M.'s).

p. 98, line 5: ܝܥܡܘ (not: ܢܥܡܘ; i.e. Syriac "yudh", not: "nun").

p. 102, The right col., line 4 from bottom should read: ἐν τῇ ὑψηλῇ] so also א*Aq. (Vulg.).

p. 102, The left col. on same line, and following lines add:
Targum Jonathan
קלא ברום עלמא אשתמע בית ישראל דבכן ומתאנחין בתר ירמיה גביא
כד שלח יתיה נבוזראדן רב קטוליא מרמתא . . .

p. 108, last line of Syriac: ܚܥܥܠ (� for ܣ).

p. 110, note 6, line 2: חביב (not: חריב).

p. 111, line 15: unparalleled (not: umparalleled).

p. 123, note 3, line 11: Bryennios (not: Byrennios).

p. 125, line 11: אוצר (not: אואר).

p. 136, note 4, line 1: ἀνατολῇ (not: ...ή).

p. 140, last line of Syriac in *both* columns: Syr. "lamad" (not ʿe).
ܠܘܡܠܐܩܘ ܠܘܡܠܐܩܘ

p. 162, line 8: of their actual or ... (not: virtual).

p. 163, line 9 should read: ...Jesus himself in 13₁₈ and 15₂₅, cf. also 19₂₈. Jn. 2₁₇, about Jesus, is.

p. 164, note 1, line 2: possibility.

p. 191, note 1 on p. 190 continued on p. 191, line 3: A similar view to that of ... (not: as that of ...).

p. 192, note 3, line 1: CDC 85–9; col. vi, 4–9, ... (not: col; vi, 4–9).

p. 212, line 7 of Greek: πολλῆς (reverse letter "pi").

p. 217, line 17: prior to (not: primary to).

p. 217, line 21: prior to Matthean context (not: primary to their context).

p. 220, 10th listing: Funk (not: Funck).

p. 237, under Williams, A.L.: Judaeos (not: Judaeous).

p. 239, between Credner and Cullmann: Cross 73.

p. 248, col. 1, line 3 from bottom: 2 Timotheus (not: Thimotheus).

p. 249, col. 3, line 6: Porphyry (not: Prophory).

THE SCHOOL

Introduction

"Matthew as rabbi and catechist" was the title of a short article by E. von Dobschütz, published in 1928.[1] It was not only the general Jewish character of the First Gospel which led the German scholar to his view. He also stressed Matthew's preference for repeating coined words and arranging the material systematically. He maintained that in his gospel, Matthew intended to offer his church a manual of discipline and a catechism of Christian behaviour.[2]

von Dobschütz's conclusions were that the author of the gospel ascribed to Matthew was a rabbi — probably trained in the school of Jochanan ben Zakkai — who had become a Christian teacher and who made use of his Jewish training in presenting the Christian gospel. Because von Dobschütz was thinking in the terms of individual authorship[3] he was not forced to determine or even conjecture what kind of audience or pupils the author had to face in his teaching activities.

When the N.T. studies are considered in the light of form-criticism, the conception of individual authorship, while it does not disappear, is felt to be an oversimplified approach to the gospels.[4] Thus our curiosity is heightened when, for instance, Ph. Carrington explicitly speaks about the Matthaean school, whose teachers are to be compared with the "elders" and *tannaim* of contemporary Judaism.[5]

Yet the interest in gathering some information about a school as a background to the First Gospel is not dependent upon a denial of individual authorship. Regardless of whether the gospel is assigned to an

---

[1] Matthäus als Rabbi und Katechet, *Zeitschr. f. d. neutest. Wissensch.* 27 (1928), p. 338–348.

[2] *op. cit.*, p. 344 f., cf. R. Bultmann, *Die Geschichte der synoptischen Tradition* (1931²), p. 382 f., B. W. Bacon, *Studies in Matthew* (1930), p. 132.

[3] ". . . dass Matthäus bei der Lesung des Lukas sich einzelnes an den Rand seines Markusexemplars notiert hatte", *op. cit.*, p. 347.

[4] Cf. the well balanced statements of G. D. Kilpatrick, *The Origins of the Gospel according to St. Matthew* (1946), p. 2, 69, 71.

[5] *The Primitive Christian Catechism* (1940), p. 69.

ex-rabbi or not, it is worth investigating whether the type of work he undertook was a unique feature in the primitive church or whether his methods of teaching and handling the traditions as well as the Scriptures were merely a remnant of his past life. Or was there in the church where he lived and served any counterpart to his old milieu?

It is not with the intention of combining into a new pattern the scarce and over-interpreted material about Matthew as the author of the First Gospel that we propose to investigate the possibilities of such a school. What can be found out along these lines affords little clue to the enigma of why this gospel was headed by Matthew's name. Our object is rather to trace the influences of a school on the composition and the actual material of the gospel. Because we concentrate on Matthew, this in no way implies a presupposition of its priority or its greater affinity to the genuine traditions of the church. Matthew's dependence upon Mark is evident, not least in his rendering of the quotations from the O.T.[1] But the traces of a school are best discernible in the First Gospel. Once we have examined them, we may find they have some relevance to the other gospels also. As any one of the Synoptics can never be treated separately, we shall start our study by considering the attitude of form-criticism towards the church as the creative milieu of the gospels.

---

[1] See below, p. 148 and 151–156.

The creative milieu of the gospels

Form-criticism claims to define the "Sitz im Leben" of the different parts and units of biblical literature. M. DIBELIUS, whose work *Die Formgeschichte des Evangeliums* has been most influential in N.T. research and teaching on the continent[1], once coined the expression "Im Anfang war die Predigt"[2], and in his Formgeschichte he treats the whole gospel material from the point of view of preaching. When considered more closely it is nevertheless striking how vaguely this original setting is defined and how little of the material composing our gospels can be linked with the preaching so much spoken of.

The German word "Predigt" has the meaning of both "sermon" and "preaching", but to Dibelius it has a still wider sense. It is used to cover all the activities of the church through which it promoted its message and doctrine: "Wenn ich also die Predigt als den Ursitz aller Tradition von Jesus bezeichne, so denke ich an alles das, was hinter dem Ausdruck Lk. 14 stehen kann: 'wovon dir Kunde geworden ist'."[3]

The preaching is spoken of in a still wider sense, however, when the term is used to emphasize that the intention of the gospels was never to preserve or state biographical facts. From the beginning these facts were expressed in order to convince unbelievers and strengthen the faith

---

[1] 1st ed. 1919, 2nd ed. 1933. DIBELIUS's method is a constructive one in contrast to the analytic procedure of R. BULTMANN, *Die Geschichte der synoptischen Tradition* (1921[1], 1931[2]). This explains why the common views on this matter have been more influenced by the more sweeping statements of Dibelius than by Bultmann's detailed struggle with the texts. Cf. V. TAYLOR, *The Formation of the Gospel Tradition* (1933), *e.g.*, p. 12.

[2] Die alttestamentlichen Motive in der Leidensgeschichte des Petrus- und des Johannes-Evangeliums, *Zeitschr. f. d. alttest. Wissensch.*, Beih. 33 (1918), p. 146 and in more general form p. 125: "Am Anfang aller geistigen Produktion im Urchristentum steht die Predigt, Missions- und Gemeindepredigt, Erzählung und Paränese, Prophetenrede und Schriftauslegung". Cf. IDEM, *Die urchristliche Überlieferung von Johannes dem Täufer* (1911), p. 4 ff., and "Herodes und Pilatus", *Zeitschr. f. d. neutest. Wissensch.* 16 (1915), p. 113.

[3] DIBELIUS, *Formgeschichte*, p. 13, cf. p. 25 on the catechism as "preaching".

of the faithful. The Sitz im Leben was that of preaching and not that of chronicles or biographies.[1]

Thus "die Predigt" is neither the sermon nor the preaching as a definite activity within the church, as opposed to other means of teaching or instruction. The Sitz im Leben is given an abstract definition which says that the material was formed in a church with the intention of converting and of claiming the legitimacy of Jesus as the Messiah.

Here and there, however, the ambiguity of the word "Predigt" has led to ambiguity in Dibelius's train of argument and "die Predigt" actually becomes the sermon proper. Dibelius draws the line between the activity of story-tellers and teachers as against that of preachers.[2] In his study of the Gospel of Peter he refers to the school as a background.[3] Moreover, when such a distinction is introduced, very little of the gospels is actually genuine preaching material.

According to DIBELIUS, the paradigms, or to use V. TAYLOR's term the pronouncement-stories[4], i.e. stories culminating in a saying of Jesus whose sole object was to lead up to such a saying, were the illustrations used by the preachers. The economy of the story favours such a view. But the rest of the material, even to Dibelius, has another Sitz im Leben within the church. The more elaborate stories (die Novellen) were told by story-tellers and used in the Christology of the gospels[5]; only a few of the legends have any relation "zur Predigt".[6] The passion narrative cannot have acquired its form within the realm of "Predigt".[7] The parenetic material is said to be the preaching itself and not only proof-texts and illustrations for the sermons[8], but at the same time there was, as we saw, a distinction between preachers and teachers of parenetic material.

The lack of interest in a concrete understanding of the Sitz im Leben might be due to sound insight into the fact that the material does not permit of closer determination, but at the same time Dibelius's interest

---

[1] DIBELIUS, *Die alttest. Motive*, p. 125 f., cf. *Formgeschichte*, p. 12 f., 34 f. and especially p. 25 on the passion narrative.

[2] DIBELIUS, *Formgeschichte*, p. 66 f. and 241.

[3] *Die alttest. Motive*, p. 137 and 148 with a reference to W. BOUSSET, *Jüdisch-Christlicher Schulbetrieb in Alexandria und Rom* (1915).

[4] *The Formation of the Gospel Tradition* (1933), p. 63. "Pronouncement-Stories" is actually the equivalent to what Bultmann calls *apophthegmata*.

[5] DIBELIUS, *Formgeschichte*, p. 66 f. and 128.

[6] *op. cit.*, p. 128.   [7] *op. cit.*, p. 25.   [8] *op. cit.*, p. 262–264, cf. p. 36.

in the forms of literature to some extent rules out his interest in the activities of which these forms were the issue and the basis.[1]

In this respect R. BULTMANN, with his analytic method, as against the constructive approach of Dibelius, gives a more differentiated background to the gospel. "Dass am Anfang aller geistigen Produktion des Urchristentums die Predigt steht, dass sie es war, die die Tradition schuf, halte ich für eine starke Übertreibung, die das Verständnis zahlreicher Traditionsstücke gefährdet, wie es sich bei den Schul- und Streitgesprächen zeigte. Apologetik und Polemik wie Gemeindebildung und Disziplin sind ebenso in Rechnung zu setzen und daneben schriftgelehrte Arbeit."[2]

Dibelius's concentration on the preaching is due to his conviction that this was the only one of these conditions which mattered in the first period of the church. Here Dibelius's hypothesis seems to include a statement of values, and when he proves the novelistic and legendary trends to be "wordly", it is not only a matter of literary forms.[3]

Given that there were different purposes and activities in the early church which formed the gospel material, there is yet another Sitz im Leben which we must discover. Where "in the church" was this material collected and worked on? Even Dibelius admits that there are a lot of texts which have but a very slight relation to the preaching activity. Yet there are good reasons for the view of Dibelius — and here Bultmann agrees with him — that the paradigms were used as illustrations in sermons and thus homiletic interests have left their imprint on the material, but from what source did the preachers derive their examples? Is it not possible to go back beyond individual memory, homiletic predilections and the adaptations of the preachers?

The view that preaching is the Sitz im Leben of the gospel material may also be checked from the opposite angle. What is found in the earliest texts which could be considered as sermons or as material with close affinity to the preaching of the church?

It is a well-known fact that very little of the gospel material is found in the other books of the N.T. In spite of the fact that the kerygma has been found as the link between the gospels and apostolic preaching, it remains

---

[1] Cf. BULTMANN, op. cit., p. 373.

[2] BULTMANN, op. cit., p. 64. On the difference between Dibelius and Bultmann in this respect as well as on form-criticism until 1937, see K. GROBEL, Formgeschichte und Synoptische Quellenanalyse (1937), cf. TAYLOR, op. cit., p. 1–21.

[3] Formgeschichte, p. 65 f. compared with p. 100.

a problem that most of the gospel material is not referred to in the Epistles or other early Christian literature. The view of Dibelius on preaching as the original setting of the gospel material finds support only in the slight references to the Galilean and Judaean career of Jesus in Acts 10 38 and 2 22. There is little reason to set the Pauline churches in a special group apart from the others; the lack of direct reference to gospel material is a common feature of the early church. Important theological problems are involved in this issue. The direct relation to the Holy Spirit and the eschatological outlook of the church made its adherents less inclined to look back towards the details of the incarnate history of the Messiah. His work had its culmination in the Cross and the Resurrection, which proved him to be the designated judge of mankind, and the Messiah in his fullness was still to come. The gospel history was to a certain extent only a prelude; but at the same time it is obvious that there existed even amongst the common members of the church a knowledge of the words and deeds of Jesus.[1]

Traces of the words of Jesus are found in parenetic context and the sayings are used especially in matters of church discipline, 1 Cor. 7 10, 9 14, cf. 7 25 — 1 Clem. 46 8. *Verba Christi* are also found in the ethical teaching of James, Peter and other N.T. epistles, as in most of the Apostolic Fathers.[2]

The Second Epistle of Clement is often regarded as the first Christian sermon and the First Epistle of Clement and Barnabas may contain material relevant to the content of early preaching. They all refer to words of Jesus but nothing is said of His deeds. Very typical is the position of the parables of Jesus up to the time of Irenaeus. Apart from the Similes of Hermas, where the N.T. parables are woven together and have influenced the imagery, *e.g.* Sim. v, 2, the parable of the Sower is the only one referred to (1 Clem. 24 5) but it appears as an argument for the resurrection. Otherwise only the final words are given without any suggestion of the parable with which they are linked, 2 Clem. 8 5, Barn. 4 14, 6 13, 19 3, Did. 16 1.[3] Even if C. F. D. MOULE is correct in his suggestion

---

[1] O. MOE, *Paulus und die evangelische Geschichte* (1912), especially the chapter "Welche Kenntnis der evangelischen Geschichte setzt Paulus bei seinen Lesern voraus?", p. 71–130.

[2] E. G. SELWYN, *Comm. 1 Peter* (1949), p. 366 ff., D. VAN DEN EYNDE, *Les Normes de l'Enseignement Chrétien dans la littérature patristique des trois premiers siècles* (1933), especially p. 39. For Matthew see É. MASSAUX, *Influence de l'Évangile de saint Matthieu sur la littérature chrétienne avant saint Irénée* (1950).

[3] Cf. A. JÜLICHER, *Die Gleichnisreden Jesu* I (1910²), p. 203 f. His explanation

of the use of the parables and sayings as illustrative material in early Christian catechism[1], this material lies below the actual surface of the text. It is not transmitted by this type of teaching.

The first time more extensive use is made of gospel material is in Justin's First Apology and in his Dialogue with the Jew Trypho and in the Epideixis of Irenaeus. It is significant that it is not in the homiletic tradition that we find any consistent material from the gospels, but in these works which are clearly of a more scholarly nature. Observations of this kind led HARNACK to make the private reading of Scripture, both O.T. and N.T., the decisive feature in the promotion of biblical knowledge[2], but we are told about a study of the Scriptures which was supervised by the church authorities at the time of Irenaeus. He says: "And then the whole teaching will be clear and convincing to him if he also reads carefully the Scriptures with those who are the presbyters of the church with whom lies the apostolic doctrine."[3] There was also a study for mature Christians in the regular life of the church as the Apostolic Tradition of Hippolytus informs us: "But if any instruction in God's word is held, everyone ought to attend it willingly ... any godly man ought to count it a great loss if he does not attend the place of instruction, *especially if he can read.*"[4] These last words bring out the school character of the instruction. In spite of the late date of these examples, they are relevant to our question, since the lack of gospel material in other types of literature is not affected by the acceptance of the gospels as official documents.[5] On the contrary, it is a constant feature in the

---

that the reluctant attitude among the Fathers to the parables is due to the abuse of the parables by the gnostics has less relevance in the earliest period.

[1] The Use of Parables and Sayings as Illustrative Material in Early Christian Catechesis, *Journ. of Theol. St.*, New Ser. 3 (1952), p. 75–79.

[2] *Über den privaten Gebrauch der heiligen Schriften in der alten Kirche* (1912), *e.g.*, p. 29.

[3] Adv. haer. iv, 32₁ (MPG vii, col. 1071): Post deinde et omnis sermo ei (*i.e.* the faithful Christian) constabit, si et Scripturas diligenter legerit apud eos qui in Ecclesia sunt presbyteri, apud quos est apostolica doctrina.

[4] iv, 2 (35), translation of B. S. EASTON, *The Apostolic Tradition of Hippolytus* (1934), p. 54.

[5] It is a matter of debate whether or not the later schools of Alexandria and other places can be considered a continuation of the school activities in the early church. BOUSSET, *op. cit.*, has given arguments for a consistent school tradition; for the earliest period see p. 308–319. The opposite view is held by K. H. RENGSTORF, art. διδάσκειν κτλ., *Theol. Wörterb. z. N.T.* II, p. 162. Rengstorf's argument is somewhat biased by a theological pattern in which the Semitic concept of למד has been rein-

life of the early church. Thus the provocative verdict of R. P. Casey seems to be sound when he says (confining himself to the canonical material): "It is curious indeed that no evidence of their (*i.e.* the words and deeds of Jesus) use survives if, in the gospels, so many stories with a moral were invented for homiletic purposes, in however broad a sense. Why, if the gospel sections were in constant circulation for homiletic purposes, do they survive only in non-homiletic form? Why do we have so many materials for one kind of sermon, but, in the early period, only sermons of other kinds?"[1]

Second century literature adds still further emphasis to these questions. Melito of Sardes in his Homily on the Passion keeps strictly to the O.T. as the basis of his preaching.[2] How the N.T. scriptures were read in those days is known from Justin's famous account in 1 Apol. 67. The exposition of the "memoirs of the apostles", however, seems to follow the same line as that indicated in the use of the parables: the ethical implications of the text were extracted and underlined, as may already be seen in the N.T. when the facts of the *kerygma* are used as a model for Christian humility, Phil. 2₅, 1 Peter 2₂₁, Heb. 12₃. The actual facts were not proclaimed in the sermons, they were referred to as well-known.[3]

---

forced by Jesus and the early church as against the Hellenized understanding which had crept into rabbinism and was the self-evident concept in Hellenistic Judaism and Christianity, see *e.g.*, p. 143: ". . . nimmt Jesus in dem διδάσκειν, wie es von ihm ausgesagt wird, die Linie wieder auf, die למד zunächst einhielt. Auf ihr handelte es sich um eine Beanspruchung des ganzen Menschen durch Gott in einer Weise, dass nicht nur jeder Wiederspruch gegen sie, sondern auch jede theoretische Reflexion über sie von vornherein ausgeschlossen war." Otherwise the interpretation of Clement is the main object for the criticism of Bousset, see J. Munck, *Untersuchungen über Klemens von Alexandria* (1933), and G. Bardy, Pour l'histoire de l'École d'Alexandrie, *Vivre et Penser* 2 (1942), p. 80–109. — As to the treatment of the O.T. Bousset shows how the school tradition of the second century is mainly one of testimonies, which were taken over from generation to generation. The typical trend of the Matthaean school on the other hand is to work with the Scriptures themselves on the basis of the Hebrew text, thereby creating a type of testimonies unparalleled in the later schools, cf. below, p. 200 f.

[1] Some Remarks on Formgeschichtliche Methode, in *Quantulacumque. Studies presented to* K. Lake (1937), p. 115 f.

[2] ed. C. Bonner, *Studies and Documents* 12 (1940). On the relation of this homily to the reading of the O.T. text, see G. Zuntz, On the Opening Sentence of Melito's Paschal Homily, *Harv. Theol. Rev.* 36 (1943), p. 299–315 and Bonner, *ibm.*, p. 317–319.

[3] Cf. K. Stendahl, Kerygma und Kerygmatisch, *Theol. Lit. Zeit.* 77 (1952), col. 715–720.

Thus it is difficult to assume the Sitz im Leben of gospel material within the form of sermons in the primitive church and there are clearly great problems involved in the common view emanating from the statement "Im Anfang war die Predigt". Obviously the preaching activity was one of the factors which influenced the gospel material; yet it was hardly the only one; nor can the activity of preaching afford a concrete milieu for the selection and composition of the different parts of the gospels. Awareness of the limitations of Dibelius's statement seems to lead Casey back to the view of individual authorship for the gospels. In this move he is not alone. The old concept of individual authorship is worked out in a most ingenious manner — maybe too ingenious a manner — by A. FARRER in his study of Mark.[1] There are, however, other alternatives.

---

[1] *A Study in St. Mark* (1951). On form-criticism, see especially p. 21–23.

The Gospel of Matthew as a handbook issued by a school

When we turn to the Gospel of Matthew we are fortunate in having a balanced and thorough study in G. D. KILPATRICK's *The Origins of the Gospel according to St. Matthew* (1946). We may gain much by making Kilpatrick's results the basis and the starting point of our inquiry. A comparison between B. W. BACON's *Studies in Matthew*, in 1930, and the work of Kilpatrick sixteen years later is most illuminating in understanding what has taken place in N.T. research during the last decades. In many respects the conclusions are the same, yet they take on another meaning, since the whole process of growth is absorbed into the organic life of the early church.

Although Bacon was able to refer to the practice of targumizing the gospel, to him this was purely a category of literature and he "never treated contemporary liturgical custom as an important element in its production".[1] This is exactly what Kilpatrick has done, and in his reference to the Sitz im Leben of the gospel there is none of the same vagueness and ambiguity that we found in Dibelius. KILPATRICK's view may be summarized as follows: At the time when Matthew was compiled, Mark had been used for liturgical purposes for some years[2], as had Q and M (the discourse material peculiar to Matthew), while the narrative material peculiar to Matthew was first put into writing by the evangelist himself.[3] The liturgical use of the Scriptures was the focus of the church's use of the gospel material. In expounding the texts read in the services the needs of the church were connected with the words and works recorded in the gospel. The exposition was repeated time and again and developed into a more or less fixed tradition, which in its turn was admitted to liturgical use. At this stage, traditions of the Matthaean church were combined into a revised edition of the gospel.[4]

Kilpatrick finds supporting parallels in the liturgical background of Judaism, both in its Palestinian and Hellenistic forms. In Palestinian

---

[1] KILPATRICK *op. cit.*, p. 78, BACON, *op. cit.*, p. 21—23.

[2] *op. cit.*, p. 78.

[3] *ibm.*, p. 70 and 35.

[4] *ibm.*, p. 67 and 71.

Judaism the Targums break down the sharp distinctions between Holy Writ and the interpretations of *halakah* and *haggadah*.[1] In Hellenistic Judaism, with its looser concept of the canon, the material used in the actual exposition becomes the literature admitted to liturgical use.[2]

There seem to be two chief weaknesses in Kilpatrick's view:

a) A liturgical recitation of gospels or gospel material in the period presumed by Kilpatrick (65–100 A.D.) is by no means an unchallenged fact. It presupposes a liturgical practice of the same type as that of the synagogue with its reading of the Scriptures. Now O. CULLMANN has seriously challenged the view that there was a "service of the Word", as in the liturgy of the synagogue (recitation of the Scriptures — prayers — preaching), apart from celebration of the Eucharist.[3] The type of service mentioned by Justin in 1 Apol. 67 is usually looked upon as a stage at which these two liturgical acts had been combined. Cullmann rather considers it evidence that the teaching of the church had taken on a more definite form inside the frame of the Eucharist, which was the only Christian service in the N.T. period (apart from Baptism). Even if the early church's liturgy is taken as a parallel to that of the synagogue, a recitation of Mark and other gospel material cannot be taken for granted.[4]

b) Clearly Matthew is an enlarged edition of Mark, and to BACON the rearrangement of the Marcan material, together with the additions, had the character of "sermons" on Marcan or Q texts[5], and Kilpatrick deliberates at length on the homiletic influence on the Matthaean text. As a whole, however, the gospel lacks the character of a liturgical text. The fivefold structure of the gospel must be regarded as the most striking feature in its composition.[6] This could be made an argument for its liturgical use, namely that it was the Christian counterpart to the Torah,

---

[1] *ibm.*, p. 61.

[2] *ibm.*, p. 62 f.

[3] *Urchristentum und Gottesdienst* (1950²), p. 29 ff., cf. G. DELLING, *Der Gottesdienst im Neuen Testament* (1952), p. 132 f.

[4] The view of Kilpatrick is brought to its extreme by PH. CARRINGTON, *The Primitive Christian Calendar* (1952), who interprets Mark as a lectionary in accordance with a liturgical year. An early liturgical reading of gospel material is maintained by W. BAUER, *Der Wortgottesdienst der ältesten Christen* (1930), p. 54, but it was not probable to P. GLAUE, *Die Vorlesung heiliger Schriften im Gottesdienste* (1907), p. 28, cf. 31 ff.; DELLING, *op. cit.*, p. 91 f. considers it an unproved suggestion.

[5] *op. cit.*, *e.g.* p. 97. On the further implications of this view see M. S. ENSLIN, *Harv. Theol. Rev.* 24 (1931), p. 77 f.

[6] See below, p. 24 ff.

which was read in the synagogues.[1] Yet as we shall find, the structure of the five parts, with its systematic aims, points rather to a milieu other than the homiletic or liturgical one.

The alternative against which Kilpatrick defends his liturgical approach is the catechetical purpose of the gospel, which he takes seriously since "it might be argued that the evidence which might seem to indicate a liturgical purpose would indicate equally well a didactic one".[2] Kilpatrick's arguments against such a view are as follows:

a) The word διδάσκειν and its derivatives are used less often in Matthew than in Mark.[3]

b) Since Mark was used liturgically, in its revised edition it had the same purpose.

c) A catechetical work, even if very good, was not given official approval since its use was of a more private nature.

d) Matthew "has direction suitable to all classes within the Church. For example, much of Mt. 18, as it stands, is intended for the leaders of the community rather than those on its threshold ... Just as Mt. 18 was addressed to the Church authorities, so Mt. 9 35–11 1 is addressed to the Christian evangelist and teacher ... The Petrine stories are frequently associated with the giving of a ruling on what must have been a disputed issue in the Church." Thus "the book has a much wider audience in view than the catechumenate".[4]

Of the four points the last is of the greatest relevance. It is quite convincing, especially if one takes the word "catechetical" in its narrowest sense, *viz.* pre-baptismal instruction. It is, however, open to question whether the basic instruction was pre-baptismal at this early stage.[5]

---

[1] So KILPATRICK, *op. cit.*, p. 135 f.

[2] *op. cit.*, p. 78.

[3] Here word statistics lead astray. The terms of the διδάσκειν are used in a very distinct way by Matthew and the teaching is considered the task of the disciples, 5 19, 28 20; cf. 10 25, 23 8. In Mark there is no explicit command to teach, though it is taken for granted, Mk. 6 30.

[4] *op. cit.*, p. 79.

[5] W. ROBINSON, Historical survey of the church's treatment of new converts with reference to pre- and post-baptismal instruction, *Journ. of Theol. St.* 42 (1941), p. 42–53, denies pre-baptismal instruction for the N.T. period. So also J. LEIPOLDT, *Die urchristliche Taufe* (1928), p. 6 ff., with reference to proselyte baptism without instruction. — CARRINGTON, *The Primitive Christian Catechism* (1940), p. 89, leaves the question open, and so does W. JENTSCH, *Urchristliches Erziehungsdenken* (1951), p. 260 ff. For the earlier discussions, see A. OEPKE, *Die Missionspredigt des Apostels Paulus* (1920), p. 9. A. SEEBERG, *Der Katechismus der Urchristen-*

Even if catechetical instruction had a place within the constituency of the church, Kilpatrick is certainly right in denying that the catechetical function is the principal one of the gospel. In doing this he lays stress upon the material intended for the leaders of the church and its character as a manual of discipline. This material, which to some extent constitutes the difference between Matthew and the other gospels, might lead to a more relevant alternative to the liturgical aspect than does the catechetical one.

According to von Dobschütz and Bultmann, Matthew intended to offer his church a manual of discipline and a catechism of Christian behaviour. "Manual of discipline" has a familiar ring in modern biblical studies. In the cave at Qumran such a manual was found (DSD). Though the formal differences between the First Gospel and this Hebrew manuscript are vast, there are similarities as to form and compass. In addition to the actual rules of discipline — with a most striking parallel to Mt. 18 15 f.: "Indeed a man shall not bring accusation against his fellow in the presence of the many (the congregation), who has not been subject to reproof before witnesses" (DSD vi, 1)[1] — DSD contains both the dogmatics and the ethics of the Sect. The scroll begins with the moral standards for those joining the Sect worked out negatively and positively in the style of "The Two Ways"[2], with "to love" and "to hate" as technical terms. Though "Manual of Discipline" is a perfectly correct description of the manuscript, it also contains a summary of the doctrines of the Sect, iii, 13 — iv, 26, and the whole of the book is marked by the eschatological and even the apocalyptic atmosphere in which the Sect professed to live.

Comparison may also be made with another manual, the *Didache*. Kilpatrick calls it "a kind of handbook for beginners" and through the differences between Didache and Matthew he supports his denial of the merely catechetical purpose of the gospel.[3] To be sure, the Didache contains material for beginners, especially in 1–6, but 7–15 is a real manual of discipline where the leaders of the church are addressed. This is most

---

heit (1903), *e.g.* p. 212 f., presumed pre-baptismal instruction and catechetical formulae woven into the baptismal liturgy.

[1] See below, p. 138 f.

[2] A detailed study of the relation of DSD to "The Two Ways" is that of J.-P. AUDET, Affinités littéraires et doctrinales du "Manuel de Discipline", *Rev. Bibl.* 59 (1952), p. 219–238.

[3] *op. cit.*, p. 79.

obvious in ch. 7. The Didache is scarcely a book to be used by beginners, but is rather a handbook for teachers and church leaders dealing with catechetical instruction and church order, and in ch. 16 it concludes with an eschatological "mark of exclamation" which has close affinities to Mt. 24.[1] The relation between ethical teaching and eschatology which is predominent in the inter-testamental literature is also found in the pattern of Jewish catechism for proselytes.[2]

No one would say that Matthew is merely a handbook as is the Didache or the Manual of the Qumran Sect. Of course, Matthew is a gospel, and from the point of view of literary form the gospel is an unparalleled feature, an *ad hoc* creation of a church which claimed a more absolute doctrine of the incarnation than is found in other accounts of religious heroes; on the other hand, this incarnation is more closely related to very recent historical facts than is the case in other mythological systems. Yet when we consider what is most typically Matthaean in Matthew's treatment of the gospel material, we get the impression that the pattern which guided him in systematizing his material was that of a handbook.

The idea of the five books of Matthew seems to have been evoked by speculations on the relation between the five books of Papias and the Gospel of Matthew.[3] At first the observations are linked up with the hypothesis of a Book of Testimonies. In BACON's convincing treatment of Matthew as the five-fold gospel this idea is no longer a parasite on the weak branch of the over-interpreted words of Papias.[4] It stands on its own. The division is marked by an almost identical phrase which occurs five times in Matthew, each time as a concluding remark at the end of the speeches. At the same time those phrases lead on to the following

---

[1] Cf. E. STAUFFER, *Die Theologie des Neuen Testaments* (1948[4]), p. 213 and 299, where he compares the triple character of Didache (Sittenkatechismus–Agende–Apokalypse) with the traces of catechetical summaries in the N.T., *e.g.* Heb. 5₁₂, 6₁ f.

[2] G. KLEIN, *Der älteste christliche Katechismus und die jüdische Propaganda-Literatur* (1909), p. 142.

[3] Papias, in *Eusebius*, Hist. eccl. iii, 39₁. See below, p. 209. In addition to the literature mentioned there: E. NESTLE, Die Fünfteilung im Werk des Papias und im ersten Evangelium, *Zeitschr. f. d. neutest. Wissensch.* 1 (1900), p. 252–254, and J. A. FINDLAY, The Book of Testimonies and the Structure of the First Gospel, *The Expositor* viii, 20 (1920), p. 388–400.

[4] BACON, *op. cit.*, p. 80–82, cf. Bacon's previous article in *The Expositor*, viii, 15 (1918), p. 56–66, where however the apologetic character was more emphasized, Matthew being a work "against the Jews", cf. below, p. 209.

part of the gospel. The five parts in their turn start with narrative material and end with a discourse. In broad outline it looks like this:

Preamble: ch. 1–2.

Part i:

a) 3₁–4₂₅ Narrative material.

b) 5₁–7₂₇ The Sermon on the Mount.

καὶ ἐγένετο ὅτε ἐτέλεσεν ὁ Ἰησοῦς τοὺς λόγους τούτους, ἐξεπλήσσοντο οἱ ὄχλοι ἐπὶ τῇ διδαχῇ αὐτοῦ· ἦν γὰρ διδάσκων αὐτοὺς ὡς ἐξουσίαν ἔχων, καὶ οὐχ ὡς οἱ γραμματεῖς αὐτῶν (7₂₈₋₂₉).

Part ii:

a) 8₁–9₃₅ Narrative material.

b) 9₃₆–10₄₂ Discourse concerning Mission and Martyrdom.

καὶ ἐγένετο ὅτε ἐτέλεσεν ὁ Ἰησοῦς διατάσσων τοῖς δώδεκα μαθηταῖς αὐτοῦ, μετέβη ἐκεῖθεν τοῦ διδάσκειν καὶ κηρύσσειν ἐν ταῖς πόλεσιν αὐτῶν (11₁).

Part iii:

a) 11₂–12₅₀ Narrative and debate material.

b) 13₁–₅₂ Teaching on the Kingdom of Heaven.

καὶ ἐγένετο ὅτε ἐτέλεσεν ὁ Ἰησοῦς τὰς παραβολὰς ταύτας, μετῆρεν ἐκεῖθεν (13₅₃).

Part iv:

a) 13₅₄–17₂₀ Narrative and debate material.

b) 17₂₂–18₃₅ Discourse concerning church administration.

καὶ ἐγένετο ὅτε ἐτέλεσεν ὁ Ἰησοῦς τοὺς λόγους τούτους, μετῆρεν ἀπὸ τῆς Γαλιλαίας . . . (19₁).

Part v:

a) 19₂–22₄₆ Narrative and debate material.

b) 23₁–25₄₆ Discourse concerning eschatology. Farewell address.

καὶ ἐγένετο ὅτε ἐτέλεσεν ὁ Ἰησοῦς πάντας τοὺς λόγους τούτους, εἶπεν τοῖς μαθηταῖς αὐτοῦ . . . (26₁ f.).

Epilogue: 26₃–28₂₀.

It might be argued that the five similar concluding remarks do not indicate actual divisions of the gospel, but represent Matthew's way of terminating his discourses. There is, however, one long and distinct discourse which lacks such a concluding remark, namely the speech against the Pharisees in Mt. 23₁–₃₉. This being so, the significance of the five-fold division is still further underlined and thus the speech in ch. 23 is

rather an enlarged edition of debate material, considered as preparatory
to the concluding discourse of the fifth part of the gospel. Thus Matthew
collected the words of Jesus under five headings: Ethics (5–7)[1], Apostle-
ship — Mission — Martyrdom (10₅–42)[2], Teaching on the Kingdom of
God, both in public and private[3] (13₁–52), Church discipline, particularly
so far as it concerned re-establishment within the church (17₂₄–18₃₅)[4],
Eschatology and Farewell address[5] (24₁–25₄₆).

These groups of sayings are related to the narrative material, the
disposition of which mainly follows the outline given in Mark. But it
is skilfully done in such a manner that the narrative parts have the
function of leading up to the discourses, and the narrative together with
the discourse constitutes a "book".[6] Yet the way in which Matthew
follows Mark makes it impossible strictly to consider the narrative and

---

[1] On the composition of the Sermon on the Mount in relation to the ethical
forms of the Synagogue and the church, see below, p. 136. When the ethical teaching
in the Sermon on the Mount is compared with that of the epistles an illuminating
observation of D. DAUBE should be remembered (Participle and Imperative in
1 Peter. Appended note to SELWYN, *Comm. 1 Peter*, p. 484 ff.). He shows how Mishnah Aboth in contrast to the rest of the Talmud does not use the participle as imperative. The reason for this is that Aboth is a "historical" text and not a code
as the rest of the Mishnah. Cf. C. H. DODD, *Gospel and Law* (1951), p. 19.

[2] S. KRAUSS, Die Instruktion Jesu an die Apostel, *Angelos* 1 (1925), p. 96–102;
on the martyrological aspects, see E. PETERSON, *Zeuge der Wahrheit* (1937), especially p. 9–29.

[3] For this distinction, see especially T. W. MANSON, *The Teaching of Jesus*
(1935²), p. 18 and the appendices *ibm.*, p. 320–324.

[4] W. VISCHER, *Die evangelische Gemeindeordnung* (1946), p. 47–76. R. BOHREN,
Das Problem der Kirchenzucht im Neuen Testament (1952), cf. L. VAGANAY, Le
schématisme du discours communautaire à la lumière de la critique des sources,
Rev. Bibl. 60 (1953), p. 203–244.

[5] On farewell addresses as a homiletic form, see B. REICKE, A Synopsis of Early
Christian Preaching, *The Root of the Vine* (A. FRIDRICHSEN *et al.*, 1953), p. 153–155,
cf. J. MUNCK, Discours d'adieu dans le Nouveau Testament et dans la littérature
biblique, *Aux sources de la tradition chrétienne, Mélanges Goguel* (1950), p. 155–170.
— In the simile on the Last Judgement the point seems to be neither to tell the
terms on which man will be judged nor to stress the unconsciousness in the doing
of good. When leaving earthly life Jesus makes "the little ones" his representatives,
his continous incarnation: "what you have done to them you have done to me!"
That gives the speech its character of a testament, a farewell address.

[6] This structure of the five parts in Matthew is a striking example of the pattern
kerygma + didache, which DODD considers a consistent feature of early Christian
theology, *op. cit.*, p. 6 and 10–12, cf. p. 66. At the same time it becomes clear that
the *didache* is not only ethical instruction, cf. below, p. 29.

debate material as an introduction to the following discourse. For example in ch. 19 a good deal of *halakah* concerning church discipline is given, in spite of the fact that this had been the subject of the discourse in the preceding part of the gospel. Matthew's procedure also adds an important factor to the interpretation of the doublets so typical of him, which are usually explained as due to overlapping material in Mark and Q.

On the other hand it is hardly possible to make a detailed division of the gospel into five consistent books with five distinct headings, as BACON and FINDLAY do, for they fail to recognize strongly enough Matthew's nature as a revised Gospel of Mark. The disposition which Matthew accounts for is primarily that of the discourses. In part iii, however, there is a striking relation between preparatory material and discourse, and here Findlay's observations are enlightening.[1] The teaching on the Kingdom of Heaven, hidden and yet revealed, is combined with the interpretation of Jesus as Wisdom, Mt. 11 19, 25–30, cf. 23 34 compared with its Lucan parallel.[2] In our study of the Matthaean quotations we shall be led to the assumption that the Wisdom literature was familiar to the Matthaean church and that it considered Jesus as the Wisdom of God.[3] Thus Findlay's heading of part iii "Jesus, the Sophia and the Logos", explains why Matthew incorporated the material now in ch. 11 into the same part as the parables on the Kingdom.

In DSD we have found counterparts to the first, third and fourth points in Matthew's five-fold pattern, and in the Didache to the first, fourth and fifth. Some of the rules concerning itinerant teachers in Didache have affinity to the second discourse of Matthew. For our inquiry we may confine ourselves to these rather general observations.

Yet the most obvious tendency towards a manual is found in Mt. 18 10–35. In Lk. 15 the lost sheep is the sinner and publican over against the righteous man, and much speaks for the originality of this function of the parable.[4] In Matthew the parable concerns the zeal for a brother who has become an apostate, and the phraseology is coloured by that function. It is not a matter of μετάνοια — which Matthew looks upon as a single action — but a question of winning back (cf. κερδαίνειν, v. 15) the brother who has gone astray (πλανᾶσθαι, vv. 12 and 13).

---

[1] *op. cit.*, p. 392–394.

[2] See below, p. 92.

[3] See below, p. 142.

[4] JOACH. JEREMIAS, *Die Gleichnisse Jesu* (1947), p. 20 f., cf. KILPATRICK, *op. cit.*, p. 28 f.

It may be that the words on binding and loosing in 16 19 have the sense of promulgating *halakah*[1], and thus Peter is given the authority of a chief rabbi. Yet in Mt. 18 18 the same saying clearly has the sense of a matter of discipline; it is the terminology of excommunication. It may not be taken for granted that the saying is intended to have the same function in both contexts. On the contrary, its repetition in ch. 18 is due to the fact that Matthew intends to alter its implications. The statement on prayer, which originally might have had a more general meaning, is confined to the prayers for the apostate, particularly prayers offered by the two or three "witnesses", cf. vv. 16 and 20.[2] It is to these very prayers the presence of the Christ is related, a most striking parallel to the practice of church discipline according to 1 Cor. 5 4: ἐν τῷ ὀνόματι τοῦ κυρίου Ἰησοῦ συναχθέντων ὑμῶν καὶ τοῦ ἐμοῦ πνεύματος σὺν τῇ δυνάμει τοῦ κυρίου ἡμῶν Ἰησοῦ . . .[3] Compared with the general words on reconciliation in Lk. 17 4, Mt. 18 21–22 is an exhortation to a generous handling of church discipline.

In a similar manner we might continue with our observations showing the changing of function and emphasis. Many similar changes as to context and focal interest, mutatis mutandis, are pointed out by Kilpatrick as arguments for the liturgical function of the gospel. We have spent a short time on the church discipline material, since these changes are least favourable to the liturgical interpretation.

If our observations are considered to be sound, then Kilpatrick's alternative between liturgical and catechetical is over-simplified. Clearly, the gospel cannot be explained as merely catechetical. Even if this word is given a wider sense as post-baptismal, it hardly covers the whole of the material. Nor does it help if we emphasize that "catechetical" is not to be taken in an ethical sense alone. In the studies on primitive Christian catechism as we find them skilfully treated by CARRINGTON and SELWYN[4], some of the important results of the investigations of A. SEEBERG half a century ago[5] have been omitted. He considered that the term "catechism" covered both ethics and dogmatics. The distinction between

---

[1] STRACK-BILLERBECK, *Kommentar zum N.T. aus Talmud und Midrasch* I (1922), p. 739.

[2] Cf. below, p. 139.   [3] Cf. BOHREN, *op. cit.*, p. 109.

[4] CARRINGTON, *The Primitive Christian Catechism*, SELWYN, *Comm. 1 Peter*, Essay II, p. 365–466.

[5] *Der Katechismus der Urchristenheit* (1903), *Das Evangelium Christi* (1905), *Die beiden Wege und das Aposteldekret* (1906), *Die Didache des Judentums und der Urchristenheit* (1908).

kerygma and didache found already in Dibelius, and elaborated with convincing force particularly by Dodd, has led to the understanding of didache as ethical teaching.[1] It may be that the actual content of the book Didache is responsible for such a limited terminology among scholars. The tendency is already obvious in DODD's *The Apostolic Preaching*[2] and in his *Gospel and Law* "didache" is understood as the mere moral instruction.[3] Here it is linked with the parallelism halakah = ethical instruction, over against haggadah = exposition of religious truth, a distinction also used by Dibelius[4], in spite of the fact that haggadah was all but free from moral instruction. From a formal point of view it was most typically teaching, whereas halakah was the direct message from God and thus rather "kerygmatic".[5]

Even if freed from the limitations of the definitions "pre-baptismal" and "ethical instruction", the term "catechetical" falls short of a definition of the Sitz im Leben of the First Gospel.

The same seems to be true, however, of the liturgical character, if this is offered as the final explanation of typical trends in Matthew. A handbook might hardly have been the ideal of those who intended to render the gospel more suitable for liturgical use. It is at this point that the school may be invoked as a more natural Sitz im Leben. The systematizing work[6], the adaptation towards casuistry instead of broad statements of principles[7], the reflection on the position of the church leaders and their duties, and many other similar features, all point to a milieu of study and instruction.

---

[1] DIBELIUS, *Formgeschichte*, p. 15 f.: "Kerygma" (as against "Paränese"), DODD, *The Apostolic Preaching* (1950[2]) and *Gospel and Law* (1951), cf. the critical remarks of F. V. FILSON, The Christian Teacher in the First Century, *Journ. of Bibl. Lit.* 60 (1941), p. 325 f.

[2] p. 7, and about didache = the (book) Didache, see p. 53.

[3] p. 11 f., cf. p. 6 on Matthew. The narrow ethical compass of the term didache leads Dodd to concentrate on the Sermon on the Mount.

[4] DIBELIUS involves himself in difficulties since on the one hand the words of Jesus are = halakah and the deeds = haggadah (*Formgeschichte*, p. 26), while on the other hand a typical feature of the halakah is to be attached to stories (p. 135 f.) just as the words of Jesus are found in the paradigms (p. 54), *i.e.* the most typical N.T. haggadah according to the distinction of Dibelius.

[5] On the confusion inherent in the term kerygma, see K. STENDAHL, *op. cit.*

[6] As against Mark, on whom Papias said ἔγραψεν, οὐ μέντοι τάξει, *Eusebius*, Hist. eccl. iii, 39 15.

[7] The most typical example is naturally the Matthaean statements on divorce, 5 31–32 and 19 9, see below, p. 137.

The Matthaean school and similar features
in the primitive church

There is no a priori reason why the Matthaean revision of Mark was not the ingenious work of one man, "the author", whether his name was Matthew or not. VON DOBSCHÜTZ suggested that he might have been a converted rabbi. If this is so, the concluding remarks in Mt. 13 52 may be a veiled reference to the author, just as in Mk. 14 52 the verse about the young man who left his mantle and fled is often considered to be such a reference. Yet, for the understanding of the gospel and for our knowledge of the early church another question is of great importance: How does such a Christian scribe fit into the context of his church?

The rapid and outstanding success of the First Gospel in the early church, and the well-known fact that the spiritual and religious atmosphere of this gospel is most nearly akin to post-apostolic Christianity is hard to explain, however, if what Matthew did was a unique feature in the life of the early church. It is much more probable that the First Gospel was the product of closer affinity to the centre of early church life than could have been the case if it were the outcome of the unusual chance fact that there happened to be a converted rabbi who succeeded in combining the old forms and the new faith. If we owe the gospel to a converted rabbi, we must suppose that he was not working entirely alone, but that he took an active part in the life of the church where he lived and served.[1] This is tantamount to saying that there was a school at work in the church of Matthew.

When Jesus is said to have forbidden his disciples to be called rabbi, father or teacher, Mt. 23 8–10, this is in no way a challenge to the existence of a school. On the contrary, it is only if something similar to the schools of the rabbis existed that the saying has any real significance.[2]

---

[1] KILPATRICK, op. cit., p. 136 f., stresses most strongly how the gospel was a product sponsored by the church where "the converted rabbi" worked as a Christian scribe. The scribal gifts were the "gift of style and construction, . . . ability to adapt varied materials to his purpose". These are, however, hardly the most typical gifts of a rabbi, though they are the only ones useful in re-editing a lectionary.

[2] A. SCHLATTER, Die Kirche des Matthäus (1929), p. 24, does not interpret the

In the epilogue which A. FRIDRICHSEN wrote to the last issue of *Svensk Exegetisk Årsbok* which he edited, he used the term *chaburah* in defining the early church, especially with reference to its production of biblical literature.[1] In spite of the temptation to over-stress the relevance of the Qumran Scrolls just now when they are so new to us, it may not be a mistake to refer to these once again. In them we get an insight into an actual Jewish *chaburah*.[2] That this brotherhood acted as a school which preserved and expounded the doctrines and rules of its founder is seen already in its Manual of Discipline. The scholarly work of the Sect can be sampled and tested in its commentary on Habakkuk. The main object of our study on the school of Matthew will be to prove the close affinity between the type of O.T. interpretation to be found in a certain group of Matthew's quotations and the way in which the Sect of Qumran treats the book of Habakkuk.[3]

Should this hypothesis prove to be valid, we venture to consider it as an almost decisive argument in favour of the existence of a school in the early church. Thus, too, the general observations we have cursorily suggested in this introductory chapter are endorsed, and we are able to go further back and look for traces of school activity even outside the limits of the Matthaean milieu.

When Fridrichsen spoke about the apostolic *chaburah* as the creative milieu of N.T. literature, he may have had the Fourth Gospel in mind since he held the view that this gospel was produced in the Johannine school at Ephesus.[4] As we shall see, this view of his also finds support in the manner in which the Fourth Gospel deals with the O.T.[5]

Matthaean emphasis on teaching as a trace of a "handbook" for teachers. Therefore he concludes that "diese Pflicht (to teach) ist aber allen aufgelegt" and consequently there was no "Lehrstand" in the Matthaean church.

[1] 13 (1948), p. 123, cf. IDEM, *Markusevangeliet* (1952), p. 25 f.: the closest analogy to the transmission of gospel material is the way in which the disciples of the O.T. prophets handled the traditions of their Master.

[2] For the implication of this term, "geschlossene Gemeinschaft", see JOACH. JEREMIAS, *Jerusalem zur Zeit Jesu* II B (1937), p. 116–121.

[3] See our chapter "The formula quotations and the Habakkuk Commentary from Qumran. — The *pesher* manner of quoting Scripture", p. 183 ff.

[4] FRIDRICHSEN, *Johannesevangeliet* (1939). The reference to a school behind the Fourth Gospel was given by W. HEITMÜLLER, Zur Johannes-Tradition, *Zeitschr. f. d. neutest. Wissensch.* 15 (1914), p. 207. His intention was to determine the authorship. He did not consider the function of the school in the framework of primitive church life. This was done, however, by BOUSSET, *op. cit.*, p. 316, where he makes use of Heitmüller's arguments.   [5] See below, p. 163.

As to the Gospel according to Luke, little will be added to our understanding of its character and compilation in presuming the existence of a school. Luke alone of the evangelists sets out to write literature and to maintain Hellenistic standards and the ideals of LXX Greek. In this case, too, his manner of handling O.T. quotations will be found to support this commonly held view of the character of this gospel.[1]

Nevertheless, it is possible that Luke gives a clue to the problem of the most primitive Christian school in his use of the term ὑπηρέτης. In his preamble he refers to the eye witnesses and to the ὑπηρέται τοῦ λόγου, and according to Acts 13₅ John (Mark) was used by Paul and Barnabas as a ὑπηρέτης when they preached the gospel in the synagogues of the Jews. In Lk. 4₂₀ the same term is used of the חזן of the synagogue who takes care of the rolls from which the text for the day was read, and this Greek term is consistently used for חזן.[2] Elsewhere in the N.T. the ὑπηρέται are connected with the court (Mt. 5₂₅) or with the Sanhedrin (Mt. 26₅₈, John 9 times, Acts 5₂₂, ₂₆). חזן also has this meaning.[3] In Acts 26₁₆ Paul may refer to the officers and witnesses present in the court, and in 1 Cor. 4₁ ὑπηρέται Χριστοῦ is combined with οἰκονόμοι μυστηρίων θεοῦ. Thus the term has the connotation of an official of some kind. In the papyri the term is used of men who guarded or wrote documents. B. T. HOLMES stresses this last fact[4] and makes it an argument for an extremely early date for Mark's gospel, since he thinks that Acts 13₅ meant that Mark had even then brought his gospel with him "substantially as it exists to-day".[5] If his interpretation of the significance of the term is correct, it is rather an anachronistic reference to the Marcan gospel.

R. O. P. TAYLOR takes a somewhat different line.[6] He considers Mark as the חזן of the apostles. Now the duties of this Jewish official were many, especially in small congregations. He not only guarded and unrolled the holy texts, but he was also the person who gave primary instruction in the Law[7]; he was the catechist. So Mark had "to undertake

---

[1] See below, p. 157.

[2] *Epiphanius*, Haer. xx, 11 (on the Ebionites, MPG xli, col. 424): ... Ἀζανιτῶν τῶν παρ' αὐτοῖς διακόνων ἑρμηνευομένων ἢ ὑπηρετῶν. — J. KLAUSNER, *Von Jesus zu Paulus* (1950), p. 273, takes the other line equating the חזן with the διάκονος.

[3] M. JASTROW, *A Dictionary of the Targumim* . . . (1926), s. v.

[4] Luke's Description of John Mark, *Journ. of Bibl. Lit.* 54 (1935), p. 63–72.

[5] *ibm.,* p. 63.

[6] *The Groundwork of the Gospels* (1946), p. 21–26.

[7] It must be admitted that the duties of the חזן in the school seem to have been

the drudgery of teaching this new chapter of history" which told about Jesus the Messiah.[1]

If this is true, the ὑπηρέται τοῦ λόγου in Lk. 1 2 are the instructors and the term is not only synonymous with the term for eye-witnesses.[2] Furthermore, this offers a most concrete Sitz im Leben for the gospel material, namely the school.

The synagogue was an undefined combination of a house of worship and a school.[3] Even the so-called homiletic *midrashim* do not therefore contain sermons, but are rather manuals in which are collected various ways of expounding a homiletic theme, as can be seen *e.g.* in the Pesikta Rab Kahana, where "the sermonic form is perhaps most nearly represented".[4] The language of these homiletic *midrashim* is Hebrew. Yet the school type of the homiletic material is not exclusively confined to the collection of material; it is found in the sermon itself. There is good reason to believe that the introductory formula ילמדנו רבנו, "Let our master teach us", with which a question on the *halakah* was prefaced, was the oldest form for beginning a sermon.[5] Thus the distinction between a house of worship and a school is hard to draw even in the homiletic material, though the balance is definitely in favour of the school. The basic instruction of the חזן, however, was entirely a matter for the school, and if we dare to consider the ὑπηρέτης as his Christian counterpart in the earliest period of the church, then it is possible to look upon the school as the Sitz im Leben of the gospel material from its earliest stages.

The evidence for such a hypothesis may appear to be rather weak, but having found that preaching as the Sitz im Leben of the gospel

---

the least important of his many tasks, S. KRAUSS, *Synagogale Altertümer* (1922), p. 126. See *bShabbath* 11 a (*mishnah*), where the *Tosephta* replaces חזן by רב. The little support in Rabbinics of חזן = "teacher" is certainly due to the fact that he had that task in synagogues without higher standing or influence on the rabbinic traditions.

[1] TAYLOR, *op. cit.*, p. 24.

[2] Against DIBELIUS, *Formgeschichte*, p. 11, and F. VOGEL, *Neue Kirchl. Zeitschr.* 44 (1933), p. 203–205, cf. H. SAHLIN, *Der Messias und das Gottesvolk* (1945), p. 39–42. — Note κατηχήθης in verse 4.

[3] Cf. L. J. SHERRILL, *The Rise of Christian Education* (1944), p. 44–47.

[4] G. F. MOORE, *Judaism* I (1927), p. 305, cf. III (1930), p. 101. *Pesikta Rab Kahana*, ed. S. BUBER (1868), transl. A. WÜNSCHE (1885).

[5] S. MAYBAUM, *Die ältesten Phasen in der Entwicklung der jüdischen Predigt* (1901), p. 5–6.

material is open to serious criticism, it is certainly worth while searching elsewhere for the origins of the gospel. The school does have the advantage of agreeing with the practice of the synagogue out of which the primitive church grew.

Finally, "one of the most firmly fixed elements in the Synoptic tradition is the fact that Jesus was regularly addressed as 'Rabbi'", and that a group of disciples gathered around him.[1] It sounds a mere truism to recall this fact, but in recent form-criticism it is often overshadowed by the stress on missionary preaching. There is every reason to assume that the social pattern of the rabbi and his disciples made a deep impression on early church life. There is no need for any conflict between this pattern and the messianic claims of the church. The character of Jesus as a teacher was not a kenotic feature in his incarnation[2], and discipleship would always imply not merely acceptance of his messianic claim and personal commitment to obedience to Him. There is no single part of the N.T. where knowledge of His teaching and of the significance of His person in the context of sacred history is not a self-evident demand.

There may therefore be an unbroken line from the School of Jesus via the "teaching of the apostles", the "ways" of Paul[3], the basic teaching of Mark and other ὑπηρέται τοῦ λόγου, and the more mature School of John to the rather elaborate School of Matthew with its ingenious interpretation of the O.T. as the crown of its scholarship.[4]

---

[1] B. S. Easton, The First Evangelic Tradition, *Journ. of Bibl. Lit.* 50 (1931), p. 148, cf. O. Moe, Fra skole til kirke, *Tidsskrift for Teologi og Kirke* 19 (1948), p. 93–98.

[2] The Messiah as teacher, see J. Bonsirven, *Le Judaisme Palestinien au temps de Jésus-Christ* I (1934), p. 454, cf. below, p. 190 f.

[3] 1 Cor. 4 17. On the catechetical significance of the Pauline expression, see Seeberg, *Der Katechismus der Urchristenheit*, p. 6 ff.

[4] Already the existence of διδάσκαλοι in the early church points to its character as a school. There are, however, few means for establishing their exact duties as opposed to those of other officials of the church. See Rengstorf, *Theol. Wörterb. z. N.T.* II, p. 160–162, and F. V. Filson, The Christian Teacher in the First Century, *Journ. of Bibl. Lit.* 60 (1941), p. 317–328. — For the Matthaean problem the Christian γραμματεῖς, Mt. 13 52 and (together with the σοφοί, חכמים) Mt. 23 34, are of more interest. This very title can be said to determine the character of the gospel, see J. Hoh, Der christliche γραμματεύς, *Bibl. Zeitschr.* 17 (1925/26), p. 256–269. — The hypothesis of the school as the Sitz im Leben of the gospels may have some bearing on the originally rather venerable function of the *lector*, who later on was one of the minor officials of the church, see Harnack, Über den Ursprung des Lectorats, in *Die Quellen der sogenannten apostolischen Kirchenordnung* (1886), p. 57–89.

Clearly, these stages do not emerge out of each other, and "unbroken" has no evolutionary meaning. In the Jewish school system there were various degrees.[1] The basic teaching in the reading of the Scriptures was given in the בית הספר attached to the synagogue. Higher education was the concern of the בית המדרש. It was to the former that the חזן was confined, while Matthew's treatment of the O.T. text brings him closer to the latter.

Thus the Matthaean school must be understood as a school for teachers and church leaders, and for this reason the literary work of that school assumes the form of a manual for teaching and administration within the church. As we shall see, the Matthaean type of midrashic interpretation is not principally the halakic or the haggadic one favoured by the rabbinic schools, but it closely approaches what has been called the *midrash pesher* of the Qumran Sect, in which the O.T. texts were not primarily the source of rules, but the prophecy which was shown to be fulfilled.

---

[1] MOORE, *Judaism* I, p. 308–322, and also L. J. SHERRILL, *op. cit.*, p. 47–72, and B. HAREIDE, Undervisninga i Palestina på Jesu tid, *Tidsskrift for Teologi og Kirke* 20 (1949), p. 77–93.

THE QUOTATIONS FROM THE OLD
TESTAMENT

The study of quotations in Matthew

From ORIGEN onwards we can trace how Matthew's manner of quoting the O.T. has presented special problems to his interpreters.[1] CELSUS had criticized the N.T.'s use of the Scriptures[2] and again in PORPHYRY († 305) we find a similar criticism of wrongly cited quotations in Mk. 1 2 and Mt. 13 35.[3] EUSEBIUS replies to the charge; his work *Against Porphyry* is lost, but in his commentary on the Psalter we find an echo of opposition to Porphyry's argument. Eusebius's reasoning is that of textual criticism, but he is also the first to explain Matthew's particular rendering by calling attention to the Hebrew text.[4]

It should be possible to refer to a still earlier witness, namely JUSTIN. In his *Dialogue* with the Jew Trypho, he sets out a comprehensive vindication of the LXX text used by him and the Christians he represents. This will also be relevant to such a quotation as Mt. 1 23, but Justin's starting point is not specifically the text of the gospel, but of the O.T.[5]

It was JEROME, however, who first dealt with the quotation problem more exhaustively. A passage in his letter *ad Aglasisam* will serve to illustrate this.[6] His starting point is the quotation from Is. 42 1–4 in

---

[1] ORIGEN, *Comm. in Mt.* ad 21 5 (ed. KLOSTERMANN I, 1935–37, p. 522) mentions the differences between Matthew and John, but he does not discuss their relation to Greek or Hebrew O. T. text. — *ibm.* ad 27 9 (ed. KLOSTERMANN II, 1933, p. 249 f.) the reference to Jeremiah is said to be either a mistake for Zechariah or to refer to an apocryphal text of Jeremiah. For those offended at this explanation Origen points to the extra-canonical quotations in 1 Cor. 2 9 and 2 Tim. 3 8. Cf. JEROME, *Comm. in Mt.* ad 27 9 (MPL xxvi, col. 205).

[2] In Mt. 1 23, JEROME, *epist.* lvii, 9 (MPL xxii, col. 575, cf. PORPHYRY, *Against the Christians*, ed. HARNACK, *Abhandl. d. königl. preuss. Akad. d. Wissensch.* 1916, Phil.-hist. Kl. 1, p. 46).

[3] Fragments *2* (Mt. 1 23), *9* (Mk. 1 2, cf. JEROME, *Comm. in Mt.* ad 3 3, referring the reading "Isaiah" in Mk. 1 2 to scribal error, MPL xxvi, col. 29), *10* (Mt. 13 35) and *15* (Mt. 27 46) in PORPHYRY's *Against the Christians*.

[4] *Comm. in Ps.* ad 77 2 (MPG xxiii, col. 901 and 904), see below p. 116.

[5] See below, p. 98 and 182.

[6] *Epist.* cxxi (MPL xxii, col. 1010 f.), cf. JEROME, *Comm. in Is.* ad 42 1–4 (MPL xxiv, col. 421 f.).

Mt. 12 18–21. Jerome successively cites the text of Matthew, the LXX, and the Hebrew text, and points out that Matthew, who omits the LXX's "Jacob" and "Israel", has as a Hebrew gone to the Hebrew text, not only in this case, but also, for example, in 2 15 : Hos. 11 1.[1] But when Matthew finds in the Hebrew text "et in lege ejus sperabit insulae", he prefers to reproduce the meaning and substitutes "nomen" and "gentes" for "lex" and "insulae". This occurs not only here. Wherever the evangelists and apostles quote the O.T. it should be noted that they do not follow the wording but the meaning, and where the LXX and the Hebrew texts differ, they render the meaning of the Hebrew.[2]

Biblical research has never ceased to be occupied with this problem since Eusebius and Jerome raised it. The study of quotations from the O.T. standing in the N.T. can have many functions and the way in which it is handled is in part coloured by the purposes the various students had behind their studies. It is of value to note this to arrive at a true estimate of the different results. The various functions of the modern study of quotations can be grouped into the following main divisions:

I. LXX research and in particular studies in the "proto-LXX". To this group belong some of the most thorough investigations. The N.T. quotations thus come to be added to that material which Philo, Josephus, Justin and others have contributed to our knowledge of the

---

[1] This and the avowed quotation in Mt. 2 23, are the typical ones in Jerome's treatment of Matthew's manner of quoting the O.T., *epist.* xx (*ad Damasum*, MPL xxii, col. 376) and *Comm. in Is.* ad 6 9 (MPL xxiv, col. 98 f.), where a similar manner is observed in Jn. 7 38 and 19 37 and in Hebrews. — The text of Mt. 2 15 and 2 23 as signs of Hebrew text are also stated in the famous passage in *De vir. ill.* 3 (ed. HERDING): In quo (*scil.* the Hebrew gospel shown to Jerome by the Nazarenes) animadvertendum quod ubicumque evangelista sive ex persona sua sive ex Domini Salvatoris veteris scripturae testimoniis abutitur, non sequitur septuaginta translatorum auctoritatem, sed hebraicam. E quibus illa duo sunt: "ex Aegypto vocavi Filium meum" et "quoniam Nazaraeus vocabitur".

[2] Et hoc non solum in praesenti loco, sed ubicumque de veteri Instrumento Evangelistae et Apostoli testimonia protulerunt, diligentius observandum est: non eos verba secutos esse sed sensum: et ubi Septuaginta ab Hebraico discrepant, Hebraeum sensum suis expressisse sermonibus. (MPL xxii, col. 1011) — Cf. the notes in the margin of cod. 86 to Zech. 12 11, see *Duodecim prophetae* (ed. ZIEGLER), *ad loc.*

Other Jerome passages: *Comm. in Is.* ad 9 1 (MPL xxiv, col. 124), *Comm. in Jer.* ad 31 15 (MPL xxiv, col. 876 f.), *Comm. in Mich.* ad 5 2 (MPL xxv, col. 1196 f.) and the passages referred to above.

Greek text of the O.T. before the Uncials, Origen, and the time of most of the papyri.[1]

II. The massoretic problem and the establishment of the *hebraica veritas*. This aspect has to a certain extent lost its significance in view of the greater reliance which modern research places on the M.T. Arising out of this, most scholars are more hesitant in drawing any conclusions about the Hebrew text from what they find in the LXX or in other Greek texts, including the N.T. quotations.[2]

III. For N.T. research the study of quotations has one or more of the following functions:

a) For the Synoptics the study of quotations is an essential to the understanding of the sources and composition of the gospels.[3] For instance, work on the LXX in this case becomes quite another matter than for students of the LXX who pursue the original text. From the N.T. point of view it is a question of finding the O.T. text used in the

---

[1] W. STAERK, Die alttestamentlichen Citate bei den Schriftstellern des Neuen Testaments, *Zeitschr. f. wissenschaftl. Theol.* 35 (1892), p. 464–85; 36:1 (1893), p. 70–98; 38 (1895), p. 218–30; 40 (1897), p. 211–68. H. B. SWETE, *An Introduction to the Old Testament in Greek* (1900), p. 381–405. A. SPERBER, New Testament and Septuagint, *Journ. of Bibl. Lit.* 59 (1940), p. 193–293, cf. *Tarbiz* 6 (1934/35), p. 1–29. — Also in P. KAHLE, *The Cairo Geniza* (1947), the N.T. material is used as arguments in the proto-LXX discussion, cf. below, p. 174.

[2] See below, p. 166, cf. p. 81.

[3] Remarks of this kind are found in most introductions and commentaries, see especially TH. ZAHN, *Einleitung in das Neue Testament* II (1899[1]), p. 314–20 (cf. the 3rd edition, 1907, p. 321–24. For our study the 1st ed. is to be preferred because the 3rd is abbreviated at this point and the material is scattered in Zahn's commentary on Matthew). J. MOFFATT, *An Introduction to the Literature of the New Testament* (1918), p. 258, W. C. ALLEN, *Comm. Mt.* (1907) in the *Intern. Critic. Comm.*, p. lxi f., M.-J. LAGRANGE, *Comm. Mt.* (1927[3]), p. cxvii–cxxiv. Other works with special reference to Matthew: R. ANGER, Ratio qua loci Veteris Testamenti in evangelio Matthaei laudantur, quid valeat ad illustrandum hujus evangelii originem, I–III, *Leipziger Programme* 1861 and 1862, E. HAUPT, *Zur Würdigung der alttestamentlichen Citationen im Evangelium Matthaei* (1870), cf. IDEM, *Die alttestamentlichen Citate der vier Evangelien* (1871), E. MASSEBIEAU, *Examen des citations de l'Ancien Testament dans l'Évangile selon Matthieu* (1885), A. H. McNEILE, Our Lord's use of the Old Testament, *Cambridge Biblical Essays* (1909), p. 214–50, B. W. BACON, *Studies in Matthew* (1930), p. 470–77, CH. C. TORREY, The Biblical Quotations in Matthew, *Documents of the Primitive Church* (1941), p. 41–90, SH. E. JOHNSON, The Biblical Quotations in Matthew, *Harv. Theol. Rev.* 36 (1943), p. 135–53, G. D. KILPATRICK, *The Origins of the Gospel according to St. Matthew* (1946), p. 56 f. and 95, T. W. MANSON, The Old Testament in the Teaching of Jesus, *Bull. of J. Ryl. Libr.* 34 (1951/52) p. 312–32.

N.T., whether uncorrupted or not, whether it can be related to an archetype or not. If fundamental differences are found in the quotations, then we have a solid basis on which to form a judgement on synoptic questions. Our purpose is thus, as far as possible, to separate from the rest of the arguments in the synoptic question any indications of quotations.

b) Closely linked to *a*) is the question of the original language — in our case Matthew's.[1] The quotations might afford one of the most decisive tests in this matter.

c) The function and significance of the quotations from the Scriptures, that is, the hermeneutic aspect, can be studied either for its own sake or for its contribution to the N.T.'s attitude to the O.T.[2]

d) In this connection there is a fourth aspect, which is distinct from *c*), *viz.* the question of the quotation's *Sitz im Leben*.[3] What picture of the church's study of the Scriptures do Matthew's quotations give us?

The purpose of our study of the quotations in Matthew is in the main twofold: to throw light upon the relations between the sources and their development, and to see how the form of the quotations helps to explain the milieu of the gospel.

For the earlier phases of research into quotations, reference may with advantage be made to VOLLMER's work of 1895 on the Pauline quotations from the O.T. The literature there cited and referred to partly covers the question of quotations in the N.T. in general.[4]

---

[1] The works of ANGER, ZAHN, LAGRANGE and TORREY, referred to in the preceding note and J. H. A. EBRARD, *Wissenschaftliche Kritik der evangelischen Geschichte* (1842[1]), p. 927 f. (1868[3]) p. 999–1001, F. BLEEK, *Beiträge zur Evangelien-Kritik* (1846), p. 56–58, E. BÖHL, *Die alttestamentlichen Citate im Neuen Testament* (1878).

[2] This aspect dominates one of the last studies of the quotations, C. SMITS, Oud-Testamentische Citaten in het Nieuwe Testament I, Synoptische Evangeliën, *Collect. Francisc. Neerlandica* 8:1 (1952), as is the case also with another Dutch work, A. VIS, *The Messianic Psalm Quotations in the New Testament* (1936). D. M. TURPIE, *The New Testament View of the Old* (1872), cf. IDEM, *The Old Testament in the New* (1868), TH. HAERING, Das Alte Testament im Neuen, *Zeitschr. f. d. neutest. Wissensch.* 17 (1916), p. 213–27, J. HÄNEL, *Der Schriftbegriff Jesu* (1919), G. H. GILBERT, *Jesus and his Bible* (1926), L. GOPPELT, *Typos* (1939), W. VISCHER, *Das Christuszeugnis des Alten Testaments* I–II (1946 and 1942).

[3] The vast literature on the hypothesis of testimonies belongs partly to this group, see below, p. 207 ff. The *Sitz im Leben* is considered by C. H. DODD, *According to the Scriptures* (1952).

[4] H. VOLLMER, *Die Alttestamentlichen Citate bei Paulus* (1895), p. 1–9. In

The nature of the material may be illustrated in a preliminary way by the word statistics which J. C. Hawkins has given in *Horae Synopticae*.[1]

I. Quotations avowedly introduced by the author or editor of the gospel:

---

addition to the literature classified above and mostly also to Vollmer, these works may be mentioned:

a) technical means: W. Dittmar, *Vetus Testamentum in Novo* (1903) and R. Chasles, *L'Ancien Testament dans le Nouveau* (1937).

b) general studies: A. Th. Hartmann, *Die enge Verbindung des Alten Testaments mit dem Neuen* (1831), F. A. G. Tholuck, *Das Alte Testament im Neuen Testament* (1836[1], 1849[3]), C. H. Toy, *Quotations in the New Testament* (1884), A. Clemen, *Der Gebrauch des Alten Testamentes in den neutestamentlichen Schriften* (1895), E. Hühn, *Die alttestamentlichen Citate und Reminiscenzen im Neuen Testamente* (1900), F. H. Woods, art. Quotations, *Hastings's Dictionary of the Bible*, IV (1902), p. 184–88, G. H. Box, The Value and Significance of the Old Testament in Relation to the New, *The People and the Book* (ed. A. S. Peake, 1925), p. 433–67, L. Venard, art. Citations de l'Ancien Testament dans le Nouveau Testament, *Dictionnaire de la Bible*, Suppl. II (1934), col. 23–51, R. V. G. Tasker, *The Old Testament in the New Testament* (1946).

c) special studies: M. Black, The Problem of the Old Testament Quotations in the Gospels, *Journ. of the Manchester Egyptian and Oriental Society* 23 (1942), p. 4, T. W. Manson, The argument from Prophecy, *Journ. of Theol. St.* 46 (1945), p. 129–36, idem, The Cairo Geniza, *Dominican Studies* 2 (1949) p. 183–92, D. Sidersky, Les citations de l'Ancien Testament dans les Évangiles, *Actes du congrès intern. d'hist. des rel. 1923*, II (1925), p. 256–60, F. K. Feigel, *Der Einfluss des Weissagungsbeweises und anderer Motive auf die Leidensgeschichte* (1910), K. Weidel, Studien über den Einfluss des Weissagungsbeweises auf die evangelische Geschichte, *Theol. St. u. Krit.* 83 (1910), p. 83–109, 163–95, K. F. Euler, *Die Verkündigung vom leidenden Gottesknecht aus Jes. 53 in der griechischen Bibel* (1934), W. Hasenzahl, *Die Gottverlassenheit des Christus nach dem Kreuzeswort bei Matthäus und Markus und das christologische Verständnis des griechischen Psalters* (1937), H. W. Wolff, *Jesaja 53 im Urchristentum* (1942). — A. H. Franke, *Das Alte Testament bei Johannes* (1885). — J. Dupont, L'utilisation apologétique de l'Ancien Testament dans les discours des Actes, *Ephemer. Theol. Lovan.* 29 (1953), p. 289–327. — O. Michel, *Paulus und seine Bibel* (1929). — G. Harder, Die Septuagintazitate des Hebräerbriefs, *Theologia Viatorum* (1939), p. 33–52. — A. Schlatter, *Das Alte Testament in der johanneischen Apokalypse* (1912).

The best bibliographies are to be found in the articles of Venard and Dupont.

[1] 2nd edition (1909), p. 154–56, cf. below, p. 143.

	Words in LXX	Words not in LXX		Words in LXX	Words not in LXX
Mt. 1 23	13	2	8 17	2	7
2 15	2	4	12 18–21	20	31
18	14	6	13 35	6	4
23	...	...	21 5	10	7
4 15, 16	20	13	27 9, 10	4	21
				100	95

II. One quotation recorded as spoken by the scribes in the introductory chapters 1 and 2:

	Words in LXX	Words not in LXX
Mt. 2 6	8	16

III. Quotations recorded as spoken in the part of the Sermon on the Mount peculiar to Matthew:

	Words in LXX	Words not in LXX		Words in LXX	Words not in LXX
Mt. 5 21	2	...	5 33	2 (?)	7
27	2	...	38	6	1
31	3	6	43	4	5
				19	19

IV. Quotations occurring in the course of the double or triple narrative, and found also in Mark or Luke or both of them:

	Words in LXX	Words not in LXX		Words in LXX	Words not in LXX
Mt. 3 3	13	1	21 13	6	...
4 4	15	...	42	20	...
6	18	1	22 24	7	12
7	6	...	32	11	2
10	8	1	37	14	7
11 10	9	7	39	6	...
15 4	13	...	44	18	1
8, 9	23	...	24 15	3	...
19 5	20	1	26 31	3	3
			27 46	6	2
				219	38

V. Quotations occurring in the course of the double or triple narrative, but not themselves recorded by either Mark or Luke:

	Words in LXX	Words not in LXX		Words in LXX	Words not in LXX
Mt. 9 13	3	2	13 14, 15	47	1
12 7	3	2	21 16	7	...
				60	5

Even a hasty study of these statistics shows that quotations with parallels in one or both of the Synoptics have a rather pure LXX text, while the so-called *formula quotations*[1] have a text form differing noticeably from the LXX. A closer study of the material, however, yields a more complicated picture.

Quotation and allusion.

The question of where to draw the line between quotations and allusions is a problem in itself. NESTLE sets both out in heavy type and thus broadly follows WESTCOTT-HORT who marked with capitals both quotations in a wider sense and allusions, and in a few places characteristic single words.[2]

We already come across the idea of marking the quotations in the text in the Uncials from the 4th century. In the margins of for instance codices ℵ, B and A we find signs consisting of small horizontal cursive *nu* (>), standing beneath each other.[3] It is difficult to decide whether these signs are inserted into the manuscripts at a later date; those in cod. B could be contemporaneous, while those in cod. A appear to be more carelessly written than the neat script in the rest of the MS.

---

[1] The term is SH. JOHNSON's synonym to the German "Reflexionscitate" (*e.g.* M. DIBELIUS, *Die Formgeschichte des Evangeliums*, 1933 [2], p. 188) for Hawkins's 1st (and 2nd) group, *Harv. Theol. Rev.* 36 (1943), p. 135.

[2] WESTCOTT-HORT, *The New Testament in Greek* II (1882), p. 316, E. NESTLE, *Novum Testamentum Graece* (1950 [20]), p. 8*.

[3] Greek O.T. MSS available to me in facsimile were: *Biblorum SS. Graecorum, Codex Vaticanus 1209 (Cod. B)*. Denuo phototypice expressus ... (1904), *Codex Sinaiticus Petripolitanus*, Facsim. ed. H. and K. LAKE (1911) and *Codex Alexandrinus*. Reduced photographic facsimile ed. (1909). — Nearly the same signs are used in non Greek MSS as *e.g.* in L'*Évangile Arménien*. Édition phototypique du manuscr. 229 de la Bibliothèque d'Etchmiadzin (ed. F. MACHER, 1920). In *Syrus sinaiticus*, however, such quotation marks are wanting, see A. HJELT's facsimile edition (1930).

Cod. B has the greatest number of such signs — twenty-five of them in Matthew, but even here only for quotations in the strict sense.[1] It may be observed that the signs are lacking in the quotations about marriage in chaps. 5 and 19, as also in 18 16, 21 9, 13, and 22 24. On the other hand 2 23 is marked as a quotation — the only case where cod. B goes beyond Nestle and Westcott-Hort.

We are confining our actual investigation to the strict quotations, by which we mean partly those passages introduced by a formula[2], and partly those which, although lacking such formula, are nevertheless conscious quotations, judging from the context, or which agree verbatim with some passage in the O.T. in its Greek or Hebrew form. This is the demarcation line drawn by SWETE which practically agrees with Hawkins's.[3] We shall bring all of these texts into our discussion.

We should first examine the quotations with synoptic parallels, and treat separately quotations with parallels only in Luke. This is because amongst other things the distinction between quotation and allusion is more complex in the material common to Matthew and Luke than in the rest of the material.[4] Of this type Hawkins only noted the quotations in the homogeneous tradition on the temptation of Jesus.

During the course of our inquiry, in spite of the uncertainty it involves, we shall be compelled to make use of even the allusive references, whose significance has been given particular prominence by SH. JOHNSON.[5] Obviously that very material is of special importance for the question which most interests Johnson, namely the relation between Matthew and Q.

---

[1] 1 23, 2 6, 15, 18, 23, 3 3, 4 4, 6, 10, 15–16, 8 17, 11 10, 12 18–21, 13 14–15, 35, 15 4, 8–9, 19 18–19, 21 5, 16, 42, 22 32, 37–39, 44, 27 9.

[2] That is not only formula quotations in the sense just mentioned above. On the different introductory formulae, see E. HÜHN, *Die alttest. Citate*, p. 271–77, cf. SWETE, *Introduction to the Old Testament in Greek*, p. 382, and for the Pauline texts, O. MICHEL, *Paulus und seine Bibel*, p. 72.

[3] SWETE, *loc. cit.*

[4] See below, p. 88 ff.

[5] *Harv. Theol. Rev.* 36 (1943), p. 136.

The texts

1. Quotations with parallels in Mark or in Mark and Luke

Mt. 3₃ ≠ Mk. 1₃ ≠ Lk. 3₄: Is. 40₃; cf. Jn. 1₂₃.

Mt.

(οὗτος γάρ ἐστιν ὁ ῥηθεὶς διὰ Ἠσα-
ίου τοῦ προφήτου λέγοντος·)

φωνὴ βοῶντος ἐν τῇ ἐρήμῳ· ἑτοιμά-
σατε τὴν ὁδὸν κυρίου, εὐθείας ποιεῖτε τὰς τρίβους αὐτοῦ.

εὐθ. — αὐτοῦ] om. syr^sin.
αὐτοῦ] "of our God" syr^cur.

Jn. 1₂₃ ἔφη ['Ιωάννης]· ἐγὼ φωνὴ
βοῶντος ἐν τῇ ἐρήμῳ· εὐθύνατε τὴν
ὁδὸν κυρίου, καθὼς εἶπεν Ἠσαΐας
ὁ προφήτης.

Is. 40₃ LXX = Mt. except αὐτοῦ]
τοῦ θεοῦ ἡμῶν. — Aquila has εὐθύνατε, but for the rest he differs from
the N. T.

Mk., see below, Mt. 11₁₀.

Lk.: ὡς γέγραπται ἐν βίβλῳ λόγων
Ἠσαΐου τοῦ προφήτου·

Mk. and Lk. = Mt.   Variants:
αὐτοῦ] Mk.: τοῦ θεοῦ ὑμῶν D; Lk.:
ὑμῶν D. In Lk. syr^sin cur is closer
to M. T., due to influence from
the O.T. Peshitta (בערבה:ܚܣܡܐ).[1]
— The text in Lk. continues with
Is. 40₄₋₅. Lk.'s εἰς ὁδοὺς λείας =
LXX^A as against LXX^B. Lk.'s text
somewhat abbreviated.

M.T.

קול קורא במדבר פנו דרך יהוה
ישרו בערבה מסלה לאלהינו

The quotation is unique within its group since it is the only formula
quotation with synoptic parallels.[2] Admittedly the introductory formula
lacks ἵνα πληρωθῇ, the term typical of Matthew, or some other form of
the verb πληροῦν, even if the formula in Matthew is suited to this
gospel's phraseology. In all three Synoptics, however, the clear inten-

---

[1] See F. C. Burkitt, *Evangelion Da-Mepharreshe* II (1904), p. 204.

[2] Lagrange, *Comm. Mt.*, p. cxix, therefore assigns it to a class akin to Hawkins
first group: Textes au compte de l'évangéliste. — It is worth noticing that Matthew
uses an introducing formula similar to those usually used by him instead of the
more technical formulae of Mk. and Lk.

tion is to express the fulfilment of prophecy by a quotation, introduced
by the evangelists themselves. It is worth noticing that also in its form
this synoptic quotation shows similarity to the formula quotations
peculiar to Matthew.

The text is exactly the same in all three Gospels, even in the form
αὐτοῦ as against the LXX's τοῦ θεοῦ ἡμῶν and the M.T.'s לֵאלֹהֵינוּ.
Justin, Dial. 50₃ follows the LXX with τοῦ θεοῦ ἡμῶν, but has the
reading τὰς ὁδούς peculiar to him.

Apart from this deviation the text of the gospels is clearly LXX;
this is most evident in that it follows the LXX's syntactical division
"A voice crying in the wilderness: Prepare the way of the Lord, make
straight his paths." When the LXX combines "in the wilderness" with
"a voice", it drops the parallel expression "in the desert". This is the
text the N.T. reproduces and its understanding of the prophecy is
necessary to its function in the gospels.[1] But this is not the meaning
of the M.T. or of the Targum as is obvious from the parallel "in the
wilderness" — "in the desert". How the Hebrew text in its turn could
be used as concretely in the signs of fulfilment, we can see in the Manual
of Discipline of the Qumran Sect. The sect which lived in the desert
applied to their lives and their work the words: Prepare in the desert
Yahweh's way . . . (DSD viii, 14).[2]

The quotation's LXX character is thus not only clear but also necessary, and the variant αὐτοῦ, common to the Synoptics must be a theological adaptation to their Christology. Here as in so many other cases
the LXX's κύριος is not the M.T.'s Yahweh, but Christ, and from this
new interpretation of the prophecy the quotation has received its form.[3]

In this first quotation of our study we already come across two other
features which we shall meet again in several places. Firstly, in Mark,
the words from Is. 40₃ form part of a composite quotation since they
are preceded by Mal. 3₁, this in spite of the fact that the introductory
formula to the whole refers to Isaiah. The words from Malachi are also
quoted in Matthew and Luke, likewise with reference to John the
Baptist, but in another context and as if they were an utterance of
Jesus, Mt. 11₁₀, Lk. 7₂₇.

---

[1] Stressed already by Hühn, *Die alttest. Citate*, p. 4.

[2] See below, p. 191.

[3] Cf. below to Mt. 22₄₄, p. 79. It is a delicate task to determine if this interpretation might be attached to the *qere* "Adonai".

Secondly, Luke's quotation from Is. 40₃ continues to 40₅. His text is thereby in agreement with LXX^A.[1]

Mt. 11₁₀ ≠ Mk. 1₂ ≠ Lk. 7₂₇: Mal. 3₁ (and Ex. 23₂₀).

Mt.	Mk.: καθὼς γέγραπται ἐν τῷ
(οὗτός ἐστιν περὶ οὗ γέγραπται·)	Ἡσαΐᾳ τῷ προφήτῃ (ἐν τοῖς προφήταις ℜ W *pm.*). Lk. = Mt.

ἰδοὺ ἐγὼ ἀποστέλλω τὸν ἄγγελόν μου πρὸ προσώπου σου, ὃς κατασκευάσει τὴν ὁδόν σου ἔμπροσθέν σου.

Mk. and Lk. = Mt. Variants:
ἐγὼ] Mk.: om. BD Θ *pc.* it; Lk.: om.
ἀποστέλλω] Mk.: ἀποστελῶ ℵΘ it.
ἔμπροσθέν σου] Mk.: om. all except ℜ *pm.*; Lk.: om. D *pc.* it.

Mal. 3₁ LXX^B

ἰδοὺ ἐξαποστέλλω τὸν ἄγγελόν μου, καὶ ἐπιβλέψεται ὁδὸν πρὸ προσώπου μου.

M.T.

הנני שלח מלאכי ופנה דרך לפני

ἰδού] add. ἐγώ ℵ^c AQF.
καὶ] om. ℵ*.

Ex. 23₂₀ LXX

καὶ ἰδοὺ ἐγὼ ἀποστέλλω τὸν ἄγγελόν μου πρὸ προσώπου σου, ἵνα φυλάξῃ σε ἐν τῇ ὁδῷ.

M.T.

הנה אנכי שלח מלאך לפניך לשמרך בדרך

All three Synoptics have κατασκευάσει which is foreign to the LXX. With reference to ἐγὼ the text is too uncertain to allow of any conclusions.

The N.T.'s reading lies closest to the M.T.,[2] but with its suffix/pronoun

---

[1] The first part of the *parallelismus membrorum* in Is. 40₅ is omitted both in LXX^A and Luke. The reading εἰς ὁδοὺς λείας and the omission of the obelized πάντα they also have in common. This case is important to SPERBER in his argument for "the Bible of the Apostles" being in accordance with the asterisk type of LXX text (cf. below, p. 176), *Journ. of Bibl. Lit.* 59 (1940), p. 280. ZIEGLER accepts the reading of A as *the* LXX text in his edition of Isaiah, *ad loc.*

[2] On the relation between the M.T. and the Hebrew text of the 1st century A.D., see below, p. 166. — For convenience the abbreviation "M.T." will occasionally be used for denoting the Hebrew text of the evangelists where there are no reasons to presume another Hebrew reading.

for the first person changed to the second person. However, Ex. 23 20 has almost the same prophetical oracle, with the suffix for the second person. This combination of pentateuchal and prophetical text opens an interesting perspective. As LOHMEYER points out, the combination may be pre-Christian, since it agrees with rabbinic exegesis in bringing together these two texts; he is referring to ExR. 32 where the two texts are given.[1] Now MICHAELIS disputes the weight of the evidence of this instance. Certainly both texts are given in ExR. 32, but without any interweaving of the wording.[2] However, MANN has shown how the sermon in the synagogue was based as much upon the *haftaroth* as on the Torah section itself.[3] According to Mann the homiletic literature to Ex. 23 20 (seder 61 a) shows that the sermon was given on Mal. 3 1–8 + 23 + 24.[4] Such a homiletic tradition, inspired by the prophetic text connected with the Pentateuch, forms a possible background to the adaptation and fusion of the two texts. In this way we get more concrete material for MCNEILE's hypothesis that the application of the passage to the Messiah points to an Aramaic version in the synagogues.[5]

The quotation formula in Matthew is identical with that in Luke. Although the formula is attached to the context, it is difficult to characterize it as either synoptic, Matthaean, Lucan or of Q type.[6] Its closest parallel is in Matthew, in 3 3. In Mark (1 2) where we have this quotation in another context and in conjunction with Is. 40 3 the formula refers to Isaiah,[7] and LAGRANGE looks upon the quotation from Mal. 3 1 in Mk.

---

[1] *Comm. Mk.* (1937), p. 11. — So also JOACH. JEREMIAS, arguing from the theology implied, art. Ἡλ(ε)ίας, *Theol. Wörterb. z. N.T.* II, p. 938: "Die Deutung von Mal. 3 1 auf den Vorläufer des Messias, die Mk. 1 2, Mt. 11 10, Lk. 7 27 dadurch sicherstellt, dass (statt LXX Mal. 3 1: πρὸ προσώπου μου) mit LXX Ex. 23 20 πρὸ προσώπου σου gelesen wird, ist also nicht erst christliches Theologumenon."

[2] The article ὁδός, *Theol. Wörterb. z. N.T.* V, p. 71, cf. STRACK-BILLERBECK, *Kommentar z. N.T. aus Talmud und Midrasch* I (1922), p. 597.

[3] J. MANN, *The Bible as Read and Preached in the Old Synagogue* I (1940), p. 6 f. and 11–15.

[4] *op. cit.*, p. 479.

[5] *Comm. Mt.* (1915), p. 154.

[6] SH. JOHNSON, *Harv. Theol. Rev.* 36 (1943), p. 144, and BACON, *Studies in Matthew*, p. 472, consider it typical of the Q material.

[7] Cf. Mt. 13 35 and 27 9. The Old Syriac text, which in 27 9 does not have the disputed reference to Jeremiah, is wanting to Mk. 1 1–12 b. Mrs. A. S. LEWIS suggested it would have been a support for the variant of the 𝔎 group. (*Light on the Four Gospels from the Sinai Palimpsest*, 1913, p. 63.) In 27 9, however, the Peshitta went with the Old Syriac texts and in Mk. 1 2 the Peshitta has "Isaiah".

1 2 as a gloss or an interpolation.[1] Such a hypothesis is supported also by the lack of agreement between the possessive pronoun σου in the Malachi quotation in v. 2 and αὐτοῦ in the Isaiah quotation in v. 3, although both are in disagreement with the LXX and the M.T. This lack of agreement is striking if the fusion is original to Mark and a christological adaptation to the context is presumed. Further, the Isaiah quotation is most naturally understood as coming from the LXX text while a merging is best comprehended from the Hebrew text as we shall see. To be sure, sign stands against sign.

Faced with such composite citations, it is reasonable to count on the possibility of testimonies, whereby a plausible explanation may be found for Mark's assignation to the wrong author. If the quotations originate from an oral or a written collection of testimonies, we can easily see how these two quotations were collected under one author's name.[2] A stronger argument for such an interpretation (that they come from testimonies) is that both the Malachi and Isaiah texts contain the phrase פַּנֵּה־דֶרֶךְ. In fact, this only occurs in Mal. 3 1 and Is. 40 3 (and in two closely related Isaiah passages, 57 14 and 62 10).[3] The N.T. translation κατασκευάσει (Aq. σχολάσει, Symm. ἀποσκευάσει, Th. ἑτοιμάσει) assumes the massoretic reading (piel) while the LXX reads qal: ἐπιβλέψεται, for which reason the Synoptics' dependence on the Hebrew text is obvious.[4] Even the N.T. ἔμπροσθέν σου requires the same explanation. The juxtaposition of such texts agrees with the tradition of rabbinic homiletics;[5] in this case, these two prophetic sayings would have been

---

[1] LAGRANGE, Comm. Mt., p. cxx ("un glossateur très ancien"), and p. cxxii.

[2] So especially J. R. HARRIS, Testimonies I, (1916), p. 49.

[3] I. ABRAHAMS, Rabbinic aids to Exegesis, Cambridge Biblical Essays (1909), p. 179, says: "except in this context in Isaiah and in the one place in Malachi the phrase (פנה דרך) nowhere else occurs". "This context" occurs however also in Is. 57 14 and 62 10 but the quotation is not influenced by these parallels. Secondly the statement of Abrahams is limited to piel. Qal: Num. 21 33, Deut. 2 8, 31, 1 Sam. 13 17, 18, Job 24 18, Is. 56 11, Ezek. 43 1, et passim. For the piel cf. Ps. 80 10.

[4] Cf. A. RESCH, Aussercanonische Paralleltexte zu den Evangelien II (1895), p. 113 f. — ἐπιβλέπειν is the usual rendering of פנה in qal in the LXX.

[5] ABRAHAMS, ibm., see also D. DAUBE, Rabbinic Methods of Interpretation and Hellenistic Rhetoric, Hebr. Union Coll. Ann. 22 (1949), p. 241: "It is safe to conclude that there existed, before Hillel, collections of ἅπαξ λεγόμενα, δὶς λεγόμενα etc. The norm of gezera shawa (inferences from analogy, in accordance with the second of Hillel's norms of interpretation) would have been impracticable without them." Daube refers to the similar aids in Rome (Varro, 100 B.C.) and to Greek models. Cf. below, p. 215 f.

combined in a Semitic milieu, whether Jewish or Christian. A Semitic background would also be appropriate to the fact that Jn. 1 23 offers a third synonym to the Hebrew פנו (*piel* as in the M.T. and the Synoptics): εὐθύνατε. We may further note that the quotation from Malachi is the only quotation common to the Synoptics which clearly shows influence from the Hebrew text (apart from Mt. 26 31 with its parallels) a fact which points in the same direction.

To judge the latest hypothesis in research on quotations, it is interesting to note that only a few verses below (v. 14) we find an allusion to Mal. 3 23 concerning Elijah. Recently, DODD has put forth the view that the primitive church did not merely fall back on isolated, disconnected quotations, but had their favourite chapters as a foundation for their theology, teaching and preaching.[1] The two references to Mal. 3 in Mt. 11 might support this view of Dodd's. The natural link between Matthew's sayings is, however, so close that Dodd's thesis cannot be considered to explain anything otherwise hard to understand.[2] In this case one may rather speak of a *theologoumenon* than of a conscious allusion to the Scriptures. The allusion to Mal. 3 23 is found several times, *e.g.* Mt. 17 10–12 (Mk. 9 11–13), and Lk. 1 17. In this last text, as in Lk. 1 76, we can see how the quotations in Mt. 3 3 and 11 10 are woven into the theology of the primitive church. DST and the hymns at the end of DSD now afford striking parallels to the allusive method by which this is done.[3]

In order to come closer to an answer to the question whether Mark's combination of the two quotations on John the Baptist is original or the result of an interpolation, we must get to know the method of

---

[1] C. H. DODD, *According to the Scriptures* (1952), p. 126. "These (selected large) sections were understood as *wholes*, and particular verses or sentences were quoted from them rather as pointers to the whole context than as constituting testimonies in and for themselves. At the same time, detached sentences from other parts of the Old Testament (than Isaiah, Jeremiah and certain minor prophets and the Psalms) could be adduced to illustrate or elucidate the meaning of the main section under consideration. But in the fundamental passages it is the *total context* that is in view, and is the basis of the argument."

[2] Dealing with the quotations from Malachi, DODD does not count this vague allusion. He thinks that Malachi on the whole did not belong to the primary body of Scriptures, which supplied testimonies. It was added as explication to the Isaiah testimony on the voice. Dodd's argument here follows an interesting theological line, tracing differences in the attitudes of the primitive church as to the sayings about Elijah. *op. cit.*, p. 71 f.

[3] See below, p. 158 f.

quotation of the gospels on the whole. Such a comparison is likewise necessary for a closer consideration of the two quotations separately. We shall find that the two show general agreement with the type which is characteristic of Matthew's formula quotations, and that they are the only quotations common to the Synoptics which offer such striking features. We have also to keep in mind that the two are connected with John the Baptist.[1]

Apart from the way in which the quotation in Mt. 11 10 is explained, the almost complete agreement of the Synoptics amongst themselves and the influence of the Hebrew text is clear. It is more difficult to decide whether the quotation has been influenced by the LXX and in that case at what stage this occurred. The hypothesis of testimonies would permit us to assume an independent tradition, without direct influence from either the Hebrew or Greek biblical text, while at the same time it naturally presupposes indirect influence from both.

These first two quotations have already presented us with a number of facts which we shall again meet in several places, mostly, however, only in Matthew's formula quotations.

1. The changing of the possessive pronoun or suffix.

2. The weaving together of quotations, bringing about a change in wording and meaning.

3. The combination of quotations without such interweaving.

4. The assignment to a wrong author, in this case (Mk. 1 2) with a composite quotation.

5. The varying of the compass of otherwise parallel quotations.

6. The agreement of the N.T. quotations with the LXX^A as against LXX^B.

7. An interpretation of the given text, in this case in agreement with the LXX, which differs syntactically from the M.T.

8. The N.T.'s use of a quotation presupposing its LXX form for it to fulfil its function.

9. Dependence on the Hebrew text.

10. An interpretation differing from the LXX on the reading of the Hebrew consonant text, in this case in agreement with the M.T.

11. The evident influence of the Hebrew text combined with the fact that the LXX form in the text is a necessary qualification for its function

---

[1] See below, p. 215.

in context and theology (if we understand the two quotations as an original unity in their Marcan form).

Mt. 154a $\neq$ Mk. 710a: Ex. 2012, Deut. 516 = Mt. 1919a see below, p. 61 ff.

The text, which agrees with Mt. 1919a, consists of a passage from the Decalogue. Like other texts used for catechism, it is LXX in nature, especially in Mark, who has the LXX's (πατέρα) σου (except in cod. D).

Mt. 154b $\neq$ Mk. 710b: Ex. 2117 (Lev. 209).

Mt.   Mk. = Mt.

ὁ κακολογῶν πατέρα ἢ μητέρα θανάτῳ τελευτάτω.

Ex. 2117 LXX[1]   M. T.

ὁ κακολογῶν πατέρα αὐτοῦ ἢ μη-   ומקלל אביו ואמו מות יומת
τέρα αὐτοῦ τελευτήσει θανάτῳ.

2nd αὐτοῦ] om. Lucian (75)[2].

τελ. θαν.] θανάτῳ τελευτάτω AF Lucian (75).

Both Mark and Matthew here lack the possessive pronouns, as compared with the M. T., the Targum and the LXX (but the second of these is missing in Lucian, as the first is missing in cod. F in the parallel saying, Lev. 209). But the presence or absence of the possessive pronoun is no indication in the case where the meaning is not thereby affected. This is already true of the original Semitic text, and in the versions we see traces in various manuscripts of different principles of translation in respect of the Hebrew suffixes.[3] Moreover,

---

[1] Our O.T. references are to the chapters and verses of the M.T. Where the text might be difficult to find in the LXX, there is also a reference to the chapter and verse of the Greek version, cf. below, p. 55, note 1.

[2] The Lucianic text edited by PAUL DE LAGARDE (*Libri veteris testamenti canonici* I, 1883) does not give the pure text of Lucian until Ruth 411, P. KATZ, *Theol. Zeitschr.* 5 (1949), p. 20, cf. SWETE, *Introduction*, p. 83, and B. J. ROBERTS, *The Old Testament Text and Versions* (1951), p. 141 ff. — Manuscript 75 represents the Lucianic text well, see RAHLF'S edition of *Genesis* (1926), p. 28 f., and it will be noticed when this manuscript supports the vaguer reference to the Lucianic text. — For the Lucianic text in Isaiah and the minor prophets, see the editions of ZIEGLER, *Isaias*, p. 73—92, *Duodecim prophetae*, p. 70—89.

[3] ZIEGLER, ed. *Isaias*, p. 86. — This kind of a change is common and quite natural in catechetical material. — ZAHN, *Comm. Mt.*, p. 436 and 516, gives another

the uncertainty of the evidence is especially obvious and easily under-
standable in the catechetical material.

More important is the N. T.'s unambiguous text θανάτῳ τελευτάτω,
which is found in LXXᴬ and LXXᶠ as well as in Lucian's readings.
The question thus arises as to whether this text was corrected from
the N. T. In the M. T. Ex. 21₁₅, ₁₆, ₁₇ all have the formula-like מוֹת
יוּמָת which the LXXᴮ renders by three different expressions: (15)
θανάτῳ θανατούσθω, (17) τελευτήσει θανάτῳ, (16) θανάτῳ τελευτάτω.[1]
On the other hand Lucian, in agreement with A and F, reads θανάτῳ
θανατούσθω in vv. 15 and 16, but θανάτῳ τελευτάτω in v. 17 (the
verse which is quoted in Mark and Matthew). To construe θάνατος
with τελευτᾶν is unique in these two cases, together with Ex. 19₁₂,
where θανάτῳ τελευτήσει also corresponds to the M. T.'s מות יומת.
θανάτῳ θανατούσθω is the usual translation in the LXX,[2] and the
nearest possible linguistic reproduction of the M. T. with retention
of both the passive and the *paronomasia*. The LXX has taken the
M. T.'s infinitive absolute[3] as a noun (מָוֶת) if the Greek translation
is not just a free rendering intended to preserve some of the assonance of the Hebrew. The form most remote from the M. T. (and the
Targum) is the N. T.'s θανάτῳ τελευτάτω.[4] This, however, reproduces
the sound of the M. T.'s *paronomasia*.

If LXXᴮ had not obviously made use of the verb τελευτᾶν in
v. 17 and of its imperative in v. 16, the reading of cod. A would
naturally appear as an emendation to make it agree more closely with

---

explanation, *viz.* "dass in paläst. Aramäisch (Galiläisch?) das Kind Vater und
Mutter nicht mit dem Possessiv anzurufen pflegte", cf. *Theol. Wörterb. z. N. T.* III,
p. 469. It is not likely that this habit did affect the use of possessive pronouns
in 3rd person.

[1] The number of the verses are those of the M. T., the order that of the LXX.
These changes might have caused some confusion in the Greek MSS.

[2] *e. g.* Lev. 20 2,9,10,11, etc., 24 16,17,31, 27 39. — In the LXX two opposite tendencies were at work: *a)* Under the influence of Greek style, the translators aimed
at greater variation than was natural to the Hebrew. *b)* The liturgical and catechetical function of the texts produced a fixed terminology. (The variation is
most obvious in cod. B, Roberts, *op. cit.*, p. 155.) See J. L. Seeligmann, *Jaarber. Ex
Oriente Lux* 7 (1940), p. 375. L. Rost found the tendency *b)* especially at work in
the nouns, *Die Vorstufen von Kirche und Synagoge im A. T.* (1938), p. 133 f.

[3] Gesenius-Kautzsch, *Hebräische Grammatik* (1909²⁸), § 113 w.

[4] Against Dittmar, *Vetus Testamentum in Novo*, p. 34 and T. W. Manson,
The Old Testament in the Teaching of Jesus, *Bull. of J. Ryl. Libr.* 34 (1951/52),
p. 315.

the N. T. Now the matter is not so clear; both the LXX texts are peculiar, not least B with its splitting up of a *terminus technicus* into three translations. If the quotation from v. 17, as Matthew and cod. A have it, is an example of material coming from the catechism, it can have influenced the LXX text before and independently of the N. T.[1]

There is complete agreement with Mark and the LXX character of the text is apparent from ὁ κακολογῶν which is scarcely the self-evident translation of the M. T.[2] On the other hand the question of the influence of the M. T. is dependent upon whether the LXX^A is considered as primary or secondary in relation to the N. T. This question will arise more frequently than any other in considering the N. T.'s quotations. It cannot be answered by any generalization, nor can the question always be settled in the individual cases. In our quotation from Ex. 21₁₇ a third factor is added, namely the tradition from the catechism.

Mt. 15₈₋₉ ≠ Mk. 7₆₋₇: Is. 29₁₃.

Mt.

ὁ λαὸς οὗτος τοῖς χείλεσίν με τιμᾷ, ἡ δὲ καρδία αὐτῶν πόρρω ἀπέχει ἀπ' ἐμοῦ· μάτην δὲ σέβονταί με, διδάσκοντες διδασκαλίας ἐντάλματα ἀνθρώπων.

ἀπέχει] ἐστίν D.

Mk.

ὁ λ. οὐ.] Mk.: οὗτος ὁ λαός, but BD *pc.* = Mt.

τιμᾷ] Mk.: ἀγαπᾷ D W it.

ἀπέχει] Mk.: ἄπεστιν Θ L (1 Clem. 15₂); ἀφέστηκεν D.

Is. 29₁₃ LXX^B

ἐγγίζει μοι ὁ λαὸς οὗτος ἐν τῷ στόματι αὐτοῦ, καὶ ἐν τοῖς χείλεσιν αὐτῶν τιμῶσίν με, ἡ δὲ καρδία αὐτῶν πόρρω ἀπέχει ἀπ' ἐμοῦ· μάτην δὲ σέβονταί με διδάσκοντες ἐντάλματα ἀνθρώπων καὶ διδασκαλίας. (διὰ τοῦτο ἰδοὺ . . .)

1st ἐν — 2nd ἐν] om. ℵ A Q (= Mt.).

M. T.

יען כי נגש העם הזה בפיו ובשפתיו כבדוני ולבו רחק ממני ותהי יראתם אתי מצות אנשים מלמדה (לכן הנני . . .)

Aq. Symm. Theod.

. . . ἐδόξασάν με . . . καὶ ἐγένετο τοῦ φοβεῖσθαι αὐτοὺς ἐμὲ ἐντολὴ ἀνθρώπων διδακτή.

---

[1] To W. Staerk, who was strongly opposed to the view that the N. T. had influenced the LXX^A, this was nevertheless one of the four texts where this might have been the case (the others are Mt. 4₁₀, 15₈ and Heb. 1₇), *Zeitschr. f. wissenschaftl. Theol.* 40 (1897), p. 255 and 265.

[2] The usual translation of קלל in the LXX is καταρᾶσθαι but κακολογεῖν occurs in Ex. 21₁₆, 22₂₈, 1 Kings 3₁₃, Prov. 20₂₀. — ὁ κακολογῶν is in accordance with rabbinic exegesis, *Theol. Wörterb. z. N. T.* III, p. 469.

The difference between Matthew and Mark is limited to a changing of the word order in the first sentence, which may be due to the difference in the prefatory formulae; it need not be taken as a sign of Matthew's greater fidelity to the LXX. The reading of D W, ἀγαπᾷ, may be original to Mark[1] but since on the one hand it lacks support in the M. T. and the Targum, and on the other hand the function of the quotation presupposes its LXX form, it must be considered as an inner-Greek variant. This is the more natural since the quotation at this point is an adapted abbreviation of the O. T. passage.

The text may be taken as a compressed form of the LXX^B. It is closer to the LXX^A, however, but differs from it in that the predicate ἐγγίζει to ὁ λαὸς οὗτος is missing and in its place we have the predicate from the second line, but in the singular form τιμᾷ.

The passage is found in this shorter form in 1 Clem. 15 2, in the form of the Θ L text of Mark[2]. The presence of the quotation in Justin, too, shows that it constituted an important text for argument in Jewish-Christian polemics. When the whole of the passage Is. 29 13–14 is quoted in Dial. 78 11, the text contains the verb ἐγγίζει and has the same short form as the LXX^A.[3] This is surely the Greek text which was known also to Mark and Matthew, and the longer reading in cod. B is a hexaplaric emendation.[4] It is the LXX^A which is compressed to the quotation which the gospels have.[5] The quotation occurs in Papyrus Egerton 2 as a citation on the lips of Jesus, without ἐγγίζει but with stronger traces of the LXX^A (τιμῶσίν με).[6]

---

[1] So MANSON, op. cit., p. 317 f.

[2] É. MASSAUX, Influence de l'Évangile de saint Matthieu sur la littérature chrétienne avant saint Irénée (1950), p. 23, takes the Marcan text of Koridethi to be influenced by 1 Clement. This he does in order to claim Matthew instead of Mark as responsible for the text of 1 Clement.

[3] Cf. the allusions in Dial. 27, 39, 80 and 140.

[4] See ZIEGLER, ed. Isaias and Hexapla (ed. FIELD), ad loc., cf. STAERK, Zeitschr. f. wissenschaftl. Theol. 40 (1897), p. 246. In spite of that, Staerk was not sure about the integrity of the text of cod. A, p. 254.

[5] E. HATCH, Essays in Biblical Greek (1889), p. 177 f., explains the text of the N. T. and of 1 Clement as a shortened and concentrated expression for times of religious revival and previous to N. T. time. Thus it crept into the LXX. — The distinction must however be kept between a) the shorter text of LXX^A, which was completed by the hexaplaric recension in LXX^B, and b) the still shorter text of the N. T.

[6] See DODD, Bull. of J. Ryl. Libr. 20 (1936), p. 80 f.: in the fragment the in-

The line of thought in the quotation is wholly dependent upon the LXX's translation of μάτην which must revert to וְתֹהוּ instead of the M. T.'s וַתְּהִי. The Targum agrees with the M. T. Even the syntactical form rests on the LXX. In the M. T., as in the Targum, the sentences are joined thus: Since this people approach me with their mouth . . . therefore I shall . . ., while the LXX turns the causal clause into an affirmative clause; the quotation is based on this. It is impossible to decide whether Jesus referred to this passage in its Semitic form, or if the quotation is added in a church where the LXX scriptures were used. In the former case we must suppose that the LXX form appeared to fit even better than the Semitic one, and thus influenced the Greek rendering; there is no direct way from the one to the other. In any case the LXX form is a *sine qua non* for the narratives of Mark and Matthew.[1]

The mutual order of διδάσκοντες, διδασκαλίας, ἐντάλματα and ἀνθρώπων is different in the LXX texts, the gospels, Col. 2 22, Papyrus Egerton 2 and Justin, Dial. 78 — an abundance of variants which puts any argument out of the question.[2]

To summarize, there is almost complete agreement between Mark and Matthew and equally clear is their dependence on the LXX; there is no dependence upon the M. T. Even LAGRANGE repudiates ZAHN's assumption of such dependence.[3]

---

troductory formula is the same as in Matthew (and Mark) but the same formula is also found in Acts 28 25 and may have been a customary way of citing prophecy. Dodd is inclined to take the quotation as a testimony, its context being quite different from that in the gospels. The text is somewhat closer to the LXX and in line 52 there is an allusion to Is. 29 13 a — a point in favour of Dodd's most recent view on the quotations, *According to the Scriptures*, p. 84 and 126, cf. above, p. 52. Dodd's article in the Bulletin has been republished in his *New Testament Studies* (1953), p. 12—52. It has just been reprinted and no remarks as to his view on quotations are added.

[1] Cf. W. G. KÜMMEL, Jesus und der jüdische Traditionsgedanke, *Zeitschr. f. d. neutest. Wissensch.* 33 (1934), p. 122. Kümmel wants to show that Matthew has a better understanding of the discussion than has Mark. According to Matthew the charge for disregard of the cleansing rules is answered by the reference to the *korban*. Kümmel's view of Mk. 7 9—13 as a consistent unit is supported by his remark that the text of Is. 29 13 is useful only in its LXX form.

[2] ZAHN, *Einleitung* II[1], p. 317, *Comm. Mt.*, p. 518, takes the text of Matthew to be closer to the M. T. than to the LXX in putting διδασκαλίας before ἐντάλματα. He translates: Menschengebote als Lehren lehrend.

[3] ZAHN, *Einleitung, loc. cit.*, LAGRANGE, *Comm. Mt.*, p. cxx: "Mais si Mt. s'était ici inspiré de l'hébreu, aurait il laissé intact le μάτην δὲ σέβονταί με, dû

Mt. 19₄₋₅ ≠ Mk. 10₆₋₈: Gen. 1₂₇ and 2₂₄.

a) Mt.   Mk. = Mt.

ἄρσεν καὶ θῆλυ ἐποίησεν αὐτούς.

LXX (M. T.) = Mt.

b) Mt.   Mk.

ἕνεκα τούτου καταλείψει ἄνθρωπος   ἕνεκα] Mk.: ἕνεκεν.
τὸν πατέρα καὶ τὴν μητέρα καὶ   πατέρα] Mk.: add. αὐτοῦ (D = Mt.).
κολληθήσεται τῇ γυναικὶ αὐτοῦ, καὶ   μητέρα] Mk.: add. αὐτοῦ ℵ; ἑαυτοῦ
ἔσονται οἱ δύο εἰς σάρκα μίαν.   D.

Variants, see below.   κολλ. — αὐτοῦ] Mk.: om. (see be-
                                          low).

Gen. 2₂₄ LXX^A   M. T.

ἕνεκεν τούτου καταλείψει ἄνθρωπος   על כן יעזב איש את אביו ואת אמו
τὸν πατέρα αὐτοῦ καὶ τὴν μητέρα   ודבק באשתו והיו לבשר אחד
αὐτοῦ καὶ προσκολληθήσεται τῇ
γυναικὶ αὐτοῦ, καὶ ἔσονται οἱ δύο
εἰς σάρκα μίαν.

μητέρα αὐτοῦ] om. αὐτοῦ Lucian,
for the rest cf. below.

In Matthew the quotation from Gen. 1₂₇ is separated from the
quotation from Gen. 2₂₄ by καὶ εἶπεν, while Mark has them both
together without such separation. Mark's version of the quotation is
slightly closer to the LXX, especially to the LXX^Lucian if the possessive pronouns are taken into account.[1] The Marcan text in cod.
D is that of Matthew, however.[2] The Attic form ἕνεκα is found, as
against the Ionic and Hellenistic form ἕνεκεν in the LXX and in
Mark.[3] Both Matthew and Mark read οἱ δύο as does the LXX, on

à une fausse lecture des LXX, qui a été évitée par le Targum, le syriaque et
saint Jérome?" Cf. below, p. 155.

[1] Note H. M. ORLINSKY's discussion with SPERBER on these differences. *Journ.
of Amer. Orient. Society* 61 (1941), p. 87, where Orlinsky stresses the abundance
of variants, especially in the N. T. text, cf. above, p. 54.

[2] Parallel influences are common in cod. D, see *e.g.* Mt. 3₁₇: cod. D = Mark,
and Mt. 27₄₆ ζαφθανει without the corresponding translation ὠνείδισας while both
are given in Mk.

[3] BLASS-DEBRUNNER, *Grammatik des neutestamentl. Griechisch* (1943⁷), § 35:3.

which this reading probably depends, though there are reasons for taking it as a variant already in the Hebrew text.[1]

Matthew gives a more complete text, and it is indeed worth noticing that this seems to have been supplemented from the LXX. Nevertheless, the N. T. text contains variants. The reading of Mt.[B] is most free in relation to the LXX and for this reason, too, is the more to be credited. The quotation from Gen. 2₂₄ also occurs in the epistles. As in Matthew, it is given in full in Eph. 5₃₁ and the last sentence is used in 1 Cor. 6₁₆.

LXX[A] (LXX[B] missing)	LXX[pap. 911 D E Lucian]
καὶ προσκολληθήσεται τῇ γυναικὶ αὐτοῦ.	καὶ προσκολληθήσεται πρὸς τὴν γυναῖκα αὐτοῦ.

Mt. BD𝔎WΘφ: κολληθήσεται τῇ γυναικὶ αὐτοῦ.

Mt. ℵCλ
Mk. A(C)λ   } = LXX[A]
Eph. pap. 46 ℵAD

Mk. (C)DΘ pl. 𝔎 } = LXX[pap. 911 etc.]
Eph. rell.

Mk. ℵB pc. syr[sin]: om.

The quotation is of LXX character and in spite of the slight deviation in Matthew according to cod. B, Matthew might have supplemented the Marcan text from the LXX, though it is just as probable that he knew the statement in the longer form from catechism and church discipline, as did Paul.[2] In Mt. 18₁₆ a similar instance is found in the material peculiar to Matthew.[3]

---

[1] ZAHN, Einleitung II¹, p. 317, claims this reading for Matthew's Hebrew Bible. So also LAGRANGE, Comm. Mt., p. cxx, and MANSON, op. cit., p. 315 and 317. It is found in the Samaritan Pentateuch, Targum Jerushalmi, Peshitta, Vulgate, Philo. The text of M. T. is retained in Targum Onkelos and in Jubilees 3₇. Cf. the translational μόνῳ in Mt. 4₁₀, added in order to emphasize the statement.

[2] Cf. TORREY, Documents of the Primitive Church, p. 73 f.: "That the added clause was present in the Hebrew (viz. the Hebrew quotations in the Aramaic Matthew), and not merely inserted in the Greek, is evidenced by the κολληθήσεται." Torrey takes Mk. 10₆ as an example of how on the other hand an insertion from the LXX was made. It is dubious if the "προσ-" is sufficient evidence for such a basic difference between what happened in Matthew and in Mark. — Both renderings of דבק are common in the LXX, cf. e.g. Ruth 2₂₁, where A has προσκολλᾶν while B has κολλᾶν.

[3] See below, p. 139.

Mt. 19₁₈₋₁₉ ≠ Mk. 10₁₉ ≠ Lk. 18₂₀: Ex. 20₁₂₋₁₆, Deut. 5₁₆₋₂₀; cf. 24₁₄.

Mt.	Mk.	Lk.
οὐ φονεύσεις· οὐ μοιχεύσεις· οὐ κλέψεις· οὐ ψευδομαρτυρήσεις· τίμα τὸν πατέρα καὶ τὴν μητέρα, καὶ ἀγαπήσεις τὸν πλησίον σου ὡς σεαυτόν.	μὴ φονεύσῃς· μὴ μοιχεύσῃς· μὴ κλέψῃς· μὴ ψευδομαρτυρήσῃς· μὴ ἀποστερήσῃς· τίμα τὸν πατέρα σου καὶ τὴν μητέρα.	μὴ μοιχεύσῃς· μὴ φονεύσῃς· μὴ κλέψῃς· μὴ ψευδομαρτυρήσῃς· τίμα τὸν πατέρα σου καὶ τὴν μητέρα.
οὐ μοιχ., οὐ κλέψ.] om. ℵ*. Mt. 19₁₉b, see below, p. 76.	μὴ φον., μὴ μοιχ.] μὴ μοιχ., μὴ πορνεύσῃς D; μὴ μοιχ., μὴ φον. ℜΘ *pm.* lat. μὴ ἀποστ.] om. B*W *pm.* syr^{sin}. μητέρα] add. σου ℵ*CW Θ *al.*	μὴ μοιχεύσῃς etc.] οὐ -σεις D. μητέρα] add. σου ℵℜ *al.*

Ex. 20₁₂₋₁₆ LXX^B	Deut. 5₁₆₋₂₀ LXX^B
τίμα τὸν πατέρα σου καὶ τὴν μητέρα . . . οὐ μοιχεύσεις· οὐ κλέψεις· οὐ ψονεύσεις· οὐ ψευδομαρτυρήσεις κατὰ τοῦ πλησίον σου μαρτυρίαν ψευδῆ.	τίμα τὸν πατέρα σου καὶ τὴν μητέρα σου . . . οὐ μοιχεύσεις· οὐ φονεύσεις· οὐ κλέψεις· οὐ ψευδομαρτυρήσεις κατὰ τοῦ πλησίον σου μαρτυρίαν ψευδῆ.
οὐ μοιχ., οὐ κλέψ., οὐ φον.] οὐ φον., οὐ μοιχ., οὐ κλέψ. AF.	οὐ μοιχ., οὐ φον.] οὐ φον., οὐ μοιχ. AF.

Ex. M. T.	Deut. M. T.
לא . . .: כבד את אביך ואת אמך תרצח: לא תנאף: לא תגנב: לא תענה ברעך עד שקר:	= Ex., except: ולא תגנב and ולא תענה.

Pap. Nash, line 16—19.[1]

כבד את אביך ואת אמ]ך [. . .] לוא תנאף לו]א תרצח לו]א תג]נב לוא [תע]נ]ה ברעך עד שוא

---

[1] S. A. Cook, A Pre-Massoretic Biblical Papyrus, *Proceedings of the Society of Bibl. Archaeol.* 25 (1903), p. 34—56 (with facsimile), cf. W. F. Albright, *Journ. of Bibl. Lit.* 56 (1937), p. 172—176.

The list of commandments from the Decalogue given in the Synoptics is not suitable for an exact comparison since the manuscripts both of the O. T. and the N. T. are rich in variants. The variety is certainly due to the fact the different forms of catechism have made their way into the wording of the Decalogue. The place of the fourth commandment[1] after the eighth is in accordance with Jewish catechetical tradition.[2] Particularly in Mark the text shows independence of biblical text. Thus $\mu\grave{\eta}$ $\dot{\alpha}\pi\text{o}\sigma\tau\epsilon\rho\acute{\eta}\sigma\eta\varsigma$ is inserted. The commandment not to defraud was well-known in Jewish ethical teaching and belongs to the terms of "The Ways".[3] In Deut. 24 14 it has even pressed itself into the LXX (LXX[B]: $\text{o}\grave{\text{u}}\varkappa$ $\dot{\alpha}\pi\alpha\delta\iota\varkappa\acute{\eta}\sigma\epsilon\iota\varsigma$, LXX[A] $\text{o}\grave{\text{u}}\varkappa$ $\dot{\alpha}\pi\text{o}\sigma\tau\epsilon\rho\acute{\eta}\sigma\epsilon\iota\varsigma$, M. T. לֹא תַעֲשֹׁק). The same impact of catechism also explains the split LXX tradition both in Ex. 20 and in Deut. 5, where most manuscripts render the order found in the Nash papyrus (adultery — murder — stealing). This order is also that of most N. T. readings in the Synoptics and in Rom. 13 9, cf. James 2 11. Yet the LXX[A] retains the order of the M. T. and the Targums (murder — adultery — stealing) and that is also the order of Matthew.[4] Matthew's close relation to the LXX — in the form of cod. A — is the more obvious in his use of $\text{o}\grave{\text{u}}\varkappa$ with the future indicative (as also in Romans) over against Mark's and Luke's $\mu\acute{\eta}$ with the subjunctive. Now LXX[A] is usually considered as corrected in order to agree with the N. T. or as a witness of the hexaplaric recension. To SH. JOHNSON the B text seems correct and he finds support in the fact that the Chester Beatty papyrus (pap. 963), contrary to what is usually the case, agrees with cod. B against A and F in placing the sixth commandment before the fifth.[5] It is however worth remembering that both the Nash and the Chester Beatty papyri are of Egyptian origin, while the LXX[A] will often be found to have retained or picked up Palestinian readings.[6] That this is what has happened in this case is the more probable since Jo-

---

[1] According to Roman and Lutheran tradition: 4. On parents, 5. On murder, etc.

[2] A. SEEBERG, *Die beiden Wege und das Aposteldekret* (1906), p. 10 f.

[3] *ibm.*

[4] The Marcan variant with this order may be due to influence from Matthew, cf. SH. JOHNSON, *Harv. Theol. Rev.* 36 (1943), p. 150 f., TORREY, *Documents*, p. 74 f.

[5] *loc. cit.*

[6] See below, p. 171 f. The term "Palestinian" is not used in its strict geographical sense. These types of LXX text may have been revised in Palestine but they were current in Syria and Asia Minor also.

sephus has the order of the M. T., LXX[A] and Matthew over against
e. g. Philo.[1]

If Matthew is drawing on catechetical sources known to him, these
are more purely LXX in their form than those of Mark. More probably he consciously conformed Mark's wordings to the biblical text.[2]
We will find that the catechetical quotations of Matthew are LXX in
form even where they occur in material peculiar to the First Gospel.[3]

The additional quotation from Lev. 19 18 is peculiar to Matthew
in this context, but the same words are combined with the *shema*
in all the Synoptics, Mt. 22 39 with parallels. Thus it looks like one
of the doublets typical to Matthew, but there are good reasons not
to consider it so.[4] The catechetical tradition of Judaism had its main
source in the Law of Holiness, especially in Lev. 18—19. These chapters constitute the biblical basis of the "Two Ways", and thereby
they have influenced the catechism of the early church.[5] The combination of the latter part of the Decalogue with a Leviticus text
as well-known as that of Lev. 19 18 was certainly in accordance with
Jewish tradition.[6] It may not be without relevance that the affinity
to the material of the "Two Ways", that of Life and that of Death,
occurs in a context where the thing that matters is to find the way
to eternal life. Nor is it by mere chance that only the latter part
of the Decalogue is quoted. The same is true for the rest of the
N. T. too[7], as for the tradition of the early church. B. S. Easton

---

[1] *Josephus*, Ant. iii, 5; *Philo*, de decalogo 12.

[2] Even the list of vices in Mt. 15 19 is more closely related to the commandments
of the Decalogue than is the parallel in Mk. 7 21 f. It tallies with the Matthaean order
within the Decalogue and the structure of the Marcan list corresponds to the Marcan order. The same correspondence will be found between the Matthaean Decalogue and the commandments in the Sermon on the Mount, see below, p. 137.

[3] See below, p. 138.

[4] In James 2 8–11 the commandment from Lev. 19 18 is combined with two from
the Decalogue. At the same time there is an affinity to Mt. 22 39 since it is taken
as a *summa* of the Law.

[5] A. Seeberg, *Das Evangelium Christi* (1905), p. 111 f., cf. Ph. Carrington,
The Primitive Christian Catechism (1940), p. 13—21 and E. G. Selwyn, *Comm.
1 Peter* (1947), p. 369—375.

[6] Seeberg's arguments for an independence of Matthew in the later combina-
tions of these two items are not conclusive, *Die beiden Wege*, p. 11 f.

[7] Eph. 6 2 presupposes the Decalogue as a consistent unit. It quotes the fourth
commandment and adds a hermeneutic observation: it is the first commandment with a promise.

explains this startling fact by theological considerations, but his negative approach[1] is ruled out by the strong positive fact of a consistent Jewish and Christian tradition of catechetical teaching.

Mt. 21₉ ≠ Mk. 11₉₋₁₀ ≠ Lk. 19₃₈: Ps. 118₂₅₋₂₆.

Mt.	Mk.	Lk. (cf. 21₄)
ὡσαννὰ τῷ υἱῷ Δαυίδ· εὐλογημένος ὁ ἐρχόμενος ἐν ὀνόματι κυρίου· ὡσαννὰ ἐν τοῖς ὑψίστοις.	ὡσαννά, εὐλογημένος ὁ ἐρχόμενος ἐν ὀνόματι κυρίου· εὐλογημένη ἡ ἐρχομένη βασιλεία τοῦ πατρὸς ἡμῶν Δαυίδ· ὡσαννὰ ἐν τοῖς ὑψίστοις.	εὐλογημένος ὁ ἐρχόμενος, ὁ βασιλεὺς ἐν ὀνόματι κυρίου· ἐν οὐρανῷ εἰρήνη καὶ δόξα ἐν ὑψίστοις.
	1st ὡσαννά] om. DW it; add. τῷ ὑψίστῳ Θφ pc. 2nd ὡσαννά] εἰρήνη W (Θ) syr^{sin}.	D: εὐλ. ὁ ἐρχ. ἐν ὀνόματι κυρίου, εὐλογημένος ὁ βασιλεύς· ἐν οὐρανῷ ...

Mt. 21₁₅
ὡσαννὰ τῷ υἱῷ Δαυίδ.

Mt. 23₃₉ ≠ Lk. 13₃₅
εὐλογημένος ὁ ἐρχόμενος ἐν ὀνόματι κυρίου (Mt. D: θεοῦ).

Jn. 12₁₃
ὡσαννά, εὐλογημένος ὁ ἐρχόμενος ἐν ὀνόματι κυρίου, καὶ ὁ βασιλεὺς τοῦ Ἰσραήλ.

Did. 10₆
ὡσαννὰ τῷ θεῷ Δαυίδ ... μαρὰν ἀθά.

Ps. 118₂₅₋₂₆ LXX	M.T.
ὦ κύριε, σῶσον δή· ὦ κύριε, εὐόδωσον δή. εὐλογημένος ὁ ἐρχόμενος ἐν ὀνόματι κυρίου.	אנא יהוה הושיעה נא אנא יהוה הצליחה נא ברוך הבא בשם יהוה

Ps. 118 ₂₅₋₂₆ is reproduced in all the Synoptics and in John in the words of the LXX. Both Mark and Matthew, moreover, give the

---

[1] *The Apostolic Tradition of Hippolytus* (1934), p. 5: "The reason for this appears to be that at this period the Fourth (third) Commandment was conceived to be wholly 'ceremonial', and to 'keep the Sabbath' was regarded as Judaizing." Cf. O. Moe, *Die Apostellehre und der Dekalog im Unterrichte der alten Kirche* (1896), p. 57 ff.

shout Hosanna[1] without translation. They have both taken it as an expression of praise and not as a cry of prayer. The explanation of this must be that the word Hosanna, like Hallelujah, belonged to the language of the Christian cultus which they knew, and there it had lost its meaning of "deliver".[2] ἐν τοῖς ὑψίστοις, Matthew's dative τῷ υἱῷ Δαυίδ[3] and Did. 10₆ τῷ θεῷ Δαυίδ all point in this direction.[4]

It is thus not a quotation from the O.T. in the ordinary sense, but the rendering of a liturgical hymn, possibly in use in the churches of the various evangelists, and freely connected with the final verses of the Jewish *Hallel*. This is made the more likely by the repetition of Hosanna, with the superlative addition "in the highest".[5] Luke and cod. W in Mark have deleted the Hebrew term altogether[6], and all have added their interpretations to the quotation. Matthew omits Mark's additional comments on the coming kingdom, possibly in closer dependence upon the text of the Psalter.[7] The form the quotation has in Mark and Matthew is of Greek creation; it is not

---

[1] In its shorter form נא הושע, which was used in Jewish liturgies, G. DALMAN, *Die Worte Jesu* I (1930²), p. 182.

[2] F. C. BURKITT, W and Θ: Studies in the Western text of St Mark: Hosanna, *Journ. of Theol. St.* 17 (1915/16), p. 146, DALMAN, *op. cit.*, p. 181. To Dalman this proves Matthew to be an original Greek work.

[3] A favourite term of Matthew, BURKITT, *ibm.*, McNEILE, *Comm. Mt.*, to 12₂₃, "Son of David" being Matthew's typical equivalent to Mark's "kingdom" and Luke's "king".

[4] See DALMAN, *op. cit.*, p. 181 on the parallel in Ps. 20₁₀ and p. 182 on the supposed parallel in 2 Sam. 14₄ which must be supplication not homage. TORREY, *Documents*, p. 77 f. stresses the sense of "save" and the influence from Ps. 20. He characterizes the whole verse as "a most unfortunate specimen of translation Greek", cf. E. WERNER, 'Hosanna' in the Gospels, *Journ. of Bibl. Lit.* 65 (1946), p. 97—122.

[5] H. BORNHÄUSER, ed. *Mischna: Sukka* (1935), p. 106 f. On the relation between this part of the Hallel and the feast of Tabernacles, see also H. RIESENFELD, *Jésus transfiguré* (1947), p. 60, and STRACK-BILLERBECK I, p. 845 f. — BURKITT too stresses the cultic function in Judaism but relates the hymn to the feast of Dedication, *op. cit.*, p. 142. This view of his depends upon his conviction that Ps. 118 in its entirety was written for the dedication of the Temple by Judas Maccabaeus. — J. S. KENNARD JR., *Journ. of Bibl. Lit.* 67 (1948), p. 173, combines both views by showing specially in the Books of Maccabees how "the language of Succoth" was used regardless of the time of the year, but with special affinity to the cleansing of the Temple.

[6] Cf. BURKITT, *op. cit.*, p. 139 f.

[7] SH. JOHNSON, *Harv. Theol. Rev.* 36 (1943), p. 149.

a translation from the Aramaic but of hymnic origin from the use of Hosanna as a shout of praise. With this may be compared the use of αἶνος in this context, 21₁₆, which also depends on the LXX interpretation of the Psalms. The relation of Ps. 118 to the Feast of Tabernacles and its triumphal procession has prepared the way for such a use as has also the combination of vv. 25 and 26 of the Psalm. So הושענא could well be in itself a shout of praise at the time of Jesus.[1] But with the addition לבן דויד it could not mean other than "deliver the son of David". Only in Greek the Matthaean sense of a hymn of praise was possible.

For our inquiry, therefore, we note that the form is of Greek origin and so far as the strict quotation is concerned, it is LXX.

Mt. 21₁₃ ≠ Mk. 11₁₇ ≠ Lk. 19₄₆: Is. 56₇ and Jer. 7₁₁.

a) Mt.
ὁ οἶκός μου οἶκος προσευχῆς κληθή-σεται.

Mk. = Mt. with the addition πᾶσιν τοῖς ἔθνεσιν. This longer text occurs in syr^cur in Mt. and Lk.

Lk.: καὶ ἔσται ὁ οἶκός μου οἶκος προσευχῆς.

ἔσται] ἐστιν (post προσευχῆς) A C D it syr.

Is. 56₇ LXX
ὁ γὰρ οἶκός μου οἶκος προσευχῆς κληθήσεται πᾶσιν τοῖς ἔθνεσιν.

M. T.
כי ביתי בית תפלה יקרא לכל העמים

b) Mt.
ὑμεῖς δὲ αὐτὸν ποιεῖτε σπήλαιον λῃστῶν.

Mk.: ὑ. δ. πεποιήκατε αὐτὸν σπ. λῃ.
Lk.: ὑ. δ. αὐτὸν ἐποιήσατε σπ. λῃ.

Jer. 7₁₁ LXX
μὴ σπήλαιον λῃστῶν ὁ οἶκός μου.

M. T.
המערת פרצים היה הבית הזה

This is a composite quotation in which both texts are clearly LXX. The combination is perhaps more natural if the texts are taken in their LXX form where both have οἶκός μου, whereas the T. M. has ביתי in Isaiah, but בית הזה in Jeremiah. Such an argument, however, has not the same weight here as in Mk. 12₃ where the combination may be based upon the Hebrew. Is. 56₇ belonged to the sayings

---

[1] So McNeile, *Comm. Mt.*, *ad loc.*

interpreted messianically by the synagogue.[1] It is therefore very un-likely that the combination of the texts is Jewish. In the N. T. the future form becomes of secondary importance, as is clear from the variant readings in Luke, provided this reading does not lay stress on the messianic accomplishment.

Luke inserts the quotation into his complex sentence and in this way the exact wording undergoes a change of form, while Matthew and Mark agree — with one important difference. Mark's πᾶσιν τοῖς ἔθνεσιν most clearly shows that this gospel's quotation is primary and that Matthew left it out as less important in the context. In the quotation from Ps. 83 in Mt. 21 16, the attribute ἕνεκα τῶν ἐχθρῶν σου is likewise omitted. One should therefore be cautious in repeating the common statement that Matthew's manner of abbre-viating Mark's text reveals his views on missions to the heathen. Obviously Matthew's attitude to his material is remarkably free in the passage 21 10-17, a fact of interest also with regard to the purely LXX citation in 21 16, which is peculiar to Matthew.[2]

Mt. 21 42 (44) ╪ Mk. 12 10 f. ╪ Lk. 20 17 f.: Ps. 118 22 f.; cf. 1 Peter 2 6 ff.

Mt. = Mk. Lk.	1 Peter
λίθον ὃν ἀπεδοκίμασαν οἱ οἰκοδο-μοῦντες, οὗτος ἐγενήθη εἰς κεφαλὴν γωνίας· παρὰ κυρίου ἐγένετο αὕτη, καὶ ἔστιν θαυμαστὴ ἐν ὀφθαλμοῖς ἡμῶν.	ἰδοὺ τίθημι ἐν Σιὼν λίθον ἐκλεκτὸν ἀκρογωνιαῖον ἔντιμον, καὶ ὁ πιστεύ-ων ἐπ᾽ αὐτῷ οὐ μὴ καταισχυνθῇ. ὑμῖν οὖν ἡ τιμὴ τοῖς πιστεύουσιν· ἀπιστοῦσιν δὲ λίθος ὃν ἀπεδοκίμα-σαν οἱ οἰκοδομοῦντες, οὗτος ἐγενήθη
γων.] Lk.: add.: πᾶς ὁ πεσὼν ἐπ᾽ ἐκεῖνον τὸν λίθον συνθλασθήσεται· ἐφ᾽ ὃν δ᾽ ἂν πέσῃ, λικμήσει αὐτόν. In Mt. this text is missing in D 33 it syr^sin with two variants: πᾶς] καὶ, and ἐπ᾽ ἐκεῖνον] ἐπί.	εἰς κεφαλὴν γωνίας καὶ λίθος προσ-κόμματος καὶ πέτρα σκανδάλου· οἱ προσκόπτουσιν τῷ λόγῳ ἀπειθοῦν-τες, εἰς ὃ καὶ ἐτέθησαν.
παρὰ — ἡμῶν] Lk.: om.	The longer text in Lk. alludes on Is. 8 14. As it occurs in 1 Peter (and in Romans 9 33) the allusion is more exact than in Lk.[3] Cf. Is. 28 16 and Barn. 6 2-4.

The text of Ps. 118 22 f. as given in the gospels is exactly that of the LXX.

---

[1] See STRACK-BILLERBECK I, p. 852 f, and A. EDERSHEIM, *The Life and Times of Jesus the Messiah* II (1884), p. 728 and 724.

[2] See below, p. 134 f.

[3] Cf. the table of the texts in SELWYN, *Comm. 1 Peter*, p. 270 f.

The quotation about "the stone" occurs both in the Synoptics and outside the framework of the gospels. Mark and Matthew agree exactly and — as often in quotations from the Psalter — even agree entirely with the LXX. The longer text from Luke adds to it a very free allusion to Is. 8 14. This longer text is found in most of the manuscripts to Matthew, namely in v. 44. It is lacking in D 33 it syr[sin] (though not in syr[cur]) and its agreement with Luke suggests the influence of parallelism. Certain differences, however, argue against this (Mt. καὶ ὁ ... ἐκεῖνον; Lk. πᾶς ὁ ... τοῦτον). It is true that v. 43 breaks in upon what is almost a composite quotation in Luke, but it cannot wholly be ruled out that Matthew knew the tradition of testimonies which we see in more elaborate form in 1 Peter and in Romans.[1]

In 1 Peter 2 7 and Rom. 9 33 the allusion to Is. 8 14 is clearer. Both have the term πέτρα σκανδάλου instead of the LXX's πέτρα πτώματι for the M. T.'s צור מכשול, an interpretation which is certainly not found in the younger Greek versions, but these have a wealth of instances of the term σκάνδαλον where the LXX uses other expressions.[2] In 1 Peter the quotation from Ps. 118 includes a complicated combination with the above-mentioned Is. 8 but especially with Is. 28 16. In this form it becomes one of the composite quotations from the later collections of testimonies.[3] In its composite form it is mainly LXX though only the text from Psalms is purely LXX[4], while the passages from Isaiah are reproduced with LXX's terminology but otherwise are closer to the M. T.[5]

E. G. SELWYN, who closely investigated the quotation from the point of view of 1 Peter, is of the opinion that the words from Ps. 118 formed

---

[1] S. G. F. BRANDON, *The Fall of Jerusalem and the Christian Church* (1951), p. 244 f., claims v. 44 as Matthaean in his criticism of Streeter's view that Matthew was the gospel of Antioch and thus best represented in the syr[sin]. Brandon takes Matthew as a gospel of Alexandria.

[2] N. T.'s and Symmachus's preference for this term is found also in the allusion to Zeph. 1 3 in Mt. 13 41, cf. MANSON, *Bull. of J. Ryl. Libr.* 34 (1951/52), p. 322.

[3] See HARRIS, *Testimonies* I, p. 26—32 and II p. 66, with 31 patristic references.

[4] ZAHN, *Einleitung* II[1], p. 318, remarks that the LXX coincides with the M. T. This hardly affects the overwhelming LXX impression in so long a quotation. The last καί is in accordance with the LXX but against the M. T.

[5] VOLLMER, *Die Alttest. Citate bei Paulus*, p. 29 f. and 41; cf. below p. 159 f. and 212. SELWYN, *op. cit.*, p. 272 f.

the nucleus of the quotation as a *verbum Christi*.[1] That this part of the quotation also occurs alone in Acts 4₁₁ points in the same direction. Selwyn thinks that we are here dealing with a part of a hymn, known to both 1 Peter and Paul. This should also provide an explanation of both the similarities and the differences in relation to the LXX. The assumption of such a hymn, however, makes it hard to explain the differences between Romans and 1 Peter, especially so far as concerns the exclusion of Ps. 118 from Romans.

It seems equally possible that we have here a *verbum Christi* which is enlarged into a compound testimony by being supplemented by other sayings about "the stone". The knowledge of the Hebrew text is worth noting in this connection, the more so as the nucleus is the purely LXX quotation from the Psalter. Here we get a glimpse of how a testimony grew and took shape; thus, for instance, v. 22b of Ps. 118 has disappeared as of less importance for the function of the testimony.

The introductory formulae in the gospels agree in substance but differ in form. They are essential to the discussions between Jesus and the Pharisees, which is more obvious in Matthew than in Mark, though even Luke shows it in some measure, since the answer is there given by the opponents, Mt. 21₄₁ with its parallels.

Mt. 22₂₄ ≠ Mk. 12₁₉ ≠ Lk. 20₂₈: Gen. 38₈, Deut. 25₅.

Mt.	Mk.	Lk.
ἐάν τις ἀποθάνῃ μὴ ἔχων τέκνα, ἐπιγαμβρεύσει ὁ ἀδελφὸς αὐτοῦ τὴν γυναῖκα αὐτοῦ καὶ ἀναστήσει σπέρμα τῷ ἀδελφῷ αὐτοῦ.	ἐάν τινος ἀδελφὸς ἀποθάνῃ καὶ καταλίπῃ γυναῖκα καὶ μὴ ἀφῇ τέκνον, ἵνα λάβῃ ὁ ἀδελφὸς αὐτοῦ τὴν γυναῖκα καὶ ἐξαναστήσῃ σπέρμα τῷ ἀδελφῷ αὐτοῦ.	ἐάν τινος ἀδελφὸς ἀποθάνῃ ἔχων γυναῖκα, καὶ οὗτος ἄτεκνος ᾖ, ἵνα λάβῃ κτλ. = Mk.

Gen. 38₈ LXX^A
εἴσελθε πρὸς τὴν γυναῖκα τοῦ ἀδελφοῦ σου καὶ γάμβρευσαι αὐτήν, καὶ ἀνάστησον σπέρμα τῷ ἀδελφῷ σου.

M. T.

בא אל אשת אחיך ויבם אתה
והקם זרע לאחיך

γάμβρ.] ἐπιγάμβρευσαι Lucian (75).

---

[1] *loc. cit.*

Deut. 25₅ LXX   M. T.

ἐὰν δὲ κατοικῶσιν ἀδελφοὶ ἐπὶ τὸ
αὐτό, καὶ ἀποθάνῃ εἷς αὐτῶν, σπέρμα δὲ μὴ ᾖν αὐτῷ, οὐκ ἔσται ἡ γυνὴ
τοῦ τεθνηκότος ἔξω ἀνδρὶ μὴ ἐγγί-
ζοντι· ὁ ἀδελφὸς τοῦ ἀνδρὸς αὐτῆς
εἰσελεύσεται πρὸς αὐτὴν καὶ λήμψεται αὐτὴν ἑαυτῷ γυναῖκα καὶ συνοι-
κήσει αὐτῇ.

כי ישבו אחים יחדו ומת אחד מהם
ובן אין לו לא תהיה אשת המת
החוצה לאיש זר יבמה יבא עליה
ולקחה לו לאשה ויבמה

συνοικ. αὐτῇ] ἐπιγαμβρεύσει αὐτήν
Aquila, cf. vv. 5a and 7.

The quotations which are introduced by the words Μωϋσῆς εἶπεν
or similar ones in Mark and Luke can scarcely be regarded as quotations in the strict sense in spite of this, but certain terminological
details in the allusions are of interest. All the Synoptics, for example,
use the word τέκνα or a word from the same root as compared with
the LXX's (Deut. 25₅) σπέρμα for the M. T.'s בן. Matthew has apparently not taken Mark's text as a quotation, but he seems to have
coined the wording more on the terminology in Gen. 38₈, which also
influenced Mark and Luke. Matthew has made use of the technical
term ἐπιγαμβρεύειν, which occurs in Lucian's text to Gen. 38.

However, the passage is of little interest because of Matthew's
free treatment. It is one of the misleading points in HAWKINS's table,
when he gives 12 words against, and 7 for the LXX.[1] Apart from
the term ἐπιγαμβρεύειν little similarity is found between Matthew
and the M. T. The N. T.'s τέκνα for the M. T.'s בן is common to all
the Synoptics and Mark stands somewhat closer to the M. T. with
his collective singular τέκνον, while Matthew's quotation does not point
to a direct dependence upon the M. T. On the contrary, his use of
the term ἐπιγαμβρεύειν might indicate that he stood within the
compass of Greek-speaking Judaism in Palestine or Syria. The word
which is *hapax legomenon* in the N. T. occurs in Aquila in Deut. 25₅.
As in Lucian's text of Gen. 38₈, it there reproduces the M. T.'s וְיִבֵּם,
a form which only occurs in these two places.[2] This entitles us to

---

[1] See above, p. 44. DITTMAR, *Vetus Testamentum in Novo*, p. 48 f., does not
classify the verse as quotation.

[2] In the LXX[pap. 911 A] to Gen. 34₅ ἐπιγαμβρεύειν stands for התחתן without
reference to the brother-in-law's marriage. Cf. Theodotion 1 Sam. 18₂₁ and LXX
1 Kings 18₂₂ etc., 2 Chron. 18₁, Ezra 9₁₄ (not B), 1 Macc. 10₅₄,₅₆.

take ἐπιγαμβρεύειν as a *terminus technicus,* and to associate it with Palestinian Greek tradition. It even opens up the possibility of explaining Matthew's text without assuming the influence of the parallel passage in Genesis.

Mt. 22₃₂ ≠ Mk. 12₂₆ ≠ Lk. 20₃₇: Ex. 3₆; cf. Acts 7₃₂.

Mt.	Mk.	Lk.
ἐγώ εἰμι ὁ θεὸς 'Αβραάμ καὶ ὁ θεὸς 'Ισαάκ καὶ ὁ θεὸς 'Ιακώβ.	ἐγὼ ὁ θεὸς 'Α. καὶ ὁ θεὸς 'Ι. καὶ ὁ θεὸς 'Ι.	κύριον τὸν θεὸν 'Α. καὶ θεὸν 'Ι. καὶ θεὸν 'Ι.
2nd and 3rd ὁ] om. ℵ.	1st ὁ] om. DW. 2nd and 3rd ὁ] om. BDW.	1st and 2nd καὶ] add. τὸν A.

Acts 7₃₂

ἐγὼ ὁ θεὸς τῶν πατέρων σου, ὁ θεὸς 'Α. καὶ 'Ι. καὶ 'Ι.
1st and 2nd καὶ] add. θεὸς D; ὁ θεὸς ℵ.

Ex. 3₆ LXX^B	M.T.
ἐγώ εἰμι ὁ θεὸς τοῦ πατρός σου, θεὸς 'Αβραάμ καὶ θεὸς 'Ισαάκ καὶ θεὸς 'Ιακώβ.	אנכי אלהי אביך אלהי אברהם אלהי יצחק ואלהי יעקב

τοῦ πατρός] τῶν πατέρων 58 72 bo aeth, cf. vv. 15 and 16. — 2nd θεὸς] ὁ θεὸς A Lucian (75). — 3rd and 4th θεὸς] om. Lucian (75).

Of the Synoptics Matthew here stands the closest to the LXX, especially to the text of Lucian and to a certain extent to that of cod. A. The differences between the Synoptics and Acts, however, are confined to the articles and to the εἰμί in Matthew.[1] Nevertheless it would be rash to take this as an example of Matthew's supplementing of the quotation from the LXX, since the brief formula-like quotation renders stricter argument impossible. Matthew's greater measure of agreement with the LXX may even depend upon the improvement of Mark's Greek. When this has not occurred in Luke, it is because he incorporated the quotation in another complex sentence. The formula style in the citation makes it possible that it had an oral existence without reference to the LXX, as may be seen in Acts 7₃₂, where the text has affinities even to the Samaritan

---

[1] TORREY's statement is therefore wrong, *Documents*, p. 80: "there is no possible variation in the Greek translation".

Pentateuch.[1] Justin, 1 Apol. 63₇ has Ex. 3₆ in a peculiar compressed quotation which does not give much material for comparison. The lack of the articles would most nearly suggest the LXX of the B type.

Contrary to what one would have expected, Luke and still more Mark, in their introductory formulae give one of the few examples of typical quotation terminology.[2] Mark: . . . οὐκ ἀνέγνωτε ἐν τῇ βίβλῳ Μωϋσέως ἐπὶ τοῦ βάτου πῶς εἶπεν αὐτῷ ὁ θεὸς λέγων· Luke: . . . καὶ Μωϋσῆς ἐμήνυσεν ἐπὶ τῆς βάτου, ὡς λέγει . . . On the other hand Matthew makes use of a formula of polemical type: . . . οὐκ ἀνέγνωτε τὸ ῥηθὲν ὑμῖν ὑπὸ τοῦ θεοῦ λέγοντος.

Mt. 22₃₇ ≠ Mk. 12₂₉f.(33) ≠ Lk. 10₂₇: Deut. 6₄₋₅ (2 Kings 23₂₅).

Mt.	Mk.	Lk.
	ἄκουε, ᾿Ισραήλ, κύριος ὁ θεὸς ἡμῶν κύριος εἶς	
ἀγαπήσεις κύριον τὸν θεόν σου ἐν ὅλῃ τῇ καρδίᾳ σου καὶ ἐν ὅλῃ τῇ ψυχῇ σου καὶ ἐν ὅλῃ τῇ διανοίᾳ σου.	ἐστιν, καὶ ἀγαπήσεις κύριον τὸν θεόν σου ἐξ ὅλης τῆς καρδίας σου καὶ ἐξ ὅλης τῆς ψυχῆς σου καὶ ἐξ ὅλης τῆς διανοίας σου καὶ ἐξ ὅλης τῆς ἰσχύος σου.	ἀγαπήσεις κύριον τὸν θεόν σου ἐξ ὅλης τῆς καρδίας σου καὶ ἐν ὅλῃ τῇ ψυχῇ σου καὶ ἐν ὅλῃ τῇ ἰσχύϊ σου καὶ ἐν ὅλῃ τῇ διανοίᾳ σου.
1st τῇ] D L pm.; om. Bℵ*ℜΘ. 2nd τῇ] om. ℜΘ al. ψυχῇ σου] add. καὶ ἐν ὅλῃ τῇ ἰσχύϊ σου Θφ al.	1st τῆς] om. B D* pc. 2nd and 3rd τῆς] om. B. κ. ε. ο. τ. διαν.] om. D pc. it.	κ. ε. ο. τ. διαν. σ.] om. D pc. it. ἐξ] ἐν D λ it sa. 1st, 2nd, 3rd ἐν] ἐξ AC WΘφℜ.[3]

---

[1] The text of Ex. 3₆ as given in Acts shows coincidence with the Samaritan Pentateuch as is the case in other details of Stephen's speech, H. HAMMER, *Traktat vom Samaritaner-Messias* (1913), p. 35 f. P. KAHLE, *Theol. St. u. Krit.* 88 (1915), p. 400 f., rescued these observations from their fantastic context in Hammer's book and claimed the existence of Greek O. T. texts with affinities to the Samaritan text, cf. below, p. 161.

[2] See B. M. METZGER, Formulas introducing Quotations of Scripture in the New Testament and in the Mishnah, *Journ. of Bibl. Lit.* 70 (1951), p. 304 f., cf. HARRIS, *Testimonies* II, p. 66.

[3] The text given above is nearest to that of ℵ and B, though B has the 1st σου added over the line and lacks the 1st τῆς. To SH. JOHNSON, *Harv. Theol. Rev.* 36 (1943), p. 147, this "indicates that something may have happened to the text".

Deut. 6₄₋₅ LXX^B

M. T.

ἄκουε, Ἰσραήλ, κύριος ὁ θεὸς ἡμῶν
κύροις εἷς ἐστιν· καὶ ἀγαπήσεις κύ-
ριον τὸν θεόν σου ἐξ ὅλης τῆς δια-
νοίας σου καὶ ἐξ ὅλης τῆς ψυχῆς
σου καὶ ἐξ ὅλης τῆς δυνάμεώς σου.

שמע ישראל יהוה אלהינו יהוה אחד
ואהבת את יהוה אלהיך בכל לבבך
ובכל נפשך ובכל מאדך

διανοίας] καρδίας A F.

Here there occurs the Jewish creed, the *shema*, a liturgical text,[1]
a fact to be kept in mind when the text is taken as an example
of synoptic quotations influenced by the M. T. or the LXX. In so
far as one dares to draw conclusions from the differences, Mark
stands closest to the LXX with the preposition ἐκ in all manuscripts throughout the passage. Mark alone gives the famous first
sentence of the *shema*, there too adhering to the LXX text. All
the Synoptics agree in the use of καρδία for the M. T.'s לבב, found
in the LXX only in cod. A etc. and in the LXX version of 2 Kings.
Otherwise the Synoptics differ from each other, from the LXX and
from the M. T. in the translation and the order of the nouns enu-
merated in the quotation. The variation is most striking in Mark
with its two different forms of the *shema*, the latter, according to
most manuscripts, without a single word in agreement with the LXX.
As with other forms of the *shema*, these give us an impression of
a deliberate intention to vary, akin to the delight of the LXX itself
in the use of synonyms.[2] The wealth of variation is obvious from
this table:

Deut. and 2 Kings M. T.	מאד — נפש — לבב — ב
Deut. Targ. Onk.	ריכסא³ — נפשא — לבא — ב
Deut. Peshitta	مבسמ — نבعמ — لحا — מ

---

[1] I. ELBOGEN, *Der jüdische Gottesdienst* (1913), e. g. p. 25 f. — The combination of the Decalogue and the *shema* in the Nash papyrus might be due to liturgical practice, though the catechetical function is as probable. It is a pity that
the text corresponding to what occurs in the gospels is wanting in the papyrus,
see the facsimile in *Proceedings of the Society of Bibl. Archaeol.* 25 (1903), p. 56.
Cf. now the phylactery from Murabaat, *The Bibl. Archaeol.* 17 (1954), p. 7. Verse
5 of Deut. 6 is, however, difficult to read from the photograph. — Cf. also the
order of the commandments and their relation to different O. T. and N. T. texts,
above, p. 62 f.

[2] See above, p. 55, note 2.

[3] "Goods", "property", basic meaning: "flock", a translation using *concretum
pro abstracto* which applies well to the synagogue's doctrine on almsgiving. In

Deut. LXX$^{B \text{ pap. } 963.}$	ἐκ — διάνοια — ψυχή — δύναμις[1]
Deut. LXX^{A}	ἐκ — καρδία — ψυχή — δύναμις
2 Kings LXX^{B}	ἐν — καρδία — ἰσχύς — ψυχή
2 Kings LXX^{A}	ἐν — καρδία — ψυχή — ἰσχύς
Mt.	ἐν — καρδία — ψυχή — διάνοια
Mt.$^{Θ φ}$	ἐν — καρδία — ψυχή — ἰσχύς — διάνοια
Mt. syr$^{\text{sin cur}}$	ܣܠܝ — ܢܦܫ̈ — ܚܠܟ — ܡ
Mk.	ἐκ — καρδία — ψυχή — διάνοια — ἰσχύς
Mk.^{A}	ἐκ — καρδία — διάνοια — ψυχή — ἰσχύς
Mk.^{D}	ἐκ — καρδία — ψυχή — ἰσχύς
Mk. syr^{sin}	ܣܠܝ — ܪ̈ܥܝܢܟ — ܢܦܫ̈ — ܚܠܟ — ܡ
Lk.$^{\aleph B}$	ἐκ, ἐν — καρδία — ψυχή — ἰσχύς — διάνοια
Lk.^{ACWΘφℜ}	ἐκ — καρδία — ψυχή — ἰσχύς — διάνοια
Lk.^{D}	ἐν — καρδία — ψυχή — ἰσχύς
Lk. syr^{sin}	= Mt. syr.
Lk. syr^{cur}	ܢܦܫ — ܚܝܠ — ܚܠܟ — ܡ
Mk. (v. 33)	ἐκ — καρδία — σύνεσις — (ψυχή) — ἰσχύς
Mk.^{D} (v. 33)	ἐκ — καρδία — δύναμις — ψυχή — ἰσχύς
Mk. syr^{sin} (v. 33)	= Mt. syr.

The only definite point in the N. T. rendering of the *shema* is the adherence to καρδία[2], as against διάνοια of the LXX^{B}.[3] Both

---

Biblical Aramaic the word is used in Ezra 6$_8$ and 7$_{26}$ for "goods" and for "fine". Particularly in Luke the pericope on the Great Commandment has much in common with that on the Rich Ruler, cf. *e.g.* 10$_{28}$ and 18$_{18}$. — Targum Jonathan to 2 Kings has the same words.

[1] *Hexapla* (ed. FIELD), ad Deut. 6$_5$: Ἄλλος· ἰσχύος. So cod. 55 and 75. The total disappearence of the LXX's δύναμις from the N. T. texts is a startling fact. It is found, except in D's text of Mk 12$_{33}$, in *Clement Alexandrinus*, Quis dives 27, see LEGG, *Novum Testamentum Graece*, ad Mk. 12$_{30}$, cf. *Clem. Alex.*, Pæd. iii, 12$_{88}$ (LEGG, ad Mt. 22$_{37}$). TORREY, *Documents*, p. 81, tries to rescue the accuracy of Matthew by accusing a scribe of having changed ΔΥΝΑΜΕΙ into ΔΙΑΝΟΙΑΙ, unconsciously influenced by the Greek of Mark, Luke and the LXX. The total disappearence of the δύναμις does not favour this explanation.

[2] The patristic parallels consistently use καρδία. These parallels contain other features of interest: in 2 Clem. 3$_4$ the quotation is combined with that found in Mt. 15$_{8-9}$. — In *Justin*, 1 Apol. 16$_6$ the verse from the *shema* is combined with Deut. 6$_{13}$ in the form of LXX^{A} as in Mt. 4$_{10}$. Cf. A. SEEBERG, *Die Didache des Judentums und der Urchristenheit* (1908), p. 71, on the words by which the Double

διάνοια and δύναμις[1] as against καρδία and ἰσχύς appear to be terms of a more philosophical style. The simpler terms are found even in LXX[B] in the less influential text in 2 Kings.[2] In Aquila διάνοια is found only in Eccles. 1₁₆, i.e. just in a type of literature of a more philosophical style. The LXX[A] as well as the N.T. may therefore be assumed to have preserved a Palestinian reading in its rendering καρδία as against the διάνοια of the Alexandrian tradition.[3]

Matthew seems to stand closest to the Hebrew text or, at least, to Semitic tradition with his preposition ἐν, but in spite of that Matthew must be dependent upon Mark. In his solicitude for the "three tones" in the Hebrew (and the LXX) *shema* he allows ἰσχύς to drop out.[4] It is noteworthy that all the Synoptics, except the D text in Mark and Luke, include the synonyms καρδία and διάνοια, both translations of the Hebrew לבב.[5] It is very unlikely that any

Commandment is introduced in Did. 1₂ πρῶτον ἀγαπήσεις τὸν θεὸν τὸν ποιήσαντά σε. — In *Justin*, Dial. 93₂, the nouns are καρδία and ἰσχύς and the pronoun ἐκ. The quotation is introduced thus: ἐν δυσὶν ἐντολαῖς πᾶσαν δικαιοσύνην καὶ εὐσέβειαν πληροῦσθαι ... as if it were a conflation of Mt. 22₄₀ and 3₁₅. On all these references to the Fathers, see Massaux, *Influence de l'Évangile de saint Matthieu*, p. 154, 485, 606 and 530 f.

[3] Hatch, *Essays in Biblical Greek*, p. 102 f., registers 4 cases where Aquila uses καρδία as against the LXX's διάνοια. He finds however, in his study in the psychological terms of the LXX no sharp distinction between the sense of the terms καρδία — πνεῦμα — ψυχή. As to καρδία — ψυχή he says that the former is most commonly used of will and intention, the latter of appetite and desire. No consequences are expressly drawn from the use of διάνοια — καρδία, p. 108.

[1] No statistics on the LXX's renderings can be made since מאד as noun is found only in these two texts of Deuteronomy and 2 Kings and in Ecclus. 7₃₀ (LXX δύναμις).

[2] McNeile, *Comm. Mt.*, ad. loc., not questioning the text of the LXX[B] in Deuteronomy, thinks that the N.T. wording was probably influenced by 2 Kings. It is highly improbable, that what was to the Jews *the* text, the *shema* of Deuteronomy, could be influenced by a passage as that in 2 Kings.

[3] Sh. Johnson, *op. cit.*, p. 147, points to the fact that pap. 963 supports the reading of LXX[B] while it usually goes with LXX[AF] in Deuteronomy. Thus he takes the A text to be influenced by the N.T.

[4] So Lagrange, *Comm. Mt.*, p. cxx, and p. 432: ... on peut croire que ne voulant conserver que trois termes ... il (the Greek translator of the Aramaic Matthew) a préféré "l'ésprit" qui correspondait mieux à l'âme et au cœur que la force, qui est un mode.

[5] διάνοια is a frequent translation of לבב in the LXX, though καρδία is far more common. The different LXX texts show no particular preference as to one of these terms. A has διάνοια for καρδία e.g. in Ex. 35₉, Josh. 14₈ and καρδία as

form of the *shema* containing such a repetition was known to the evangelists. The text of Matthew must therefore be a revision of the Marcan text.[1] The readings of D are accordingly later corrections of the same type as the hexaplaric corrections in the LXX.

It is surprising that the Greek text of the *shema* occurs in such a completely inconsistent form, the more so since we know that it was permissible to read the *shema* in Greek.[2] In the rendering of the Decalogue in Mt. 19₁₈–₁₉ with its parallels, there was similarly inconsistency as to the order and imprint of catechetical tradition. Yet the terminology was unanimous even in Greek. It may be that the wording of catechetical instruction on the basis of the *shema* has left its marks. Nevertheless the wealth of variants indicates that there was no authorized Greek form of that part of the Jewish liturgy in the days of the evangelists or that there were different forms, which influenced the N. T. texts in different ways. Not one of the gospels, however, gives one of those more or less authorized forms as may be seen from the combined use of the synonyms καρδία and διάνοια.

Mt. 22₃₉ (= 19₁₉b) ≠ Mk. 12₃₁ (₃₃b) ≠ Lk. 10₂₇b: Lev. 19₁₈.

Mt.

ἀγαπήσεις τὸν πλησίον σου ὡς σεαυ-τόν.

σεαυτόν] ἑαυτόν Θ *al.*

Mt. 19₁₉b has the same text with the same variant in Θ *al.*

Mk. 12₃₁ = Mt. — Mk. 12₃₃: τὸ ἀγαπᾶν τὸν πλησίον ὡς ἑαυτόν.

ἑαυτόν] σεαυτόν ℵ A D *al.*

Lk.: (καὶ) τὸν πλησίον σου ὡς σεαυ-τόν.

σεαυτόν] ἑαυτόν A.

Lev. 19₁₈ LXX

ἀγαπήσεις τὸν πλησίον σου ὡς σεαυ-τόν.

σεαυτόν] ἑαυτόν Lucian (75).

M.T.

ואהבת לרעך כמוך

---

against B's διάνοια except in Deut. 6₅ also *e.g.* in 28₄₇. — The later Greek versions to Deut. 6₅ are missing.

[1] So also SH. JOHNSON, *op. cit.*, p. 147 f. He thinks that Matthew conflated the Mark and Q form while Luke retained Q's reading. This to Sh. Johnson is an argument for Q's independence of the LXX.

[2] E. SCHÜRER, *Geschichte des jüdischen Volkes* III (1909⁴), p. 141, cf. II (1907⁴), p. 26, STRACK-BILLERBECK IV, p. 196. According to S. LIEBERMAN, *Greek in Jewish Palestine* (1942), p. 30, there is, however, no evidence of the recitation in Greek within the borders of Palestine until the 4th century.

The agreement of the Synoptics with each other and with the LXX is complete. In the LXX as well as in Matthew and Luke is found the variant reading ἑαυτόν, a Hellenized feature in the N. T.[1], supported only by the less reliable manuscripts. What contributes to this reading is, however, the character of a general rule, and this is most apparent in Mark., v. 33.

In Matthew this commandment about loving one's neighbour is not only associated with the *shema*. Matthew, in 19₁₉b, was the only one to add it to the Decalogue. For him it was not exclusively associated with the double commandment known from the Testaments of the Twelve Patriarchs.[2] He attributes the combination of the commandment and the *shema* to Jesus. Luke takes it for granted, partly in that to him it is the scribe who quotes the double commandment, and partly in that these two elements are joined together with the unstressed καί.

Mt. 22₄₄ ≠ Mk. 12₃₆ ≠ Lk. 20₄₂f.: Ps. 110₁ (Ps. 87); cf. Acts 2₃₄f. Heb. 1₁₃.

Mt.

εἶπεν κύριος τῷ κυρίῳ μου· κάθου ἐκ δεξιῶν μου ἕως ἂν θῶ τοὺς ἐχθρούς σου ὑποκάτω τῶν ποδῶν σου.

κύριος] BℵDZ; *rell.* ὁ κύριος.
ὑποκάτω] ὑποπόδιον ℜ *pm.*

Mk. = Mt.   **Variants:**

εἶπεν] λέγει AD.
κύριος] BD; ὁ κύρ. 𝕳ℜΘ *pl.*
κάθου] κάθισον B.
θῶ] θώσω D*, θήσω D².
ὑποκάτω] BD *pc.*; ὑποπόδιον ℵℜΘλφ.

Lk. = Mt. except ὑποκάτω] D it syr^cur; *rell.* ὑποπόδιον. Variants:
εἶπεν] λέγει D it.
κύριος] BD 579; *rell.* ὁ κύριος.
ἕως ἂν θῶ] ἕως τιθῶ D.

---

[1] BLASS-DEBRUNNER, *Grammatik*⁷, § 64: 1, and W. BAUER, *Wörterbuch z. N. T.* (1952⁴), s. v. ἑαυτοῦ, 2.

[2] Test. Issachar 5₂, cf. 7₆, see R. EPPEL, *Le piétisme juif dans les Testaments des douze Patriarches* (1930), p. 146, and C. EDLUND, *Das Auge der Einfalt* (1952), p. 69.

Ps. 110₁ LXX   **M. T.**

εἶπεν ὁ κύριος τῷ κυρίῳ μου· κάθου   נאם יהוה לאדני שב לימיני עד אשית

ἐκ δεξιῶν μου ἕως ἂν θῶ τοὺς ἐχ-   איביך הדם לרגליך

θρούς σου ὑποπόδιον τῶν ποδῶν σου.

Ps. 8₇

πάντα ὑπέταξας ὑποκάτω τῶν πο-   כל שתה תחת רגליו

δῶν αὐτοῦ.

The quotation in the discussion on the Scriptures, usually called the Question about the Son of David, is of LXX type. The only positive deviation from the LXX is ὑποκάτω in Matthew and Mark, and this is usually considered to be influenced by the cognate Ps. 8₇.[1] Cod. B and D in Mark have the same text as Matthew, which certainly is the genuine Marcan text.[2] In Matthew the reading κύριος without the article has a slightly better support than in Mark and Luke, but this scarcely bears out ZAHN's argument for the deviation from the LXX.[3] Both the agreement between the Synoptics and the dependence upon the LXX is clear.

The type of argument we come across is expressed by the introductory formula, which is lacking in Luke, however. David spoke "in the spirit" and thus it was a prophecy, though it could not have been fulfilled in David's time or since. The hermeneutics of the primitive church often uses this principle of *deductio ad absurdum*. The prophetic sayings in the O. T. which have not been accomplished in the old covenant still remain as promises and prophetic sayings of the Messiah — Christ and His community. We find this same thought in the introductory formulae to our quotation in Acts and Hebrews[4],

---

[1] In Hebrews both these texts are quoted without any confusion, 1₁₃ and 2₈.

[2] Cf. the verdict of MANSON, *Bull. of J. Ryl. Libr.* 34 (1951/52), p. 316. Cod. D is otherwise a weak support since it contains obvious influences from parallels (above, p. 59) and even from theological deliberations (below, p. 85).

[3] *Einleitung* II¹, p. 318. Zahn finds it to be a special Matthaean trend to use κύριος without the article for the name of Yahweh. In the examples given by him (Mt. 1₂₀,₂₂ 3₃), however, κύριος is part of a fixed term, where the other gospels also make use of the same wording. Only example in point is 1₂₂. On the whole question, see B. WEISS, Der Gebrauch des Artikels bei den Gottesnamen, *Theol. St. u. Krit.* 84 (1911), p. 319—392 on θεός and 503—538 on κύριος, for our question particularly p. 503—505. Cf. *Theol. Wörterb. z. N. T.* III, p. 1085 f. and for the LXX evidence, p. 1057.

[4] On the Jewish interpretation see, in addition to STRACK-BILLERBECK IV, p. 452—460, G. H. Box, in *The People and the Book*, p. 456.

and this type of argument becomes a characteristic of second century exegesis, as is seen *e.g.* in Justin.[1]

The argument of the N. T. is most natural from the LXX text with its κύριος referring to Christ[2], but it is not impossible on a Semitic basis, if we presume the *qere* אדני instead of the *ketib* יהוה.

The synoptic apocalypse.

Mt. 24 is rich in allusions but lacks quotations in the strict sense. This agrees with the nature of that chapter. The apocalyptic style is characterized by allusive references and this in a way which seems to imply a deliberate unwillingness to cite exactly.[3] Most allusions in Mt. 24 are common to the Synoptics; at times they bear the imprint of the Semitic Bible in their Greek text.

Mt. 24₇ ≠ Mk. 13₈ ≠ Lk. 21₁₀: Is. 19₂.

Mt. = Mk. Lk.	LXX[B]	M. T.
ἐγερθήσεται γὰρ	καὶ ἐπεγερθήσονται	... וסכסכתי
ἔθνος ἐπὶ ἔθνος	... καὶ πολεμήσει	... ונלחמו
καὶ βασιλεία ἐπὶ	... πόλις ἐπὶ πόλιν	עיר בעיר
βασιλείαν.	καὶ νομὸς ἐπὶ νομόν.	ממלכה בממלכה

γὰρ] Lk.: D *pc.* it syr; ἐπεγερθ.] –εται א*.–Aא^ca
om. *rell.*   repeats ἐπεγερθήσεται
   before πόλις.

Aquila, Theodotion and Symmachus all give variants to ἐπεγερθήσονται.

The allusion to Is. 19₂ agrees with the M. T. as opposed to the LXX in βασιλεία ἐπὶ βασιλείαν but differs from every O. T. text known to us by talking of ἔθνος ἐπὶ ἔθνος.

In Mt. 24₁₅ and Mk. 13₁₄ we find the set term τὸ βδέλυγμα τῆς ἐρημώσεως and Matthew (and likewise Mark in a few manuscripts) refers expressly to Daniel, the prophet. The words quoted are exactly in the terms of both the LXX and Theodotion[A] of Dan. 12₁₁. In other places where the "abomination" is referred to, there are slight differences as to number and article. Luke is as usual more free in

---

[1] Cf. below, p. 118.

[2] So *e.g.* J. DUPONT, *Ephemer. Theol. Lovan.* 29, 1953, p. 317 f. — Cf. above to Mt. 3₃ and DALMAN, *Die Worte Jesu*, p. 150.

[3] See below, p. 158 f.

his rendering. The masculine ἑστηκότα in Mark refers the sign to a person. Matthew uses the neuter ἑστός which is more in accordance with the Jewish interpretation[1], and the context gives evidence that Matthew took over Mark's text with this and other recensional corrections.

Mt. 24 30 presents a most complex conflation of O. T. material, partly in accordance with the other Synoptics and partly in accordance with Rev. 17. The text shows both dependence upon the LXX and acquaintance with the Hebrew. As the verse may be considered the main evidence for the hypothesis on testimonies used by Matthew, it will be dealt with later when we have to come to some conclusion on the hypothesis in question.[2]

Mt. 26 31 ≠ Mk. 14 27: Zech. 13 7; cf. Jn. 16 32.

Mt.	Mk.
πατάξω τὸν ποιμένα, καὶ διασκορπισθήσονται τὰ πρόβατα τῆς ποίμνης. (... προάξω ...)	πατάξω τὸν ποιμένα, καὶ τὰ πρόβατα διασκορπισθήσονται.
	τὰ πρ. διασκ.] διασκ. τὰ πρ. Α Δ.
διασκ.] pap. 53 𝔓φ al.; –σεται pap. 37 45 ℵDΘ pm.	Jn. 16 32
	ἰδοὺ ἔρχεται ὥρα καὶ ἐλήλυθεν ἵνα σκορπισθῆτε ἕκαστος εἰς τὰ ἴδια.

Zech. 13 7 LXX[B]	LXX[A]	M.T.
πατάξατε τοὺς ποιμένας καὶ ἐκσπάσατε τὰ πρόβατα, (καὶ ἐπάξω ...).	πάταξον τὸν ποιμένα καὶ διασκορπισθήσονται τὰ πρόβατα τῆς ποίμνης, (καὶ ἐπάξω ...).	הך את הרעה ותפוצין הצאן

πάταξον] so also ℵ[cb] Q; πατάξω V 538 pc.
τὸν ποιμένα] so also ℵ[ca cb] QΓ.
διασκ.] –σθήτω ℵ[ca] Lucian; –σθήτωσαν ℵ[cb] Γ.

This quotation leads to Jesus's prediction of the reunion in Galilee. Luke lacks these traditions about Galilee[3] and consequently is also without this quotation. The difference between Matthew and Mark

---

[1] STRACK-BILLERBECK I, p. 951, for the meaning of Mark's form, see the discussion in LOHMEYER, Comm. Mk., ad loc.

[2] p. 212 ff.

[3] R. H. LIGHTFOOT, Locality and Doctrine in the Gospels (1938), p. 52 ff.

so far as word order is concerned is not important. In Mark, where Matthew's τῆς ποίμνης is missing, the chiastic position of the words belongs to an emphatic style.[1] What is more striking is πατάξω which is uniformly found in the N. T. as against the imperative forms in the M. T., the Targum and the O. T. Peshitta, as in practically all LXX manuscripts.[2] The text of the gospels, on the other hand, resemble the M. T. in the singular "shepherd", which is an indispensable condition for the function of the quotation in the N. T. The LXX witnesses are divided, however, and as a matter of fact the LXX^A agrees with Matthew in the use of the singular. Matthew's only deviation from this text is the introductory πατάξω, while LXX^Q agrees rather with Mark's text, apart from the word order. It therefore looks as in these two cases the LXX was corrected from Matthew and Mark respectively. However, as both these sources of evidence render the M. T. better through their singular form, this conclusion is not convincing. A and Q may be bearers of a Palestinian LXX tradition.[3] It would otherwise be extraordinary if the

---

[1] The text of Matthew can hardly be said to be closer to the M. T. in its reading τὰ πρόβατα τῆς ποίμνης. It might well be a stilistic change in order to stress the breaking up of a unit. So also TORREY, Documents, p. 84, arguing however on the basis of his alleged Hebrew text. — On the other hand the dependence on the Hebrew O. T. text cannot be definitely ruled out since the Matthaean text renders the collective noun הצאן ingeniously, which here as usual takes the plural, see GESENIUS-BUHL, Handwörterb. über das A. T. (1921¹⁷), s. v. — The Marcan type is found in the Fayyum (?) fragment 14 (3rd century), ed. CH. WESSELY, Patrol. Orient. IV, 2, p. 173—177.

[2] The common emendation אכה (Wellhausen, Nowack, Marti, Kittel) coincides with the N. T. but has its only support in this quotation and in some less reliable MSS of the LXX. (On cod. V, see ZIEGLER, ed. Duodecim prophetae, p. 37—39: V. gives a blended text and is often "sehr eigenwillig".) These LXX texts are most probably influenced by the N. T. — The emendation of הך is evoked by the lack of correspondence with the feminine form עירי. It is equally possible, however, not to consider "the sword" the conscious subject of הך also. The M. T. is strongly supported by the same reading in the Damascus Document (CDCb 93; col. xix, 8). — Other emendations are made by Kahle, Sellin (הכי), Mitchell (הכות הך אח < הכוה), Th. Robinson (הכה אכה).

[3] Against J. HÄNEL, Der Schriftbegriff Jesu (1919), p. 114, and TORREY, Documents, p. 84. — To SPERBER, Journ. of Bibl. Lit. 59 (1940), p. 281, this is one of the cases where the reading of the "al. ex." in the Hexapla retains the text of the apostles. — It is worth noting that the latter part of the same verse (Zech. 137) in Lucian's text has been corrected from the M. T., ZIEGLER, op. cit., p. 84. Thus a correction from the N. T. also is less probable and at the same time the coincidence with the N. T. lessens the suspicion of hexaplaric influence.

introductory imperative had not also been corrected to agree with the N. T. From the point of view of contents this would have been all right, since the following sentence in Zech. 13 7 is introduced by ἐπάξω. The current emendation אכה in the commentaries on Zechariah shows how natural this had been in the context.

The reading of LXX^AQ in its entirety is now by no means simply motivated by adaptation to the N. T. As a matter of fact the LXX^B gives a most peculiar interpretation of the M. T. in rendering פורץ by ἐκσπᾶν. This is the only place in the LXX where this occurs. In the LXX this verb tends to be used *in bonam partem* with the meaning "to save", "to redeem", as for example (in connection with the work of the shepherd) in Amos 3 12. Otherwise the LXX^A has a certain predilection for ἐκσπᾶν (7 times it is the variant reading in A and only here in Zech. 13 does LXX^B read ἐκσπᾶν in opposition to A). In 1 Sam. 19 10 it is A's synonym for B's διασώζειν, even there in connection with πατάσσειν. Only in Judges 20 32 has it the sense "to coax out of" (the town). LXX^B to Zech. 13 thus appears to be a tendentious interpretation which lays stress on "the remnant", the godly in the land, as the good ones who will be redeemed, unlike their wicked leaders. Thus, for example, the Ethiopic translation has interpreted ἐκσπᾶν as *congregare*. LXX^A on the other hand gives an interpretation which is more closely connected with the Hebrew text. Since Justin supports this reading, it does not seem to be a hexaplaric adaptation to the Hebrew text but merely a Palestinian form, the form which was familiar to the evangelists and which underlies the formation of the passion story at this point.

On the other hand, the transformation of the imperative into the indicative has no foundation in the Greek O. T., but must be attributed to Christian adaptation of the type we have seen proof of earlier. From the theological point of view the activity of God is emphasized thereby as the subject in the passion story. In the same direction points the σκανδαλισθήσεσθε ἐν ἐμοὶ (v. 31a) which might have the instrumental meaning[1]: "By me you will be made to stumble". It may be objected that the adaptation was not necessary for its function as a Christian testimony, as may be seen in Justin and Irenaeus.[2] The first person singular is the more noteworthy as v. 28

---

[1] BLASS-DEBRUNNER, *Grammatik*, § 219.

[2] In *Justin*, Dial. 53 6 the quotation occurs in fuller context from Zech. 13 7. Its form is nearly that of LXX^Q, though it is also close to cod. A. — In *Irenaeus*,

in Mark and v. 32 in Matthew have προάξω with Jesus as the subject. The possibility that the shepherd here in question may be Peter and not Jesus cannot be entirely eliminated. The context is the foretelling of Peter's denial. It is, however, more credible that the quotation in its Christian form with the πατάξω was primary to the context it received in the passion story in Mark, and that it was taken over in the same form by Matthew. Consequently we may speak of a testimony which had an independent existence.[1]

Mt. 27₄₆ ≠ Mk. 15₃₄: Ps. 22₂.

a) Mt.

ἠλὶ ἠλὶ λεμὰ σαβαχθάνι.

Mk.

ἐλωΐ ἐλωΐ λαμὰ σαβαχθάνι.

	Mt.	Mk.
B	ελωει ελωει λεμα σαβακτανει	ελωι ελωι λαμα ζαβαφθανει
ℵ	ελωι ελωι λεμα σαβαχθανει	ελωι ελωι λεμα σαβακτανει
A	ηλι ηλι λιμα σαβαχθανει	ελωι ελωι λιμα σαβακθανει
W	ηλι ηλι μα σαβαχθανει	
D	ηλει ηλει λαμα ζαφθανει	ηλει ηλει λαμα ζαφθανει
Θ	λ: ηλει ηλει λαμα σαβαχθανει	Θ: ηλει ηλει λαμα σαβαχθανι

syr^sin ܘܠܡܢܐ ܠܡܐ ܐܠܝ ܐܠܝ   ܘܠܡܢܐ ܠܡܐ ܐܠܗܝ ܐܠܗܝ

b) Mt.

θεέ μου, θεέ μου, ἱνατί με ἐγκατέλιπες;

Mk.

ὁ θεός μου, ὁ θεός μου, εἰς τί ἐγκατέλιπές με;

1st μου] om. ΑΘλφ sa.

2nd ὁ θ. μ.] om. B 565.

ἐγκ.] ὠνείδισας D.

Epideixis 76, the quotation is of the same length and the text seems to have been that of the LXX^A. — Barn. 5₁₂ on the other hand is a free rendering, adapting the quotation to the context of the epistle, and the text shows no direct dependence on the LXX, cf. MASSAUX, *Influence de l'Évangile de saint Matthieu*, p. 70.

[1] Against DODD, *According to the Scriptures*, p. 65 f., cf. below, p. 217. — Otherwise the hypothesis of Dodd is most convincing particularly when dealing with Zech. 9—14 as a text book used as a whole in the early church. There might however be a difference between the quotations in the passion story and in the other parts of the gospels. — On the difficulties into which this quotation forces LAGRANGE, see below, p. 154 f.

Ps. 22₂ LXX

ὁ θεός, ὁ θεός μου, πρόσχες μοι,
ἱνατί ἐγκατέλιπές με;

M. T.

אלי אלי למה עזבתני

πρόσχες μοι] sub obelo in Hexapla
but retained in nearly all MSS.

Targum

אלי אלי מטול מה שבקתני

Aquila

ἰσχυρέ μου, ἰσχυρέ μου, ἱνατί ἐγκατέλιπές με;

O. T. Peschitta

ܐܠܗܝ ܐܠܗܝ ܠܡܢܐ ܫܒܩܬܢܝ

a. *The Hebrew-Aramaic text.* From the point of view of textual criticism, this is for natural reasons the most uncertain element in Matthew's and also in Mark's quotations. Two extremes may be distinguished. Cod. D, followed to a certain extent by cod. Θ, seems to render the M. T. text in both Matthew and Mark, while cod. W gives a text for Matthew which practically agrees with the Targum. These consistent types of text are, however, the fruit of later revision.

The reading ελωι supposes the Aramaic אלהי but the Targum, as we have it, reads אלי[1]; as in the Targum Onkelos this form occurs as an accepted Hebraism.[2] The words uttered by Jesus were certainly current in Aramaic form, and not in that of the Targum, but in the purer Aramaic form, which was used by Mark, who is known to be the evangelist who preserved Aramaic words.[3] By reading ηλι

---

[1] So ed. LAGARDE and the *London Polyglott*, ed. WALTON. I cannot find the source of D. SIDERSKY's reading אלהי in the Targum, *Journal Asiatique* 11: 3 (1914), p. 233 (he may have got it from v. 3, where it is found). — In this article he puts forth the view that the שבקתני of Matthew is the שבחתני of Ps. 42₁₀, though the translator of Matthew rendered the text of Ps. 22. He supports his view by pointing to the irregular transliteration χ for ק, but that rendering is due to the ϑ, cf. above: κ + τ or χ + ϑ, see DALMAN, *Die Worte Jesu*², p. 43. On Greek transliteration of Hebrew see SWETE, *Introduction to the O. T. in Greek*, p. 67, cf. below to Mt. 2₂₃, p. 103 f. and 198 f.

[2] DALMAN, *op. cit.*, p. 42 f.

[3] Mark's λαμα as an Aramaic form, see J. LEVY, *Wörterb. z. Talmud u. Midrasch*, s. v. מָה. — H. BIRKELAND, *Språk og religion hos jøder og arabere* (1949), p. 28 f., has put forth a revolutionary view on the language of Palestine in the time of Jesus. He thinks that the Aramaic phrases in Mk. 5₄₁ and 7₃₄ were retained because in these two cases Jesus spoke Aramaic as against his habit of speaking the vernacular Hebrew of the *am-ha-ares*. The words on the cross were uttered in this language, though Mark already held the false view that the usual language of Jesus had been Aramaic. The more detailed arguments for this revolutionary hypothesis have not been published yet. As far as the words on the cross are con-

Matthew obtains a clearer reference to the misunderstanding of the bystanders at the Cross, who thought that Jesus spoke to Elijah. This difference between Matthew and Mark is preserved in the Syriac of syr[sin], naturally without any translation corresponding to the latter part of the verse in Greek.

Considerable confusion made its way into the manuscripts, however, partly through lack of knowledge of Hebrew and Aramaic, and partly through intentional changes. The Western text does not afford any help in restoring the original text of Matthew, nor that of Mark, though many scholars have claimed D's text in Mark to be genuine.[1]

---

cerned they are scarcely able to support any theory about the actual language of Jesus. Partly they are a quotation and partly there is no firm basis from the point of view of textual criticism. Thirdly the gospels do not lead us further back than to the *a priori* fact that the words from the earliest stage of the tradition existed in both Hebrew and Aramaic (and Greek) form, cf. MANSON, *Bull. of J. Ryl. Libr.* 34 (1951/52), p. 327.

[1] Whether the reading of D is accepted as the genuine text of Mark (HARNACK, *Sitzungsber. Akad. Berlin* 1901:1, p. 261 ff. = *Arbeiten zur Kirchengeschichte* 19, 1931, p. 98 ff., cf. MANSON, *op. cit.*, p. 318 and 326—28) or is considered a later correction, it shows the signs of theological uneasiness with the words of the Psalm used by Jesus, cf. MANSON, p. 328: "it means that Mark offered an interpretation of the cry rather than a translation; for ὠνείδισας cannot be regarded as a translation either of the Hebrew or the Aramaic".

Thus D's reading is hardly due to mere misunderstanding or mistranslation caused by Syriac influence (so F. H. CHASE, *The Syro-Latin Text of the Gospels*, 1895, p. 107). The way which led to the translation ὠνείδισας might, however, be best understood as leading through a Syriac milieu. D's ζαφθανει is usually taken as a rendering of the M. T. עזבתני (*e.g.* DALMAN, *loc. cit.*, HARNACK, *loc. cit.*, A. MERX, *Comm. Mt.*, p. 424), where the initial α was dropped (as it is also in the Old Latin texts which follow D). It might, however, be that this Hebrew word was never in the text but was only the starting point for the theologians who promulgated the D text. They intended to lessen the offence of the desolation of Christ. Starting from the Hebrew עזב, a root not found in Syriac, they changed it intentionally into זעף — ܚܣܢ. In Hebrew this meant "to be angry" and the LXX never renders it by ὀνειδίζειν. That translation is more natural if the whole theological process is presumed to have taken place in a Syriac milieu since the Syriac ܚܣܢ is less strong and takes on the meaning of "to be indignant". It is used in the Christian Palestinian for ἐμβριμᾶσθαι (Mt. 9 30, Mk. 1 43) and ἐπιτιμᾶν (Mt. 17 18, 20 31 *et al.*), see CHASE, *loc. cit*, cf. DALMAN, *loc. cit.*, (M. BLACK's criticism of Chase, *An Aramaic Approach to the Gospels and Acts*, p. 29 f. touches hardly this special case where both the Semitic and the Greek text is extant in the N. T.) — HARNACK, *loc. cit.*, strengthens his view that ὠνείδισας was the genuine reading in Mark by pointing to the place of ὀνειδισμός in the Christology

This is rendered less probable especially when it is remembered that Mark is the gospel with retained, untranslated Aramaic wordings. It is also weakened by the fact that the Hebrew text led to the interpretation ὠνείδισας instead of the LXX ἐγκατέλιπες, which is found in the rest of the N. T. manuscripts. This translation is surely deliberate in order to diminish the theological offence in the desolation of Jesus. The transliteration of D is found also in Matthew, but without the translation, so that it is obviously due to parallel influence. What happened in the Western text was similar to the intentional change in the Gospel of Peter (5 19). Its reading ἡ δύναμίς μου depends either upon taking אלי to have the same meaning as Aquila: ἰσχυρέ μου, or more probably upon reading חילי instead of אלי.[1] In both cases, however, the changes are clearly deliberate, though based on linguistic methods. This type of interpretation is found in Jewish hermeneutics and we shall come across instances of it in the formula quotations in Matthew, though in Mark, where it exists side by side with other readings, it definitely bears the mark of later theological deliberations.

b. *The Greek text* affords a clearer picture from the point of view of textual criticism. Even here Matthew and Mark do not coincide. In common they both differ from the LXX in the absence of its characteristic πρόσχες μοι which Origen marked with an obelus. It is true that these words are also missing in Aquila's text, but since all LXX manuscripts worth noting agree in their pre-Hexapla text, it is less probable that a Greek text of the type found in Matthew and Mark was taken from the evangelists' Greek O. T.[2] Neither is the common form ἐγκατέλιπες conclusive of such influence, since this is the LXX's usual translation of עזב (שבק). Matthew's vocative θεέ is an Attic form, added in the margin of certain LXX manuscripts[3],

of the gospels, *e.g.* Mk. 15 32 and also in the 22nd Psalm (v. 7). This may also support the view of a later correction in the quotation. — On this kind of theological treatment of the biblical text, see below, p. 112 and 183 ff.

[1] W. HASENZAHL, *Die Gottverlassenheit des Christus*, p. 77–94: the Gospel of Peter depends directly on a Greek text of the type found in Aquila. — F. ZIMMERMAN, *Journ. of Bibl. Lit.* 66 (1947), p. 465 f.: In Galilean pronounciation the "gutturals" א, ח and ע were scarcely distinguishable. — L. VAGANAY, *L'Évangile de Pierre* (1930), p. 255 f.

[2] The text in *Justin* (Dial. 98 2, 99 1a = LXX; 99 1b = N. T.), see HASENZAHL, *op. cit.*, p. 105 f.

[3] P. KATZ, *Philo's Bible* (1950), p. 152 f., cf. BLASS-DEBRUNNER, *Grammatik*[7] § 44: 2, 147: 3.

perhaps due to influence from this very passage in the N.T. On this point Mark's text is in closer agreement with the LXX, but in the latter part of the quotation Matthew, together with the LXX and Aquila, has ἰνατί while Mark's εἰς τί is a striking example of N. T. translation Greek.[1]

In the evangelists' use of the Scriptures this is a special case, since the Hebrew-Aramaic text is given and the differences between Matthew and Mark depend upon the fact that each gave his own interpretation. The freedom in relation to the LXX is at the same time bound up with the earlier insertion of Ps. 22 into the passion story[2], as appears also from the quotation in Mt. 2743[3]. It is thus misleading to speak of testimonies, if by that is meant texts which had an existence independent of their context.

---

[1] M. BLACK, *op. cit.* p. 88. — In spite of Matthew's εἰς τί in 1431, ἰνατί could be a correction on mere linguistic ground, without conscious influence from the LXX.

[2] On the difference between a quotation of this kind in the passion narrative and in the formula quotations, see M. DIBELIUS, *Formgeschichte*[2], p. 188, and HASENZAHL, *op. cit.*, p. 146.

[3] See below, p. 104 f.

2. Quotations with parallels in Luke

And now let us turn to the quotations common to Matthew and Luke which lack a counterpart in Mark. Here to draw the line of distinction between quotation and allusion is more difficult than ever HAWKINS only registered the four quotations in the passage on the temptation, while DITTMAR counted also Mt. 7 23 ≠ Lk. 13 27 : Ps. 6 9 and Mt. 23 39 ≠ Lk. 13 35 : Ps. 118 26, cf. Mt. 21 9, 15. Allusions bordering upon quotations and of interest to our study are Mt. 10 35f. ≠ Lk. 12 53 : Micah 7 6; Mt. 11 5 ≠ Lk. 7 22, cf. Lk. 4 18f. : Is. 61 1 and others; Mt. 11 23 ≠ Lk. 10 15 : Is. 14 11, 13, 15; Mt. 23 34–36 ≠ Lk. 11 49–51 : 2 Chron. 24 20ff.; Mt. 24 38f. ≠ Lk. 17 27 : Gen. 7 6f.

The passage on the temptation constitutes a complete unity, and to an even greater degree than the passion story is moulded on the basis of quotations from the O. T. Apart from the quotations, indeed, the dependence on the O. T. is considerable. The forty days and forty nights are an allusion to Moses's similarly long fast, Deut. 9 9, 18 ≠ Ex. 34 28 and 24 18. That this allusion is a conscious one is emphasized by the fact that three of the four express quotations are taken from Deuteronomy.

Mt. 4 4 ≠ Lk. 4 4. In the first quotation, taken from Deut. 8 3, Matthew and Luke are in complete agreement with the LXX and even with each other, so long as they follow one another, but here, as in Mt. 19 5, Matthew has a longer text. The eight additional words also agree entirely with the LXX and dependence upon the M. T. is excluded[1], but the LXX interpretation is in agreement with rabbinic tradition.

---

[1] The M. T.: על כל מוצא פי יהוה, but the LXX: ἐπὶ παντὶ ῥήματι τῷ (om. A F Lucian) ἐκπορευομένῳ διὰ στόματος θεοῦ. The Targums read *"memra of Yahweh"*, however, see STRACK-BILLERBECK I, p. 150.

On the difference as to the length of a quotation, cf. above to Mt. 3 3, 19 4–5, and below, p. 110, note 1. It was a rabbinic method to imply the continuation of a given quotation, see DODD, *According to the Scriptures*, p. 47, J. DUPONT, *Ephemer. Theol. Lovan.* 29 (1953) p. 315, cf. J. MANN, *The Bible as Read and Preached in the Old Synagogue* I, p. 12, on the use of the "skipped" parts of the *haftaroth*.

On the other hand Mt. 4₆ has a somewhat longer gap than the corresponding passage in Lk. 4₁₀₋₁₁ in the LXX text, which is otherwise followed word for word (Ps. 91₁₁₋₁₂).[1]

Mt. 4₇ ≠ Lk. 4₁₂ : Deut. 6₁₆ are identical with each other and with the LXX, while the M. T. has the verb in the plural.[2]

Even Mt. 4₁₀ ≠ Lk. 4₈ : Deut. 6₁₃ are identical with each other but both differ from the LXX[B] which has φοβηθήσῃ for the M. T.'s תירא and also lacks the N. T.'s μόνῳ. Both this and the N. T.'s προσκυνήσεις are found in the LXX[A] (and similarly in Lucian). Also in Deut. 10₂₀ LXX[A] has these two variants. This translation of ירא (the Targum's: דחל) is otherwise non-existent in the LXX. Since pap. 963 has the reading μόνῳ, A's reading cannot simply be dismissed as a correction from the N. T.; it may render the Greek text as the N. T. knew it.[3] The assumption that cod. A might have been corrected according to the N. T. may, however, find support in the fact that προσκυνεῖν occurs in the preceding context of the gospels, Mt. v. 9, Lk. v. 7.

In any case the quotations are without influence from texts other than the LXX and their LXX character is almost a literal one. In spite of the lesser differences between Matthew's and Luke's passages on the temptation, even in their quotations, they presuppose a common source and not merely material from an oral tradition or a framework consisting only of the four quotations as testimonies.

Mt. 7₂₃ ≠ Lk. 13₂₇ shows a singular relation to Ps. 6₉:

Mt.	Lk.
ἀποχωρεῖτε ἀπ' ἐμοῦ οἱ ἐργαζό-μενοι τὴν ἀνομίαν.	ἀπόστητε ἀπ' ἐμοῦ πάντες ἐργάται ἀδικίας.

LXX	M. T.
ἀπόστητε ἀπ' ἐμοῦ πάντες οἱ ἐρ-γαζόμενοι τὴν ἀνομίαν.	סורו ממני כל פעלי און

---

[1] See SH. JOHNSON, *Harv. Theol. Rev.* 36 (1943), p. 144 f., criticizing TORREY, *Documents*, p. 56.

[2] TORREY, *loc. cit.*: "A better Hebrew text" had the singular. Thereby Torrey rescues his hypothesis of the Matthaean independence of the LXX. — BACON, *Studies in Matthew*, p. 472, stresses the reading of D in Matthew as possibly a free rendering of the Hebrew.

[3] One of the texts where W. STAERK admitted LXX[A] to have been corrected from the N. T., *Zeitschr. f. wissenschaftl. Theol.* 40 (1897), p. 256 f., cf. p. 265.

The first half of the quotation is thus LXX in Luke while the second half is LXX in Matthew. That we should have two types of Greek O. T. text in such a case of chiastic parallelism is scarcely credible. If we add to this the pure LXX form running through the N. T. quotations from the Psalms, it naturally comes about that we cannot speak of more than a mode of expression influenced by the LXX. ἀφιστάναι is common in Luke while it is lacking in Matthew. (Lk. 4₁₃ ≠ Mt. 4₁₁: ἀφιέναι, Lk. 8₁₃ ≠ Mt. 13₂₁: σκανδαλίζεσθαι). ἀποχωρεῖν is, however, *hapax legomenon* in Matthew. When the quotation occurs in 2 Clem. 4₅, it is closest to Luke. In Justin, 1 Apol. 16₁₁, it is an independent revised blending of Matthew and Luke, so that it differs in all respects from the LXX.[1] This only emphasizes the impression of uncertainty. The various deviations from the LXX do not imply any greater proximity to the M. T.; neither Matthew nor Luke seem to have understood it as a regular quotation.

It is, however, worth noting that the citation is included in an apocalyptic saying. We have already had occasion to point out that in material of such a type the quotations are treated with great freedom; this seems to belong to the characteristic style of apocalyptics.[2]

Mt. 10₃₅ ≠ Lk. 12₅₃: Micah 7₆.

The same text in another context. The differences between Matthew and Luke are considerable and indicate that we have here another allusion in a saying of apocalyptic type. For neither Matthew nor Luke is unequivocally closer to any O. T. text known to us. The deviations from the LXX do not necessarily imply greater proximity to the M. T. or knowledge of the Hebrew text. The different prepositions (Matthew: κατά, Luke: ἐπί) depend upon the use of different verbs.[3] The term οἱ οἰκιακοί αὐτοῦ, which lacks a counterpart in Luke,

---

Sh. Johnson, *op. cit.*, p. 145, finding support in Kenyon's evaluation of pap. 963, considers the reading of the LXX[A] pre-Matthaean. See F. G. Kenyon, *Recent Developments in the Textual Criticism of the Greek Bible* (1933), p. 108.

[1] Massaux, *Influence de l'Évangile de saint Matthieu*, p. 150 and 489. Cf. *Justin*, Dial. 76₅ = Matthew, *ibm.*, p. 522.

[2] On quotations and apocalyptic style see below, p. 158 f. Manson, *Bull of J. Ryl. Libr.* 34 (1951/52), p. 321, suggests that Luke gave the quotation another meaning and used the allusion still more loosely. If so Luke's text is read with a comma after ἐμοῦ (with Westcott-Hort): "Depart from me; you are all workers of iniquity." So syr[sin cur].

[3] διχάζειν is a *hapax legomenon* in Matthew as in the N. T. Luke's διαμερίζειν is used (in its concrete sense) by Matthew, 27₃₅.

is not in itself nearer to the M. T.'s אנשי ביתו (= the Targum Jonathan) than the LXX's οἱ ἐν τῷ οἴκῳ αὐτοῦ, since Matthew uses the term οἰκιακοί also in 10 25 in quite another context. Yet dependence upon the M. T. is not precluded.[1] The readings of the later versions are not preserved.

Luke's allusion is marked by his deliberate calculation of the number[2] and, as so often, it is more integrated into the context. It is possible that we here have Q material which was influenced by the LXX without being definitely modelled on it.

Mt. 11 5 ≠ Lk. 7 22: Is. 6 11 and others.[3]

In the answer to John the Baptist's question a reference is made to the Messiah's deeds as known from Isaiah in particular. The main passage from which the allusion is taken is Is. 611[4], which is found more literally quoted in Lk. 4 18. Both this citation and our allusion have a noticeable suggestion of the LXX in that the reading of the M. T. (followed also by Symmachus and Theodotion) "freedom for the captives", is replaced by the LXX's "sight for the blind".

The allusive character of this quotation may most nearly be compared for type to Is. 6 9f. in Mt. 13 13 and parallels.[5] There we will trace retained wording from an Aramaic Targum in the Marcan text, but there is no question of something similar in this quotation. The Targum to Is. 6 11 reinforces the captivity aspect which Q together with the LXX completely eliminated.

Mt. 11 23 ≠ Lk. 10 15: Is. 14 11, 13, 15.

This is another example of biblical allusion in apocalyptic language without the exact nature of a citation and without definite indications of influence from either the LXX or the M. T. The N. T.'s

---

[1] LAGRANGE, Comm. Mt., p. cxxi, expresses himself carefully: "il semble que le mot οἰκιακοί (in 10 35) indique l'influence de l'hébreu".

[2] B. REICKE, Svensk Exegetisk Årsbok 12 (1947), p. 302. In Judaism the text was interpreted as a messianic prophecy, ibm., p. 289 ff.

[3] Cf. Ginza 303 ff. = 487 ff. REITZENSTEIN claimed that the Q text depended upon the source of Ginza. Contrary to this view H. SCHLIER stated that the Ginza passage belonged to late Mandaean traditions and was dependent upon the N. T., Theol. Rundschau 5 (1933), p. 9 and 32 f.

[4] This is in fact the only text of those in question where ἀναβλέπειν is used to express the healing of the blind, cf. Is. 35 5 and 29 18.

[5] See below, p. 130 f.

ὑψωθήσῃ differs from both. The text in Luke is uncertain but hints at a free treatment of the phrases without a conscious tendency to conform the text to that of the LXX.[1]

Mt. 23 34–36 ≠ Lk. 11 49–51 (in a similar context).

This saying has its background in the Jewish view on the murder of the prophets.[2] The O. T. text which it most closely resembles is 2 Chron. 24 20–22 [3], not, however, the text according to the LXX which reads Ἀζαρίαν[4] τὸν τοῦ Ἰωδάε for the M. T.'s Zechariah, son of Jehoiada. Matthew's υἱοῦ Βαραχίου is a mistake not unparalleled in the extremely complex Jewish tradition-literature linked with the martyr name Zechariah.[5] In Is. 8 2 Uriah, the priest, and a Zechariah, son of Jeberechiah, are found in juxtaposition as עדים-μάρτυρες, but when the LXX here reads Zechariah, son of Barachiah, this is partly due to the fact that the term "martyr" has here caused the LXX to put together two biblical figures of martyrs, and partly that the

---

[1] On the variants in Matthew, see McNEILE, *Comm. Mt.*, ad loc.

[2] H. J. SCHOEPS, *Die jüdischen Prophetenmorde* (1943), p. 17–21, cf. IDEM, *Theologie und Geschichte des Judenchristentums* (1949), p. 266. The idea of the persecuted prophets occurs — except in the following 23 37 — also in Mt. 5 12 ≠ Lk. 6 23, cf. on John the Baptist as the Second Elijah (Mt. 17 12 ≠ Mk. 9 13 with the explicit reference καθὼς γέγραπται ἐπ' αὐτόν): "they handled him as they liked"; on Jesus in Nazareth, Mt. 13 57, and "it would never do for a prophet to perish except in Jerusalem", Lk. 13 33. — In *Justin*, Dial. 16 4, 73 6, 93 4, 95 2, 126 5 this view of the martyrdom of the prophets is self-evident also to the opponent, the Jew Trypho.

[3] Luke's introductory formula ἡ Σοφία τοῦ θεοῦ εἶπεν could refer to an apocryphal scripture as *e.g.* Jubilees 1 12: "And I shall send witnesses unto them, that I may witness against them, but they will not hear, and will slay the witness also, and they will persecute those who seek the law . . ." (transl. CHARLES), cf. BACON, *Studies in Matthew*, p. 476. If one compare Mt. 23 34 and Lk. 11 49, it is, however, striking that according to Matthew Jesus is the acting subject, ἰδοὺ ἐγὼ ἀποστέλλω. Thus "The Wisdom of God" in Luke might be another name for Jesus (Tatian: I, the Wisdom of God . . .). So HARRIS, *Testimonies* II, p. 98, J. H. A. HART, *The Expositor* vii, 1 (1906), p. 203 f. — Cf. 1 Cor. 1 24, see V. TAYLOR, *The Names of Jesus* (1953), p. 150—152.

[4] Ζαχαρίαν in LAGARDE's Lucianic text, supported by 15, 19, 53, 57, 72, 135, cf. above, p. 54, note 2.

[5] SH. A. BLANK, The Death of Zechariah in Rabbinic Literature, *Hebr. Union Coll. Ann.* 12/13 (1937/38), p. 327–346, cf. CH. C. TORREY, The Lives of the Prophets, *Journ. of Bibl. Lit.*, Monogr. Ser. 1 (1946), p. 31 and 47 and E. NESTLE, *Zeitschr. f. d. neutest. Wissensch.* 6 (1905), p. 198–200.

character of a martyr could be ascribed to Zechariah, son of Barachiah.[1]

From the point of view of citation, this passage yields very little. The quotation, which is inserted into a saying of Jesus, has been formed without conscious influence from either the M. T. or the LXX.[2]

Mt. 23 39 $\neq$ Lk. 13 35 is a quotation from Ps. 118 26, which even appears in exactly the same form in connection with the entry into Jerusalem (for the form and dependence of the quotation see Mt. 21 9, cf. Mk. 11 9, Lk. 19 38). In Lk. 13 35 the quotation alludes to the entry of Jesus and is included in the Account of the Journey; it links the words on Jerusalem with the answer to the Pharisees' exhortations, vv. 31–33, for which reason we find λέγω δὲ . . . in v. 35.[3] The parallel passage in Matthew has another context and follows after the entry, so that both the expression λέγω γὰρ . . . and ἀπ' ἄρτι (note the close agreement with the passage on the Last Supper, 26 29, but also with 26 64) call up thoughts of the Parousia.

Mt. 24 38f. $\neq$ Lk. 17 27: Gen. 7 7, cannot be regarded as a quotation, but the choice of words is in agreement with the LXX. Matthew and Luke are in substantial agreement in Mt. v. 38 and the parallel.

The Lucan text is of interest since in its entirety (vv. 22–37) it is a composite Genesis commentary. The example from Noah is followed by an example from Lot. They are coordinated in style by means of the homophony καὶ ἀπώλεσεν πάντας, vv. 27 and 29, and also by the description of this improvident life on the eve of the catastrophe, vv. 27 and 28. In Luke's exposition, the prohibition to

---

[1] This is the earliest example of the term "martyr" in the technical meaning of "bloodwitness", not mentioned by E. GÜNTHER, ΜΑΡΤΥΣ (1941), see p. 79–82. To H. STRATHMANN, Theol. Wörterb. z. N. T. IV, p. 486, μάρτυς in Is. 8 2 is an "eye-witness". Cf. K. STENDAHL, Martyr. Ordet och saken, Svensk Teologisk Kvartalskrift 27 (1951), p. 28–44.

[2] The Gospel of the Hebrews read Zechariah, the son of Jehoiada, see ZAHN, Einleitung II[1], p. (308 and) 314: "Korrektur eines auf mangelhafter Kunde des A. T.:s beruhenden Fehlers hat das Hebräerevangelium nachweislich nur zu Mt. 23 35 angebracht." The other inaccurate references (13 35, 27 9) were retained also in the Gospel of the Hebrews.

[3] So BℵDΘ, while pap. 45 ℵ omit δέ.

turn back (Gen. 19 17) is included, v. 31. Luke's text, more than either Mark's or Matthew's, thus has an element of parenetical *midrash*, and this development of Q material seems to be the work of Luke, though he might be drawing on other traditions unknown to us.[1] The allusion in v. 31 is not intended as a quotation but as a description μὴ ἐπιστρεψάτω εἰς τὰ ὀπίσω for the M. T.'s אל תביט אחריך and the LXX's μὴ περιβλέψῃς εἰς τὰ ὀπίσω. The expression εἰς τὰ ὀπίσω possibly indicates influence from the LXX. In Mt. 24 18 and Mk. 13 16 there is no express reference to Lot's wife, cf. Lk. 17 32. Matthew only has ὀπίσω and likewise Mk. אD *pc.*, while the rest of the witnesses in Mark agree with Luke and the LXX.

In Luke there is another allusive reference to the Lot story, Gen. 19 24: Luk. 17 29, ἔβρεξεν πῦρ καὶ θεῖον ἀπ' οὐρανοῦ, with inversion of the order of the two nouns in relation to the M. T., the Targum and the LXX, and with a different preposition from that in the LXX (ἐκ).[2] These allusions are thus both free and dependent upon the LXX, and we have reason to look upon the passage both in its Matthaean and Lucan form as an apocalyptic composition formed in a LXX milieu, for none of the minor differences point to primary contact with the Semitic text.

We have only two quotations in the strict sense of the word in the material peculiar to Luke, namely in 4 18f. and 22 37. They both show slight traces of the M. T., in contrast with the general LXX character of the gospel.

Lk. 22 37 is a citation from Is. 53 12. It is quoted as coming from Jesus and its introductory formula refers to the fulfilment, with the term τελεσθῆναι: καὶ μετὰ ἀνόμων ἐλογίσθη — LXX: καὶ ἐν τοῖς ἀνόμοις ἐλογίσθη — M. T.: ואת פשעים נמנה. We find here signs which indicate that Is. 53 had been the subject of early Christian translation and interpretation in connection with its significance for Christology. In certain cases this interpretation seems to be dependent on existing Greek texts, though whether the N. T. readings support the assumption of a LXX text other than the one we have, is hard to decide.[3]

---

[1] To F. HAUCK, *Comm. Lk.*, *ad loc.*, and BULTMANN, *Geschichte der synoptischen Tradition* (1931²), p. 123, vv. 28–30 might have been original in Q.

[2] MANSON, *op. cit.*, p. 320. The N. T. order of these nouns is found in Ezek. 38 22, 3 Macc. 2 5, in cod. א to Is. 30 33 and in DSH, col. x, 5.

[3] See below, p. 180 f.

Certain of these interpretations may just as well have won recognition on the authority of the apostle Peter.[1] Our quotation does not admit of such far-reaching constructions as we have it in the passion narrative, where there are other traces of retained Semitic wording, not wholly conformed to the LXX.[2]

Lk. 4₁₈₋₁₉: Is. 61₁₋₂ and 58₆.

Lk.	Is. 61₁₋₂ LXX[B]
πνεῦμα κυρίου ἐπ' ἐμέ, οὗ εἵνεκεν ἔχρισέν με εὐαγγελίσασθαι πτωχοῖς, ἀπέσταλκέν με κηρῦξαι αἰχμαλώτοις ἄφεσιν καὶ τυφλοῖς ἀνάβλεψιν, ἀποστεῖλαι τεθραυσμένους ἐν ἀφέσει, κηρῦξαι ἐνιαυτὸν κυρίου δεκτόν.	πνεῦμα κυρίου ἐπ' ἐμέ, οὗ εἵνεκεν ἔχρισέν με εὐαγγελίσασθαι πτωχοῖς, ἀπέσταλκέν με ἰάσασθαι τοὺς συντετριμμένους τὴν καρδίαν, κηρῦξαι αἰχμαλώτοις ἄφεσιν καὶ τυφλοῖς ἀνάβλεψιν, καλέσαι ἐνιαυτὸν κυρίου δεκτὸν καὶ ἡμέραν ἀνταποδόσεως...
ἀπέσταλκέν με] add. (ex Is. 61₁, cf. Lk. 4₂₃) ἰάσασθαι τοὺς συντετριμμένους τὴν καρδίαν ℵΘ pm.	πτωχοῖς] ταπεινοῖς ℵ*. τὴν καρδίαν] B Lucian; rell. τῇ καρδίᾳ.

Is. 61₁₋₂ M.T.

רוח אדני יהוה עלי יען משח יהוה אתי לבשר ענוים שלחני לחבש לנשברי לב לקרא לשבוים דרור ולאסורים פקח קוח: לקרא שנת-רצון ליהוה ויום נקם לאלהינו לנחם כל אבלים

Is. 58₆ LXX(in similar context)	M.T.
ἀπόστελλε τεθραυσμένους ἐν ἀφέσει ...	ושלח רצוצים חפשים

---

[1] H. W. WOLFF, *Jesaja 53 im Urchristentum* (1942), neither poses nor answers this question. He registers nevertheless the deviations from the LXX from case to case *e.g.* p. 50 (Lk. 22₃₇) and p. 64 (Mt. 8₁₇) and concludes, p. 70: "Ganz allmählich beginnt dann die Gemeinde in Palästina, sich selbst mit dem hebräischen Text von Jes. 53 zu befassen. Ein allererstes Anzeichen dafür ist Matthäus 8₁₇." Here the background of Wolff's statement is his view that the early and genuine — his account is rich in value statements — use of Is. 53 was not an "atomistic" one where the text was adduced as separate quotations: "Er (Jesus) benutzt nicht die Schrift sondern er lebt die Schrift", p. 62 f., cf. p. 132 f. — O. CULLMANN argues for a more definite Christian form of Is. 53 when he makes Peter the first to interpret the death of Jesus in the categories of Is. 53, *Petrus. Jünger, Apostel, Märtyrer* (1952), p. 69–72. The quotations from Is. 53 in 1 Peter do not offer a pure LXX text. — On Mt. 8₁₇, see below, p. 106 f.

[2] Cf. below, p. 140.

Luke's marked dependence upon the LXX is especially apparent
if one compares Luke's text with the later Greek versions.[1] This
relates particularly to the N. T. and LXX reading τυφλοῖς ἀνάβλεψιν,
mentioned above with reference to Mt. 11₅, an interpretation which
may be connected with the Targum's reference to the light (". . . to
prisoners: Come forth to light!"). The only agreement with the M. T.
against the LXX might be that Luke reproduces the M. T.'s קרא
the second time, too, by κηρῦξαι when, as usual, the LXX prefers a
change to the synonymous καλέσαι. However, Luke's rendering is
natural since the two verbs are separated by a sentence from the
related prophecy in Is. 58₆.[2] Such an interweaving is most natural
from the Greek text since both prophecies in the LXX have the
term ἄφεσις in common, while they have different Hebrew corresponding terms in the M. T. So the quotation is the work of Luke
and his freedom in matters of citation permits us to set to his own
account even the κηρῦξαι, without conscious influence from the Hebrew text.

The combination of prophecies of this kind was a feature of the
haftaroth, but it is contrary to rabbinic tradition to go backwards
in a scroll.[3] The Greek and LXX character of the quotation therefore renders it more probable that we should take the text of Luke
as a literary composition of his own. This is the more likely since
the quotation acts as a vignette to Luke's account of the words and
deeds of Jesus.[4]

---

[1] See *Hexapla*, ed. FIELD, *ad loc.*, or *Isaias*, ed. ZIEGLER, *ad loc.*

[2] Barn. 14₈ has the quotation from Is. 61 without any insertion or influence
from the text of Luke.

[3] *bMegillah* 24a (*gemara*). The *mishnah* gives regulations on skipping in the
prophets (on the *haftaroth*, cf. p. 50 and 217) but without considering the question of direction. In the *gemara* the prohibition of "skipping" backwards on
the one hand is introduced in a special case (concerning a scroll which contains
the minor prophets), but on the other hand it seems to state a self-evident fact.

[4] Cf. T. W. MANSON, *The Teaching of Jesus* (1935²), p. 44.

3. The formula quotations

Matthew's formula quotations are of quite another type than those so far treated. The differences between the LXX[B], other LXX manuscripts and readings preserved in the younger Greek versions certainly contribute at times to the explanation of their form, but are by no means sufficient when it comes to dealing with the considerable differences which are found here. At times the closeness of the formula quotations to the M. T. is striking, but often they show deviations from all Greek, Hebrew and Aramaic types of text known to us, while at the same time they intermingle influences from these. HAWKINS counted ten such formula quotations and under a special heading he adds 2 6.[1] We shall examine these eleven citations which are all without synoptic parallels.[2]

Mt. 1 23: Is. 7 14.

Mt.	LXX[B]	M.T.
ἰδοὺ ἡ παρθένος ἐν γαστρὶ ἕξει καὶ τέξεται υἱόν, καὶ καλέσουσιν τὸ ὄνομα αὐτοῦ Ἐμμανουήλ.	ἰδοὺ ἡ παρθένος ἐν γαστρὶ λήμψεται καὶ τέξεται υἱόν, καὶ καλέσεις τὸ ὄνομα αὐτοῦ Ἐμμανουήλ.	הנה העלמה הרה וילדת בן וקראת שמו עמנו אל

καλ.] –σεις D pc.

λήμψ.] ἕξει אAQ.
καλ.] –σει א; –σετε Q*; –σ(ουσι)ν Γ.

Aquila, Symmachus: ἰδοὺ ἡ νεᾶνις (so also Theodotion) ἐν γαστρὶ (om. Symm.) συλλαμβάνει καὶ τίκτει υἱόν, καὶ καλέσεις ὄνομα αὐτοῦ Ἐμμανουήλ.

---

[1] As it stands in the gospel, it is a saying of the scribes. Even ZAHN, *Einleitung* II¹, p. 315, emphasizes its character of Matthaean formula quotation. Naturally it lacks the typical reference to fulfilment found in the other formula quotations in Matthew, since the introductory words are spoken by the scribes.

[2] Mt. 2 15 has a parallel in Jn. 12 15. On formula quotations in John, see below, p. 163. — The quotation from Is. 40 3 common to the Synoptics was introduced by a formula akin to that peculiar to Matthew, see above, p. 47, cf. Lk. 22 37, above, p. 94.

Matthew and the LXX agree in the translation παρθένος for עלמה, a translation which the early church fought a bitter struggle to defend against Jewish scholars, although they had taken over the reading from the synagogue.[1] On the other hand the variant ἕξει (LXX^A, Mt.)[2] — λήμψεται (LXX^B) does not seem to have played a larger part and neither can it be said to be an indication of Matthew's greater proximity to the M. T., even if ἐν γαστρὶ λαμβάνεσθαι is the LXX's usual translation of הרה.

Of greater significance is the apparently lesser difference καλέσουσιν in Matthew, as against the LXX's and the M. T.'s second person singular.[3] This is an intentional change, depending upon the fact that Immanuel was not the name which the parents gave their child. Instead it is interpreted as one of the messianic titles symbolically ascribed to Jesus: "they (i.e. one) will call him Immanuel". In Lk. 1 31, the language is coloured by Is. 7 14, but the explicit reference to the virgin is not given and Luke merges the O. T. command to name the child Immanuel with the order in the N. T. to name Him Jesus. In Matthew the two are kept distinct, 1 23 and 1 21.[4]

---

[1] On *Justin*'s apology for the LXX and Christian reading, see below, p. 182. — ZAHN, *Einleitung* II¹, p. 314 f., maintains Matthew's independence of the LXX: Out of the context and in accordance with Jewish tradition the translator rendered his Greek wording, cf. IDEM, *Comm. Mt., ad loc.* — The old dispute on the meaning of עלמה has been revived lately in the U.S.A. when the *Revised Standard Version* (1952) translated it "young woman", see e.g. C. H. GORDON, *Journ. of Bible and Rel.* 21 (1953), p. 106, and E. R. LACHEMAN, *ibm.* 22 (1954), p. 43.

[2] ZIEGLER, ed. *Isaias*, who values cod. A rather highly in Isaiah, gives its reading as that of the LXX. — *Irenaeus* was only interested in the disputed alternatives παρθένος — νεᾶνις and thus reports Aquila and Theodotion to have read ἕξει as the N. T., *Eusebius*, Hist. eccl. v, 8 10.

[3] *Justin*, Dial. 43 5 καλέσεται, 66 2 καλέσουσι, both times nevertheless in longer context from Isaiah. — A. BAUMSTARK, *Zeitschr. d. Deutsch. Morgenl. Gesellsch.* 89 (1935), p. 116, assumes two different Targum renderings, both originating from T. M.'s קרא־ת: a) יתקרא = O. T. Peshitta, syr^{cur pesh} ܢܠܩܐ and O. T. Vulgate *vocabitur*; b) יקראי = Christian Palestinian Lectionary ܢܩܒܐ, "Ur-Matthäus" and Greek Matthew. The reading of the lectionary is more probably influenced from the N. T. than *vice versa*. To be sure, Baumstark has good reasons for his reluctant attitude to the N. T.'s influence on this and other texts, but in our case it is *petitio principii* to rule out that explanation, particularly since the Targum Jonathan does not support any of the readings Baumstark presumes, cf. below, to Mt. 2 6.

[4] G. D. KILPATRICK, *The Origins of the Gospel according to St. Matthew*, p. 57

Thus Mt. 1 23 probably shows influence from the LXX, though not against the Hebrew text. Furthermore, it follows the Jewish-Greek tradition. At the same time it is adapted to the fulfilment of the prophecy by Christ.

Mt. 2 6: Micah 5 1 (3) (2 Sam. 5 2).

Mt.	LXX[B]	M.T.
καὶ σὺ Βηθλέεμ, γῆ ᾽Ιού- δα, οὐδαμῶς ἐλαχίστη εἶ ἐν τοῖς ἡγεμόσιν ᾽Ιούδα· ἐκ σοῦ γὰρ ἐξελεύσεται ἡγούμενος, ὅστις ποιμα- νεῖ τὸν λαόν μου τὸν ᾽Ισ- ραήλ.	καὶ σὺ Βηθλέεμ οἶκος ᾽Εφράθα, ὀλιγοστὸς εἶ τοῦ εἶναι ἐν χιλιάσιν ᾽Ιού- δα· ἐξ οὗ μοι ἐξελεύσεται τοῦ εἶναι εἰς ἄρχοντα τοῦ ᾽Ισραήλ. . . .[3] καὶ στήσε- ται καὶ ὄψεται καὶ ποι- μανεῖ τὸ ποίμνιον αὐτοῦ ἐν ἰσχύϊ κύριος . . .	ואתה בית־לחם אפרתה צעיר להיות באלפי יהודה ממך לי יצא להיות מושל בישראל: ועמד ורעה בעז יהוה
γῆ ᾽Ιούδα] τῆς ᾽Ιουδαίας D it.		
ἐκ σοῦ] ἐξ οὗ ℵCD.	ἐξ οὗ] ἐκ σοῦ B[bc]AQ. — ἐξελεύσ.] add. ἡγούμενος A. — τοῦ ᾽Ισρ.] ἐν τῷ ᾽Ισρ. AQ.	

2 Sam. 5 2 LXX	M.T.
σὺ ποιμανεῖς τὸν λαόν μου τὸν ᾽Ισ- ραήλ.	אתה תרעה את עמי את ישראל

Matthew differs entirely from both the M.T. and the LXX, with the latter of which Matthew has only six words in common. It is a composite quotation or rather a citation from Micah supported by a similar expression from 2 Sam. 5 2, a text connected with Davidic claims. The reference to the prince's function as a shepherd, which is expressed in this composite verse, is, however, found in Micah 5 3, though there expressed in other words. It agrees with rabbinic tradition that the word is put into the mouths of the scribes, for the Micah text belonged to Jewish sayings of messianic interpretation.[1] This is even apparent from a משיחא inserted into the Targum.

γῆ ᾽Ιούδα may be an explanatory geographic interpretation of the

---

and 93, presumes that the introductory formula in 1 22 originally belonged to 1 21, a quotation from Ps. 130 8, which got its form in Semitic milieu, *ibm.* p. 53. His argument is less credible if one considers that the Hebrew equivalent of Matthew's σώσει is not ישע but פדה (LXX: λυτρώσεται).

[1] Cf. Jn. 7 42.

type we know from the LXX.[1] On the other hand the reading
ἡγεμόσιν for the LXX's χιλιάσιν is a remarkable intentional interpretation of the M. T.'s אַלְפֵי which has been vocalized אַלֻּפֵי.[2] In addition the M. T.'s saying about the insignificance of Bethlehem, which
is modified to a largely rhetorical question in the LXX, is pressed
a stage further in the direction of messianic interpretation in Matthew,
so that it constitutes a statement emphatically negatived by οὐδαμῶς
— γάρ, which stresses the significance of Bethlehem.[3]

Matthew's ἡγούμενος (as in LXX[A], due to Christian influence)[4],
is created from the Christian reading ἡγεμόσιν and is necessary as
a link with the following relative clause taken from 2 Samuel. At
the same time the Matthaean text renders the meaning of Micah 5₃.
The variant ἐκ σοῦ — ἐξ οὗ (scribal errors were inevitable in such
words), both in the LXX and in Matthew, hardly gives a basis for
determining the relation to the Hebrew text.

In general the M. T. and the LXX agree as against Matthew,
whose interpretation clearly has a specific object, namely to point
out the fulfilment in Christ; neither does it agree entirely with the
messianic interpretation of the Targum or with the O. T. Peshitta,
which here, as often, stands close to the Targum. In addition it is

---

[1] Cf. I. L. SEELIGMANN, *The Septuagint Version of Isaiah*, p. 80 f.

[2] See E. HÜHN, *Die alttest. Citate*, p. 2 and 279. — To SWETE, *Introduction to
the Old Testament in Greek*, p. 394, this and the quotation in Mt. 27₉f. are the
typical examples of "substitution of a gloss for the precise words which the writer
professes to quote". — BAUMSTARK, *op. cit.* p. 115 (cf. above, p. 98, note 3),
here also assumes a Targum tradition on two scores, starting from the reading
אַלֻּפֵי: a) מדברני = Matthew's τοῖς ἡγεμόσιν; b) מלב = syr[sin pesh]. These readings
however lack the support both of Targum Jonathan and the O. T. Peshitta, where
the verse is rendered quite differently with the reading "the thousands of Judah('s
cities)".

[3] TORREY's translation of the M. T., *Documents*, p. 49f., "And art thou, Bethlehem Ephrathah, too small to be among the clans of Judah?", would require
צעיר מחיות and the interrogative form cannot be taken for granted. J. PEDER-
SEN's translation is to be preferred: And thou ... tiny as thou art among the
houses of Judah ..., *Israel* III/IV (1934), p. 73, cf. Eng. ed. (1940), p. 92. It
is rather in the LXX that the sentence virtually is a rhetorical question. The negative assertion in Matthew seems to be a free rendering in order to emphasize
the messianic interpretation, but it could be that Matthew read intentionally
לא היית לחיות as לֹא הִיִית.

[4] ZIEGLER, ed. *Duodecim prophetae*, p. 43: one of the two cases of influence
from the N. T. in cod. A to the Minor Prophets. The other example is Hos. 10₈
(Lk. 23₃₀), cf. below, p. 173.

not only the tendentious adaptation which causes the great divergence from the LXX, since its text might be able to serve Matthew's purpose, though the adaptation renders the citation more appropriate. It may seem strange that Matthew could put such a reading into the mouths of the scribes, but the insight we have received into Jewish interpretation of the Scriptures through the scrolls of the Qumran Sect will make this less offensive.[1]

Mt. 2₁₅: Hos. 11₁.

Mt.	LXX	M.T.
ἐξ Αἰγύπτου ἐκάλεσα τὸν υἱόν μου.	ἐξ Αἰγύπτου μετεκάλεσα τὰ τέκνα αὐτοῦ.	ממצרים קראתי לבני

The LXX codex 86 gives the whole material of the Hexapla at this verse and points out that Mt. and Aquila both agree with the M.T. Theodotion is more close to the LXX and Symmachus departs from both. Aquila reads καὶ ἀπὸ Αἰγύπτου ἐκάλεσα τὸν υἱόν μου.

Matthew, as distinct from the LXX, renders an exact translation of the M.T., as does Aquila. Like the LXX, the Targum has the plural "sons" together with another construction: "Out of Egypt I have called them sons", a construction found also in Theodotion. This, together with Mt. 2₂₃, was JEROME's pattern of Matthew's use of the M.T. instead of the LXX in the Hebrew Gospel.[2] There are no means for deciding whether Matthew knew a Greek rendering of the prophecy like that of Aquila or if he formed the quotation directly out of the Hebrew. Similar cases in other Matthaean quotations make the former alternative plausible. The Matthaean form of the prophecy is necessary for its function as a messianic proof-text in the context of the gospel.

---

[1] In his *Comm. in Mich.* (MPL xxv, col. 1197) JEROME explained the deviation from all known O. T. text: Matthew wanted to show how carelessly the scribes handled the holy Scriptures. In *epistula* lvii (MPL xxii, col. 574 f.), however, he gives his more usual explanation that the evangelists and apostles followed the sense, not the wordings of Scriptures. — Justin and Irenaeus took the Matthew text as a true rendering of Micah. *Justin*, Dial. 78, 1 Apol. 34, follows Matthew and *Irenaeus*, Epideixis 63, seems to have had the D text to Matthew. He retains the rhetorical question of the LXX so far as can be judged from J. A. ROBINSON's translation (*St Irenaeus, The Demonstration of the Apostolic Preaching*, 1920).

[2] See above, p. 40.

Mt. 2₁₈: Jer. 31₁₅.

Mt.

φωνὴ ἐν Ῥαμὰ ἠκούσθη, κλαυθμὸς
καὶ ὀδυρμὸς πολύς· Ῥαχὴλ κλαίουσα
τὰ τέκνα αὐτῆς, καὶ οὐκ ἤθελεν
παρακληθῆναι, ὅτι οὐκ εἰσίν.

ἠκούσθη] add. θρῆνος καὶ C𝔑D *pl.*
syr^sin cur.

Jer. 31₁₅ M.T.

קוֹל בְּרָמָה נִשְׁמָע נְהִי בְּכִי תַמְרוּרִים
רָחֵל מְבַכָּה עַל בָּנֶיהָ מֵאֲנָה לְהִנָּחֵם עַל
בָּנֶיהָ כִּי אֵינֶנּוּ

LXX^B (Jer. 38₁₅)

φωνὴ ἐν Ῥαμὰ ἠκούσθη, θρήνου
καὶ κλαυθμοῦ καὶ ὀδυρμοῦ· Ῥαχὴλ
ἀποκλαιομένη οὐκ ἤθελεν παύσα-
σθαι ἐπὶ τοῖς υἱοῖς αὐτῆς, ὅτι οὐκ
εἰσίν.

LXX^A

φ. ἐν τῇ ὑψηλῇ ἠκ., θ. κ. κ. κ. ὁ.· Ῥ.
ἀποκλαιομένης ἐπὶ τῶν υἱῶν αὐτῆς
καὶ οὐκ ἤθελεν παρακληθῆναι, ὅτι
οὐκ εἰσίν.

ἐν τῇ ὑψηλῇ] so also ℵ*Aq. Targ.
θ. κ. κ. κ. ὁ.] θ-ος κ. κ-ὸς κ. ὁ-ός Q
ἀποκλαι.] so also ℵQ.
ἐπὶ τ. υ. α. κ.] so also Q.

Matthew comes the nearest to giving an abbreviated translation
of the M.T., possibly with some influence from the LXX.[1] The Targum is quite different with reference to the exile and the dispersion.
Justin, Dial. 78₈ follows Matthew word for word, but it seems rash
to take this as an argument in favour of the existence of this text
form as an independent testimony or a pre-Matthaean Greek O.T.
text, since in Justin it stands in a section which reproduces the
contents of Mt. 2 in its entirety.[2]

Matthew's use of τέκνα as against υἱοί occurring in a united LXX

---

[1] If so, mostly in the form of LXX^A, whose text is closer to the M.T. as is
Aquila. Both in Aquila and in the variants of the LXX we find traces of Palestinian biblical tradition (O.T. Peshitta = LXX^A) which has left no imprints in
Matthew. Even υἱοί of LXX^A as against τέκνα of Matthew speaks against the N.T.
influence on the LXX text. There is however no influence in the opposite direction, since LXX^A lacks the retained Rama, which is less satisfactory to Matthew's use of the text. The coincidences of Matthew and LXX^A thus are due to
the hexaplaric character of LXX^A and Matthew's dependence on the Hebrew text.
— ALLEN, *Comm. Mt.*, p. lxii, claims the Matthaean text to be mainly LXX with
a slight influence from the Hebrew text (τὰ τέκνα αὐτῆς).

[2] J. A. FINDLAY, *Amicitiae Corolla*, p. 61, denies it for an alleged Book of
Testimonies, and thinks that Justin quoted Matthew directly. It is not found in
the testimonies of Cyprian.

tradition, is similar to what we found in Mt. 22₂₄ and parallels.[1] Matthew gives his own rendering of the expressions of lament and consolation. In this and other respects, the text is close to what we find in the O. T. Peshitta, and could thus depend on the Targums, but the Syriac reading may also be due to influence from the N. T. On the whole, Matthew seems to give his own translation, though there are no signs of intentional changes.

Mt. 2₂₃: Is. 11₁ (Judges 13₅).

Mt.	LXX	M.T.
(ὅπως πληρωθῇ τὸ ῥηθὲν διὰ τῶν προφητῶν)	καὶ ἐξελεύσεται ῥάβδος ἐκ τῆς ῥίζης Ἰεσσαί, καὶ ἄνθος ἐκ τῆς ῥίζης ἀναβήσεται.	ויצא חטר מגזע ישי ונצר משרשיו יפרה
ὅτι Ναζωραῖος κληθήσεται.		

	O. T. Peshitta	Targum Jonathan
syr^sin cur pesh : ﺍﺯﻳﻞ ﻳﺜﻘﺮﺍ	ﻭﻧﻔﻮﻕ ﺷﺒﻮﻗﺎ ﻣﻦ ﺟﺰﻋﻪ	ויפוק מלכא מבנוהי דישי ומשיחא מבני בנוהי יתרבי
	ﻭﻧﻮﺭﺍ ﻣﻦ ﻋﻘﺮﻳﻪ ﻧﻔﺮﻉ	

Judges 13₅ LXX^B	M.T.
ὅτι ναζὶρ θεοῦ ἔσται τὸ παιδάριον ἀπὸ τῆς κοιλίας.	כי נזיר אלהים יהיה הנער מן הבטן

ναζὶρ] ἡγιασμένον ναζιραῖον A; ναζιραῖον Lucian.

The introductory formula is the usual one for formula quotations, but with the more vague reference διὰ τῶν προφητῶν without mention of the name, together with the prefatory word ὅτι. The discussion on the aim of this introductory formula is extremely comprehensive.[2] The most common explanation appears to be unquestionably the right one: the reference concerns the term נצר in Is. 11; this assumes a Semitic linguistic background. The Greek variant to this citation seems to be the reference to Jesus as τὸ ἄνθος, borne out, for example, in Justin, and in the later testimony literature[3], cf. ἐγώ εἰμι ἡ ῥίζα καὶ τὸ γένος Δαυίδ, Rev. 22₁₆. It is, however, remark-

---

[1] See above, p. 70.

[2] See below, p. 198 f.

[3] *Justin*, Dial. 126, *Cyprianus*, Testimonia ii, 11. — See V. BURCH in *R. Harris*, *Testimonies* II, p. 62 f. and FINDLAY, *op. cit.*, p. 61 f.

able that this translation does not exist in the Matthew text, which
ought to have made of the quotation a testimony of the same type
as Mt. 1 23 with its translation of Immanuel. The difficulty with the
comparison of נצר with ναζωραῖος — since the Hebrew ṣade is usually
represented by the Greek *sigma*[1] — does not need to be a conclusive
argument in the bilingual milieu which we must assume for Matthew, nor in the light of Jewish interpretation of the Scriptures, as
we shall find it in the Sect of Qumran. In that connection we shall
have to deliberate in greater detail on our quotation.[2]

Mt. 4 15–16: Is. 8 23–9 1.

Mt.	LXX^B (9 1–2)	M.T.

γῆ Ζαβουλὼν καὶ γῆ Νε-
φθαλίμ, ὁδὸν θαλάσσης,
πέραν τοῦ Ἰορδάνου, Γα-
λιλαία τῶν ἐθνῶν, ὁ λαὸς
ὁ καθήμενος ἐν σκοτίᾳ
φῶς εἶδεν μέγα, καὶ τοῖς
καθημένοις ἐν χώρᾳ καὶ
σκιᾷ θανάτου, φῶς ἀν-
έτειλεν αὐτοῖς.

τοῦτο πρῶτον πίε, ταχὺ
ποίει, χώρα Ζαβουλών, ἡ
γῆ Νεφθαλίμ, καὶ οἱ λοι-
ποὶ οἱ τὴν παραλίαν καὶ
πέραν τοῦ Ἰορδάνου, Γα-
λιλαία τῶν ἐθνῶν· ὁ λαὸς
ὁ πορευόμενος ἐν σκότει
ἴδετε φῶς μέγα, οἱ κατοι-
κοῦντες ἐν χώρᾳ σκιᾷ
θανάτου, φῶς λάμψει ἐφ'
ὑμᾶς.

כעת הראשון הקל
ארצה זבלון וארצה
נפתלי והאחרון
הכביד דרך הים עבר
הירדן גליל הגוים:
העם ההלכים בחשך
ראו אור גדול ישבי
בארץ צלמות אור
נגה עליהם

σκοτίᾳ] B (D); σκότει
𝕭ℜΘ pl.
τοῖς καθ.] οἱ καθήμενοι
D it syr sa.

Νεφθ.] add. ὁδὸν θαλάσσης ℵ^{ca}AQ.
παραλίαν] add. κατοικοῦντες ℵ^{ca}AQ.
πορευόμενος] καθήμενος A.

Matthew clearly departs from both the M. T. and the LXX, though
he shows dependence on both. To a certain extent Matthew translates
independently; he takes the quotation out of its context, and uses
γῆ twice where the LXX has χώρα and γῆ. As in Lk. 4 18, this may
be understood as a N. T. preference of Semitic monotony as against
the LXX's fondness for synonyms. The term γῆ in its narrower
geographical sense is peculiar to Matthew (cf. 2 6, 2 20f., 10 15, 11 24).
Instead of using the verbs in the future, as the LXX does, Matthew

---

[1] Swete, *Introduction to the Old Testament in Greek*, p. 67. Gesenius-Buhl,
Wörterbuch[17], sub צ.

[2] See below, p. 198 f.

uses the past tense, thereby stressing the fulfilment of the prophecy, clearly an intentional change.

The reading Γαλιλαία τῶν ἐθνῶν shows, however, that Matthew knew the interpretation given in the LXX against those of Aquila and Symmachus. Matthew's reading ὁ καθήμενος, which is opposed to both the M. T. and the LXX (cod. A may be irrelevant in this case)[1] certainly intends to stress again the local, geographical intention of his interpretation. It was to the people actually settled there in such a position that the light of the Messiah came. As an alternative explanation the preference for monotony might even be at work here. The phrase occurs elsewhere in the O. T., as in Ps. 107 10, alluded to in Lk. 1 79.

Matthew's ὁδὸν θαλάσσης is found in the LXX[A] and also in Aquila and Theodotion.[2] This raises the problem of a "pre-Theodotion" text, and it gives good reason to trust codex. A on this point, as preserving a Palestinian reading of the Greek O. T., known to Matthew.[3] His ἀνέτειλεν could be a free rendering of the M. T. It is, however,

---

[1] ZIEGLER, ed. Isaias, ad loc., see below, p. 173.

[2] The reading Γαλιλαία τῶν ἐθνῶν is common to the LXX and Matthew as against (the M. T.) Aquila and Symmachus, while the reading ὁδὸν θαλάσσης is common to Matthew, the LXX[A], Aquila and Theodotion. Even if we presumed that the Greek O. T. of Matthew could be restored by putting together Palestinian LXX readings scattered in different LXX MSS and in the later versions, a case like that in our quotation makes it more natural to consider the Matthaean text to emanate from the Hebrew but under influence of different Greek traditional translations. — Both in favour of and against such a view ALLEN's remark can be repeated (Comm. Mt., ad loc.): "Matthew obviously depends carelessly and uncritically on a Greek translation since the accusative ὁδόν is inappropriate." But ὁδόν followed by a genitive is the literal translation of Hebrew דרך = versus, BLASS-DEBRUNNER, Grammatik[7], § 161: 1; so also FINDLAY, op. cit., p. 62. — The dependence on a translation is obvious but the scholarly treatment of different traditions is anything but careless.

[3] See below, p. 173. To SH. JOHNSON, Harv. Theol. Rev. 36 (1943), p. 138 ff., this is the typical example of "Ur-Theodotion". He concludes: ". . . while in the formula citations Matthew is not directly dependent on the LXX and cannot be dependent on the Theodotion, he often follows an exegetical or translational tradition akin sometimes to the one and sometimes to the other. This would be Montgomery's Hellenistic oral Targum" (on Montgomery's Targum, see below, p. 178). — It is a misleading statement if it means that the text now in Matthew was that available to the evangelist. But giving his own Christian interpretation he used this and other Greek traditions where they seemed useful to him.

the interpretation also given in the O. T. Peshitta, which might preserve the text of a Targum lost to us.[1]

Thus when working with the Hebrew text, Matthew depends on different Greek interpretations, but also gives his own interpretation from the point of view of the fulfilment by Jesus. This renders it impossible to presuppose that he quoted one consistent Greek — or Semitic — text.

Mt. 8 17: Is. 53 4.[2]

Mt.	LXX	M. T.
αὐτὸς τὰς ἀσθενείας ἡμῶν ἔλαβεν καὶ τὰς νόσους ἐβάστασεν.	οὗτος τὰς ἁμαρτίας ἡμῶν φέρει καὶ περὶ ἡμῶν ὀδυνᾶται.	אכן חלינו הוא נשא ומכאבינו סבלם׃

Aquila (cod. 86) or Symmachus	Targum Jonathan
ὄντως αὐτὸς τὰς νόσους ἡμῶν ἀνέλαβεν καὶ τοὺς πολέμους (Symm.: πόνους) ἡμῶν ὑπέμεινεν.	בכין על חובנא הוא יבעי ועויתנא בדיליה ישתבקן ואנהנא חשיבין כתישין מחן מן קדם יהוה ומענן

(βαστάζειν occurs in Aq. Is. 53 11).

Here we have the exact text of the M. T. where the LXX and the Targum give a more spiritualized interpretation.[3] The text of the LXX occurs in 1 Clem. 16 4. Matthew's rendering has influenced Ignatius, To Polycarp 1 3 (πάντων τὰς νόσους βάσταζε). The text of Matthew has been taken as evidence of an earlier stage of the LXX text of Is. 53 4, but as its wording has no parallel in the other Greek

---

[1] O. T. Peshitta ܕܢܚ, "to rise", sometimes, however, = LXX λάμπειν, PAYNE SMITH, *Thesaurus Syriacus* (1879), s. v. Thus the O. T. Peshitta might be uninfluenced by the N. T. and have retained a Targumic interpretation. In Targum Jonathan (אזדהר) the interpretation concerns the exodus and the exile.

[2] This and the following formula quotations (to some extent also that in Mt. 4 15 f.) are woven into a synoptic context and thus akin to those of our fourth group (= Hawkins's class v.), cf. below, p. 128.

[3] The same spiritual interpretation of the healing is found in Mark's ἀφεθῇ αὐτοῖς (4 12) for M. T. לו רפא LXX (and Mt. 13 15) ἰάσομαι αὐτούς. The Marcan interpretation is that of the Targum Jonathan, cf. below, p. 131.

[4] H. S. NYBERG, *Svensk Exegetisk Årsbok* 7 (1942), p. 13, denies such a direct relation to the Hebrew text. His argument is that Jn. 12 38, Acts 8 33, Rom. 10 16 and 15 21 obviously are based on the LXX, and thus the text in Mt. 8 17 must be an older reading of the LXX. Nyberg does not raise the question whether the principles of quoting the O. T. are consistent throughout the N. T. — Now Ny-

versions — though its meaning comes close to that in Aquila, due
to the fact that both follow the M. T. — we should take it as
Matthew's own rendering of the Hebrew. The spiritualizing ἁμαρτία
for חלי is not found elsewhere in the LXX, but neither is Matthew's
ἀσθένεια. As the LXX coincides with the Targum there is still less
reason to consider the LXX reading a later correction. Matthew's
νόσους and βαστάζειν are likewise not found in the LXX style of
translating, but they correspond to Matthew's phraseology.[1] Even if
we have found some hints of a Christian pre-gospel rendering of Is. 53
in Greek[2], this formula quotation shows less affinity with the LXX
than the other Christian readings from this important chapter of
Isaiah and it is closely linked up with the context and the phraseology of the gospel.

Mt. 12 18–21 : Is. 42 1–4.

Mt.	LXX[B]	M. T.
ἰδοὺ ὁ παῖς μου ὃν ᾑρέ-	Ἰακὼβ ὁ παῖς μου, ἀντι-	הן עבדי אתמך בו
τισα, ὁ ἀγαπητός μου ὃν	λήμψομαι αὐτοῦ· Ἰσραὴλ	בחירי רצתה נפשי
εὐδόκησεν ἡ ψυχή μου·	ὁ ἐκλεκτός μου, προσεδέ-	נתתי רוחי עליו
θήσω τὸ πνεῦμά μου ἐπ᾽	ξατο αὐτὸν ἡ ψυχή μου·	משפט לגוים יוציא:
αὐτόν, καὶ κρίσιν τοῖς	ἔδωκα τὸ πνεῦμά μου ἐπ᾽	
ἔθνεσιν ἀπαγγελεῖ.	αὐτόν, κρίσιν τοῖς ἔθνε-	
	σιν ἐξοίσει.	

berg's intention is to warn against retranslation from the LXX as a means of
restoring the *hebraica veritas,* and that is in any case out of question here where
the LXX has a typical spiritualized reading, noticeable even in the Targum.
K. F. EULER, *Die Verkündigung vom leidenden Gottesknecht* (1934), p. 59–63, also
held the view that Mt. 8 17 rendered the original LXX text. SEELIGMANN, who
is in favour of a rich differentiation in the proto-LXX tradition (see below,
p. 175 f.) states however: "The text of Matthew shows such great divergence from
ours that it either hails from sources other than the LXX, or should be explained
as being an improvised version based on a vague reminiscence of the Hebrew text;
an alternative applying to many other N. T. texts", *The Septuagint Version of
Isaiah,* p. 29. It is hard to see that the reminiscence is vague in this case. The
text of Matthew is certainly based on the M. T. So also WOLFF, *Jesaja 53 im
Urchristentum,* p. 64.

[1] See A. SCHLATTER, *Der Evangelist Matthäus* (1929), p. 282 f., cf. WOLFF,
loc. cit.

[2] See above, p. 95.

¹⁹οὐκ ἐρίσει οὐδὲ κραυγά-
σει, οὐδὲ ἀκούσει τις ἐν
ταῖς πλατείαις τὴν φωνὴν
αὐτοῦ. ²⁰ κάλαμον συντε-
τριμμένον οὐ κατεάξει
καὶ λίνον τυφόμενον οὐ
σβέσει, ἕως ἂν ἐκβάλῃ
εἰς νῖκος τὴν κρίσιν. ²¹καὶ
τῷ ὀνόματι αὐτοῦ ἔθνη
ἐλπιοῦσιν.

2nd ὅν] Bℵ* pc.; εἰς ὃν
ℵΘ pm.; ἐν ᾧ C*D al.
v. 21] om. 33.

² οὐ κεκράξεται οὐδὲ ἀν-
ήσει, οὐδὲ ἀκουσθήσεται
ἔξω ἡ φωνὴ αὐτοῦ.
³ κάλαμον τεθλασμένον
οὐ συντρίψει καὶ λίνον
καπνιζόμενον οὐ σβέσει,
ἀλλὰ εἰς ἀλήθειαν ἐξοίσει
κρίσιν.
⁴ ἀναλάμψει καὶ οὐ θραυ-
σθήσεται, ἕως ἂν θῇ ἐπὶ
τῆς γῆς κρίσιν· καὶ ἐπὶ
τῷ ὀνόματι αὐτοῦ ἔθνη
ἐλπιοῦσιν.

'Ιακὼβ and 'Ισραὴλ] sub
obelo in the Hexapla.
κεκράξεται] κράξεται A.
τεθλ.] συντεθλ. A.

לא יצעק ולא ישא
ולא ישמיע בחוץ
קולו:
קנה רצוץ לא ישבור
ופשתה כהה לא
יכבנה לאמת יוציא
משפט:
לא יכהה ולא ירוץ
עד ישים בארץ
משפט ולתורתו איים
ייחלו

DSIa:
1st [משפט] משפטי
[ירצעק] יזעק
[ולתורתו] לתורתיו
[וייחלו] ינחילו

Is. 42 1–4. Targum Jonathan

הא עבדי אקרבניה בחירי דאתרעי ביה מימרי אתין רוח קודשי עלוהי דיני
לעממין יגלי: לא יצוח ולא יכלי ולא ירים בברא קליה: ענותניא דכקני רעיע
לא יתבר וחשיכיא דכבוצין עמי לא יטפי לקושטיה יפיק דינא: לא יהלי ולא
ילאי עד דיתקין בארעא דינא ולאורייתיה נגוון יכתרון:

Is. 42 1a Theodotion¹	Aquila	Symmachus
ἰδοὺ ὁ παῖς μου, ἀντι-λήψομαι αὐτοῦ, ὁ ἐκλεκ-τός μου, ὃν εὐδόκησεν ἡ ψυχή μου·	ἰδοὺ (ὁ) δοῦλός μου, ἀντιλήψομαι ἐν αὐτῷ·	ἰδοὺ ὁ δοῦλός μου, ἀνθ-έξομαι αὐτοῦ, ὁ ἐκλεκτός μου ὃν εὐδόκησεν ἡ ψυχή μου·

Is. 42 2 O.T. Peshitta   Mt. 12 19 syr^sin cur   N.T. Peshitta

ܠܐ ܢܬܚܪܐ ܘܠܐ ܢܒܓܢ ܘܠܐ ܢܫܡܥ   ܠܐ ܢܬܚܪܐ ܘܠܐ ܢܒܓܢ ܘܠܐ ܐܢܫ   ܠܐ ܢܬܚܪܐ ܘܠܐ ܢܒܓܢ ܘܠܐ ܐܢܫ
ܩܠܗ ܒܫܘܩܐ   ܢܫܡܥ ܩܠܗ   ܢܫܡܥ ܩܠܗ ܒܫܘܩܐ

[ܩܠܗ] add. ܒܫܘܩܐ cur.

---

¹ "So Q und die syrohexaplarische Übersetzung. Nach Theodoret von Cyrus
hat Theodotion jedoch auch Js. 42 1 עבד mit δοῦλος übersetzt. Für die Richtigkeit
der Lesart δοῦλος spricht, dass Theodotion עבד stets mit δοῦλος wiederzugeben
scheint und dass παῖς in der erhaltenen Bruchstücken bei ihm (ausser als vl. zu
Js. 42 1) überhaupt nicht vorkommt", JOACH. JEREMIAS, Theol. Wörterb. z. N. T.
V, p. 682.

This is the longest quotation in Matthew and it affords important features for our inquiry. It offers a text which is neither the M. T.'s nor the LXX's, but gives evidence of elements from both. At the same time it contains features which make it likely that it is dependent upon a number of other types of text. When the texts given above are compared we will find coincidence with the M. T., the LXX, Theodotion, the Targum, the O. T. Peshitta, and this upon points where such similarities cannot be explained as being due to some basic text, such as, for example, the M. T.[1] It is therefore natural to look upon it as a targumizing translation of Christian origin, but this targumizing process has not taken place independently, but in connection with traditions of interpretation known to the Matthew school. It gives an example of an ingenious Christian text interpretation. The startling coincidence with the O. T. Peshitta cannot be explained as an erroneous translation in the ordinary sense, but must be a conscious Christian interpretation, although with doubtful lexical and grammatical methods according to modern standards.

The citation therefore seems to be a typical example of Matthew's genuine quotation technique. If one wishes to call this a "testimony", of course one may do so, but scarcely in the sense of a text embodied in a collection of "proof-texts" created before Matthew; and this for two reasons. Partly the text is not supported in this form outside the First Gospel, and partly the Matthew school itself seems to be the most natural place for the moulding of such a text both from a geographical and a theological point of view.

V. 18 a and b. In the form the quotation has in Matthew, it contains two designations for Jesus which are of interest, παῖς μου (= θεοῦ) and ἀγαπητός. The first of these is also found in the LXX, but Matthew's freedom in general gives us reason to consider his choice of words as deliberate. It only occurs here in the Synoptics and further in Acts 3₁₃, ₂₆, 4₂₇, ₃₀, i.e. in material acknowledged as early.[2]

There is reason to suppose that the words spoken by the voice

---

[1] To KAHLE, *The Cairo Geniza*, p. 166 f., this is the typical example of a Greek Targum, quoted by Matthew. On this view, see below, p. 174.

[2] A recent statement on the significance of the term in these texts is found in CULLMANN, *Petrus. Jünger, Apostel, Märtyrer*, p. 70, cf. HARNACK, *Sitzungsber. Akad. Berlin*, Phil. Hist. Kl. 1926, p. 234, on παῖς θεοῦ as confined to the liturgical language of prayers.

from the heavens at the baptism and transfiguration of Jesus are considered as a quotation from Is. 42 1[1], in spite of the fact that the actual term παῖς is replaced by δοῦλος. In these passages the quotation has come into Matthew via Mark, and thus received its form adapted to non-Jewish readers.[2] The LXX's insertion of Jacob and Israel (cf. Is. 44 1, 2, 21 and 45 4) serves to stress the LXX's collective interpretation of Ebed Yahweh. Origen marks the inserted names with an obelus.[3] Matthew's object is the opposite and thus he finds support in the M. T. and even in the textual tradition of which the Targum and Theodotion give examples.

On the other hand ὁ ἀγαπητός lacks a counterpart in any Greek version of Is. 42. When Matthew gives his targumizing interpretation, he uses the verb αἱρετίζειν (which may have the meaning "to adopt")[4] and thereby ὁ ἐκλεκτός has been anticipated. It is replaced by the typically N. T. ὁ ἀγαπητός[5], perhaps due to the influence of Mk. 1 11 and 9 7.[6] Similarity to Theodotion's reading does not necessarily signify dependence, for both give the most natural translation of the M. T., but it is possible that Matthew knew the Greek text precisely in Theodotion's form. In the continuation of the translation we do

---

[1] JOACH. JEREMIAS, op. cit., p. 698 f., particularly p. 699, line 23 ff. "Wie so oft in alttestamentlichen Zitaten, z. B. der rabbinischen Literatur, ist der Fortgang des Zitates: θήσω τὸ πνεῦμά μου ἐπ' αὐτόν (Js. 42 1 nach Mt. 12 18c) mitgedacht, aber nicht mitzitiert", cf. above, p. 88. Only such an interpretation makes the "quotation" suitable as a proof-text about the Spirit descending upon the Messiah.

[2] See P. KATZ, Theol. Zeitschr. 5 (1949), p. 17, on the disappearance of παῖς already in the younger books of the LXX.

[3] The difference between the texts with and without obelus is used by SPERBER, Journ. of Bibl. Lit. 59 (1940), p. 280, cf. p. 198 f, for his thesis on the "Bible of the Apostles", see below, p. 176.

[4] BAUER, Wörterbuch z. N. T.[4] s. v.

[5] In the LXX it occurs 7 times for יָחִיד, 5 times for יָדִיד and once for הֹד, יַקִּיר and נָאֶה (twice without exact equivalent in Hebrew and 5 times in the Greek part of the LXX). Aquila Is. 41 8 about Abraham (אֹהֵב) as LXX Gen. 22 2 (יָחִיד). — On υἱὸς ἀγαπητός = "Only Son", see C. H. TURNER, Journ. of Theol. St. 27 (1926), p. 113–29.

[6] D. PLOOIJ, in Amicitiae Corolla, p. 248 f. takes the ἀγαπητός in these texts as a retained Targum reading. The Targum Ps. 2 7: "Beloved (חָבִיב) as a son to his father thou art to me," see MANSON, Bull. of J. Ryl. Libr. 34 (1951/52) p. 323 ff. — Plooij himself referred also to Mt. 12 18, op. cit., p. 249 f.

come across further points in common with the Palestinian LXX
text which Theodotion and the related versions exemplify.[1]

V. 18 c shows similarity with the Targum in its future form ϑήσω
— if we dare to determine the feeling of tense expressions in Aramaic
in such a way — and in its use of ἀπαγγέλλειν.[2] At the same time
Matthew's interpretation is the natural one for the evangelist's purpose and understanding of the prophecy.

V. 19. Even here we have reason to consider Matthew's text as
an interpretation rather than as a translation. Matthew's ἐρίσει[3] must
in some way be connected with the ܢܨܐ found in the O. T. Peshitta
(and in syr[sin cur]); its meaning (in aphel) is "to cry", but in Western
Aramaic and Hebrew it means "to contend".[4] E. NESTLE made this
an argument for an Aramaic Matthew where the root רוב meant
"to be loud", but by mistake was rendered "to strive".[5] The Eastern
Aramaic meaning "to be loud" is, however, umparalleled in Western
Aramaic.[6] Thus it is unlikely that the text in Matthew is due to a
mere mistranslation. That is only possible if the Greek Matthew is
considered a translation from the Syriac.[7] The change of order among
the three negative statements on the behaviour of the Messiah indicates that something else has happened to the quotation[7], and the

---

[1] If Theodotion had δοῦλος instead of παῖς (see above, p. 108, note 1) it would
be still more difficult to consider Matthew to quote one consistent Greek text.

[2] So ZAHN, Einleitung II¹, p. 316. — Whatever is the true meaning of the
Hebrew "tenses", the LXX consistently renders the imperfect by the future tense.

[3] Hapax legomenon in the N. T. In the LXX ἐρίσει is the rendering of חתנ־ה
and ריה.

[4] M. BLACK, An Aramaic Approach, p. 177, calls attention to this puzzling
fact, cf. IDEM, Journ. of the Manchester Egyptian and Oriental Society 23 (1942),
p. 4, but he does not tell us how to explain it. His view on the syriacisms in
the N. T. are of no help in a case like this, Aram. Appr., p. 30.

[5] Exp. Times 20 (1908/09), p. 92 f. Num. 14ı M. T.: את קרׁיב אשׁתׁיׁ; O. T.
Pesh.: ܘܢܬܟܬܫܘܢ.

[6] M. JASTROW, A Dictionary of the Targumim etc. (1926), sub ריב gives more
references than J. LEVY in his Dictionaries to the Targums (1881) and to Talmud
and Midrasch (1924²). Cf. E. BREDEREK, Konkordanz zum Targum Onkelos (1906),
p. 112.

[7] D. S. MARGOLIOUTH, Exp. Times 38 (1926/27), p. 278 f., calls it a foundation
stone of synoptic criticism and uses it as a proof for A. Merx's view that the
Greek Matthew was a translation of syr[sin] or its archetype.

[8] The Bohairic version of Isaiah and the min. 534 (11th century) support this
order, but they are certainly influenced by the N. T. The O. T. Peshitta has
the order of the M. T. and the LXX.

word ἐρίσει is suitable in the context of Matthew, when he shows how Jesus retires from the place when the Pharisees plotted against him, v. 15, cf. Mk. 3 6f., 12.

Thus there are reasons to presume that the form of the text in Matthew is an interpretation of the prophecy in the light of what happened to Jesus. This interpretation was not made without textual support. The school of Matthew might have been acquainted with an Eastern Aramaic Targum to Isaiah, where the word נריב was used, and this they rendered in accordance with Western Aramaic understanding.[1] They were not "mistaken": they knew exactly what they were doing. A proceeding of this kind was neither unusual in a milieu where different languages and dialects were used[2], nor was it felt to be unjust.[3] We have found a parallel to this procedure in the Western text to Mk. 15 34, but in Matthew it does not only belong to a branch of the textual tradition.[4] It is the result of the work of the Matthaean school, since the reading ἐρίσει is unanimous in all manuscripts.[5]

It might be that the reading of Matthew does not require a supposed knowledge of Syriac O. T. tradition, but builds only on dialectal conditions in the area where the gospel took shape. It is more probable, however, that the reading now found in the O. T. Peshitta was the starting point for the theological work behind Matthew's translation of the quotation.

In v. 19 b ἐν ταῖς πλατείαις is an interpretation of the M. T.'s

---

[1] On the age of the O. T. Peshitta to the prophets and its Targumic predecessors, see B. J. ROBERTS, *The Old Testament Text and Versions* (1951), p. 217 ff. Since the Syriac text of Isaiah is widely paraphrasing it is surely dependent on Targums, Western and Eastern, see below, p. 167 f.

[2] The same procedure, working in the opposite direction, is well known in the Peshitta, L. HAEFELI, *Die Peschitta des Alten Testaments* (1927), p. 50 (on the Isaiah text): "Das hebräische Wort wird gelegentlich in der Bedeutung genommen, die es seinem Stamme nach in Syrischen hat", cf. RAHMANI, *Les liturgies orientales et occidentales* (1929), p. 108 f., "dans des mots de langue araméenne ayant une double signification, l'une primitive, l'autre dérivée, le texte grec les exprime par des termes ayant le sens primitif, plutôt que le sens dérivé, diversement de l'intention de l'auteur", e.g. ܡܚܢ, "to be gracious", but with a noun or pronoun preceded by *lamad* = "far from", ἵλεώς σοι, Mt. 16 22.

[3] See below, p. 190 ff.

[4] See above, p. 85, note 1.

[5] Also ܢܚܒ in the O. T. Peshitta without variants, G. DIETTRICH, *Ein Apparatus criticus zur Pešitto zum Propheten Jesaia* (1905), ad loc.

בחוץ (Targum בברא), which is also peculiar to Matthew. The "correct" and natural translation is the adverbial one of the LXX, but Matthew splits up the adverbial expression into its component parts and obtains something more concrete which fitted into the context where the reluctant attitude of Jesus to publicity is stressed. This preference for the concrete is further shown by the active construction "nobody will hear his voice" for the M. T.'s "he will not let his voice be heard" and the LXX's "his voice will not be heard".

In v. 20 b Matthew's line of thought is brought to a conclusion by an abbreviation of Isaiah's text. In contrast to the period of secrecy is placed the open proclamation and the final victory, as, for example, in 10 26, 17 9. V. 3 b and 4 a in the M. T. and the LXX have no value as an argument in this instance. Thus Matthew's quotation goes directly over to 4 b, where one usually presumes parallel influence from an expression of the type we find in Hab. 1 4, ויצא לנצח משפט[1], but with the translation of לנצח which is found consistently throughout Aquila: εἰς νῖκος.[2] This interpretation is also found in five passages in the LXX instead of the usual εἰς τέλος or similar expression in the LXX (2 Sam. 2 26, Amos 1 11, 8 7, Jer. 3 5 and Lam. 5 20), but is more common in the later versions. It is easiest to understand as an Aramaism since the Aramaic נצח means "victory".[3] When Paul in 1 Cor. 15 54 quotes Is. 25 8, he also has this interpretation along with Aquila and Theodotion. This is usually cited as one of the clearest agreements between Theodotion's text and the N. T. quotations.[4] RAHLFS, in an exhaustive study, has shown

---

[1] LXX: διεξάγεται εἰς τέλος κρίμα. — BAUERNFEIND, Theol. Wörterb. z. N. T. IV, p. 944, takes εἰς νῖκος as a translation of לאמת in the part of the O. T. which was omitted in Matthew's quotation, but the temporal ἕως ἄν indicates that Matthew intends to render the sense of עד ישים באריץ משפט, and in the process of abbreviation the inference from a set term like that of Habakkuk is the more probable.

[2] Aquila to Hab. 1 4 is missing. The material collected by RAHLFS, Zeitschr. f. d. neutest. Wissensch. 20 (1921), p. 186–89.

[3] See MCNEILE, Comm. Mt., ad loc. — To LAGRANGE, Comm. Mt., ad loc. and ZAHN, Einleitung II¹, p. 317, νῖκος for נצח indicates an Aramaic Matthew. 1 Cor. 15 54 and the younger Greek versions, which even in other respects are closer to the milieu of the gospels, show that this translation was the self-evident rendering in a Palestinian milieu.

[4] VOLLMER, Die alttest. Citate bei Paulus, p. 24 ff., SCHÜRER, Geschichte des jüdischen Volkes III (1909⁴) p. 441, cf. above, p. 105. On the implications of the active verb of the LXX and Aquila and in Rabbinics as against the passive

that Theodotion's reading probably differed in other respects from
Paul's and that the coincidence between Paul's text and Theodotion's
translation cannot be a valid argument for Paul's dependence upon
the latter.[1] It is, however, a strong indication that the interpretation which the later versions (and also Lucian) have is the one that
was known by N. T. authors as distinct from the LXX's.

ἐκβάλλειν occurs elsewhere in the LXX as a translation of הוֹצִיא
but in that case with the connotation of violence[2], 2 Chron. 23 14,
29 5, 16, Ezra 10 3. It is striking that Matthew's choice of words,
differing from the LXX, is found in the chapter which is dominated
by the question of ἐκβάλλειν τὰ δαιμόνια 12 24, 26, 27 (bis), 28, cf. ἐκβάλλειν
without the connotation of violence in v. 35 (bis). κρίσις here means
"justice", as in 23 23 and elsewhere.[3]

V. 21 (lacking in min. 33 and often considered an interpolation[4]).
In the final words of the quotation we suddenly have complete accord with the LXX. The dependence upon the LXX is obvious in
ἔθνη = the LXX for the M. T.'s אִיִּים, a translation which the LXX
only has here and in Is. 41 5, and which is a typically geographical
and theological adaptation[5], together with the "translation" ὄνομα
for תּוֹרה given in the same sentence.[6] The grammatical construction

---

κατεπόθη of Paul, Theodotion (and Symmachus), see A. F. Puukko, *Studia Orien-
talia* 2 (1928), p. 57 f.

[1] Über Theodotion-Lesarten im Neuen Testament und Aquila-Lesarten bei
Justin, *Zeitschr. f. d. neutest. Wissensch.* 20 (1921), p. 182–99, cf. below, p. 179 ff.
A. F. Kautzsch, *De Veteris Testamenti locis a Paulo Apostolo allegatis* (1869), p.
104, maintained that the Hexapla by mistake referred to the Pauline text as that
of Theodotion, cf. Vollmer, *op. cit.*, p. 26. — In 1 Cor. 15 55 LXX's δίκη (M. T.
רבֶ-) is substituted by another νῖκος, a "contamination chrétienne", J. Bonsirven, *Exégèse rabbinique et exégèse paulinienne* (1939), p. 333.

[2] Particularly in Matthew ἐκβάλλειν is used without any such connotation,
Blass-Debrunner, *Grammatik*[7] § 126: 2.

[3] *Theol. Wörterb. z. N. T.* III, p. 943.

[4] In addition to the commentaries, see Bacon, *Studies in Matthew*, p. 475, Joach.
Jeremias, *Zeitschr. f. d. neutest. Wissensch.* 34 (1935), p. 119 f., Kilpatrick,
The Origins, p. 94, Manson, *Bull. of J. Ryl. Libr.* 34 (1951/52), p. 323. — From a
theological point of view there is no reason to suppress this positive statement
about the gentiles, see B. Reicke, Den primära israelsmissionen och hednamissionen enligt synoptikerna, *Svensk Teologisk Kvartalskrift* 26 (1950), p. 77–100.

[5] Seeligmann, *The Septuagint Version of Isaiah*, p. 80. Cf. above to Mt.
4 15 f., p. 105, cf. p. 100.

[6] Joach. Jeremias, *Theol. Wörterb. z. N. T.* V, p. 698, and Ziegler, ed. *Isaias,*
assume a scribal error for ἐπὶ τῷ νόμῳ αὐτοῦ. The generalized, abstract expressions

is, however, slightly different in Matthew and shows a certain freedom in its rendering of the LXX text.[1] Matthew has accepted the LXX's interpretation as being the one most suited to his requirements and most significant to the position of the church, that is to say, the prophecy's fulfilment. As we have seen, the LXX's geographical adaptation was useful to Matthew in the Isaiah quotation, Mt. 4 15. The LXX influence does not therefore justify the assumption of a later interpolation in Matthew's text.[2]

The unique interweaving of traditions of interpretation supported on different sides, and the completely original readings, render it difficult to understand the quotation in 12 18–21 as a "free citation" or to be satisfied that it shows dependence upon the M. T.[3] It can only have a satisfactory explanation as a targumized text which is the fruit of reflection and acquaintance with the interpretation of the Scriptures.[4]

---

are, however, common in the LXX. There might be a tendency of the same kind behind the plural noun in DSIa. A scribal error of this kind in the LXX would have been extremely welcome to the N. T., too suitable to be considered an error accepted throughout all MSS.

[1] The classical ἐλπίζειν τινί only here in the N. T. (cod. D ἐν τῷ) as against the LXX ἐπὶ τῷ, BLASS-DEBRUNNER, *Grammatik*[7] § 187: 6, Anhang, p. 33.

[2] In spite of the obvious dependence on LXX Is. 42, the LXX's understanding of Gen. 49 10 may have some relevance: M. T.: וְלוֹ יִקְּהַת עַמִּים (= Targ. Onk.); LXX: καὶ αὐτὸς προσδοκία ἐθνῶν (= O. T. Peshitta and Vulgate). The prophecies in Gen. 49 were a focus of messianic expectation, A. EDERSHEIM, *The Life and Times of Jesus the Messiah* II (1884[2]), p. 712 f. Their relevance for the early church can be studied in *Justin*, Dial. 52–53, cf. to Mt. 21 5, below, p. 119 and 200.

[3] Cf. SWETE, *Introduction*, p. 394, classifying it as "recensional". In adding Mk. 12 29 f. (the *shema*), where quite other conditions led to the "recension" (see above, p. 74 f.), Swete uses the term recensional in a rather vague sense.

[4] *Justin's* text (Dial. 123 and 135) cannot in its entirety be advanced as an example of the Greek text used by Matthew. It must have been influenced by Matthew here, as in many other passages, but to a certain extent it might give evidence of the tradition of interpretation used by him, see A. RESCH, *Aussercanonische Paralleltexte zu den Evangelien* I, 2 (1894), p. 140–42, E. HATCH, *Essays in Biblical Greek*, p. 199–201, W. BOUSSET, *Die Evangeliencitate Justins des Märtyrers* (1891), p. 39 f., MASSAUX, *Influence de l'Évangile de saint Matthieu*, p. 542 f.

Mt. 13₃₅: Ps. 78₂.

Mt.

(ὅπως πληρωθῇ τὸ ῥη-
θὲν διὰ τοῦ προφήτου λέ-
γοντος·)

| | LXX^B | M. T. |

ἀνοίξω ἐν παραβολαῖς τὸ   ἀνοίξω ἐν παραβολαῖς τὸ   אפתחה במשל פי
στόμα μου, ἐρεύξομαι   στόμα μου, φθέγξομαι   אביעה חידות
κεκρυμμένα ἀπὸ κατα-   προβλήματα ἀπ' ἀρχῆς.   מני קדם
βολῆς.

παραβολαῖς] –λῇ א*.

διὰ] add. Ἡσαΐου א*
Θλφ al.
καταβολῆς] B pc. it; add.
κόσμου א*ℜDΘ pl.

| Aquila | Symmachus |

a) ἐν παραβολῇ   διὰ παροιμίας

b) ὀμβρήσω αἰνίγματα ἐξ ἀρχῆθεν.   ἀναβλύσω προβλήματα ἀρχαῖα.

A quotation from a psalm of Asaph. The words are introduced as spoken by a prophet — according to cod. א and the Caesarean text by the prophet Isaiah. It was in connection with this quotation Eusebius referred to, that Matthew, as a Hebrew, used ἡ οἰκεία ἔκδοσις, which must signify the Hebrew text.[1]

The first part of the verse of the quotation agrees with the LXX, even in understanding משל collectively and rendering it with the plural, while Aquila on the other hand retains the M. T.'s singular (as does the LXX^{א*}). Even if this LXX feature in Matthew does not necessarily signify dependence, since the translation is grammatically correct[2], it is worth noting. The LXX character is undeniable even in Matthew's formula quotations.

Differing entirely from the LXX and the later Greek versions, Matthew reproduces the second half of the verse of the quotation. ἐρεύξομαι κεκρυμμένα is an intentional interpretation of the Hebrew text in con-

---

[1] Comm. in Ps. 77₂ (MPG xxiii, col. 904), see above, p. 39. — On the meaning of ἔκδοσις, see H. DÖRRIE, Zeitschr. f. d. neutest. Wissensch. 39 (1940), p. 90.

[2] GESENIUS-KAUTZSCH, Grammatik²⁸, § 123. — So also the O. T. Peshitta and the Vulgate. This understanding is verified by the plural חידות in the second half-verse, while Aquila's singular is in accordance with his principles of translation.

nection with Matthew's context, by which the parables as signs of the Messiah are accentuated (cf. Mk. 4 22 and parallels). Both the participle and ἀπὸ καταβολῆς (κόσμου) express the aspect of sacred history more concretely than the LXX translation.[1] The verbal significance in the participle is made full use of, a possibility permitted by the Greek. It is not the eternal mysteries which are pronounced, but it is the Messiah who has come and who reveals what had been hidden up to that time. The train of thought in Matthew is thus the same as that in 1 Peter 1 10 ff.[2] (note πρὸ καταβολῆς κόσμου in 1 20) and in Col. 1 26. The Sect of Qumran associated this work of revelation with the Teacher of Righteousness, DSH vii, 4 f.[3]

ἐρεύγεσθαι, "to belch out" for the M.T.'s הביע (idem) is also found in the LXX, Ps. 19 3, with the meaning "to announce", but usually has the signification of "to roar", "to bellow" in the LXX = the M.T. שאג.[4] Its use in Matthew shows clear dependence upon the Hebrew text and is a literal translation of the type for which Aquila is known, even if in this case it is Symmachus who gives a similar interpretation. The Aramaic נבע in aphel has the same double meaning.

The quotation is entirely dependent upon the form it has in Matthew to fulfil its purpose in the context. Thus it is an ad hoc Christian interpretation, which, moreover, is closely bound up with its context.

The introductory formula διὰ τοῦ προφήτου — without reference to Isaiah, which may be later, even though it is rather difficult to explain why it was completed so wrongly[5] — can have two possible explanations acting together:

---

[1] Syr^sin cur: "from of old", derived from the O. T. Peshitta, BURKITT, Evangelion Da-Mepharreshe II, p. 204.

[2] Cf. T. W. MANSON, Journ. of Theol. St. 47 (1946), p. 220, on 1 Peter 1 10–12 as a midrash on a form of a Q saying more primitive than that given in Lk. 10 23 f. and Mt. 13 16 f.

[3] The parallelism חידות — משל is found in Hab. 2 6, but in another sense, cf. DSH viii, 6.

[4] In HARRIS's argument for a Book of Testimonies (see below, p. 208) the order of the quotations in relation to one another is important. From that point of view it might be worth noting that in the preceding formula quotation שים was the Hebrew equivalent of the Targum's אבא, Is. 42 2. There is also a more general similarity between these two quotations in Mt. 12 and 13. They are both concerned with the hidden and revealed character of the Messiah and his teaching.

[5] The textual support for the wrong ascription is weaker in this case than in Mk. 1 2 and Mt. 27 9. The Gospel of the Hebrews also read "Isaiah", cf. above, p. 93, note 2.

a) Asaph, to whom this psalm is ascribed, is considered as a prophet, 1 Chron. 25₂, according to earlier Jewish tradition. The Massoretes have here adapted the text in accordance with a stricter theological distinction between the prophets in the proper sense and prophetically inspired men in a wider meaning.[1] Of the Greek versions it is Aquila who most unambiguously calls Asaph and the men like him prophets.

b) The prophetic nature of the word in itself could mislead or rather give rise to the understanding of the text as a prophecy. That the Psalms were considered prophecies is obvious in Justin, 1 Apol. 38 and 40–41.[2] But it is as obvious in the N.T. itself. We have seen Ps. 110 so used in the gospels, in Acts and in Hebrews, and in Mt. 22₄₃ there is a formal reference to David speaking "in the Spirit".

Mt. 21₅ ⧣ Jn. 12₁₅: Is. 62₁₁ and Zech. 9₉.

Mt.	Jn.
εἴπατε τῇ θυγατρὶ Σιών· ἰδοὺ ὁ βασιλεύς σου ἔρχεταί σοι πραῢς καὶ ἐπιβεβηκὼς ἐπὶ ὄνον καὶ ἐπὶ πῶλον υἱὸν ὑποζυγίου.	μὴ φοβοῦ, θυγάτηρ Σιών· ἰδοὺ ὁ βασιλεύς σου ἔρχεται καθήμενος ἐπὶ πῶλον ὄνου.
ὑποζυγ.] –ιον D* it.	θυγάτηρ] BDL *al.*; θύγατερ ℵℜΘ *pm.*

Is. 62₁₁ LXX^B	M. T.	Targum Jonathan
εἴπατε τῇ θυγατρὶ Σιών· ἰδοὺ ὁ σωτήρ σοι παραγέγονεν …	אמרו לבת ציון הנה ישעך בא …	אימרו לכנשתא דציון הא פריקיך מתגלי …
παραγ.] –γίνεται A; –γίνετε ℵ*.		

Zech. 9₉ LXX	M. T.	Targum Jonathan
χαῖρε σφόδρα, θύγατερ Σιών, κήρυσσε, θύγατερ Ἰερουσαλήμ· ἰδοὺ ὁ βασιλεύς σου ἔρχεταί σοι δίκαιος καὶ σώζων αὐτός, πραῢς καὶ ἐπιβεβηκὼς ἐπὶ ὑποζύγιον καὶ πῶλον νέον.	גילי מאד בת ציון הריעי בת ירושלם הנה מלכך יבוא לך צדיק ונושע הוא עני ורכב על חמור ועל עיר בן אתנות	follows the meaning of M. T. except in בת = כנשתא

The words from Is. 62 almost serve as introductory words or a form of address. The actual quotation is taken from Zech. 9 9, but in a somewhat abbreviated form. That this abbreviation leads to the omission of the adjectives δίκαιος καὶ σώζων is surprising, since those words would be more appropriate to Matthew's picture of Jesus as the Messiah, indeed, would constitute the very epitome of Matthew's Christology. However, if one turns to the rabbinic texts where Zech. 9 9 is used as a messianic prophecy, it becomes clear that greatest stress is laid on the words "poor and riding on an ass".[1] It is to a Jewish tradition that Matthew wants to relate his argument for the prophecy as fulfilled by Jesus's entry.

The final words of the quotation, the Greek form of which shows affinities with readings in Aquila and Theodotion, renders the M.T. with the literalness of an Aquila.[2] It is surprising that in this way Matthew seems to overlook the significance of the M.T.'s *parallelismus membrorum*, but it is in no way a sign that he was unfamiliar with Jewish exegesis, but on the contrary gives evidence of his acquaintance with the hermeneutic methods of the rabbis. Yet in this case the rabbis only counted with one ass in connection with Gen. 49 11.[3] Thus it is unlikely that Matthew is the originator of the tradition of two asses, vv. 2 and 7, or that this was created on the basis of this quotation from Zechariah.[4]

In the form the quotation has in John, the introductory words from

---

[1] STRACK-BILLERBECK I, p. 842 f., O. MICHEL, *Theol. Wörterb. z. N. T.* V, p. 284 f.

[2] While the LXX renders only two of the M. T.'s three synonyms for "ass", all of them are found in the later versions, yet nowhere exactly in the Matthaean form. The Quinta comes nearest with: ἐπὶ ὑποζύγιον καὶ πῶλον υἱὸν ὄνων. The Quinta, like Symmachus, read πτωχός for πραΰς (LXX, Aquila, Matthew).

[3] See STRACK-BILLERBECK, *loc. cit.* — The relation to Gen. 49 11 is worth noting since Mt. 12 21 had some affinity to Gen. 49 10. — Gen. 49 1, 9, 10, 12, 17 messianically applied in rabbinic writings, see EDERSHEIM, *The Life and Times of Jesus the Messiah* II², p. 712 f. — The verses 10 and 11 are kept together and combined with Mt. 21 5 in *Justin*, 1 Apol. 32. "The midrashic development in 21 5 is carried a step further by Justin who binds the foal to a vine", MOFFATT, *Introduction to the Lit. of the N. T.*, p. 258.

[4] See below, p. 200 — On the whole problem, see MICHEL, *op. cit.* p. 286.

---

[1] הַזֶּה, but some MSS הַזְּבָא, cf. v. 1: *ketib* הַזִּנְבְּיאִם, *qere* הַזִּנְבָּאִים. DSH vii, 5 has הַזּבִ(־)אִם defective scriptum. Aquila is consistent in reading προφήτης.

[2] In 1 Apol. 38 1 we find the technical term for the christological interpretation of the O. T.: ῞Οταν δὲ ἀπὸ προσώπου τοῦ Χριστοῦ λεγῃ τὸ προφητικὸν πνεῦμα οὕτως φθέγγεται· . . .

Is. 62 are lacking and instead the Zechariah text has as preface a phrase which occurs several times in texts related to Zech. 9, *e.g.* Is. 40 9 or 35 4. To a greater degree than in Matthew, the quotation is concentrated to the main point of the context, the fact of the procession, and John is less dependent upon both the M.T. and the LXX. As to the question of testimonies which might have influenced the form of the quotations in the gospels, it is worth noting that there is no agreement between Matthew and John apart from their common LXX features.[1]

The quotation's form in Justin, 1 Apol. 35 11 and Dial. 53 3, shows a strange mixture of the LXX and agreement with Matthew. The text in the Apology is more in harmony with Matthew[2] in spite of the fact that there the quotation already starts with Zech. 9 9a instead of Is. 62 11. The reference of the citation is, however, to Zephaniah, where the initial words of the quotation are found in 3 14.[3] Irenaeus, Epideixis 65, has the quotation in Matthew's form.

Mt. 27 9–10 (26 15 27 5–8): Zech. 11 (12–) 13 (Jer. 18 1–2, 32 6–9).

Mt. 26 15	Zech. 11 12 LXX	M. T.
οἱ δὲ ἔστησαν αὐτῷ τριάκοντα ἀργύρια.	καὶ ἔστησαν τὸν μισθόν μου τριάκοντα ἀργυροῦς.	וַיִּשְׁקְלוּ אֶת שְׂכָרִי שְׁלֹשִׁים כָּסֶף

ἀργ.] στατῆρας D.

Mt. 27 5–9a

καὶ ῥίψας τὰ ἀργύρια εἰς τὸν ναὸν ἀνεχώρησεν, καὶ ἀπελθὼν ἀπήγξατο. ⁶οἱ δὲ ἀρχιερεῖς λαβόντες τὰ ἀργύρια εἶπαν· οὐκ ἔξεστιν βαλεῖν αὐτὰ εἰς τὸν κορβανᾶν, ἐπεὶ τιμὴ αἵματός ἐστιν. ⁷συμβούλιον δὲ λαβόντες ἠγόρασαν ἐξ αὐτῶν τὸν ἀγρὸν τοῦ κεραμέως εἰς ταφὴν τοῖς ξένοις. ⁸διὸ ἐκλήθη ὁ ἀγρὸς ἐκεῖνος ἀγρὸς αἵματος ἕως τῆς σήμερον. ⁹τότε ἐπληρώθη τὸ ῥηθὲν διὰ Ἰερεμίου τοῦ προφήτου λέγοντος·

ῥίψας] cf. Aquila. τὸν κορβανᾶν] ܠܒܝܬ ܩܘܪܒܢܐ syr^sin cur pesh. Ἰερεμίου] om. Φ 33 syr^sin bo; Ζαχαρίου 22 syr^hl mg; Ἡσαΐου 21.

---

[1] On the quotations in the Fourth Gospel, see below, p. 162 ff. — on testimonies, p. 207 ff.

[2] Bousset, *Die Evangeliencitate Justins*, p. 34 f: Influence from Matthew! But the complex character of Justin's text prevents a definite verdict, cf. below, p. 179 f.

[3] Cf. J. R. Porter, *Church Quarterly Rev.* 154 (1953), p. 230.

Mt. 279b–10	Zech. 1113 LXX	M. T.
καὶ ἔλαβον τὰ τριάκοντα ἀργύρια, τὴν τιμὴν τοῦ τετιμημένου ὃν ἐτιμήσαντο ἀπὸ υἱῶν Ἰσραήλ, καὶ ἔδωκαν αὐτὰ εἰς τὸν ἀγρὸν τοῦ κεραμέως, καθὰ συνέταξέν μοι κύριος.	καὶ εἶπεν κύριος πρὸς μέ· κάθες αὐτοὺς εἰς τὸ χωνευτήριον, καὶ σκέψομαι εἰ δόκιμόν ἐστιν, ὃν τρόπον ἐδοκιμάσθη ὑπὲρ αὐτῶν. καὶ ἔλαβον τοὺς τριάκοντα ἀργυροῦς καὶ ἐνέβαλον αὐτοὺς εἰς τὸν οἶκον κυρίου εἰς τὸ χωνευτήριον.	ויאמר יהוה אלי השליכהו אל היוצר אדר היקר אשר יקרתי מעליהם: ואקחה שלשים הכסף ואשליך אתו בית יהוה אל היוצר

ἔδωκαν] ἔδωκα ℵ al. syr.
τοῦ κεραμέως] ‎ܟ̇ܐܪܐ(ܕ)
syr^sin cur pesh.

τὸ χωνευτ.] O. T. Pesh.:
‎ܒܝܬ ܡܪܝܐ

Zech. 1113 Aquila (Symmachus)

ῥῖψον αὐτὸ πρὸς τὸν πλάστην (Symm.: εἰς τὸ χωνευτήριον)· ὑπερμεγέθης ἡ τιμή, ἣν ἐτιμήθην ὑπὲρ αὐτῶν.

Zech. 1113 Targum Jonathan

ואמר יהוה לי כתוב דוכרן עובדיהון בחלש כתבא ורמי יתיה לבית מקדשא לתחות יד אמרכלא רבא חלף דיקרת דחלתי בעיניהון וכתבית דוכרן עובדיהון בחלש כתבא ורמיתי יתיה לבית מקדשא דיהוה דיהוה לתחות יד אמרכלא רבא

Mt. 279–10 is a citation from Zech. 1113 in connection with the story of Judas. Judas's role and destiny must appear as an offensive riddle to the Christians and we see how all the evangelists are anxious to make clear the position of Judas in sacred history.[1] In the Acts of the Apostles, the record about Judas is introduced by the words of Peter "it must be fulfilled which was prophesied of the Holy Spirit by the mouth of David", 116, and Ps. 6926 and 1098 are quoted.

Also in Matthew the story of Judas is closely interwoven with O.T. prophecy. The words in 2615 and the passage 273–10 are dominated by Matthew's interpretation of Zech. 1112–13. The quotation from v. 13 terminates Matthew's passage and the form of the quotation shows that Matthew has given his own interpretation from the point of view of what he sees as the fulfilment and as the revelation of the text's partly hidden meaning. It is surely for this reason useless to try to find a Greek,

---

[1] e.g. Mt. 2624, Mk. 1421, Lk. 2222, Jn. 132.

Aramaic or Hebrew O.T. text which might contain Matthew's Zechariah text. When HAWKINS notes 4 words with, but 21 without, equivalents in the LXX (cod. B and in this case even cod. A), it does not in any way signify an overwhelming advantage to the M.T. from the point of view of word statistics, but merely means that Matthew went his own way.[1] At the same time, the express quotation formula prevents us from interpreting the citation only as an allusion or a "free quotation". As it stands in Matthew, it must have had the conclusiveness and authority of a literal quotation.

The introductory formula is, however, rather puzzling with its reference to Jeremiah.[2] Though the quotation itself is obviously from Zechariah, the association with the financial transactions of Jeremiah when purchasing a piece of land from his cousin (32 6–9. LXX 39 6–9) and his visit to the potter, 18 1ff., were certainly well-known biblical features. By combining these two texts and reading them in the light of Zech. 11 12–13, Matthew found the latter to be a prophecy about Judas. "He recognized this to be the word of God", as we actually read both in Jer. 32 8 and Zech. 11 11. So Matthew seems to have had the Jeremiah passages in mind when doing the exegetical work that led him to understand the Zechariah text as it stands in his gospel. They were auxiliary texts, or perhaps it is better to say, according to the interpretation of the historical facts about Judas's death known to the author, the prophecy of Zechariah was shown to have the same eschatological end as the action of the prophet Jeremiah. The crucial point was the purchase of the land[3], the action which the O.T. explicitly states to be a prophecy. TORREY thinks that the combination of the two Jeremiah passages was helped by the reference to the "potter's vessel" in which the deed of purchase was laid, 32 14.[4] The Hebrew term there, however, is כלי־חרש without the actual word "potter".

---

[1] HAWKINS, *Horae Synopticae*[2], p. 154. — The use both of LXX and Hebrew text and the manner in which the prophecy is woven into the context of Matthew is a strong argument in N. J. HOMMES's criticism on Harris's alleged Book of Testimonies, *Het Testimoniaboek* (1935), p. 138 ff.

[2] AGNES S. LEWIS, *Light on the Four Gospels from the Sinai Palimpsest*, p. 61 ff., argues strongly for the originality of her syr[sin] in its omission of the prophet's name. The reading is supported by Peshitta and two early Old Latin texts. — HOMMES, *op. cit.*, p. 133–135 enumerates 10 alternative views on this matter of textual criticism, cf. *ibm.*, p. 147–150.

[3] This to HOMMES, *op. cit.*, p. 152 ff. proves that Matthew was right in referring to Jeremiah, cf. TORREY, *Journ. of Bibl. Lit.* 55 (1936) p. 252.

[4] *Documents*, p. 87.

The explicit reference to God's command[1] at the end of Matthew's quotation seems to be a reference to the introductory words in Zech. v. 13, not quoted in Matthew. The retained μοι may put this beyond doubt, but we saw how also the passages alluded to in Jeremiah laid much emphasis on the command of the Lord.

Even so, the reference to Jeremiah is somewhat arbitrary and we had better take it to be a slip or rather a confusion of memory.[2] This does not mean that Matthew introduced this passage as a free quotation from memory. The complex way in which the Zechariah text is related to the whole context shows a type of elaborate exegetical work which must depend upon a detailed study of the text proper, a study which demands the use of the written Hebrew text. Scholarly books at that time could contain mistakes, just as they do to-day. Moreover Matthew's error is well supported by the facts.[3]

HAWKINS counted only 4 words of the quotation common with the

---

[1] A tentative suggestion is that this was what Matthew worked out from the Hebrew ביד יהוה > בית יהוה (cf. Targ. Onk. Num. 33 10; Targ. Jon. (and Pesh.): על יד) or בדת = "on order" (cf. Esther 1 8 a. o., Dan. 2 13 a. o.) — If so, the accusativus loci (GESENIUS-KAUTZSCH, Grammatik, § 118 d) is interpreted already in v. 5. On double interpretation of a single text, see below, p. 192.

[2] So e.g. KLOSTERMANN, Comm. Mt., ad loc., who treats the passage at length. — A priori it is not at all impossible that the Zechariah prophecy was inserted in a Jeremiah text, as e.g. E. BÖHL, Die alttest. Citate im N. T. (1878), p. 75, maintains. Böhl has collected valuable parallels to such a procedure. Cf. below, p. 126. Yet in our case the bridge between Zechariah and Jeremiah is the יוצר interpreted as "potter", an interpretation which was unknown to Jewish understanding of Zech. 11. Thus there was no reason to combine the prophecies.

[3] Another explanation is found in H. F. D. SPARKS's article: St. Matthew's reference to Jeremiah (2 17, 16 14, 27 9), Journ. of. Theol. St., New Ser. 1 (1950), p. 155 f. He points out that only Matthew mentions Jeremiah and he thinks that Matthew was accustomed to a canon of "the later prophets" in which the book of Jeremiah stood first, as that mentioned in ¡Baba Bathra 14b (baraitha) shows. — The text in question was edited and commented on by G. DALMAN (Gustavus Arminus Marx), Traditio rabbinorum veterrima de librorum Veteris Testamenti ordine atque origine (1884). Here Dalman shows that the affinity between the material of 2Kings and Jeremiah was the reason for this order. — Cf. the Aramaic booklists in Greek transliteration and with Greek translation which are found in the Byrennios MS to the Didache and in EPIPHANIUS, de mens. et pond. 23 (MPG xliii, col. 237 f.), see J.-P. AUDET, Journ. of Theol. St., New Ser. 1 (1950), p. 135–154 and TORREY-EISSFELDT, Theol. Lit. Zeit. 77 (1952), col. 249–254, cf. TORREY, Zeitschr. f. d. neutest. Wissensch. 44 (1952/53), p. 205–223. In the first of these lists Jeremiah comes first. The mutual order in these lists varies however from all canons known to us.

LXX. If we take Zech. 11 12, quoted in Mt. 26 15, together with 11 13 — and as we shall see, they belong together — we shall have to add two or three[1] LXX words, one of them rather distinctive, ἔστησαν = וישקלו in the sense of "weigh". This is, however, by far the most usual translation of שקל in the LXX. The relation to the LXX in this quotation is therefore very slight, and its form is definitely dependent on Matthew's interpretation of the Hebrew text.

Ever since WELLHAUSEN the commentaries have paid attention to the fact that Matthew shows that he knows of both the M.T.'s reading יוצר, "potter", and the reading אוצר, "treasury", an emendation which the O.T. Peshitta is said to support.[2] This latter interpretation is actually reflected in Matthew's κορβανᾶν, v. 6.

This interpretation has been strongly challenged by TORREY.[3] He thinks that the Peshitta's reading was probably a conjectural improvement[4], though it is possible that he really had a corrupt Hebrew text with אוצר. All other witnesses have read יוצר, though they knew it was a technical term, a title for the "founder", who was in olden times in charge of the melting down of precious metal given to the Temple. This is the interpretation of the LXX χωνευτήριον, "foundry" and Aquila's πλάστης, cf. the Vulgate's statuarius.[5]

In the Targum the whole passage is transformed and the יוצר is a man in charge of deposited documents called אמרכלא רבא. This seems to have been one of the officials in the treasury department of the Temple. For this reason the reading יוצר, as denoting the person in charge, was the reading which the Targum rendered and to which it gave a modernizing interpretation.

Having rejected the reading אוצר, accepted by most commentaries, Torrey does not consider Matthew's κορβανᾶς as an allusion to another reading than Matthew's κεραμεύς. So far as the M.T. is concerned, Torrey has given quite a satisfactory defence of the reading יוצר as a tech-

---

[1] Matthew's ἀργύρια as against the LXX's ἀργυροῦς (Aquila, Symmachus) might depend on Mark's ἀργύριον. It might be a sign of independence of the LXX. In Mt. 27 9 it recurs, even there against the LXX. (Jer. 32 10, LXX 39 10 : ἀργύριον.)

[2] WELLHAUSEN, Comm. Mt., p. 145, cf. below, p. 196–198 and e.g. KLOSTERMANN, Comm. Mt., ad loc., SELLIN, Comm. Zech., p. 565.

[3] The Foundry of the Second Temple at Jerusalem, Journ. of Bibl. Lit. 55 (1936), p. 247–260 and in shorter form now in Documents, p. 87 f.

[4] So already F. J. V. D. MAURER, Commentarius ... in Vetus Test. II (1838), p. 698, cf. H. G. MITCHELL, Comm. Zech., p. 310.

[5] אוצר is mostly θησαυρός in the LXX.

nical term. The sense of this term, however, was related to the treasury
and led to an understanding of the passage which even without the reading
אוצר made the Peshitta's "treasury house" quite a natural improvement
to obtain greater clarity. All the other interpretations take היוצר to be
an official of the Temple; the LXX even takes it as the institution itself,
and not the person in charge of it. Matthew alone takes היוצר to be the
usual κεραμεύς[1], and he supports his interpretation by allusions to
Jeremiah. There are therefore two quite different interpretations. For
our problem the facts remain the same if we repudiate the reading אוצר.
Matthew's κορβανᾶς is the equivalent of יוצר, and what he stood for at
the time of Jesus. Both in the Peshitta and Matthew the word אוצר was
probably in the minds of the translators, even if it was not in the text.
Matthew obviously gives both the old and a new interpretation to his
quotation.

Matthew's new interpretation bears the stamp of elaborate adaptation.
His rendering of the Zechariah text shows changes of subject as against
the M.T. and the LXX. ἔδωκαν is certainly to be preferred in connection
with the context and ἔλαβον is also to be considered as a 3rd person
plural. Thus Matthew read: "And they took ... and they gave ...".
ἔδωκα is a later correction to closer agreement with the O.T. In a citation with such a marked revision as this, this development is more credible than the reverse. The μοι, on the other hand, refers to the prophet
who received the command to perform the prophetic action, a prophecy
which was fulfilled by the high priests. In spite of the very slight influence from the LXX in the quotation, the ambiguous forms of the LXX
verbs may have supported such a change of the biblical text.

τὴν τιμὴν τοῦ τετιμημένου ὃν ἐτιμήσαντο ἀπὸ υἱῶν Ἰσραήλ. Here
it is evident that the 1st person of the M.T. has been changed into
the 3rd. The מעליהם is expounded as מבני ישראל because it had no cor-
relative. For the rest, the consonantal text is that of the M.T. and reads:
אֶדֶר הַיְקָר אֲשֶׁר יָקַר(וּ) מִבְּנֵי יִשְׂרָאֵל, "the price of the estimable (venerable)[2],

---

[1] This is the LXX word for יוצר as a trade in 2 Sam. 17₂₈, 1 Chron. 4₂₃, Ps. 2₉,
Is. 29₁₆, 30₁₄, 41₂₅, 45₉, Jer. 18₂,₃,₆, 19₁, Lam. 4₂.

[2] So TORREY, Documents, p. 86 f., who thinks that the Hebrew quotation in
the Aramaic Matthew was closer to the M. T., reading ... אֶדֶר הַיְקָר ... יָקַר,
" ... the noble price at which he was estimated by the children of Israel ...".
— The participle τετιμημένος in the sense of an adjective "venerable", see Did. 15₂
cf. 1 Clem. 44₆. It was in the interest of Matthew to personalize the meaning of
the text, cf. below, p. 200 and there is no reason to presume an intermediate
stage as that of Torrey. — Piel of יקר not in Biblical Hebrew but in the Mishnah.

which some[1] of the children of Israel had estimated." That understanding is closely related to the N.T. context.

This is true also about the insertion of the ἀγρός of the potter. The Jeremiah purchase gives Matthew the right to do so, whether he consciously interprets the cousin to be a potter or combines the two prophetic actions without such an explicit identification. Thus Matthew claims to have explored the true significance of היוצר.[2] This creates a difficulty: the words בית יהוה then have no direct meaning[3], yet they are not overlooked by him in his telling of the story. When Judas threw the coins down in the Temple, they finally came to the potter. In v. 5 where Judas is said to throw down the 30 shekels, the Greek ῥίψας is in agreement with Aquila and Symmachus against the LXX.

Thus the quotation is largely affected by the context and the context by the quotation. In this, the last of Matthew's formula quotations, we are able to get a glimpse of this mutual relation. We have found adaptations of the same type in others of these quotations, but here it is obvious that Matthew has explored a new meaning — to him the true one — and he rewrites the prophecy from his findings. At the same time he retains and refers to the old reading of the text. We will revert to these features and their importance for our study.[4]

Having examined the formula quotations, we are confronted by quite another citation technique than the quotations which had parallels in

---

Pael = "to make heavy" *e.g.* Targ. Zech. 7 11. The crux interpretum in this understanding of Matthew's translation is how אדר ("excellence") could be rendered by "price". Partly the Greek τιμή made this possible, since it had both meanings, partly "price" was given in the Hebrew text. In any case, "excellence" could give no meaning to Matthew's understanding of the text.

[1] מן interpreted as a partitive particle, GESENIUS–KAUTZSCH, *Grammatik*, § 119 w, cf. BLASS–DEBRUNNER, *Grammatik* § 164 and Mt. 23 34. This understanding of מן has theological significance. Contrary to John's οἱ Ἰουδαῖοι = the evil nation as a whole, Matthew distinguishes between the authorities and the people, putting the responsibility on the former.

[2] So TORREY, *Documents*, p. 88, and also WELLHAUSEN, *Comm. Mt.*, p. 145, though he does not make clear how Matthew meant the prophecy. Surely Matthew does not intend to show how the authorities pondered upon the different interpretations of the Zechariah passage. But in doing what they did the prophecy was fulfilled. — Cf. BÖHL, *Die alttest. Citate*, p. 73: "Der Nothbau der LXX hatte ausgedient." It was however not only the LXX which veiled the simple meaning "potter" but the whole Jewish tradition of interpretation.

[3] Cf. above, p. 123, note 1.

[4] See below, p. 196 ff.

the Synoptics. Dependence upon the M.T. is greater, but at the same time it is not sufficient to afford an explanation of the Matthaean form of the quotations.[1] The LXX features can scarcely be explained as the result of a translator's conscious or unconscious dependence upon the LXX, nor can the Hebrew element be understood as arising from the corrections of the primary LXX text to obtain a greater measure of agreement with the M.T. We have hardly found any signs of an Aramaic version, which was later rendered with greater or less use of the LXX. That would demand a larger measure of agreement with the Targum texts known to us. Certain interpretations of Matthew's require the LXX's understanding of the text for the function of the O.T. text in the Matthaean context.[2] On the whole there is scarcely any tradition of translation or interpretation which does not emerge in Matthew's manner of understanding his quotations. This leads us to presume that Matthew wrote Greek and rendered the O.T. quotations along the lines of various traditions and methods of interpretation. This gives proof of a targumizing procedure which demands much of the knowledge and outlook of the scribes. In distinction from the rest of the Synoptics and the Epistles with what seems to be their self-evident use of the LXX, Matthew was capable of having, and did have, the authority to create a rendering of his own.[3]

When we call this type of citation in Matthew a targumizing procedure, and are faced with its great freedom when adapting the texts to their fulfilment in Christ, the question arises as to how these texts could claim the authority they must have had to be useful. The Targums did not obtain that authority in Judaism.[4] We shall have to look elsewhere than in the Targum process in the synagogues to find the *Sitz im Leben* of such a rendering of O.T. prophecies. Yet, before reverting to that problem we have to study the quotations peculiar to Matthew outside the group of formula quotations.

---

[1] It is worth noting that when TORREY presumes a Hebrew form of the quotations he is compelled to assume also an intermediate stage, *viz.* a rhythmical Hebrew form arranged by Matthew, *Documents*, p. 46.

[2] *e.g.* "the Galilee of the Gentiles", Mt. 4 15. — For a discussion of the different explanations mentioned above, see below, p. 150 ff.

[3] Cf. HOMMES, *Het Testimoniaboek*, p. 165: "Mt. 27 9, 10 is, gelijk alle vervullings-citaten in dit Ev., het geheel eigene en fijn doordachte werk van den Evang. zelf".

[4] Cf. A. BERLINER, *Targum Onkelos* II (1884), p. 109.

4. Quotations peculiar to Matthew, but without his introductory formula of fulfilment

How special a feature the formula quotations are, is illustrated by the fact that there are other quotations peculiar to Matthew, but without the formula pointing to the fulfilment of prophecy, and these seem to be more in accordance with what we have seen in the other Synoptics, with their dependence upon the LXX.

Matthaean quotations in synoptic context.

There is only a gradual transition between the Matthaean formula quotations (corresponding to groups i and ii of HAWKINS), and the citations found only in Matthew but which occur in a synoptic context (Hawkins's group v). Only in the chapters on the childhood of Jesus can there be any question of a quotation entirely without such a context. Most of the remaining formula quotations have been bound up with synoptic material of the Marcan type. Thus except for the actual quotation formula, there occurs no further additional sign of recognition which distinguishes groups i and ii, just dealt with, from those we are about to consider. In group i the formula was intended to indicate that the quotations were added by the evangelist. In the texts now to be examined, the introductory formulae are found *within* the actual sayings of Jesus.

Mt. 9₁₃ and 12₇: Hos. 6₆.

Mt.	LXX^B	M.T.
ἔλεος θέλω καὶ οὐ θυσίαν.	ἔλεος θέλω ἢ θυσίαν.	הסד הפצתי ולא זבח

ἢ] καὶ οὐ AQ.

Ziegler follows the LXX^A in his edition of the LXX to Isaiah.

The quotation is too short to determine its nature with certainty. It may be directly dependent upon the M.T., but also upon a Greek rendering. Concise as it is, one could take it to be a word of Jesus where the exact wording in the O.T. source did not play any part. It should be noted that the paraphrastic form of the Targum is similar to the LXX^B, but for Matthew the markedly adversative form is conclusive of the function of the citation.[1]

The introductory formula appears to be interesting; it is purely rabbinic, particularly in the form it has in 9 13, πορευθέντες δὲ μάθετε τί ἐστιν = וּבְלַמֵד אֵי, a typical phrase from the language of debate, with parallels in the other Synoptics.[2]

Mt. 13 13–15 (≠ Mk. 4 12 ≠ Lk. 8 10 ≠ Jn. 12 40) ≠ Acts 28 26–27: Is. 6 9–10.

Mt. 13 13	Mk. 4 12	Lk. 8 10
(ὅτι βλέποντες οὐ βλέπουσιν καὶ ἀκούοντες οὐκ ἀκούουσιν οὐδὲ συνιοῦσιν. καὶ ἀναπληροῦται αὐτοῖς ἡ προφητεία 'Ησαΐου ἡ λέγουσα·)	(ἵνα βλέποντες βλέπωσιν καὶ μὴ ἴδωσιν, καὶ ἀκούοντες ἀκούωσιν καὶ μὴ συνιῶσιν, μήποτε ἐπιστρέψωσιν καὶ ἀφεθῇ αὐτοῖς.)	(ἵνα βλέποντες μὴ βλέπωσιν καὶ ἀκούοντες μὴ συνιῶσιν.)
	συνιῶσιν] συνῶσιν D*LW pc.	βλέπωσιν] ἴδωσιν DW pc.
	ἀφεθῇ] ἀφεθήσεται A pc.	
	αὐτοῖς] add. τὰ ἁμαρτήματα ADΘ φ pc.	

Mt. 13 13, cod. D (it.)

(ἵνα βλέποντες μὴ βλέπωσιν καὶ ἀκούοντες μὴ ἀκούσωσιν καὶ μὴ συνῶσιν μήποτε ἐπιστρέψωσιν· καὶ τότε πληρωθήσεται ἐπ' αὐτοῖς ἡ π. 'Η. ἡ λ.· πορεύθητι καὶ εἰπὲ τῷ λαῷ τούτῳ· . . .)

Mt. 13 14–15 = Acts 28 26–27	Jn. 12 40
ἀκοῇ ἀκούσετε καὶ οὐ μὴ συνῆτε, καὶ βλέποντες βλέψετε καὶ οὐ μὴ ἴδητε· ἐπαχύνθη γὰρ ἡ καρδία τοῦ λαοῦ τούτου, καὶ τοῖς ὠσὶν βαρέως ἤκουσαν, καὶ τοὺς ὀφθαλμοὺς αὐτῶν ἐκάμμυσαν· μήποτε ἴδωσιν τοῖς ὀφθαλμοῖς καὶ τοῖς ὠσὶν ἀκούσωσιν καὶ τῇ καρδίᾳ συνῶσιν καὶ ἐπιστρέψωσιν, καὶ ἰάσομαι αὐτούς.	τετύφλωκεν αὐτῶν τοὺς ὀφθαλμοὺς καὶ ἐπώρωσεν αὐτῶν τὴν καρδίαν, ἵνα μὴ ἴδωσιν τοῖς ὀφθαλμοῖς καὶ νοήσωσιν τῇ καρδίᾳ καὶ στραφῶσιν, καὶ ἰάσομαι αὐτούς.
	ἐπώρωσεν] ἐπήρωσεν אW pc.; πεπώρωκεν א pm.
	2nd καί] add. μὴ D it.

---

[1] The quotation from Hos. 6 6 was dear to Jochanan ben Zachai, see E. v. Dobschütz, *Zeitschr. f. d. neutest. Wissensch.* 27 (1928), p. 339, cf. above, p. 11. — The understanding of the LXX and of the Targum is that of the rabbinic literature, Strack-Billerbeck I, p. 499 f. This interpretation might have found support in Prov. 21 3, the influence of which can be traced in the Targum of Hos. 6 6.

[2] J. J. Wetstein, *Novum Testamentum Graecum* I (1751), p. 359 and W. Bacher,

Mt.:

1st ὧσὶν] add. αὐτῶν אCΘ *pc.*

Acts:

ἀκοῇ] pro add. πορεύθητι πρὸς τὸν
λαὸν τοῦτον καὶ εἰπόν·
ἐπαχύνθη] ἐβαρύνθη א*.

Is. 6₉–₁₀ LXXᴮ	M. T.	Targum Jonathan
πορεύθητι καὶ εἰπὸν τῷ λαῷ τούτῳ· ἀκοῇ ἀκούσετε καὶ οὐ μὴ συνῆτε, καὶ βλέποντες βλέψετε καὶ οὐ μὴ ἴδητε· ἐπαχύνθη γὰρ ἡ καρδία τοῦ λαοῦ τούτου, καὶ τοῖς ὠσὶν αὐτῶν βαρέως ἤκουσαν καὶ τοὺς ὀφθαλμοὺς ἐκάμμυσαν, μή ποτε ἴδωσιν τοῖς ὀφθαλμοῖς καὶ τοῖς ὠσὶν ἀκούσωσιν, καὶ τῇ καρδίᾳ συνῶσιν καὶ ἐπιστρέψωσιν, καὶ ἰάσομαι αὐτούς.	ויאמר לך ואמרת לעם הזה שמעו שמוע ואל תבינו וראו ראו ואל תדעו: השמן לב העם הזה ואזניו הכבד ועיניו השע פן יראה בעיניו ובאזניו ישמע ולבבו יבין ושב ורפא לו:	ואמר איזיל ותימר לעמא הדין דשמעין משמע ולא מסתכלין וחזן מחזא ולא ידעין: טפיש לביה דעמא הדין ואודנוהי יקר ועינוהי טמטים דלמא יחזון בעיניהון ובאודנהון ישמעון ובליבהון יסתכלון ויתובון וישתביק להון:

ἀκούσετε] ἀκούσητε ΑVΓ. — αὐτῶν] om. א*. — ὀφθαλμοὺς] add. αὐτῶν אAQ. — ἐπιστρέψωσιν] -ουσιν א. — ἰάσομαι] ἰάσωμαι V.

In v. 13 there is an allusion to the Isaiah text. Compared with Mark it is even more allusive and lacks the final sentence which in Mark has affinity to the Targum Jonathan. It could thus be supposed that this concluding sentence had been suppressed when the literal quotation received its place in Matthew. On the other hand it can be said that Luke's allusion also lacks this final sentence, although no explicit citation follows. An example of targumizing paraphrase followed by exact quotation stands in 1 Peter 2₄, ₆.[1]

The literal quotation in Matthew is now entirely LXX, precisely the same LXX text as in Acts 28₂₆f. This, however, differs from Is. LXXᴮ

Die älteste Terminologie der jüdischen Schriftauslegung (1899), p. 75: "dramatisches Element der exegetischen Terminologie".

[1] See E. G. SELWYN, *Comm. 1 Peter*, p. 269.

only in one minor detail.[1] The quotation also occurs in Jn. 12₄₀, but there it is in part more freely treated and accentuated. It is inserted into the context. The exhortation to the prophet has lost its imperative character, and has been made into an indicative, with God Himself as the subject. The Johannine form on certain points has greater affinity with the M.T.[2], though the dependence upon the LXX appears from the translation characteristic to the LXX ἰάσομαι αὐτούς for the M.T.'s רפא לו.[3]

Much indicates that in Matthew the quotation is an interpolation at a later stage than the properly Matthaean.[4] Already the pure LXX form, and even more the exact agreement with Acts 28 in such a long quotation, encourages us to such a supposition. This is strengthened by the agreement of the short allusions with Luke and by the un-Matthaean quotation formula with two *hapax legomena* in Matthew, καὶ ἀναπληροῦται αὐτοῖς ἡ προφητεία 'Ησαίου ἡ λέγουσα· . . .[5] It is also strengthened by the considerable variation between cod. D and the other manuscripts, a difference unparalleled elsewhere in Matthew.

If such were the case we should have a parallel to this procedure in Mt. 27₃₅, where the allusion common to the Synoptics διεμερίσαντο τὰ ἱμάτια αὐτοῦ βάλλοντες κλῆρον is completed according to cod. ΔΘλφ *al.* it: ἵνα πληρωθῇ τὸ ῥηθὲν ὑπὸ τοῦ προφήτου· διεμερίσαντο τὰ ἱμάτιά μου ἑαυτοῖς, καὶ ἐπὶ τὸν ἱματισμόν μου ἔβαλον κλῆρον. This is exactly Jn. 19₂₄ in its LXX quotation from Ps. 22₁₉.[6] In Mt. 27 the formula is,

---

[1] Both in Matthew and Acts the LXX's αὐτῶν in the second clause is missing.

[2] ἵνα μὴ ἴδωσιν = וראה פן and καὶ στραφῶσιν = ושב. The tendency of the LXX works in the opposite direction to that of John. In the LXX the fatness of their hearts is the reason for the lack of success in preaching. On this dogmatic tendency of the LXX, see J. ZIEGLER, *Untersuchungen zur Septuaginta des Buches Isaias* (1934), p. 108 f. There might be an influence from Deut. 32₁₅ which supported the interpretation of the LXX.

[3] On the theological implication of the LXX's translation, see TORREY, *Documents*, p. 66. — The spiritualized rendering found in Mark, ἀφεθῇ αὐτοῖς is that of the Targum, see T. W. MANSON, *The Teaching of Jesus*, p. 76, IDEM, *Bull. of J. Ryl. Libr.* 34 (1951/52), p. 315 and BLACK, *An Aramaic Approach*, p. 156.

[4] So TORREY, *op. cit.*, p. 66–68.

[5] ἀναπληροῦν only in the Pauline epistles, but not about the fulfilment of prophecy. Most close to its sense in Mt. 13. is the saying in Gal. 6₂. For the LXX, cf. 1 Esdr. 1₅₄(₅₇). — προφητεία as a term for O. T. prophecy only in 2 Peter 1₂₀. For a proper saying of a prophet only Mt. 13₁₄.

[6] Cf. also Mt. 27₄₉ according to אBC *pc.* = Jn. 19₃₄. The originality or very early interpolation of this is claimed by BRANDON, *The Fall of Jerusalem*, p. 247.

however, the Matthaean one. That this is not the case in Mt. 13₁₄ may
be due to the fact that the context requires the more gradual transition to the quotation which is obtained by the formula there used.

It is remarkable that in both these cases we are dealing with a quotation which also appears in John. The citation from Is. 6 does not show
any agreement in form in John and Matthew. This contradicts the assumption of testimonies behind the gospels, particularly if one wants to
suppose Matthew's quoting to be genuine and original on this point,
which is, however, less likely.

There is also another quotation in Matthew which appears to have
been added at a later stage than the properly Matthaean, *viz.* Mt. 12₄₀.

Mt. 12₄₀: Jonah 2₁. Matthew renders the LXX text literally: ἦν
Ἰωνᾶς ἐν τῇ κοιλίᾳ τοῦ κήτους τρεῖς ἡμέρας καὶ τρεῖς νύκτας. It is
a common assumption that this verse is foreign to Matthew's original
text. This has been argued both from the theological and the literary
critical point of view. On the other hand, the manuscripts confirm the
text unanimously. FINDLAY is one of those who emphasize that the
Jonah quotation breaks the continuity between v. 39 and v. 41, and he
refers to the fact that v. 40 is lacking in Justin's quotation of the Matthew
passage in Dial. 107₂.[1]

A closer study of Justin's text makes the assumption of an interpolation even more likely. Mt. 12₃₉ is quoted, with express reference to τὰ
ἀπομνημονεύματα, in order to establish that Christ was to rise upon the
third day after his crucifixion. But the text in Matthew which he thus
quotes, excluding v. 40, only speaks of Jonah's preaching as a messianic sign. Of this text Justin says: καὶ ταῦτα λέγοντος αὐτοῦ παρακεκαλυμμένα ἦν νοεῖσθαι ὑπὸ τῶν ἀκουόντων ὅτι μετὰ τὸ σταυρωθῆναι
αὐτὸν τῇ τρίτῃ ἡμέρᾳ ἀναστήσεται, "When he uttered this hidden saying, the hearers might realize that he would rise up on the third day
after he was crucified."[2] Justin continues by linking together Jonah's

---

He overlooks the passage in 27₃₅ when he says: "The text of Matthew generally
shows no clear signs of assimilation to the Gospel of John."

[1] *Amicitiae Corolla*, p. 58.

[2] BOUSSET, *op. cit.*, p. 103, translates "Und als er dies sagte, blieb es verborgen,
dass er . . . am dritten Tage auferstehen werde", but the allusion to the three
days Jonah dwelled in the belly of the fish (not quoted by Bousset) supports the
translation given above. So G. ARCHAMBAULT, ed. *Justin, Dialogue avec Tryphon*
(1909), *ad loc.* — In any case the implication of the Jonah sign was known to
Justin, though he does not take it from Matthew.

preaching and the resurrection by pointing out how Jesus had showed that the Jews were worse than the people of Nineveh, who ordained a fast, since Jonah, after he had been cast up out of the belly of the fish on the third day, proclaimed to them that after three days they would all be destroyed. The LXX's reading in 3₄ with "three days" — according to the M.T., Theodotion, Symmachus and Aquila it was forty days — here became the condition necessary to the gradual transition between the three days in the fish's belly and the days for repentance.

Thus Justin knew the tradition of typological interpretation which the Matthaean quotation from Jonah 2₁ clearly shows, and he refers to it with the word παρακεκαλυμμένα. It is unbelievable that Justin would have passed over or forgotten this quotation in Mt. 12₄₀ if it had been in his text, or that he has tacitly corrected Matthew.[1] Under such circumstances we receive confirmation of our assumption that we here have a later exegetic complement to elucidate the way in which Jesus, like Jonah, was a "sign".[2] The quotation's purely LXX form strengthens this assumption.[3]

---

[1] So McNEILE, *Comm. Mt., ad loc.* — LAGRANGE, *Comm. Mt., ad. loc.*, maintains the text of 12₄₀ as genuine. He thinks that Justin (and Luke) avoided the quotation because of the theological difficulty involved in the reference to the three nights. How this very difficulty has influenced the textual tradition can be seen in the marginal note of min. 899 (Uppsala Univ. Gr. 4.): τὸ Ἰουδ⟨αι⟩κὸν οὐκ ἔ⟨χει⟩ τρεῖς ἡ⟨μέρας⟩. Cf. K. BORNHÄUSER, *Zeiten und Stunden in der Leidens- und Auferstehungsgeschichte* (1921), p. 45–47: Day and night were counted according to Jewish practice: 3–6 day, 6–12 night, 12–6 night, 6–12 day, 12–6 day, 6–12 night.

[2] The most recent study in the Sign of Jonah seems to be that of P. SEIDELIN, *Studia Theologica* 5 (1951), p. 119–131. Partly following JOACH. JEREMIAS, *Theol. Wörterb. z. N. T.* III, p. 413, Seidelin lessens the contrast between "preaching of a prophet" and "dwelling in Sheol" by pointing to Jewish traditions, where the Sign of Jonah was used as a "death-life" motif. Seidelin takes the words of Jesus as an enigma, the interpretation of which is made most clear in Matthew. He does not exclude that this was the interpretation given already by Jesus, though he finds it more probable that it was added by the evangelist. Cf. *ibm.*, p. 122, on the relative sense of the term "genuine" in a text like this.

[3] Is it merely by coincidence that the Matthaean doublet on the significance of the Sign of Jonah also affords textual difficulties (Mt. 16₂b–₃ : om. B ℵ *al.* syr^sin cur sa bo)? For a plausible explanation, see LAGRANGE, *Comm. Mt., ad loc.*

Mt. 21₁₆: Ps. 8₃.

Mt.	LXX	M.T.
ἐκ στόματος νηπίων καὶ θηλαζόντων κατηρτίσω αἶνον.	ἐκ στόματος νηπίων καὶ θηλαζόντων κατηρτίσω αἶνον ἕνεκα τῶν ἐχθρῶν σου.	מפי עוללים וינקים יסדת עז למען צורריך

The form of the N.T. text in this quotation, which constitutes Jesus's answer about the children's Hosanna song, is purely LXX, and that even on a point where the LXX has a peculiar, though possible translation of the M.T.: αἶνον ("praise") for עז ("strength").[1] An interpolation of the type we presumed for Mt. 13₁₄₋₁₅ is unlikely, since the context is here dependent upon this quotation in which the passage culminates. With respect to the context, LAGRANGE assumes the meaning "praise" already in the Aramaic translation of the O.T. "Comment un écrivain araméen aurait-il traduit עז de l'hébreu exactement dans le sens des LXX? Cependant, précisément parce que cette traduction convenait mieux aux faits, étant d'ailleurs possible, elle a pu figurer en araméen."[2] This somewhat strained explanation to preserve the Aramaic Matthew cannot find support in the reference to the O.T. Peshitta's ‏ܬܫܒܘܚܬܐ‎. When this Syriac text agrees with the LXX but is opposed to the M.T. and is in this case even against the Targum, it is certainly influenced by the LXX, a feature specially common in the Psalter.[3]

It is worth noting that it is just in a quotation from the Psalter that the most literal agreements between the N.T. and the LXX appear. This is quite natural if one remembers the Psalter's unique position amongst the books of the O.T. The Psalter was more intimately linked to the cult of the synagogue and church[4] than any other parts of the Scriptures. This fidelity to the LXX renders the considerable deviation from the

---

[1] GESENIUS-BUHL, *Wörterbuch*[17], s. v.: Ps. 29₁, 68₃₅, 96₇, 1 Chron. 16₂₈, "Verherrlichung, Lobpreis, nur von Gott", cf. Ex. 15₂, Is. 12₂, Ps. 118₁₄, where the LXX differs widely in its rendering of עז in the phrase עזי וזמרת יה: Ex. βοηθός, Is. δόξα, Ps. ἰσχύς. — Ps. 8₃ Aquila, Symmachus: κράτος.

[2] *Comm. Mt.*, p. cxix, cf. ZAHN, *Einleitung* II¹, p. 318, with a tentative guess that the Targum's עושנא ("strength") might have given an intended assonance to the Hosanna of v. 15. To render this ambiguity the translator used the LXX αἶνον.

[3] B. J. ROBERTS, *The O. T. Text and Versions*, p. 221, cf. below, p. 168.

[4] See H. ST. J. THACKERAY, *The Septuagint and Jewish Worship* (1923), p. 55 ff., 67 ff. and C. W. DUGMORE, *The Influence of the Synagogue upon the Divine Office* (1945). Also in Justin the quotations from the Psalms are strikingly consistent in their form and coincide with LXX[B], BOUSSET, *Die Evangeliencitate Justins*, p. 32.

LXX which we noted in Matthew's formula quotation in 13 35 the more conclusive, since it proves the special character of these quotations in Matthew.

The Matthaean context of our quotation bears Matthew's individual stamp, as for example in the Matthaean form of the "Hosanna", v. 15. When it comes to the entry of Jesus into the Temple in Jerusalem, the three Synoptics (and also John) differ greatly from each other, and the context in which Matthew has our quotation lacks anything properly corresponding to it in any of the other gospels. The nearest parallel in Luke concerns the disciples' — not the children's — songs of Hosanna, and the Pharisees' rebuke was answered by Jesus with the words "If these should be silent the stones would speak"[1], which is combined with the prophecy of the fall of the city, the city in which not one stone will be left standing upon another, the "stones" being the link between those two sayings. Notably enough — but apparently accidentally — even here (Lk. 19 44) is found a quotation dealing with children, καὶ ἐδαφιοῦσίν σε καὶ τὰ τέκνα σου ἐν σοί (Ps. 137 9 and other passages). As in the temptation passage, Mark only has the outline to this first visit to the Temple. Since Matthew shows that he formed the whole passage with comparatively great freedom in relation to what may be thought to have been his material, the LXX form, even in this quotation peculiar to him, is the more worth notice.

HAWKINS's statistics suggested a basic LXX character in the quotations which are peculiar to Matthew, though they are woven into the synoptic context. In addition we considered Mt. 12 40. We believe we have found reason to separate this and also Mt. 13 14–15 as interpolations at a later stage than that which in the true sense can be regarded as the period when the gospel came into being. In both cases it has been a question of elucidation and as to Mt. 12 40 an indication has been found that the interpolation was in agreement with the oldest meaning of the original text. In Mt. 9 13 and 12 7 the possibility is lacking to decide whether a direct literary influence from the LXX existed. Such an influence was, however, undeniable in Mt. 21 16.

Allusions in Mt. 1–2.

The genealogical tables in Matthew also belong to the LXX material, as do the other names of O.T. figures occurring in the gospel. In the cases

---

[1] McNEILE, *Comm. Mt.*, p. 301: "Does an Aramaic original lie behind both narratives, 'stones' (Lk.) and 'children' (Mt.) representing אבניא and בניא ?"

in which the names in these two tables agree with Luke, with two exceptions[1] they have the same transcription. A detailed study is rendered especially difficult by the uncertainty in the manuscript tradition both in Matthew and in the LXX.[2]

One may even find a LXX element in the allusions in Mt. 1 and 2. Mt. 2₂ at first scarcely looks like a conscious allusion to the messianic prophecy in Num. 24₁₇, common in later Christian testimony literature, about the star to come forth from Jacob.[3] The term ἀνατολή is natural in the text without any allusion. There is, however, the startling fact that the verse in Numbers is the only one in the LXX where דרך is translated by ἀνατέλλειν.[4]

In Mt. 2₂₀ there is no difference between the M.T. and the LXX, but the plural "they who sought for the child are dead" does not fit quite naturally into the context referring to the death of Herod, v. 19. The term εἰς γῆν Ἰσραήλ also points to the exodus at the time of Moses. This makes the verbal coincidence with the LXX of Ex. 4₁₉ a striking allusion.

Such observations further strengthen the impression of the LXX as Matthew's Bible and place the formula quotations in a special class. The dependence on the Hebrew text is hardly a consistent feature in Matthew's quotations. There are, however, slight traces of Semitic text in some Matthaean quotations outside the formula quotations. Partly they are quotations related to catechism and church discipline, partly they show affinity to Wisdom.

Quotations for catechism and church discipline.

The Decalogue and Lev. 19 in the Matthaean Sermon on the Mount.

In Matthew 19₁₈f. we noted how a commandment from the Law of Holiness (Lev. 19₁₈) had been added to those of the Decalogue. We pointed out that the combination of texts from those different parts of the Pentateuch is based on Jewish tradition.[5] In the Sermon on the

---

[1] Mt. Σαλμών, Lk. Σάλα; Mt. Βόες, Lk. Βόος.

[2] The deviations from the LXX[B] are given by ZAHN, *Comm. Mt.*, p. 57–61 and LAGRANGE, *Comm. Mt.*, p. cxxii. If the LXX[A] is taken into account, Ἐσρώμ, Ἰωβήδ and Σολομών also are LXX in form.

[3] *Justin*, 1 Apol. 32, Dial. 106₄, *Irenaeus*, Epideixis 58, Adv. Haer. iii, 9₂, see HARRIS, *Testimonies* I, p. 69, II, p. 87, cf. E. BURROWS, *The Oracles of Jacob and Balaam* (1939), p. 97 f. and FINDLAY, *Amicitiae Corolla*, p. 59.

[4] This fact in its turn reinforces the translation "at its rising" for ἐν τῇ ἀνατολῇ, see MCNEILE, *Comm. Mt.*, ad loc.

[5] See above, p. 62 ff.

Mount they also are interwoven.[1] In Mt. 5 21 and 5 27 commandments of the Decalogue are quoted but in 5 33 Matthew refers to Lev. 19 12. — Ex. 21 24, Deut. 19 21 or Lev. 24 20 is quoted in Mt. 5 38 and Lev. 19 18 occurs once more in Mt. 5 43, whatever may be the biblical or rabbinical support for the additional clause καὶ μισήσεις τὸν ἐχθρόν σου. The obvious dependence upon Leviticus in the fifth chapter of Matthew makes it reasonable to take Mt. 5 48 as an adaptation of Lev. 19 2. It may be noted that the order of the ethical statements in this part of the Sermon on the Mount is that of the commandments in Mt. 19 18f., where their climax is a parallel to Mt. 5 48 when it is said εἰ θέλεις τέλειος εἶναι, Mt. 19 21.

From the point of view of form Mt. 5 21 and 5 27 follow the LXX and so does Mt. 5 38. The five words in Mt. 5 43 which HAWKINS registers as "not in the LXX" have no equivalent in the Bible. Not least do the ethical statements in the Manual of Discipline from Qumran encourage us to presume that sayings like those Jesus here refers to did exist in Jewish catechism.[2] It is only in Mt. 5 31 and 5 33 that the textual relation to the O.T. is somewhat of a problem.

Mt. 5 31, (32): Deut. 24 1.

As in the passage in Mt. 22 24 on the brother-in-law's marriage, Matthew here deviates both from the LXX and the M.T. to the extent of an allusion. He uses the LXX term ἀποστάσιον. The term παρεκτὸς λόγου πορνείας renders the Hebrew ערות דבר according to the rabbinic interpretation = דבר ערוה.[3] Thus Matthew shows dependence upon Jewish terminology, as was the case with his ἐπιγαμβρεύσει in Mt. 22 24.

Mt. 5 33 a: Lev. 19 12.

Here Matthew seems to use catechetical material known to him. The commandment not to swear falsly is rather unusual in early Christian catechism. It was probably ruled out by the commandment of Jesus not to swear at all. Yet it is found where the imprint of Jewish catechism is the greatest *viz.* in the Didache (2 3) and in the Jewish material related to the Two Ways it is a constant feature.[4] Thus it is probable that the

---

[1] See PH. CARRINGTON, *The Primitive Christian Catechism*, p. 94–96.

[2] See *e.g.* DSD i, 4 and 10, cf. iv, 1.

[3] See T. W. MANSON, *The Teaching of Jesus*, p. 292 f., cf. J. BONSIRVEN, *Le divorce dans le Nouveau Testament* (1948), p. 16 ff. — E. LÖVESTAM, *Äktenskapet i Nya Testamentet* (1950), p. 141–144 refutes the equivalence between דבר עי-וה and λόγος πορνείας.

[4] A. SEEBERG, *Die beiden Wege und das Aposteldekret*, p. 15 f., IDEM, *Das Evangelium Christi,* p. 121. Cf. A. VÖGTLE, *Die Tugend- und Lasterkataloge im*

word of Jesus alludes to catechetical material known to Matthew. The singular οὐκ ἐπιορκήσεις as against the plural of the M.T. and the LXX conforms with the other commandments in Mt. 5. The close relation between the Decalogue and Lev. 19 also favours the view that the entire quotation is taken from Jewish catechism.

HAWKINS registered 19 words of the LXX and 19 against it in the quotations in the Sermon on the Mount. None of the latter bring the text of Matthew closer to the M.T. They only indicate that the ethical statements of the scribes and of the early church were not exact quotations from the Scriptures. So far as the O.T. is quoted literally, Matthew follows the LXX.

Thus the catechetical material peculiar to Matthew has none of the dependence on Hebrew biblical texts which we have found in the formula quotations. His ethical statements are partly LXX in form, partly in accordance with Jewish tradition. As was seen in 22₂₄ Matthew's Greek terminology seems to be that of Greek-speaking Judaism.

Mt. 18₁₆: Deut. 19₁₅, cf. 2 Cor. 13₁, 1 Tim. 5₁₉.

Mt.	2 Cor.	1 Tim.
(ἵνα) ἐπὶ στόματος δύο μαρτύρων ἢ τριῶν σταθῇ πᾶν ῥῆμα.	ἐπὶ στόματος δύο μαρτύρων καὶ τριῶν σταθήσεται πᾶν ῥῆμα.	ἐκτὸς εἰ μὴ ἐπὶ δύο ἢ τριῶν μαρτύρων.

μαρτύρων] om. D.
δ.μ.ἢ.τ.] δ.ἢ.τ.μ.ℵ it syr.

καὶ] ἢ ℵ (it.).

Dt. 19₁₅ LXX^B

M. T.

ἐπὶ στόματος δύο μαρτύρων καὶ ἐπὶ στόματος τριῶν μαρτύρων στήσεται πᾶν ῥῆμα.

על פי שני עדים או על פי שלשה עדים
יקום דבר

καὶ ἐπὶ στόματος] ἢ Lucian.
στήσεται] σταθήσεται AFΘ Lucian.

Here too, Matthew draws on Jewish tradition. Both in the synagogue[1] and in the early church this was a basic statement for church discipline. The closest parallels are found in the Damascus Document (CDCa 10₂;

Neuen Testament (1936), p. 115. Vögtle criticizes (rightly) the somewhat rigid view of Seeberg, but does not deny the Jewish imprint in catechetical material, *ibm.*, p. 120.

[1] STRACK-BILLERBECK I, p. 790 f.

col. ix, 2) and in the Manual of Discipline from Qumran (DSD vi, 1). In spite of being traditional material its form is that of a literal quotation from biblical text and we have to ask whether it received its actual shape in a LXX or Semitic milieu. The answer to that question depends partly on how the different LXX readings are evaluated. Matthew's σταθῇ is necessitated by his ἵνα-clause but seems to be related to the reading of LXX^A etc., cf. 2 Cor. SH. JOHNSON gives good reasons for accepting that reading as uninfluenced by the N.T.[1] Even the shortened form common to Lucian and the N.T. can be maintained as pre-Christian. The commandment's function as a rule of discipline in Judaism may have left such a mark in the Greek text. Thus the LXX character of the Matthaean quotation seems to be certain. The additional πᾶν common to the LXX and the N.T. favours that view, though it is typical of legislative style.[2] The variation between ἤ (M.T., LXX^{Lucian}, Mt., 1 Tim.) and καί (LXX, 2 Cor.) is of less importance[3] and in the N.T. it may be due to the different contexts. Paul uses the quotation in a less technical way, *viz.* with reference to his third visit to Corinth. In that function a καί is more natural.

McNEILE points out that the brethren spoken of in Matthew hardly have the proper function of witnesses[4], and that makes the quotation even more an accepted rule, to which Matthew gives his own interpretation. SH. JOHNSON seems to be right when he finds the Matthaean church discipline more anxious to stress the forgiveness and the reconciliation than was Paul.[5]

The similarities between Matthew and Paul as to the form and compass of the quotation do not point to a literary or direct dependence. The rule of church discipline, to which the authority of a *verbum Christi* had been added, was known to both of them, and that in a form closely related to the LXX. This affords yet another argument for the LXX character of the quotations outside the group of formula quotations.

There are however slight traces of Semitic text in two other Matthaean quotations and we will follow up and end our survey of the material by drawing attention to them.

---

[1] *Harv. Theol. Rev.* 36 (1943), p. 141 f.

[2] So LAGRANGE, *Comm. Mt.*, p. xcviii. Cf. TORREY, *Documents*, p. 73, denying any influence from the LXX.

[3] The difference has not the same significance for the interpretation as it had in Mt. 9 13 and 12 7, see above, p. 128.

[4] *Comm. Mt., ad. loc.* — On the witnesses as intercessors, see above, p. 28.

[5] *loc. cit.*

Quotations related to Wisdom.

Mt. 2743: Ps. 229 (Wisdom 2 10–20).

Mt.	LXXᴮ	M.T.
πέποιθεν ἐπὶ τὸν θεόν, ῥυσάσθω νῦν εἰ θέλει αὐτόν.	ἤλπισεν ἐπὶ κύριον, ῥυσάσθω αὐτόν· σωσάτω αὐτόν, ὅτι θέλει αὐτόν.	גל אל יהוה יפלטהו יצילהו כי חפץ בו

πέποιθεν] εἰ πέποιθεν DΘλ it sa bo. τὸν θεόν] τῷ θεῷ B. νῦν] om. A; add. αὐτὸν all except אBL 33 *al.*	θέλει] ἐθέλει (ε for ει¹) U; εἰ θέλει 1221 Lucian bo sa.	

Syrˢⁱⁿ ᶜᵘʳ	O. T. Peshitta	Targum
ܠܐ ܣܒܪ ܥܠ ܐܠܗܐ ܗܘ ܟܐ ܐܠܗܐ ܢܦܨܝܘܗܝ ܐܢ ܪܓ ܐ ܒܗ	ܐܬܬܟܠ ܥܠ ܡܪܝܐ ܟܐ ܢܦܪܩܝܘܗܝ ܢܦܨܝܘܗܝ ܐܢ ܪܓ ܐ ܒܗ	ישבח קדם יהוה ושזבריה פצא יתיה מטול דאיתרעי ביה

This is yet another allusion in the passion narrative to the 22nd Psalm.[2] It is the only distinct allusion to this psalm given in Matthew which is not paralleled in the Synoptics. Compared with the LXX text it seems to be an allusion rather than a deliberate adaptation. The words as given by Matthew are, however, exactly those of the M.T. — except the νῦν which is natural in the context of Matthew — if the Hebrew כי is taken in another sense than the one in which the LXXᴮ takes it. Matthew understands it as conditional, which is possible from the grammatical point of view[3], though it is less usual and certainly not intended in the psalm. On this point Matthew coincides with the LXXᵁ ᴸᵘᶜⁱᵃⁿ.

---

[1] The classical ἐθέλει of cod. U in Dittmar, *Vetus Testamentum in Novo*, p. 69. Yet cod. U writes ε for ει 4 times in Ps. 22: vv. 1, 7, 9, and 16, see Rahlfs, *Septuaginta-Studien* II (1907), p. 149, cf. *ibm.* p. 154. — Rahlfs takes the reading εἰ θέλει as influenced from Mt. 2743. For the opposite view, see P. L. Hedley, *Harv. Theol. Rev.* 26 (1933), p. 70. — Even if Matthew knew a Greek reading like that in LXXᵁ he depends upon the Hebrew in the rest of the allusion. As Hedley points out, this fact reinforces the value of the LXXᵁ reading, cf. below, p. 174.

[2] How the use of this Psalm was followed up can be seen in *Justin*, Dial. 97–105, especially 981. Neither in 1 Apol. 388 nor in Dial. 1013 is Justin's LXX text influenced by Matthew. The same applies to wording of 1 Clem. 1616.

[3] Gesenius-Kautzsch, *Grammatik*²⁸, § 159 b, 1 and aa, כי expressing the contrary-to-fact-condition, which suits the context of the gospel. Cf. Bonsirven, *Exégèse rabbinique et exégèse paulinienne* (1939), p. 156 f.

Their reading seems to be uninfluenced by the N.T., but when the O.T. Peshitta understands the text in the same way as Matthew, it is clearly due to such influence from the N.T., since the Syriac follows Matthew as against the LXX even in the rest of the verse.

Both Matthew and the LXX have read בָּל instead of the M.T.'s imperative בֹּל. Matthew's (and the O.T. Peshitta's) "he has put his trust" is a somewhat more exact rendering of the Hebrew גֹּל, "to roll" = "to throw (oneself) on Yahweh", than is the LXX's "he has hoped". The Targum has combined the verb with the root גִּיל, "to shout for joy".

At the same time the whole situation is like a historical illustration to what is said about the thoughts of the ungodly in Wisdom 2 10 ff., a text which in its turn shows affinity to Is. 53 (e.g. when it states that the wise man is repulsive to behold, 2 14) and with allusion to Ps. 22 9, "Let us see if his words be true, and let us try what shall befall in the ending of his life. For if the righteous man is God's son, he will uphold him, and he will deliver (ῥύσεται) him out of the hand of his adversaries", Wisdom 2 17–18. In v. 16 it is said that the righteous man boasts that God is his father. The line of thought found in Wisdom is certainly met in the other Synoptics, but it seems that Matthew intentionally chose to make this allusion clearer and more conscious by his quotation from Ps. 22 9. However, the passage in Wisdom has not influenced the form of the text in Matthew, unless there is a slight influence in Matthew's omission of the Psalter's "to save" and retention of ῥύεσθαι common to Matthew and Wisdom.

Since Matthew's allusion to Ps. 22 9 is inserted in the passion story, it cannot simply be considered as an addition of Matthew's, but may have been included in the gospel tradition with its Semitic form preserved. Yet it is just as likely that Matthew, who was familiar with the Hebrew text, found this text appropriate in the context. This was not so obvious if one only approached the text in its LXX form.

Mt. 11 29: Jer. 6 16 (Ecclus. 51 23–30).

Moreover, we must ask ourselves: Is it merely by chance we find in the allusions peculiar to Matthew a text which shows slight but obvious traces of Hebrew biblical phraseology, as well as the same relation to Wisdom literature, viz. Mt. 11 29. Its εὑρήσετε ἀνάπαυσιν ταῖς ψυχαῖς ὑμῶν is opposed to the LXX[B] ἁγνισμόν and the LXX[A] ἁγιασμόν (Aquila: ἀνάψυξιν) and rightly renders the Hebrew מצאו מרגוע לנפשכם in

Jer. 6 16. Now the context in Matthew is strongly influenced by Ecclus. 51 23 ff., where Wisdom (as an hypostasis) is speaking and where the true teaching of the school will give the disciples the ἀνάπαυσις.[1]

This type of literature seems to have been studied in the school of Matthew and related to Jesus, equating Him with Wisdom, as does Luke in 11 49.[2] The Wisdom Christology may have been treated by Matthew, and in relation to those studies Matthew's eyes may have been opened to the two quotations he renders in 27 43 and 11 29; in this respect, however, only useful when found in their Hebrew form.

Thus these last two quotations form a sort of bridge between the LXX texts used by the Synoptics and by Matthew himself, and the more elaborate type of quotations introduced by the formula of fulfilment.

---

[1] On the whole problem see T. ARVEDSON, *Das Mysterium Christi* (1937), especially p. 201–204, and E. NORDEN, Das Logion Ev. Matth. 11 25-30, in *Agnostos Theos* (1913), p. 277–308. To Norden the Semitic stamp in the quotation from Jeremiah was important, see *ibm.*, p. 284.

[2] See above p. 92 and HARRIS, *Testimonies* II, p. 97 ff. (without reference to Mt. 27 43).

Discussion and conclusions

Inter-synoptic observations

The starting point for our studies was HAWKINS's statistics on quotations. These have been corrected and completed on certain points.[1] Our first question is therefore whether Hawkins's classification can be maintained. If such is the case it confronts us with a number of questions affecting the composition of Matthew and the possibility of its being a translation. Is the distinction between the formula quotations and the remaining Matthew quotations basic or can it be understood as a relative difference with parallels to what we otherwise find in synoptic (or N.T.[2]) methods of quotation?

Our examination of quotations in Matthew with parallels in Mark (and Luke) strengthens Hawkins's statistics so far as it concerns the fundamental LXX character of these quotations. Where these statistics gave the greatest number of non-LXX words it was not a question of quotations in a strict sense (22_{24}). We have further found very close agreement between Matthew and Mark, while Luke shows a tendency to deviate more from the LXX text. This he merely does in form, however, the better to merge his quotations into their context.

Mark and the LXX.

T. W. MANSON has now challenged the view that Mark's quotations follow the LXX[3]. He has put forward quite a few cases where the M.T.,

---

[1] *Horae Synopticae*[2], p. 154–56, see above, p. 43–45. — Corrections *e.g.* in Mt. 54_3, see p. 137 f., Mt. 22_{24}, see p. 70 and in Mt. 27_{9-10}, see p. 123 f. On Hawkins's LXX text, cf. below, p. 169.

[2] See below, p. 156 ff.

[3] The Old Testament in the Teaching of Jesus, *Bull. of J. Ryl. Libr.* 34 (1951/52), p. 312–22, especially p. 314 ff. During the war Manson undertook a detailed study of the quotations in the N.T. The results were given in the Grinfield Lectures in Oxford in 1945. Unfortunately I have not found more of this published than his article in the *Bulletin* and his review of Kahle's The Cairo Geniza in the *Dominican Studies* 2 (1949), p. 183–92, cf. also The Argument from Prophecy, *Journ. of Theol. St.* 46 (1945), p. 129–36.

the LXX and the Targums do not agree and where Mark opposes the LXX. Some of the cases are convincing beyond doubt; some of them are not, but when combined with the evident cases, they, too, could be significant.[1] Most of the facts have been stated above in connection with the examination of the texts.

The passages in question are:

Mk. 1 11 (Mt. 3 17, Lk. 3 22). This gives a combination of Ps. 2 7 and Is. 42 1 where the specifically Christian translation has antecedents in Semitic and Palestinian Greek texts.[2] The combination itself is similar to the *charuzim* in rabbinic interpretation.[3] As a whole, however, the text must be taken as a Christian hymnic translation coined *ad hoc*, and as such it has influenced the version of Is. 42 1 in Mt. 12 18.[4] It is not a quotation in the true sense.

Mk. 4 12 (Mt. 13 13–15). Here ἀφεθῇ αὐτοῖς is the Targum's interpretation of the M.T. רפא לו as against the LXX. The agreement with the Targum is convincing, though we have to bear in mind that the text in Mark is not more than a strong allusion to the passage in Is. 6.[5]

Mk. 4 29 (Joel 4 13, no parallel in Mt.[6]). The LXX's παρέστηκεν in Mark is in agreement also with the Targum's translation of the verb. But this is no argument for Manson's thesis, since the interpretation of the Targum clearly departs from the imagery of Joel, and in the LXX this is the only case where בשל is thus interpreted.

Mk. 10 8 (Mt. 19 5). οἱ δύο is not only the LXX's but also the Targum Jonathan's reading and Manson is in favour of the view that this was what Mark had in his Hebrew text.[7]

---

[1] MANSON, *Bulletin*, p. 315. — Mk. 7 10 (Mt. 15 4) is however insignificant, see above, p. 55 f.

[2] MANSON, *op. cit.*, p. 323 f.   [3] See below, p. 216.

[4] Cf. above, in relation to Mt. 12 18, p. 109 f.

[5] See above, p. 130 f.

[6] Mk. 4 29: εὐθὺς ἀποστέλλει τὸ δρέπανον, ὅτι παρέστηκεν ὁ θερισμός. — Joel 4 13 (LXX 3 13): ἐξαποστείλατε δρέπανα, ὅτι παρέστηκεν (ὁ cod. A) τρύγητος. — M.T.: שלחו מגל כי בשל קציר. — Targ. Jon.: אושישו בחון חרבא ארי מטא זמן קיצירהון. The change τρύγητος — θερισμός in this apocalyptic allusion is dictated by the context in the respective texts. The only trace of a Semitic O.T. in the Marcan text is the singular δρέπανον.

Other quotations peculiar to Mark: 9 48 (Is. 66 24), a free rendering in an apocalyptic saying; on its relation to the LXX^A, see below, p. 173. 12 32 (Deut. 4 35), also closer to the LXX^A than to the LXX^B. 6 23, 8 18, 12 33, and 14 18 are mere allusions without relevance for our study.

[7] See above, p. 60.

Mk. 10 19 (Mt. 19 18 f.). In the enumeration of the commandments Mark and Luke have μή + the subjunctive whereas Matthew and the LXX have οὐ + the indicative. The order of the commandments is that of the M.T., the Targums and the LXX^A in Matthew while Mark and Luke follow the LXX^B.[1]

Mk. 12 36 (Mt. 22 44). According to Manson, the reading ὑποκάτω is due to a free manner of quoting. It should be noted, however, that it is possible that we have here evidence of influence from Ps. 8 and the deviation can thus be explained as coming from another text within the LXX.[2]

Mk. 13 8 (Mt. 24 7). βασιλεία agrees with the M.T. and the Targum, as against the LXX's νομός, but at the same time Mark's ἔθνος differs from all texts known to us, for which reason we are scarcely right in taking it as a strict quotation in this case.[3]

Mk. 13 22 (Mt. 24 24: Deut. 13 2). Even here the nature of the quotation is not clear and Manson's emphasis on the fact that Mark together with the Targum Jonathan explicitly speaks of false prophets does not turn the balance, since that sense is given by the context.

Mk. 14 62 (Mt. 26 64). With the M.T. and Theodotion Mark has μετὰ τῶν νεφελῶν as against the LXX (and Matthew).[4]

Mk. 15 34 (Mt. 27 46). Mark agrees with the M.T. and the Targum against the LXX's πρόσχες μοι, which Origen marks with an obelus. It is not inconceivable that Mark's Greek text of Palestinian type lacked this LXX addition — a question of less interest since the Greek text is related to Mark's own Hebrew or Aramaic. Manson inclines to the opinion that Mark's ὠνείδισας was his original reading.[5]

To those texts dealt with by Manson may be added:

Mk. 1 2–3 (Mt. 11 10 and 3 3). This is a composite quotation of LXX type but with marked deviations from the LXX in details, and most probably some kind of Christian testimony.[6]

Mk. 12 26 (Mt. 22 32). The LXX's εἰμί is lacking in Mark and the text thus agrees rather with the M.T. in form.[7]

---

[1] The Marcan μὴ ἀποστερήσῃς, found in LXX^A to Deut. 24 14, does not occur in the other gospels, see above, p. 62.

[2] See above, p. 77 f.   [3] See above, p. 79.

[4] Mk. 13 26 has however ἐν νεφέλαις, see MANSON, op. cit., p. 316 and 319 and below, p. 212 ff.

[5] See above, p. 85.

[6] See above, p. 50 ff. and below, p. 201 and 215.

[7] See above, p. 71 f.

Mk. 12 29–30 (Mt. 22 37). Mark's form of the *shema* has a certain similarity to the M.T., but of the Synoptics Mark stands nearest to the LXX. Liturgical or catechetical sources may be presumed.[1]

Mk. 14 27 (Mt. 26 31). The form πατάξω for the M.T.'s and LXX's imperative is striking. Like 1 2–3 it carries one's thoughts most closely to testimonies.[2]

Among these cases 4 12, 10 19, 13 8, 14 62, and 12 26 may point to a dependence on the Hebrew or Aramaic text as the case may be. Mk. 1 2–3 and Mk. 14 27 raise special problems relating to testimonies and will be dealt with in that context.[3] The first four of the cases just mentioned, as the less certain cases in Manson's list, are, however, evidently not pure quotations. In 13 8, for example, we came upon the noteworthy combination of the M.T. βασιλεία with an ἔθνος, which was not supported by any O.T. text. This manner of allusion instead of strict quotation is typical of apocalyptic literature in general[4] — and we may take as apocalyptic sayings 13 8, 13 22, 14 62 and 4 29. Only in 12 26, 12 36 and 14 27 is the character of the quotation pure. In two cases we came across texts used in catechism or liturgy which had their existence outside the framework of the biblical text (10 19 and 12 29–30).

In quotations and allusions of these types we thus find that the Semitic background asserts itself and that it has not been completely harmonized with the LXX form. This is especially the case in the allusive references. It should, moreover, be added that the quotation in Mk. 7 6 f. (Mt. 15 8 f.) only has a meaning in its LXX form,[5] and even where isolated features of the Hebrew or Aramaic text penetrate Mark's text, this shows a conscious use of the LXX. The Semitic features seem, therefore, to be a survival of that Aramaic form in which the words and deeds of Jesus were originally recounted. The features cannot be interpreted as of direct literary dependence on Semitic Scriptures. They are a survival, not a conscious tendency, and it is quite natural that this survival is found in the allusive references. Neither have we found any reason for supposing that Mark's Greek text is evidence of another

---

[1] See above, p. 72 f.

[2] Cf. above, p. 80 ff.

[3] Cf. below, p. 215 ff.

[4] Cf. below, p. 158 f.

[5] When MANSON, *op. cit.*, p. 317 f., defends the reading ἀγαπᾷ in 7 6 (cf. above, p. 57), this has little bearing on Mark's supposed dependence on Semitic text. If accepted, the reading is due to inner-Greek changes.

Greek translation or yields actual variants to the Greek text of the
O.T.[1] It therefore seems possible to maintain WOODS's conclusion: "It
seems that the writer, while he had received and retained a few sayings
of our Lord as actually uttered, generally used LXX as a matter of
course."[2]

It is not clear whether Manson proposes merely to touch up this
statement by pointing out further cases of "retained sayings" or whether
he wishes to urge an essentially different view when he concludes: "I
think it a fair statement of the case .... to say that while there is a
definite tendency for O.T. quotations to be conformed to the LXX, it
does not seem to operate to any great extent in the early period."[3] It
depends on what is meant by "to be conformed": a) to use the LXX as
the main source of the O.T. text in the sayings of Jesus instead of giving
a direct ad hoc translation of the Aramaic, or b) to carry this use of the
LXX still further in a more consistent manner by suppressing all traces
of Semitic wording. The clear impression that the LXX is the Bible of
the Marcan gospel is not lessened by Manson's approach when he
considered the cases where the different O.T. texts do not agree and
the quotation in Mark "takes sides".[4] The cases where the O.T. texts do
not differ are of equal relevance where Mark's quotation literally follows the LXX. Manson has laid strong emphasis on the few but obvious
cases of retained sayings, but his material does not affect the LXX
basis of the O.T. quotations in the sayings of Jesus.

Matthew takes over Mark's quotations.

If the quotations in Mark are compared with the form they have in
Matthew, a greater measure of agreement with the LXX may be
observed in certain cases in Matthew.[5] This is so in Mt. 19 18 f. ≑ Mk. 10 19;
Mt. 21 9 ≑ Mk. 11 9–10; Mt. 22 32 ≑ Mk. 12 26; Mt. 24 30 ≑ Mk. 13 26
(Mt. 26 64 ≑ Mk. 14 62).

In Mt. 27 46b (Mk. 15 34b), sometimes the one and sometimes the

---

[1] See below, p. 180 f.

[2] HASTINGS's *Dictionary of the Bible* IV, p. 186.

[3] *op. cit.*, p. 322, cf. p. 314 and 318.

[4] MANSON, *op. cit.*, p. 314.

[5] This is strongly stressed by BACON, *Studies in Matthew*, p. 470, cf. ALLEN,
Comm. Mt., p. lxii. So also MANSON, *op. cit.*, p. 317, states 15 such cases, 12 of
which he does not register which they are. Some of these might not be relevant,
e.g. Mk. 4 12 ≑ Mt. 13 13–15, see above, p. 130 f.

other agrees more closely with the LXX.[1] Even in other respects Matthew's tendency towards the LXX in these quotations is not without ambiguity. In his form of the *shema* Mark, together with the LXX, has ἐξ while Matthew has the more Semitic form ἐν,[2] and in 22 24 Matthew, as against Mark and the LXX, uses the technical term ἐπιγαμβρεύειν, which is, however, found elsewhere in the LXX.[3] But in both these cases the material might originate from catechetical traditions and not directly from the O.T.

Of greater interest is the fact that at times Matthew offers a longer LXX text than Mark, as in 19 5,[4] but here again in catechetical material. We have the opposite case, with longer LXX text in Mark, in the parallels to Mt. 21 13 and 22 37.[5]

However, as we have seen, all these variations only relate to details. The close agreement between Matthew's and Mark's quotations, even where they differ from every O.T. text known to us (Mt. 3 3 ≒ Mk. 1 3; Mt. 11 10 ≒ Mk. 1 2; Mt. 22 44 ≒ Mk. 12 36; Mt. 26 31 ≒ Mk. 14 27), together with the slight but obvious tendency to greater fidelity to the LXX, shows that Matthew took over this material from Mark. This LXX revision does not have to be considered a single process. That the tendency is not without ambiguity speaks against this. It is more likely that Mark was in use in the Matthaean church and school, and had thereby been gradually conformed to the church's Greek O.T.[6]

Matthew — Luke.

The quotations common only to Matthew and Luke present the same picture as those common to Matthew and Mark. The Q material shows

---

[1] See above, p. 86 f.

[2] See above, p. 73 f.

[3] See above, p. 70.

[4] See above, p. 60.

[5] See above, p. 67 and 75.

[6] MANSON, *op. cit.*, p. 319, finds that "Luke is less inclined than Matthew to adapt the quotations in Mark to the text of the LXX". Mk. 12 36 ≒ Mt. 22 44 ≒ Lk. 20 42 should be the only example of the opposite. Of the other texts, however, Mk. 4 12 is hardly in case, since Matthew takes quite another line, see above, p. 130 f., and Mark's Targum reading is not retained by Luke. Mk. 10 19 ≒ Lk. 18 20 have μή in common as against Matthew, but the Marcan "addition" is wanting in Luke, see above, p. 62. On the only text which might be in case, the quotation from Dan. 7 13 in Mk. 13 26, see below, p. 214. — Thus Manson's view on the relation Mark–Luke–LXX is hard to maintain, cf. SH. JOHNSON, *Harv. Theol. Rev.* 36 (1943), p. 146.

somewhat fewer survivals of Semitic form. For the most part we have allusions rather than quotations, and these clearly show dependence on the LXX (Mt. 115, 2438).[1] Only with hesitation could we trace greater similarity to the M.T. in Matthew's form of the allusion to Micah 7 (Mt. 1035).[2] We found strict quotations only in the passage on the temptation.[3] These were purely LXX, but on one point we found how Matthew and Luke adapted the quotation to the context in the same manner (Mt. 410, Lk. 48). One quotation was somewhat longer in Matthew (44, Lk. 44), another in Luke (410, Mt. 46), but in both cases the longer text was LXX. This was similarly the case with Luke's longer text in the testimony taken over into Lk. 34.[4]

Whether one regards the quotation from Malachi in Mk. 12 as an interpolation or not, this quotation must be included in the Q material, Mt. 1110, Lk. 727.[5] When Matthew and Luke insert this quotation into the same context it cannot be explained simply by the occurrence of the quotation in Mark, where the context is quite a different one and the quotation slightly shorter. It is a quotation with a Christian adaptation, and we have found reason to take the view that it was given its form in a Semitic milieu. In this form it made its way into Q.

The matter peculiar to Luke gives an even stronger LXX impression, though it chiefly consists of allusions. This impression is disturbed in a manner that at first seems surprising, by the two strict quotations in this material, 418 f. and 2237.[6] The first of these, however, was obviously LXX in spite of minor agreement with the M.T. which may depend on a tendency towards homophony within Luke. In the latter case we have found reason to assume Christian interpretations of Is. 53, which not least have influenced the passion story.

Thus we find that not only the material peculiar to Luke but also that common to both Luke and Matthew is of the same nature as the Mark quotations, though with somewhat greater fidelity to the LXX in the cases of the strict quotations in the passage on the temptation.

---

[1] See above, p. 91 and 94.

[2] See above, p. 90 f.

[3] See above, p. 88 f.

[4] See above, p. 49.

[5] This text to BACON, *op. cit.*, p. 472, proves the Semitic basis of the quotations in Q, cf. SH. JOHNSON, *op. cit.*, p. 144. Bacon extends his suggestion to Mt. 723, 1242 and the reading of cod. D in Mt. 47.

[6] See above, p. 94 ff.

The Q and other material common to Matthew and Luke have thus been formed in a consciously LXX milieu and the small variations which occur do not point to a direct influence from a consistent tradition of Semitic quotations.

One would rather expect the Q material to contain more survivals of quotations from Semitic writings than any other material, this already from a more general point of view, but especially if one equates Q and Papias's Semitic Matthew document.[1] Nevertheless, the case is just the reverse, so that precisely those quotations which consist of the words of Jesus are most clearly LXX in their nature.

Material peculiar to Matthew.

If it were the case that the quotations in Matthew which had parallels in Mark or in both Mark and Luke agreed between themselves and with the LXX, but that the rest showed striking deviations from the LXX or even no acquaintance with Greek translations of the O.T., we should get a clear picture of Matthew's quotation technique and the growth of the gospel. Such is not the case, however, on two scores. Firstly, the Matthew formula quotations show familiarity with the LXX in a manner which makes it necessary to assume a LXX interpretation for the form of these quotations; and secondly, Matthew's peculiar material contains other quotations of pure LXX type. Mt. 21 16 (Ps. 8 3) is dependent upon its LXX form for being useful and at the same time it occurs in a context where the evangelist himself gave the material its shape.[2] Unfortunately it is the only quotation within HAWKINS's fifth group (Quotations occurring in course of the double or triple narrative, but not themselves recorded by either Mark or Luke), which allowed of any conclusion. We found reason to deny Matthew himself 13 14 f., as well as the purely LXX verse in 12 40. Even so the LXX feature in the formula quotations renders it impossible to exonerate Matthew from use of the LXX Bible. The genealogy of Jesus is likewise LXX in the forms of the names and the allusions in Mt. 1–2 give proof of a dependence upon the LXX which goes beyond the bounds of fortuitous agreement.[3] Similarly Matthew's adaptation of Mark's quotations to a closer agreement with the LXX points in the same direction. Not only the material he has taken over, but also Matthew's own material gives

---

[1] Cf. below, p. 209.

[2] See above, p. 135.

[3] Cf. above, p. 136.

evidence of a church milieu familiar with the LXX as the workshop where Matthew took shape. Thus, quite naturally, it is not least in the Psalm texts familiar through the liturgy that the LXX text occurs in its best and purest state.

Hawkins's statistics suggested a remarkable boundary between the Matthew formula quotations and other quotations in Matthew. Our detailed study has confirmed and elaborated this impression. But the lack of resemblance to the LXX in formula quotations, which is the only factor Hawkins takes note of, did not always imply a greater verbal agreement with the M.T. In all cases we could suppose a knowledge of the Hebrew text, but in its interpretation Matthew shows great freedom and a tendency to make use of readings which we could often support by examples from various LXX manuscripts, the later Greek versions, the Targums and even the O.T. Peshitta. In certain cases the quotations would not have made sense in LXX form — just as those in 15 8f. and 21 16 were dependent on this form for their function. Such was the case in 2 15, 4 15f., 8 17, 27 9. In other cases the interpretation of the LXX would have been satisfactory: 1 23, 2 6, 2 18, 12 18–21, 13 35, and 21 5.

That being so, one cannot presume that Matthew intended to follow the LXX. As the method of quoting in the formula quotations is not characteristic of the material peculiar to Matthew in its entirety, there must be some connection between the nature of formula quotations as such, and the remarkable freedom in citing, a freedom which seemingly contrasts with the explicit reference to the word of prophecy.

If such is the case, this quotation technique should constitute a significant feature of Matthew. For its quotations cannot be consigned to a special source inserted into Matthew's gospel,[1] but, as a striking feature in the composition of the gospel, they may be considered a key to the character and milieu of the gospel.

The quotations and Matthew as a consistent Aramaic unity.

It may be quite unnecessary to linger at such length over the meaning of the quotations for the synoptic problem when our result corroborates what has for long been the most generally accepted view. This may seem the more unnecessary as the quotations scarcely give any clear verdict on those points on which the two-document hypothesis is least clear, *viz.* with reference to Q's character and compass.[2]

---

[1] So *e.g.* BACON and KILPATRICK, see below, p. 204 f.

[2] Cf. SH. JOHNSON, *op. cit.*, p. 144–48.

Nevertheless, the quotation material does constitute an essential link in reasoning amongst certain scholars who maintain the view that Matthew is a Greek translation from a consistent Aramaic gospel. This is so in the studies of ZAHN, LAGRANGE, and TORREY.[1] The instances in which Matthew agrees with the M.T. as against the LXX invite such reasoning. The complexity of Matthew's quoting undeniably welcomes a third factor. In supposing an Aramaic Matthew, it is possible to refer to the M.T., of which Matthew's rendering in Aramaic was connected to a greater or a lesser degree with the Targums, but also to the Greek translator's attempt to render his original. To this add the translator's familiarity with both the LXX and Mark's Greek text, and the chances of explaining obvious agreements and deviations will be considerably increased.[2] The differences in the type of quotation in the First Gospel are thus placed to the translator's account, and the quotation material loses its meaning so far as the question of composition is concerned.

TORREY holds a special position. He wishes to prove that the Aramaic Matthew has had its O.T. quotations in Hebrew, but in a revised, and often rhythmical, form, which the translator renders literally.[3] Torrey's retroversion of Matthew's text to Hebrew, however, is scarcely supported by a single case in which this hypothesis yields a striking explanation

---

[1] B. C. BUTLER, *The Originality of St. Matthew. A Critique of the Two-Document Hypothesis* (1951), does not treat the O.T. quotations. — To A. SCHLATTER, who also maintained the originality of the First Gospel, the quotations are not felt as a problem due to his concept of the gospel's bilingual character, *Der Evangelist Matthäus* (1929), *e.g.* p. ix. — R. ANGER, Ratio qua loci Veteris Testamenti in evangelio Matthaei laudantur, quid valeat ad illustrandum huius evangelii originem I–III, *Leipziger Programme* 1861–1862, who made one of the most detailed studies in the Matthaean quotations, does not relate the LXX and the "Semitic" quotations to distinct groups as did *e.g.* Bleek (see below) and Hawkins. He minimizes the differences between the two types by emphasizing the quoting from memory and the looseness even in the LXX quotations. This he does in order to claim the originally Greek unity of the First Gospel, where sometimes the LXX wording was touched up by direct translation of the Hebrew O.T.

[2] LAGRANGE, *Comm. Mt.*, p. cxxiii: "S'il composait en araméen, il n'était lié ni par le texte hébreu, ni par le texte grec". If so, one might however expect more affinity to the readings of the Targums in the Matthaean quotations from the O.T.

[3] There were, however, some mistranslations as in 27 9–10, TORREY, *Documents of the Primitive Church*, p. 86 f, and the "unfortunate specimen of translation Greek" in 21 9 comes close to a misunderstanding, *ibm.*, p. 78.

of Matthew's text form.[1] Nevertheless, it gives valuable insight into Matthew's method in formula quotations.[2]

ZAHN's argument for the quotations as support for an Aramaic Matthew is found in a criticism of an earlier grouping of his quotations.[3] F. BLEEK had made a distinction between A) Pragmatic quotations, dependent on the Hebrew text, and B) Quotations on the lips of Jesus or others, taking over the LXX material available in Mark and elsewhere in tradition.[4] By contrast Zahn maintains that 11 10 and 26 31, and certain transcriptions of proper names, reveal independence from the LXX[5], and that 11 29 and the order of the commandments in 19 18 f. suppose reference to Hebrew or Aramaic texts though they all belong to group B.[6] On the other hand, the transfer from the LXX is clear in 1 23 and 3 3[7] of the group A. That Zahn does not find greater influence from the LXX in the "pragmatic" quotations depends on the fact that he starts from the LXX^B and regards codex A's text as generally corrected according to the N.T.[8] Holding this view, he also makes still wider the gap between the LXX and Mt. 26 31, for instance.

---

[1] SH. JOHNSON's article in *Harv. Theol. Rev.* 36 (1943), p. 135–53, to which we have referred so often, is written as a (balanced) critique of Torrey's hypothesis.

[2] See above, especially in relation to Mt. 27 9–10, p. 125.

[3] ZAHN, *Einleitung* II[1], p. 314 and 319 f. (cf. 3rd edition, p. 308 f. and 321 f.).

[4] F. BLEEK, *Beiträge zur Evangelien-Kritik* (1846), p. 57 f. Bleek classifies the quotations in Matthew in order to get an argument in his critique of J. H. A. EBRARD, who had vindicated a consistent Aramaic Matthew (*Wissenschaftliche Kritik der evangelischen Geschichte*, 1842, on the quotations, see p. 927 f.). Bleek's groups: A: "solche (Citate), wo der Evangelist pragmatische Nachweisungen über die Erfüllung alttestamentlicher Aussprüche in den von ihm dargestellten Verhältnissen und Erreignissen gibt, wie Kap. 1 23, 2 6, 15, 18, 4 15 f., 8 17, 12 18–21, 13 35, 21 5, (27 9)." — B: "solche, wo im Laufe der Erzählung in Reden der auftretenden Personen gelegentlich Stellen des Alten Testaments angeführt oder benutzt werden."

In the 3rd edition of his work, which Bleek had criticized, EBRARD answered, p. 999–1002. His arguments are the same as those we later meet from Zahn, cf. K. A. CREDNER, *Beiträge zur Einleitung in die biblischen Schriften* II, *Das alttestamentliche Urevangelium* (1838), e.g. p. 312–17.

[5] See above, p. 136.

[6] See above, p. 141 and 62.

[7] ZAHN, *Einleitung* II[1], p. 319. As against Zahn, we have classified this "formula quotation" among the common synoptic material, cf. above, p. 47, note 2. So did also BLEEK though his distinction was misleading. By referring to the parallel in Jn. 1 23 he argued that this quotation was the Baptist's statement on his mission. It was not added by the evangelist and thus it belonged to his group B, *op. cit.*, p. 168 f.

[8] See below, p. 169.

Applied to the more developed form of the grouping of quotations which we made use of, Zahn's criticism only implies that features of the LXX are not lacking in the formula quotations, and that Mt. 11 29 shows dependence upon the Hebrew text, while Mt. 11 10 remains as a specially coined testimony, which, like 26 31, may go back to an earlier stratum in the theology of the primitive church.

As Zahn's exposition took the form of a discussion with Bleek, so LAGRANGE's study consists of an examination of the implications of HAWKINS's statistics.[1] Lagrange's grouping of the quotation types most closely follows Hawkins. He emphasizes the marks of the Hebrew text in 22 24 (ἐπιγαμβρεύσει) and 22 37 (the *shema*), as in the cases mentioned by Zahn (11 10, 26 31) in which this Hebrew trait was found also in Mark. The two texts in Mt. 22 show revision of the terminology of Mark to make it agree more closely with the Hebrew terms; 22 24 is furthermore, as we have seen, an allusive reference. This rather confirms the assumption that Matthew took over Mark's quotations.

Lagrange emphasizes more strongly than Zahn the LXX's significance for Matthew in its entirety. When there was no question about the meaning of the original, the translator simply used the LXX which was his reader's Bible. He did so even where he retained in details the meaning of the Aramaic (and consequently of the Hebrew) text. His intention was, however, not so much to make use of this sacrosanct translation as to give the texts in the form in which the church knew them. For this he first and foremost used Mark's Greek form of the quotations.[2]

In two cases Lagrange is compelled to a forced reasoning. On one point he thinks that Mark — which for him is originally a Greek Gospel — is dependent upon (the Greek) Matthew[3]: Mk. 14 27 (Mt. 26 31), accord-

---

[1] LAGRANGE, *Comm. Mt.*, p. cxvii–cxxii.

[2] Cf. ZAHN, *Einleitung* II[2], p. 322: The translator knew the LXX. Where its text was familiar to him from the teaching and preaching of the church, he used it when suitable to his Aramaic original. Otherwise he gave his own translation. He also left the LXX wording "wo er wegen mangelnder oder undeutlicher oder fehlerhafter Quellenangabe die citierte Stelle nicht leicht hätte auffinden können, auch wenn er sie aufgesucht hätte". — On this last principle, cf. BACON, *op. cit.*, p. 472: It is in such obscure passages the Semitic remnants are retained, *e.g.* the quotation from Malachi in Mt. 11 10 with parallels.

[3] Otherwise LAGRANGE was a pioneer in Catholic exegetics for Mark's independence of Matthew, *Comm. Mk.*, p. xl, the view now accepted by most Catholic scholars, see A. WIKENHAUSER, *Einleitung in das Neue Testament* (1953), p. 142.

ing to Lagrange, the only place where Mark shows dependence upon the Hebrew text;[1] but as this is a common tendency in Matthew, Lagrange supposes that the quotation took on this form in Matthew and in this form it crept later into Mark.[2] This demands the Greek text of Mark, which usually influenced the Greek translator of Matthew, to have been corrected at a *later* stage according to Matthew's Greek wording. This creates a vicious circle; the more so, as the function of the quotation necessitates the form it now has. What, then, was found in Mark before this transfer from Matthew had taken place? Rather must we resort to the explanation Lagrange advances as the less probable, that both Mark and Matthew have taken the quotation from a common source.

The greatest obstacle to an original Aramaic Matthew — as far as the quotations are concerned — is, however, the LXX form of the Isaiah quotation in Mt. 15 8f. Only in the LXX form has this quotation any meaning for Mark and Matthew. Lagrange refutes Zahn's attempt at evasion[3] and says: "Comme le Matthieu araméen n'a pas dû offrir ce texte, il faut donc supposer ou qu'un écrivain grec a écrit d'après Mc. ou Mc. d'après lui, ou bien que le traducteur grec de l'araméen a traduit très largement en se rapprochant de Mc."[4]

This explanation is of fundamental interest since it gives an example of Lagrange's interpretation of the synoptic problem. When expounding his view on these matters, he emphasizes that it is in agreement with the principles of the Vatican Bible Commission to consider the Greek Matthew not only as a translation but as an enlarged Greek edition of the Aramaic Matthew.[5] This view which is creeping into Catholic exegetics, partly under cover of Lagrange's authority, has led scholars to still greater agreement with Protestant research,[6] in a man-

---

[1] The similar case in Mk. 1 2 is considered a gloss by LAGRANGE, *Comm. Mt.*, p. cxxii.

[2] LAGRANGE, *loc. cit.* and *ibm.*, p. 499. In his *Comm. Mk.*, p. 383, the quotation is treated merely as a word of Jesus and the text of LXX^A is given as support of the N.T. text. In *Comm. Mt.* the LXX^A is considered a Christian correction.

[3] ZAHN, *Einleitung* II^1, p. 317, cf. above, p. 58 and TORREY, *Documents*, p. 70f.

[4] LAGRANGE, *Comm. Mt.*, p. cxx, cf. above (about Mt. 21 16), p. 134.

[5] LAGRANGE, *Comm. Mt.*, p. xxxiv.

[6] LAGRANGE, *Comm. Mt.*, p. xli on the "catéchèse à Jérusalem". This new line of Catholic scholarship has been followed by *e.g.* P. BENOIT in his *L'évangile selon Saint Matthieu* (1950), see especially p. 27, cf. A. VAGANAY, La question synoptique, *Ephemer. Theol. Lovan.* 28 (1952), p. 238–56.

ner which is not without significance for our problem. A. WIKENHAUSER thus considers as sources of the Greek Matthew the Greek Mark and a Q, that is, the Aramaic Matthew — not consisting exclusively of *logia*, but impossible to define more exactly in its compass. To him the very quotations in Matthew, being of different types, constitute a decisive argument against the original unity of Matthew.[1]

We are certainly right, therefore, in considering Lagrange's admission with regard to Mt. 15 8 as an argument untenable in the long run. It cannot preserve the thesis of an originally Aramaic Matthew — at least not in its classical form.

The dependence upon Mark and the LXX cannot be placed to the translator's account, nor can the striking demarcation between formula quotations and the other quotations be explained on this hypothesis. As we have seen, the LXX text should have been suitable in many cases where it was not made use of, and in 15 8f. it is unadvisable to detach the passage from its LXX quotation. Neither may we assume the formula quotations to be unknown or impossible to identify. In any case this would not explain the independence of the LXX in Is. 42 1ff. as in Mt. 12 18 ff.

---

[1] *Einleitung*, p. 141, cf. p. 182 on Q = the Aramaic Matthew. Wikenhauser, differing from Benoit, does not suppose any material peculiar to Matthew.

Quotations in different types of New Testament text

How did one quote? Did one know the texts by heart? Did this take place in so far as it concerned the Hebrew text, but not the Greek? Did one look up — or to be more exact — did one unroll the manuscript to check the passage in question? Has the transition of Christian literature to the codex type anything to do with the practice of quoting?[1] We are rather badly informed on these matters. We have to look for the answers by inference from the actual texts[2] in the light of the earliest manuscripts and of iconographic data.[3]

In classical authors one finds a deliberate freedom in quoting, a kind of poetic licence which seems to have been the sign of mastery in the treatment of the material.[4] We have seen tendencies in this direction in

---

[1] On the change from rolls to codices and its implications, see C. C. McCown, *Harv. Theol. Rev.* 34 (1941), p. 219–250, C. H. Roberts, *Journ. of Theol. St.* 50 (1949), p. 155–168, cf. P. Katz, *ibm.* 46 (1945), p. 63–65, and S. Lieberman, *Hellenism in Jewish Palestine* (1950), p. 203–208.

[2] R. Gordis, Quotations as a Literary Usage in Biblical, Oriental and Rabbinic Literature, *Hebr. Union Coll. Ann.* 22 (1949) p. 157–219. L. Blau, *Studien zum althebräischen Buchwesen* (1902), p. 85f., on private ownership of biblical texts, and so also Harnack, *Über den privaten Gebrauch der heiligen Schriften in der alten Kirche* (1912), p. 21 ff., both for Jews and Christians. — In the rabbinic literature V. Aptowitzer accords the quoting from memory little importance, Das Schriftwort in der rabbinischen Literatur, *Sitzungsber. Akad. Wien*, Phil. Hist. Kl. 153:6 (1906), p. 23 and 26, cf. G. Aicher, *Das Alte Testament in der Mischna* (1906), p. 63 ff. — W. Sanday, Conditions under which the Gospels were written, in *Oxford Studies in the Synoptic Problem* (ed. W. Sanday, 1911), p. 18, referring to literary sources of the gospels: "He (the evangelist) would not have his copy before him, but would consult it from time to time".

[3] For archaeological and iconographic material, see R. Vielliard, Codices et Volumina dans les Bibliothèques juives et chrétiennes. Notes d'iconographie, *Rivista di Archaeologia Cristiana* 17 (1940), p. 143–148, C. Wendel, *Die Griechischrömische Buchbeschreibung verglichen mit der des Vorderen Orients* (1949), F. G. Kenyon, *Books and Readers in Ancient Greece and Rome* (1951²), Th. Birt, *Die Buchrolle in der Kunst* (1907).

[4] On this tendency in speeches which are incorporated in historical accounts, see M. Dibelius, Die Reden der Apostelgeschichte und die antike Geschichtsschreibung, *Sitzungsber. Akad. Heidelb.* Phil. Hist. Kl. 1949/50:1, p. 5 f. = idem, *Aufsätze zur Apostelgeschichte*, p. 120 f.

Luke. In a Jewish milieu where the translation has entered as an inter-mediate stage we may find a statement like that of Rabbi Yehuda: "Whoever translates verbally a verse of the Bible is a falsifier, whoever adds anything, is a blasphemer".[1] This, however, has quite another background than the stylistic one. It is based on the Jewish interest in maintaining a sufficiently wide gulf between the most sacred text of Hebrew Scripture and the Aramaic Targums.

Most of the quotations in the gospels have given us the impression of a conscious desire to reproduce the LXX text correctly. This is also the impression made by the N.T. in general. It gives us reason not to resort to the explanation of "free quoting from memory" as soon as any dif-ferences appear[2], especially when face to face with Matthew's formula quotations, which, contrary to what one would expect, show remarkable deviations, not only from the LXX, but from every Semitic or Greek O.T. text known to us. It is equally erroneous to consider the exact ci-tation — often given the derogatory appellation "atomistic" — as foreign to primitive Christianity.[3]

The degree to which a quotation is exactly cited cannot be deter-mined in a general statement consistent to the whole of the N.T.[4] We have already established that texts of apocalyptic nature seldom con-tain quotations in the strict sense, while at the same time, it is just these texts which are abounding in allusions which with supreme freedom and skill have been woven into the context. Revelation is itself a striking

---

[1] *Tosephta Megillah* 3₂₁, see J. L. SEELIGMANN, *Jaarber. Ex Oriente Lux* 7 (1940), p. 359.

[2] The warning against such an evasive attitude is especially emphatic in A. BAUMSTARK, *Zeitschr. d. Deutsch. Morgenl. Gesellsch.* 89 (1935), p. 114, cf. SPERBER, *Journ. of Bibl. Lit.* 59 (1940), p. 193.

[3] So H. W. WOLFF, *Jesaja 53 im Urchristentum*, p. 132 f., cf. KATZ, *Theol. Zeitschr.* 5 (1949), p. 17: "Soweit ich sehe, treten hier (in the N.T. quotations) völlig neue Momente auf, die in der ausgeprägt anti-biblizistischen Haltung des Ignatius gipfeln: hie Geist des Herrn und Prophezei, dort Buchstabendienst und Zitat-brauch". Katz may be thinking of *e.g.* Ign. Philad. 8. For the discussion of its im-plications see J. KLEVINGHAUS, *Die theologische Stellung der Apostolischen Väter zur alttestamentlichen Offenbarung* (1948), p. 98–102, and TH. CAMELOT, ed. *Igna-tius* (1951), p. 148 f.

[4] An illuminating parallel to the different methods of quoting the O.T. is given by a comparison of *Justin*'s First Apology with his Dialogue. In the former the quotations are more free than in the latter, where a more "scholarly approach" is apparent also in other respects. See K. A. CREDNER, *Beiträge zur Einleitung in die biblischen Schriften* II (1838), p. 337 f., and HOMMES, *Het Testimoniaboek*, p. 114.

example of this. Without a single true quotation, it is nevertheless interwoven with O.T. material to a greater extent than any other writing in
the N.T.[1] In the apocalypses of the gospels, as in their sayings of apocalyptic nature, we have found the same phenomenon. Consequently,
there is no attempt to quote exactly in this form, and the citing is certainly freely given from memory. The prophetic spirit creates, it does
not quote in order to teach or argue.

It is not surprising to find a close parallel to this type of allusion in
the biblical hymns, *e.g.* in Lk. 1–2, as well as in the hymns of the Qumran
Sect (DST and DSD). The hymn of Zechariah, for example, is introduced as a prophecy "in the Spirit", Lk. 1 67. These hymns do not yield
anything which can be compared exactly with O.T. texts.

Of the 78 quotations in Paul's epistles, more than a half give the exact
text of the LXX and the majority of the others are also of LXX type,
even where the LXX deviates considerably from the M.T. There are
coincidences with other Greek translations, and differences of both an
intentional and an accidental nature. In a few cases the text is influenced
by the Hebrew. On the whole, however, the Pauline material gives the
impression of an author quoting from memory, yet a memory which
was the storehouse of more than one language, and one trained in Jewish
methods of bringing together passages from different books of the O.T.[2]

In Paul the quotations from one book of the O.T. show a consistent
tendency to coincide with one type of LXX text. In Isaiah, Paul is close
to the LXX^A, in Leviticus to LXX^F and in Job he goes his own way,
or follows a translation not known to us.[3] On the other hand, there is
no difference in type of O.T. text in the letters written from different
cities.[4] T. W. MANSON intimates that the two traces of Theodotion's
interpretation, which we find in 1 Cor. 15 54 and in Jn. 19 37, might point
to the fact that Paul here made use of the O.T. text which was found in
Ephesus, the home town of both Theodotion and John, the evangelist,

---

[1] Moreover the quotations in Revelation are influenced by the Hebrew text,
CHARLES, *Comm. Rev.* I, p. lxvi, cf. lxviii–lxxxvi and xliv; SCHLATTER, *Das Alte
Testament in der johanneischen Apokalypse* (1912), with the reference to a *hag-
gadah* type in the use of the O.T. as against the *halakah*.

[2] See below, p. 216, and SWETE, *Introduction*, p. 392, L. VENARD, *Dictionnaire
de la Bible*, Suppl. II, col. 34–36, VOLLMER, *Die Alttestamentlichen Citate bei Paulus,*
especially p. 35 and 48, O. MICHEL, *Paulus und seine Bibel* (1929), p. 66–68.

[3] VOLLMER, *op. cit.*, p. 48, and below, p. 173.

[4] The Pauline Epistles of the captivity lack quotations except 5 in Ephe-
sians.

and the place from which Paul sent his First Epistle to Corinth.[1] We have also found such traces of Theodotion's text in Matthew, however. This must mean that the text which Theodotion proceeded from when carrying out his work of revision was just as well represented in Palestine as in Ephesus, and that Paul became acquainted with it already at the time of his studies under Gamaliel.[2] The rendering of the text to Job points in the same direction. All these observations reinforce the view that Paul quotes from memory.

Also in the General Epistles the quoting is LXX, though somewhat more often penetrated by influence from the Hebrew text. This is natural if we presume oral quotations here, with somewhat greater geographical and theological proximity to Palestinian Christian tradition. On the other hand we scarcely find any agreements with the later Greek versions.[3]

In most of the Epistles it is natural to suppose a more or less free quoting from memory. The very nature of the Epistles, that they were written for special occasions, speaks for this, even though to different degrees. It is also natural that we come across another picture when we reach the Epistle to the Hebrews. Here we find a thorough fidelity to the LXX, and its long quotations are often in literal agreement with the Greek biblical text, though a trace of the Hebrew text is not entirely lacking.[4] That occurs rather in allusions than in strict quotations, however, which only strengthens the impression of a desire to quote exactly according to the LXX.[5] This desire to quote exactly is related to the character of the letter as an *argumentum e scriptura*. Most of the adaptations which occur are deliberate, but also citations which give the im-

---

[1] *Dominican Studies* 2 (1949), p. 187. Favourable to Manson is the fact that the fragments now found of a Palestinian LXX are less in accord with Theodotion than with Aquila and Symmachus, see BARTHÉLEMY, *Rev. Bibl.* 60 (1953), p. 26.

[2] In the School of Gamaliel some of the pupils seem to have carried out their studies in Greek, *b Sotah* 49b, see W. L. KNOX, *Some Hellenistic Elements in Primitive Christianity* (1944), p. 30.

[3] Cf. above to Mt. 21 42, p. 67 ff. — In addition to DITTMAR, and the articles of VENARD and WOODS, see HÜHN, *Die alttest. Citate*, p. 118–143, cf. *ibm.*, p. 278 ff.

[4] 10 30, cf. Rom. 12 19, probably a well-known Greek wording, and Heb. 2 12, 13 and 10 17.

[5] C. SPICQ, *Comm. Hebr.* I, p. 334–336, denies any influence from the Hebrew text. G. HARDER, Die Septuagintazitate des Hebräerbriefs, *Theologia Viatorum* (1939), p. 33–52, shows that in many cases the LXX form is necessary for the function of the quotation in Hebrews. The form of Hab. 2 4 in Heb. 10 38 is due to an inner-Greek process, cf. below, p. 202, note 1.

pression of looser quotations from memory occur; this is clear from a comparison of the quotations from Jer. 31 33 f. in Heb. 8 11 f. and 10 16 f.

So far as Acts is concerned[1], where all quotations except that in 8 32 f. are included in the speeches, the LXX type is striking even in the material which is most often considered to offer the clearest N.T. examples of translation from the Aramaic. There is a slight influence from Semitic tradition to be found in the speech of Stephen, an influence with affinity to the Samaritan Pentateuch.[2] It is highly significant that one quotation in Hebrews also shows acquaintance with the traditions preserved in this text, as does the Book of Jubilees.[3] But in all the quotations in the first part of Acts the line of thought is nowhere dependent upon the Hebrew text, while in certain cases it presupposes the LXX text.[4] These quotations further seem to be of the type which presume a longer O.T. context than that given in Acts.[5] These texts, as those in Hebrews, give the impression that the author, or the Greek tradition on which he was drawing, intended to quote literally.[6]

Apart from the formula quotations and the manner in which Luke in-

---

[1] The quotations in Acts have been studied in detail by L. CERFAUX, Citations scripturaires et tradition textuelle dans le Livre des Actes, in *Aux sources de la tradition chrétienne, Mélanges offerts à M. Goguel* (1950), p. 43–51, and by J. DUPONT, L'utilisation apologétique de l'Ancien Testament dans les discours des Actes, *Ephemer. Theol. Lovan.* 29 (1953), p. 289–327.

[2] Observed by H. HAMMER, *Traktat vom Samaritaner-Messias* (1913), cf. KAHLE, *Theol. St. u. Krit.* 88 (1915), p. 399–402 and IDEM, *The Cairo Geniza*, p. 144. — On the coincidence with the Samaritan Pentateuch in Acts 7 4, cf. S. CARLSON, *Aggadastoff i Nya Testamentets skrifter* (1920), p. 102–105 where the similarities are explained by rabbinic material. On Acts 7 32, see above, p. 71 f.

[3] According to Heb. 9 3 f. the altar of incense was placed in the Holy of Holies, a concept which the Samaritan Pentateuch Ex. 26 35, 30 1 ff., easily evoked. This type of O.T. text common to the speech of Stephen and to Hebrews favours W. MANSON's view on a close relation between these two N.T. documents, *The Epistle to the Hebrews* (1951), p. 25 ff. — On the O.T. quotations in the Book of Jubilees, see below, p. 195, note 2.

[4] DUPONT, *op. cit.*, p. 317. The combined quotation from Jeremiah and Amos in Acts 15 16 ff. adheres clearly to the LXX even where it is furthest from the Hebrew text. This "is significant, especially when it is remembered that the speaker is St. James of Jerusalem", SWETE, *Introduction*, p. 399. Also in the Epistle of James the quotations are in accordance with the LXX.

[5] DUPONT, *op. cit.*, p. 315 f., cf. above, p. 110.

[6] W. K. L. CLARKE, in *The Beginnings of Christianity* II, p. 84–95, takes over SWETE's classification of the synoptic material (*Introduction*, p. 394) as also appropriate for Acts, but this does not seem to be in accordance with the intentions of Swete, see *ibm.*, p. 398 f.

serts his O.T. material into his gospel, the same intention is quite evident
in the Synoptics. This is not to say that there are no quotations from
memory, but the tendency in Matthew and Luke to conform Mark's text
to the LXX yields the final visible examples of a process which on the
whole was completed when the traditions were incorporated into the
gospels. There the conditions are different from those in the Epistles,
which took their form from the outset and retained it on the authority
of their virtual or supposed author. In the gospel material we are faced
with a literature which developed in the actual life of the church. This
process of making the quotations conform to the LXX was a very early
one, as can be seen from the fact that it is in the words of Jesus that we
find the LXX character to be most consistent[1], and it is hardly challenged by substantial variants in the manuscripts. This Greek Jesus
tradition does not need to be understood as a translation in the ordinary
sense. The spread of Greek even within Palestine and in Jerusalem renders it natural that the Jesus tradition took shape along parallel lines in
Aramaic and in Greek. Considering this character of the synoptic gospels
from the point of view of quotations, it must be considered a loose and
evasive manner of explaining the deviations in Matthew's formula quotations to say it is due to mere freedom combined with a knowledge of
the Hebrew text.

So far we have not dealt with the O.T. text in the Fourth Gospel except when it used the same passages as Matthew (see Mt. 11 10, 13 13–15,
21 5 and the addition in 27 35).[2] In none of these cases was there a sign of
a common source to their quotations, though the interpretation of Is.
40 3 was the same in both gospels. It is in the Fourth Gospel that we find
the greatest resemblance to Matthew's typical formula quotations. Moreover, this gospel gives in explicit terms a description of how these citations were attached to the words and works of Jesus. After having quoted
the prophecy in Zechariah on the entry upon an ass, John adds "This his
disciples did not understand at first, but when Jesus was glorified, then
they remembered how this had been written of him and how it had happened to him", 12 16, cf. 2 22. In 5 39–47 the theological basis for the Christian interpretation of the O.T. is given in equally explicit words. It
starts with the saying to the scribes "you search the Scriptures, imag-

---

[1] Cf. J. A. FINDLAY, in *Amicitiae Corolla*, p. 69.

[2] The quotations in the Fourth Gospel were studied in detail by A. H. FRANKE,
Das alte Testament bei Johannes (1885), especially p. 255–293. He emphasizes the
deviations from the LXX, particularly in the allusions, p. 287 ff.

ining to have eternal life in them" and passes on to the verdict that the Jewish interpretation leads astray: "If you believed Moses, you would believe me, since it was of me that he wrote". There is another explicit passage on this to be found in Luke, in the well-known dialogue on the way to Emmaus, 24₄₄.

There are six formula quotations explicitly introduced by the evangelist himself in the Fourth Gospel, 12₁₅, 12₃₈, 12₄₀, 19₂₄, 19₃₆, 19₃₇, all but the first introduced by the term πληροῦσθαι and this word is also used by Jesus himself in 13₁₈ and 15₂₅. Jn. 2₁₇, again in the words of Jesus, is akin to this material in character, as may be seen by the comment in 2₂₂.

Considering the text of these and other quotations in John, there are, however, quite other conditions in John than in Matthew. The distinction between the formula quotations and the remainder is not as sharp, though the greatest deviations from the LXX are found in 12₄₀, 19₃₇ and the related 13₁₈. Except for the last case, the quotations from the Psalms are in the form of the LXX, as is the phrase from Is. 53₁ in 12₃₈. On the whole John's way of quoting the O.T. is consistent in its inconsistency. He is not dependent on a tradition where the words of Jesus were conformed to the LXX — as far as the distinction between the words of Jesus in the proper sense and the words of the evangelist can be maintained in this gospel. As in Revelation he seems to work on his own, showing acquaintance with the Hebrew text as well as with the LXX. This is exactly what might be expected in a gospel which developed in the School of St. John[1], a school where the Scriptures were studied and meditated upon in the light of the preaching, teaching and debating in which the church was involved. Compared with the formula quotations of Matthew, those in the Fourth Gospel are less elaborate; but the Ephesian school possessed and used the authority to produce a translation of their own. To them this was more natural than the use of the text of the LXX in which the synoptic tradition took refuge as a matter of course. Thus the Johannine method is not what is usually meant by loose citations, or those more or less freely quoted from memory. It is rather the opposite since the form of John's quotations is certainly the fruit of scholarly treatment of written O.T. texts.

The intention to quote literally, and the practice of checking the text with the Greek text available may be taken for granted in the synoptic

---

[1] See above, p. 31.

material. The deviations in Luke are due to his desire to write good literature. The deviations from the LXX, the acquaintance with the Hebrew
text as well as the divergences from it in Matthew and John, do not lessen their relation to the O.T. texts proper.[1] They show that they were
real students in this field. This leads us to the much debated question of
what these texts looked like in the first century A.D.

First, however, we must ask how stable is the N.T. text in the quotations? The editions of NESTLE are surprisingly sparing with variants, for
such certainly occur, especially in cod. D.[2] To a great extent they depend
merely on parallel influence in the gospels. On the other hand, at the
stage of which the variants give evidence, the N.T. does not appear to
have been the object of many corrections to greater agreement with the
LXX. The text had sufficient internal authority to withstand this tendency.[3] What happened in this respect at the oldest stage eludes our

---

[1] K. W. CLARK, *Journ. of Bibl. Lit.* 66 (1947), p. 168 f., denies emphatically
the possiblity of arguing about these O.T. texts, since our knowledge of them is
insufficient. This he does in order to state that "the scriptural quotations
employed in Matthew point neither to any use of the Hebrew text nor to a
Jewish author". In the next chapter we will try to show that the O.T. texts
known to us afford sufficient material for a rather detailed comparison between
Matthew and the O.T.

[2] The value of cod. D is strongly championed by M. BLACK, *An Aramaic Approach*, p. 5–6, 25–31, partly following up the lines of A. J. WENSINCK, cf. *Journ.
of Theol. St.* 49 (1948), p. 157–165. Black refutes both the view of F. H. CHASE,
The Syro-Latin Text of the Gospels (1895), on D as a syriacized text and that of
LAGRANGE, *Comm. Mk.*, p. lxxx viii and clxxv ff., on Latin influence in the bilingual
manuscripts. The latter view was held also by BAUMSTARK, *Zeitschr. d. Deutsch.
Morgenl. Gesellsch.* 89 (1935), p. 107, who was anxious to make the distinction between the significance of D in Luke-Acts and in Matthew and Mark. KAHLE,
The Cairo Geniza, p. 206, follows Wensinck. — For further discussion, see A. F. J.
KLIJN, *A Survey of the Researches into the Western Text of the Gospels and Acts*
(1949), p. 148–150 and 162–171. — As far as the quotations are concerned, the view
of Wensinck and others, who take the text of D to be closer to Aramaic tradition, must be counterbalanced by the tendency of the Western text to complete
the quotations in accordance with the LXX as in Lk. 3₂₂, cf. T. W. MANSON
Bull. of J. Ryl. Libr. 34 (1951/52), p. 324 f., and its obvious theological correction in
Mk. 15₃₄, see above, p. 85 f. Cf. CERFAUX, *op. cit.*, p. 45 on the theological intention
of D's longer text in Acts 13₃₃f. — BRANDON, *The Fall of Jerusalem*, p. 244–248,
who holds Matthew to be the gospel of Alexandria, tries to strengthen his hypothesis by criticizing STREETER's argument (in *The Four Gospels, passim*) for the
value of the Antiochian text (represented foremost by syr^sin), cf. above, p. 68
and 131 f.

[3] KAHLE, *op. cit.*, p. 165: "The quotations in the N.T. were not altered according

judgement. The quotations in the words of Jesus have early received their authority from Jesus himself, even so far as the Greek wording is concerned.

We have come across a striking example in Mt. 12 19 where both in position and form the remarkable ἐρίσει entirely lacked variants. The most striking variants are met naturally enough in the Hebrew form of the Eli Eli quotation. Even the Greek translation of the words on the Cross contained an important variant, by reason of the fact that the transliterated Hebrew/Aramaic text gave rise to intentional changes. The D text of Mt. 13 13 f. also deviated widely from the rest of the manuscripts, but this we considered an argument for an interpolated quotation in Matthew. The important variants in these special cases only strengthens the impression of the stability of the N.T. material in the rest of the quotation material.

---

to the later standard text of the O.T., the Septuagint, as quotations in Philo, Josephus and the Church fathers were. The authors of the writings of the N.T. had their own authority." — See also STAERK's tables "Verteilung der LXX-Lesarten auf die neutestamentlichen Textfamilien", *Zeitschr. f. wissensch. Theol.* 35 (1892), p. 475, 485. — 36:1 (1893), p. 84 f., 89. — 38 (1895), p. 230. — 40 (1897), p.237 f.

The Old Testament texts

The Hebrew text.

To what extent are we justified in making use of the M.T. as the Hebrew text with which the quotations in the N.T. should be compared? From the Matthew material we have scarcely found weighty reasons to consider Matthew as evidence of another Hebrew text tradition than that we find in the M.T. In Zech. 13₇ we saw how the commentators emended the M.T. in accordance with Mt. 26₃₁, but we found this emendation unwarranted and refuted by the text in the Damascus Document. DSIa, and to an even greater extent DSIb, provide us with good reasons for trusting the Massoretes. The deviations from the M.T. in DSH — and to some extent even in DSIa — do not generally justify their use in textual criticism in the current sense of the word. As we shall see[1], these variants are often of the same type as those examples we found in Matthew's quotations, whereby the Hebrew text has been read differently from the way it is understood by the M.T. (or by the LXX). Yet this does not mean that Matthew had a Hebrew text other than the M.T. His different reading should rather be understood as an *ad hoc* interpretation of the M.T.'s consonantal text. Not even the alleged variant אוצר, which the O.T. Peshitta and Matthew might give us reason to assume in Zech. 11₁₃, needs to be an actual reading. These and other translations could be taken as interpretations of the M.T.'s יוצר. We found a similar example of different interpretations of one and the same consonantal text in the quotation from Micah 5₁ (Mt. 2₆), with the M.T.'s אַלְפֵי and Matthew's אַלֻּפֵי, which was obviously an intentional change made by Matthew. The fact that the DSS material does not show any greater similarity to the LXX makes the Nash Papyrus stand out as a special case, when its text may be described as a text-form standing midway between the M.T. and the LXX.[2] Its form must be understood in the light of two facts: the liturgical or catechetical nature of the text, and its origin in Egypt.

---

[1] Below, p. 196 ff.

[2] W. F. ALBRIGHT, *Journ. of Bibl. Lit.* 56 (1937), p. 174–176, cf. above, p. 61 f.

We can therefore confidently assume that on the whole[1] the M.T. offers good material for comparison with the N.T.'s quotations to the extent to which they show acquaintance with or dependence upon the Hebrew text of the O.T.

The Aramaic text.

Of the Aramaic Targums, the Targums to the Prophets are of greatest interest to our study.[2] Without involving ourselves in the criteria for old Palestinian material in the Targums,[3] we have adopted the interpretations in the Targum which differ from the M.T. but agree with the N.T., and we dare make the assumption that we here have material relevant to N.T. times. A post-Christian influence or a development in the tradition of interpretation along messianic lines akin to Christian interpretation is scarcely credible within the material of the Targums.

The Syriac text.

Aramaic Targum tradition, in part of a very old Palestinian type, is also found in the O.T. Peshitta[4], but there the Targum elements are

---

[1] Cf. above to Mt. 19₅ (οἱ δύο), p. 59 f. We do not think that the Hebrew text of Matthew was exactly that of the Massoretes, but it is certainly wrong to take Matthew's quotations (particularly his formula quotations) as a basis for reconstructing the *hebraica veritas* (cf. above to Mt. 8₁₇, p. 106, note 4) as does SPERBER, cf. below, p. 176.

[2] We have used the texts of P. DE LAGARDE, *Prophetae chaldaice* (1872) and *Hagiographa chaldaice* (1873); to Isaiah: J. F. STENNING, *The Targum of Isaiah* (1949). For the Pentateuch, to Onkelos: A. BERLINER, *Targum Onkelos* (1884) and to the Jerusalem Targums (incl. Pseudo-Jonathan): B. WALTON, *SS. Biblia Polyglotta* IV (1657). In the geniza-material to the Palestinian Targum, published by KAHLE, *Masoreten des Westens* II (1930), p. 1–65, there are none of the O.T. passages quoted by Matthew.

[3] See B. J. ROBERTS, *The O.T. Text and Versions* (1951), p. 197–213. — A. WIKGREN, *Journ. of Rel.* 24 (1944), p. 89–95, stresses the Targum's relevance for the N.T. study, though he does not enter into details and no reference to actual N.T. passages are given. J. R. HARRIS, Traces of Targumism in the New Testament, *Exp. Times* 32 (1920/21), p. 373–376, refers to Mt. 27₄₆ and 26₆₄.

[4] BAUMSTARK, *Zeitschr. d. Deutsch. Morgenl. Gesellsch.* 89 (1935), p. 89–95, and IDEM, *Bibl. Zeitschr.* 19 (1931), p. 257–270: the Targums on which the O.T. Peshitta relies are of an older type than the Eastern Onkelos and the Western Fragment–Jerusalem–Pseudo-Jonathan traditions; cf. KAHLE, *The Cairo Geniza*, p. 187 f., on a fragment of Palestinian Targum older than the basis for the O.T. Peshitta. — F. ROSENTHAL, *Die aramaistische Forschung* (1939), p. 199–206, takes a somewhat critical attitude to this view of Baumstark and his pupils, though he does not deny its possibility. Yet he favours Baumstark's view on the relation between the Jeru-

interwoven with both the Hebrew and the Greek tradition. Whether one assumes a Jewish or a Christian origin to the O.T. Peshitta[1], it is clear that the translation was made under the influence of the Western Aramaic Targums and was not simply a translation from the Hebrew text. To this must be added the influence from the LXX which is marked in the books of the Prophets and even more obvious in the Psalter[2], *i.e.* in the very writings which have the greatest significance for the Matthaean quotations. Where the O.T. Peshitta follows the LXX and deviates from the other texts, it is of no value for the Semitic background to the N.T. quotations such as, for example, in Mt. 21 16 (Ps. 8 3). On the other hand of great significance to our study are those cases in which the Syriac text differs from both the M.T. and the LXX, while at the same time no obvious influence from the N.T. can be assumed. One dares to suppose that it then preserves a reading which was also found in a Palestinian Targum.

The strange fact that the ܢܒܝ which influenced Matthew's understanding of Is. 42 2 in Mt. 12 19 is found in the O.T. Peshitta did not *necessarily* mean that a Syriac translation to Isaiah existed at the time of Matthew. That such a translation did exist at an early date, however, appears from the O.T. Peshitta's influence upon syr[sin cur] and even upon the Diatessaron.[3] The Syriac etymology in Mt. 12 19 could also depend upon dialectal conditions which were known or natural in the milieu of the Matthaean church.

On the other hand the targumizing feature in the O.T. Peshitta, or more correctly in one of its recensions[4], is of interest as background to Matthew's formula quotations; this is the more so if, as BACON does, one

---

salem Targum and the O.T. text in the Christian-Palestinian lectionaries, *ibm.*, p. 158 f. For the texts quoted in the N.T. these are of little interest, see H. DUENSING, *Christlich-palästinisch-aramäische Texte und Fragmente nebst einer Abhandlung über den Wert der palästinischen Septuaginta* (1906), p. 88–127, especially p. 112.

[1] For these different views, see ROBERTS, *op. cit.*, p. 222, cf. BAUMSTARK, *Geschichte der syrischen Literatur* (1922), p. 18.

[2] W. E. BARNES, *Journ. of Theol. St.* 2 (1900/01), p. 189–197, cf. KAHLE, *op. cit.*, p. 183, and on Isaiah, L. HAEFELI, *Die Peschitta des Alten Testamentes* (1927), p. 49–50.

[3] BURKITT, *Evangelion Da-Mepharreshe* II, p. 201–206. On Burkitt's later views see KAHLE, *op. cit.*, p. 204.

[4] ROBERTS, *op. cit.*, p. 219: "It can be further demonstrated that at an early period there were two recensions of the Peshitta Pentateuch, one a literal translation, and the other the production of a rendering such as is described above, namely a Targum with a considerable amount of paraphrase." These two types are repre-

assigns the Matthaean church to Syrian borders[1], or if it is localized in a town where Eastern Aramaic dialects were known. For in the Peshitta the targumized text is certainly a biblical text and not, as in Palestine, merely a semi-sacred translation without binding authority.[2]

The Greek text.[3]

Our study of the quotations in the gospels has repeatedly brought to the fore the question of the N.T.'s relation to the various text types and manuscript families of the LXX. HAWKINS's statistics, which were our starting point, built on a comparison between Westcott-Hort's N.T. text and Swete's LXX (cod. B with the gaps completed from A and א).[4] Most N.T. scholars seem to take the same view and consider agreements between the N.T. and LXX$^{A\ etc.}$ as an influence of the N.T. upon the LXX.[5]

However, the readings supported by the N.T. are often treated with greater respect among LXX scholars, a respect which is considerably strengthened by the fact that later discoveries have shaken the authority of LXX^B and shown that the readings from LXX^A and other related manuscripts often go further back than Origen's Hexapla.

The oldest fragment of LXX text (2nd century B.C.) is pap. 957 (Papyrus Ryland Gk. 458). Although the text only includes Deut. 23 24–24 3,

---

sented among the rest of the O.T. books, though not extant in parallel texts, see *ibm.*, p. 221, and more in detail by KAHLE, *op. cit.*, p. 181–183.

[1] BACON, *Studies in Matthew*, p. 23.

[2] Cf. above, p. 127.

[3] Only in a few cases have we paid attention to the *vetus latina*. Even when retaining old readings, relevant to our study, it leads to a third area of language with the Greek as an intermediate stage and thereby it becomes of minor importance for the exact comparison of quotations. — On the possibility of Jewish targums as its predecessors and on its relation to LXX^{Lucian}, see ROBERTS, *op. cit.*, p. 237–246 and F. STUMMER, *Einführung in die lateinische Bibel* (1928).

[4] *Horae Synopticae*[2], p. xv.

[5] So ZAHN, *Einleitung* II[1], p. 314, LAGRANGE, *Comm. Mt.*, p. cxviii, and particularly TORREY, *Documents*, p. 47: "As is well known, there is frequent contamination of LXX manuscripts from the Greek of the Gospels, in the passages which are quoted ... The passages in Matthew from which readings have found their way into one or more mss. of the LXX are 2 18, 4 4, 4 10, 4 15 f., 11 23, 15 4, 15 8 f., 18 16, 19 18 f., 22 37, 39 and 26 31."

As to the Pauline material VOLLMER, *Die Alttest. Citate bei Paulus*, p. 17 ff., takes a more positive view on the variants to LXX^B, and so does SH. JOHNSON, *Harv. Theol. Rev.* 36 (1943), p. 145 and 147, with reference to Mt. 4 10 and 22 37, 39. In both cases pap. 963 is the decisive factor.

25 1–3, 26 12, 17–19, 28 31–33, it allows a clear determination of the type of text. Compared with B, A and Θ it is most remote from B, while it stands closest to Θ and then to A. Its text seems to have had strong agreements with pap. 963, which are lacking, however, in the passages in question.[1] Of greatest interest are its agreements with Lucian's text, to which Θ and the minuscules 54 and 75 (*g* and *n*) here belong. With these texts pap. 957 shares the most apparent deviations from the current LXX text.[2]

From approximately the same period we have a fragment of Deut. 31 28–32 7 with the Tetragrammaton in archaic Hebrew, the Fouad papyrus 266, belonging to the Société Royale de Papyrologie in Cairo.[3] Its type of text is clear from the following record of its variants: With A F against B, once; with B against A F, three times; with A B F 75 against Θ, once; five individual readings.

The oldest of the Chester Beatty Papyri, pap. 963, is that to Numbers and Deuteronomy (probably dating from the first half of the 2nd century A.D.; a codex). Of this KENYON says: "while the text of Numbers is most akin to that of B, in Deuteronomy it is conspicuously not in agreement with B but rather with G and Θ".[4]

Cod. W from the 3rd century A.D. stands closest to Q amongst the Uncials. Moreover, 171 of the 348 readings (except in Amos and Micah), which are not found in the Uncials, coincide with the minuscules and the versions. There are also 30 accomodations to the Hebrew text, almost all of which lack counterparts in other versions. Some examples of the "sparing use" of the translations of Symmachus and Aquila, but few of Theodotion, are to be found in it. The text contains still more adaptations to the Hebrew text *secunda manu*.[5]

---

[1] C. H. ROBERTS, *Two Biblical Papyri* (1936), p. 32–37, cf. B. J. ROBERTS, *op. cit.*, p. 145 f., SEELIGMANN, *Jaarber. Ex Oriente Lux* 7 (1940), p. 374. See also A. ALLGEIER, *Biblica* 19 (1938), p. 1–18. — J. A. MONTGOMERY, *Journ. of Bibl. Lit.* 55 (1936), p. 309–311, and W. F. ALBRIGHT, *ibm.* 56 (1937), p. 174, both state that, though the fragment deviates from B, it is close to the type of text represented in this manuscript. Yet Albright adds (p. 175): "They (the fragments) do diverge more from it than we should expect if there were only one archetype translation."

[2] See A. VACCARI, *Biblica* 17 (1936), p. 504, cf. KAHLE, *Die hebräischen Handschriften aus der Höhle* (1951), p. 34.

[3] Edited (with facsimile) by W. G. WADDELL, *Journ. of Theol. St.* 45 (1944), p. 158–161.

[4] F. G. KENYON, *Our Bible and the Ancient Manuscripts* (1939), p. 64 f.

[5] H. A. SANDERS–C. SCHMIDT, *The Minor Prophets in the Freer Collection and the Berlin Fragment of Genesis* (1927), p. 26–30.

Also the Berlin Genesis (pap. 911), which belongs to the 3rd century and seems to be rather free from hexaplaric influence, to a great extent shows the same picture.[1]

Thus SWETE's statement about the relation between the N.T. and the LXX holds good to-day; indeed, it has become apparent that it has more solid foundations than Swete himself could have known when he said: "There is a considerable weight of evidence in favour of the belief that the Evangelists employed a recension of the LXX which came nearer to the text of cod. A than to that of our oldest uncial B. This point has been recently handled ... by Dr W. STAERK[2], who shews that the witness of the N.T. almost invariably goes with codd. ℵ A F and Lucian against the Vatican MS, and that its agreement with cod. A is especially close. It may of course be argued that the text of these authorities has been influenced by the N.T.; but the fact that a similar tendency is noticeable in Josephus, and to a less extent in Philo, goes far to discount this objection."[3]

This view is both strengthened by, and strengthens, other observations concerning cod. A. Its similarity to the M.T. must often be explained as due to hexaplaric influence "but it possesses a large element of ancient readings which are not hexaplaric, and which it shares, to a great extent, with the Lucianic family. Moreover, as we have already seen, the citations of the LXX in the N.T. and by Christian writers of the first three centuries often support the readings of A with a remarkable unanimity. These phenomena point to the presence in A of an underlying text of great antiquity, possibly a pre-Christian recension made in Syria".[4] Swete adds that cod. B's readings, which lack this sup-

---

[1] ibm., p. 264.

[2] Zeitschr. f. wissenschaftl. Theol. 35 (1892), p. 464–485; 36:1 (1893), p. 70–98; 38 (1895), p. 218–230; 40 (1897), p. 211–268. Staerk admits four cases where the N.T. might have influenced the LXX^A: Mk. 9 48, Mt. 4 10 and 15, 8 f., Heb. 1 7, op. cit., 40 (1897), p. 265. Of these, however, LXX^B to Is. 29, quoted in Mt. 15, is certainly hexaplaric and the reading of LXX^A in Deuteronomy, quoted in Mt. 4, is now supported by pap. 963, see SH. JOHNSON, op. cit., p. 145. On the other hand, Mk. 9 48 has certainly influenced the LXX^A, see ZIEGLER, ed. Isaias, p. 27.

[3] Introduction, p. 395, cf. ibm., p. 479: "A few traces may be found of the accidental influence of N.T. citations, e.g. the interpolation in Ps. 13 3, and perhaps also the reading σῶμα in Ps. 39 3; but apart from these, the Septuagint suffered little from Christian hands beyond errors of transcription."

[4] op. cit., p. 489, cf. ibm., p. 403: "In the Epistles, as in the Gospels, the text of the LXX which is employed inclines to cod. A rather than to cod. B. But its agreement with the A text is not without exception; and there are other elements in the

port of Christian quotations, represent a text which has not undergone such a Palestinian revision.

These general classifications have certainly been confirmed and diversified by the discoveries and research of the past half century. Even if Staerk's argument is too forced in many details and one must simply admit corrections in LXX$^{A \text{ etc.}}$ to greater agreement with the N.T.[1], there remains the impression that the LXX^A and related texts as F, Q and Lucian represent the O.T. text, which is of interest for the N.T.

Instead of the general and broad statements of Staerk, it is necessary to examine each book individually[2] and thereby cod. A shows itself to be unusually trustworthy, especially in Isaiah and in the Minor Prophets which are so important to the N.T.[3] With good reason the Lucianic text may even be considered to have preserved Palestinian material, not least with reference to its geographical place of origin, Antioch.

In yet another way, Staerk's vindication of the integrity of cod. A requires qualification. The value of the eclectic method as a principle for editions of texts must be questioned, but its significance for a diversified viewpoint upon the value of the manuscripts is obvious. It is possible to make a broad statement on the value of a manuscript, but it is impossible to transfer this to specific readings in the said manuscript. The eclectic method is inevitable.

---

problem which must not be overlooked. As in the Gospels, again, we notice from time to time a preference for Lucianic readings, or for the readings of Theodotion. It has been reasonably conjectured that the writers of the N.T. used a recension which was current in Palestine, possibly also in Asia Minor, and which afterwards supplied materials to Theodotion, and left traces in the Antiochian Bible, and in the text represented by cod. A.''

[1] On the other hand, LXX^A is more seldom corrected to closer agreement with the M.T., ZIEGLER, ed. *Isaias*, p. 27 f., IDEM, ed. *Duodecim prophetae*, p. 43: except in five readings the variants of cod. A are against the M.T.

[2] For the Pauline material, VOLLMER, *op. cit.*, p. 48, found this distinction most elucidating, see above, p. 159. In the Matthaean quotations it does not yield any distinct limits. We found the quotations from the Psalms to be in close agreement with LXX^B, but here the relation between the MSS are quite different from the rest of the O.T., see RAHLFS, ed. *Psalmi cum Odis*, p. 21 ff. This is certainly due to the liturgical function of the Psalter.

[3] On Isaiah, see especially R. R. OTTLEY, *The Book of Isaiah according to the Septuagint (Codex Alexandrinus)* I–II 1904–1906, *e.g.* I, p. 8–20; H. ST. J. THACKERAY, *Journ. of Theol. St.* 10 (1908/09), p. 299, and ZIEGLER, ed. *Isaias* on A Q as against B V, p. 21–26; on the Minor Prophets, see IDEM, ed. *Duodecim prophetae*, p. 40 and 127.

A study of the LXX text in the passages quoted by Matthew in ZIEGLER's edition of the LXX Isaiah and Minor Prophets shows that on five points he gives a LXX text which agrees with the N.T. against LXX[B].[1] a) Synoptic quotations: Mt. 11 10 (Mal. 3 1) ἐγώ. — Mt. 15 8 (Is. 29 13), the shorter text. The longer text in closer agreement with the M.T., which B has, is hexaplaric. — (Lk 3 5: Is. 40 4 ὁδοὺς λείας.) — b) Formula quotations: Mt. 1 23 (Is. 7 14) ἕξει. — Mt. 2 6 (Micah 5 1) ἐξ οὗ. — Mt. 4 15 (Is. 8 23) ὁδὸν θαλάσσης.

This does not mean that all the other cases of agreements might be due to influence from the N.T. It is inevitable that such are to be found. The most obvious example of such an influence is found outside the gospels. LXX[א*A] Is. 40 14 has a longer text without any counterpart in the M.T. but it coincides exactly with Rom. 11 35. Now the preceding verse in Romans quotes Is. 40 14, and Rom. 11 35 is a quotation from Job 41 3, either in allusive form or following a text of Job unknown to us. A priori it is quite possible that the Isaiah text had been completed from Job, but when the Job text is not that of the LXX itself this is less credible. Moreover, this and the other Pauline quotation from the Book of Job, 1 Cor. 3 19, are both singular in relation to the rest of the O.T. texts in Paul and seem to rely upon a Greek version of which we have no information.[2]

As to N.T. readings which have crept into the LXX[A] Ziegler refers to Mt. 4 16 καθήμενος and also to Mk. 9 48 τελευτᾷ.[3] But in many cases A's reading may be evidence of a "popular text" which was better known and more used than the text-tradition which led up to cod. B.[4] In a

---

[1] Cf. above in the chapter on the texts to the different passages in question.

[2] VOLLMER, op. cit., p. 18 and 23 f. — Apparently there existed widely different forms of the Book of Job. Pap. 11778 (Berliner Septuagintafragmente, ed. STEG-MÜLLER, nr. 17), deviates widely from the LXX, partly in closer agreement with the M.T., cf. KAHLE, The Cairo Geniza, p. 150, who makes this an argument for the abundance of Greek targums, but to Stegmüller it was a real LXX text, free from the glosses and misinterpretations of the Uncials. — In the gospels the Book of Job (42 2) is alluded to in Mk. 14 36, while the parallel in Mt. 19 26 is closer to Gen. 18 14. In Lk. 1 37 the same text is quoted more exactly, showing affinity to the M.T. and coincidence with LXX[Lucian], see DITTMAR, Vetus Testamentum in Novo, p. 42. — On the LXX Job, see R. GORDIS, Hebr. Union Coll. Ann. 22 (1949), p. 161 f., and S. R. DRIVER–G. B. GRAY, Comm. Job I, p. lxxvi and xlix f. lxxi ff. — Paul's Greek text may depend on the Targum which is said to have been in the hands of Gamaliel, see B. J. ROBERTS, op. cit., p. 210.

[3] ZIEGLER, ed. Isaias, p. 27, cf. above, p. 100, note 4.

[4] So also STAERK, op. cit., 40 (1897), p. 267: "entweder nämlich repräsentirt B

number of cases the question of the N.T.'s influence upon the LXX[A etc.] must be left open.[1] It is, however, obvious that the Greek text upon which the evangelists were throughout dependent was closer to A than to B.[2]

This considerably diminishes the gap between the O.T. quotations in the N.T. and the LXX; and at the same time it opens up the possibility of finding a common denominator for these quotations on a Greek basis. For in the extension of the conception that the said manuscripts might provide remains of Palestinian Greek text, lies the assumption that to a large extent the deviations of the N.T. are evidence of an alleged abundance of different Greek targums. Along these lines KAHLE makes use of the N.T. quotations and cites as an argument Is. 42 1 ff. in the form in which it stands in Mt. 12 18 ff.[3] As to this particular quotation, one should remember that it agreed in part with the LXX, in part with Theodotion and in part with the M.T. Kahle's theory, like every position adopted

einen *älteren*, in jenen Zeiten nicht mehr allgemein gebrauchten LXX-Text, während A und Genossen eine jüngere Form von LXX darstellen, die damals, vielleicht um gewisser Vorzüge willen, sich grösster Beliebtheit erfreute; oder aber die in B vorliegende Recension ist die Frucht späterer Bemühungen um Harmonisirung von LXX mit M.T. und stellt den specifisch *origenianischen* LXX-Text, also einen zwar von den Auswüchsen der κοινη möglichst gereinigten, aber auch diese selbst nicht mehr genau vertretenden dar, während A und die ihm verwandten Handschriften nebst Lucian sich enger an die alte unrecensirte LXX, wie sie bis zum dritten Jahrhundert in Gebrauch war, anschliessen". Cf. ZIEGLER, ed. *Isaias*, p. 36, IDEM, *Duodecim prophetae*, p. 30, SEELIGMANN, *The Septuagint Version of Isaiah*, p. 6.

[1] A principle of method not to be overlooked is that of L. P. HEDLEY, *Harv. Theol. Rev.* 26 (1933), p. 70: "if a N.T. quotation varies markedly from all known LXX manuscripts, agreement in some trivial point is probably not due to N.T. influence, especially if the minute agreement occurs over a wide geographical field, *e.g.* Mt. 27 43", see above, p. 140.

[2] Only once has a variant of LXX[B] made its way into the greater part of the N.T. MMS., *viz.* Mk. 15 34, a quotation from the Psalms and a singular case in the N.T. even in other respects, cf. above, p. 83 f.

[3] *The Cairo Geniza*, p. 167: "an excellent example of the character of a Greek Targum in its earlier time, before a standard text was created". Kahle adds however: "It is very remarkable that a Greek translation of Isaiah, which must have been well known in the first Christian century and was quoted by Matthew has completely disappeared in the Church." It is remarkable indeed! Cf. below, p. 181, and ALLEN, *Comm. Mt.*, p. lxii: the formula quotations and Mt. 11 10 were known to Matthew in their Greek form, but Allen suggests testimonies rather than Jewish Greek Targums, cf. below, p. 215 f.

towards the O.T. quotations in the N.T., thereby becomes dependent upon the picture which one accepts of the origin of the LXX.

The present LXX research offers two diametrically opposed conceptions of the nature of this Greek text.[1] LAGARDE treated this text with the same principles of textual criticism which are used for manuscripts of the works of classical authors. It was a matter of going back to the original LXX, the archetype behind the three recensions, those of Hesychian, Lucian and Origen. Naturally the LXX's nature of translation was taken into consideration *e.g.* when rejecting the hexaplaric glosses and other changes to a closer agreement with the Hebrew text. This is how it is referred to in Lagarde's famous second axiom: "Wenn ein vers oder versteil in einer freien und in einer sklavisch treuen übertragung vorliegt, gilt die erstere als die echte."[2] But such a reference to its nature of a translation does not weaken the thought of an archetype. Amongst others RAHLFS, MARGOLIS, ORLINSKY und KATZ follow this line.

The other point of view on the nature of the Greek text draws more essential inferences from the fact that we are here dealing with a sacred literature which had been widespread and demanded a translation for its cultic function. Here the search for an archetype is considered an

---

[1] A penetrating survey of LXX research is given by SEELIGMANN, Problemen en Perspectieven in het moderne Septuaginta-Onderzoek, *Jaarber. Ex Oriente Lux* 7 (1940), p. 359–390e, and by G. BERTRAM, *Theol. Rundschau*, N.F. 3 (1931), p. 283–296; 5 (1933), p. 173–186; 10 (1938), p. 69–80 and 133–159. Both take a sceptical attitude towards the archetype-thinking of Lagarde and his sucessors. This attitude is brought to its extreme by KAHLE, Untersuchungen zur Geschichte des Pentateuchtextes, *Theol. St. u. Krit.* 88 (1915), p. 399–439, and later in *The Cairo Geniza* (1947). Mainly the same view — with special relation to the N.T. — is found in the works of A. SPERBER, particularly "New Testament and Septuagint", *Journ. of Bibl. Lit.* 59 (1940), p. 193–293.

Another survey of the modern study of the LXX but with the opposite tendency is that of KATZ, *Theol. Zeitschr.* 5 (1949), p. 1–24, which also includes a critical review of Kahle's, *The Cairo Geniza*. — The same lines were followed by H. M. ORLINSKY, *Journ. of the Amer. Orient. Soc.* 61 (1941), p. 81–91, and IDEM, in *The Study of the Bible today and tomorrow* (ed. H. R. WILLOUGHBY, 1947), p. 144–161. In *The Biblical Archaeologist* 9 (1946) an article of ORLINSKY, "The Septuagint — its Use in Textual Criticism", p. 21–34, is followed up from the N.T. point of view by F. V. FILSON, "The Septuagint and the New Testament", p. 34–42. — A survey with reference to the quotations in the gospels is given by W. HASENZAHL, *Die Gottverlassenheit des Christus* (1937), p. 12–37.

[2] *Anmerkungen zur griechischen übersetzung der Proverbien* (1863), p. 3, IDEM, *Mittheilungen* I (1884), p. 21.

illusion.[1] A homogeneous LXX text constitutes the end of a long process of selection and the beginning is a wealth of Greek targums. The foremost representative of this viewpoint, KAHLE, writes: "We may try to edit the Jewish standard text of the Greek Tora. But can we possibly regard such a text as an 'Urtext' — a text from which all existing texts have to be derived? A standard text of a translation is always found at the *end* of the development, never in the beginning."[2] That is to say, in the time of the gospels there did not exist "a LXX text" of the O.T. This is the most radical attitude to the relation of the N.T. quotations to the Greek O.T., and Kahle has hardly faced its implications from the N.T. point of view, though as we saw, he points to the text of Mt. 12 18 ff. to prove his opinion. This radical stand is not shared by the other scholars taking the same line, except by BAUMSTARK. SPERBER holds the view that in the time of the apostles there existed two types of Greek (and Hebrew) text to the O.T.[3]

The manuscripts which show that LXX[B] is not the obvious point of comparison with the N.T. quotations all have in common that they come from Egypt, as is also the case with the oldest Uncials. Only pap. 957 and the Cairo fragment can with certainty be assigned to a Jewish origin[4], the former of which, however, in Deuteronomy shows the same

---

[1] KAHLE, *Theol. St. u. Krit.* 88 (1915), p. 439. — SEELIGMANN, *op. cit.*, p. 376: "Het streven naar de reconstructie of zelfs slechts naar de benadering van den oertekst der LXX is, naar men vreezen moet, de jacht op en illusie." So also BERTRAM, *op. cit.*, 10 (1938), p. 159. — KATZ, *op. cit.*, p. 24, on the other hand, states that the variants in the LXX are not more substantial than those found in the manuscripts of other classical authors.

[2] KAHLE, *The Cairo Geniza*, p. 175. — It must be remembered how closely Kahle's view on the LXX is related to his concept of the pre-Massoretic Hebrew texts. In both cases the pattern of development is the same, and to Kahle one single authorized Greek version of the O.T. is impossible before 100 A.D., see *ibm.*, p. 117.

[3] SEELIGMANN, *loc. cit.*; BAUMSTARK, *Zeitschr. d. Deutsch. Morgenl. Gesellsch.* 86 (1935), p. 98; BERTRAM, *Theol. Rundschau*, N. F. 10 (1938), p. 159. — SPERBER, *Journ. of Bibl. Lit.* 59 (1940), in some measure takes a way of his own. He assumes not more than two types of Greek O.T. text: a) That represented by cod. B and the obelus readings of the Hexapla and b) the "Bible of the Apostles", represented by the asterisk type of the hexaplaric LXX and often also by cod. A, p. 278–283. These two types depend in their turn up on two different types of Hebrew text, p. 283–289. For the detailed study of the Matthaean quotations this hypothesis is of little help. The N.T. readings of Mt. 9 13, 12 7 and Lk. 3 4–5 are those of the "al. ex." and thus according to Sperber of the asterisk type.

[4] There is also an inscription from the LXX (Ps. 36 8–10) on a pot found in Palestine and dated about 200 A.D. Though certainly cited from memory it is worth noting

text-type as one of the Chester Beatty Papyri, which is certainly of Christian origin.[1]

These facts make the discovery of a Greek text to the O.T. in the Wilderness of Judaea in August 1952 most welcome. The discovery concerns fragments from the Minor Prophets, from Micah, Jonah, Nahum, Habakkuk, Zephaniah and Zechariah, and the text upon paleographical grounds can be assigned to the end of the first century A.D. In addition the cave contains a deposit of manuscripts from the revolt of Bar Kochbah. BARTHÉLEMY has given a preview of these texts and shows that they stand very close to those which we find in Justin's quotations.[2] Justin has therefore cited a genuinely Jewish text and not only gone his own way.

These fragments agree in a number of readings with Aquila, and also with Symmachus and to a minor extent with Theodotion. Barthélemy even finds points in common with Hebraisms in the Coptic translations, and with Origen's Quinta. So far as the Hebrew background is concerned, in Habakkuk it stands decidedly closer to the M.T. than to DSH. The text seems to be not an independent translation but a recension of the LXX, as Barthélemy shows in a convincing manner. This is of great significance for the basic problem in present-day LXX research, the question of an archetype or abundance of Greek targums.[3]

Barthélemy looks upon the newly-discovered text as a step along the road to the later versions, Aquila, Symmachus and Theodotion, which he also considers as recensions. All these versions, however, do not merely have to be understood as a LXX corrected to a greater measure of agreement with the M.T. The edition may have been made with the help of the Palestinian Greek tradition of translation, oral and/or written. This might assume such traditions of translation alongside the LXX

---

that it goes with B R against A once, with B A against R once, and probably once with pap. 2013 A Lucian against the rest, see P. BENOIT, Rev. Bibl. 56 (1949), p. 438.

[1] KENYON, The Chester Beatty Biblical Papyri V (1935), p. ix f. and I. Bell's letter to KAHLE, The Cairo Geniza, p. 139 f.

[2] D. BARTHÉLEMY, Redécouverte d'un chaînon manquant de l'histoire de la Septante, Rev. Bibl. 60 (1953), p. 18–29. — The only substantial difference is found in Dial. 78₁, where Justin quotes Micah 5₂, but here he obviously follows Matthew.

[3] In his presentation of these fragments KAHLE, Theol. Lit. Zeit. 79 (1954), col. 81–94, considers them somewhat older than did Barthélemy but he does not discuss the French scholar's view as to their character of a revised LXX text.

and together with SWETE we might be able to suppose that it is such Palestinian material which is met with in the N.T. quotations, especially when it shows agreement with cod. A Q F etc. against cod. B.

For a long time LXX research has worked with the hypothesis of a so-called pre-Theodotion (Ur-Theodotion).[1] This problem has been most clearly stated by MONTGOMERY in his Commentary on Daniel. "That there exists some such body (as pre-Theodotion) of received translation before the Christian age lies beyond doubt, but we must not too quickly assume a written version. Very much can be explained by the hypothesis of a Hellenistic oral Targum, necessary in the first place for correction of faulty renderings, and especially of lacunae in LXX."[2] It is especially in such cases that pre-Theodotion readings occur. However, such a Greek targum was not actually produced in order to fill in the gaps and correct the mistakes of a given LXX text. In passing over to the Hellenistic synagogue Greek targums arose. The historical Theodotion in the second century was "the Hellenistic Onkelos[3], whose work was facilitated by the presence of a large amount of customary oral translation of the Scriptures, possessed by him memoriter. Of course such a theory does not exclude the possibility of literary predecessors of the historical Theodotion".[4]

Montgomery's conclusions in the first instance concerns the book of Daniel and cannot as a matter of course be stretched to cover other writings.[5] In the quotation from Dan. 7 13 (Mt. 24 30, Mk. 13 26) the textual witnesses are divided in their evidence and readings from both

---

[1] So already K. A. CREDNER, *Beiträge zur Einleitung in die biblischen Schriften* II (1838), p. 274.

[2] J. A. MONTGOMERY, *Comm. Dan.* (1927), p. 50.

[3] Or rather "Jonathan", "Theodotion" being its translation in Greek, KAHLE, *op. cit.*, p. 118.

[4] MONTGOMERY, *loc. cit.* — KATZ, *Theol. Zeitschr.* 5 (1949), p. 22, therefore seems to be wrong in using Montgomery's observations as an argument in favour of his own view, and in letting him say that the parallel readings were evoked by the actual LXX text. To Montgomery they were real parallels and not only a recensional tradition, though he did not draw the same far-reaching consequences of these oral or written Targum traditions as did *e.g.* Kahle. — SH. JOHNSON, *Harv. Theol. Rev.* 36 (1943), p. 138–140, combines Montgomery's view with that of Margolis and Orlinsky on pre-Theodotion readings in the Palestinian *koine*.

[5] Cf. IDEM, The Hexaplaric Strata in the Greek texts of Daniel, *Journ. of Bibl. Lit.* 44 (1925), p. 300, cf. THACKERAY, *The Septuagint and Jewish Worship* (1923), p. 24–28, on pre-Theodotion to the Books of Reigns as a work of an anonymous *Asiaticus*.

Theodotion and the LXX are represented. But in addition Matthew's formula quotations contain two parallels to Theodotion, 4 15 and 12 18, which cannot be explained by common proximity to the M.T. In 4 15, however, even LXX^{A etc.} have Theodotion's reading. There is also agreement with Aquila in 2 15. Outside Matthew we find coincidence with Theodotion in two passages, Jn. 19 37 (Zech. 12 10) and 1 Cor. 15 54 (Is. 25 8). Through a text-critical examination of the various witnesses to Theodotion's reading, RAHLFS confines himself to the agreement of the terms εἰς νῖκος and ὃν ἐξεκέντησαν.[1] Even if he is considered to be correct in this minimizing of the similarities, it is hard to explain that agreement entirely as a common closer resemblance to the Hebrew text.[2]

Since part of the readings of Theodotion which can come into the question are also encountered in Aquila, Rahlfs attempts to strengthen his reasoning by saying: "Übrigens könnte man . . . ebensogut auf Abhängigkeit von Aquila schliessen . . . Dann allerdings würde sich die völlige Haltlosigkeit des Schlusses nur um so deutlicher zeigen, da Aquila ganz sicher erst im II Jh. n. Chr. gelebt und ein 'Aquila vor Aquila' zweifellos nicht existiert hat."[3]

Here the fragments published by Barthélemy put the matter in quite another light. Rahlfs has himself pointed out Justin's knowledge — though a somewhat confused one — of Aquila's tradition of translation. Now a text obviously akin to the readings of Aquila and the text of Justin appears towards the close of the first century A.D.

BOUSSET draws attention to Justin's dependence upon Aquila but explains the pervading agreement, especially with the Lucianic text, as a later revision of Justin's text, made by the church, which thereby used the Lucianic recension of the LXX.[4] In quotations common with the N.T. we must count with influence from this, especially from Matthew[5], but Barthélemy's observations should call for greater caution in the former case.

---

[1] Über Theodotion-Lesarten im N.T. und Aquila-Lesarten bei Justin, *Zeitschr. f. d. neutest. Wissensch.* 20 (1921), p. 182–199.

[2] See above, p. 113, and below, p. 213, cf. VOLLMER, *op. cit.*, p. 24 f. and p. 35, with reference also to other passages: ". . . dass es vor Aquila, Symmachus und Theodotion schon andere, ihnen verwandte Versionen werde gegeben haben, die hie und da neben LXX benutzt wurden. Natürlich hat man sich dieselben nicht als vollständige Gesamtausgaben des Alten Testaments zu denken".

[3] *op. cit.*, p. 190.

[4] BOUSSET, *Die Evangeliencitate Justins des Märtyrers* (1891), p. 18–43.

[5] MASSAUX, *Influence de l'Évangile de saint Matthieu*, p. 569 f.

KATZ holds another and more radical view of this trace of Aquila in Justin and maintains that it can be ascribed entirely to a very late alteration of the longer quotations introducing Justin's arguments. Katz points out that in the context Justin follows the LXX and has certainly originally done the same in all quotations.[1] In taking this stand, Katz transfers to Justin the interpretation he put forward in his study of Philo's Bible. There he proceeded from Rahlfs's group of *catenae* and late manuscript texts which in the book of Ruth were shown to be due to a correction of Aquila type carried out long after Origen. Katz finds this same text in Philo's *lemmata* while the interpretations in the context are of LXX type.[2] So far as Justin is concerned, and even indirectly so far as Philo's quotations are concerned, the LXX fragments from the Wilderness of Judaea disproves Katz's assumption.

As to Josephus and Philo, there is little material from the Later Prophets. THACKERAY points out that Josephus seems to have made his own translation for the Octateuch, in Judges apparently following a Targum. On the other hand the Josephan biblical text is uniformly of Lucianic type from 1 Samuel to 1 Maccabees, and Thackeray assumes a "pre-Lucian". For the Later Prophets no signs are found for dependence upon a Greek text.[3]

These scattered observations from the facts of the text and modern discussion of the LXX seem to support the conception of Swete that the text in question for the N.T. is to be found in the Palestinian LXX tradition, of which we find traces in manuscripts like AQF and in the Lucianic text. But all the material we find in readings and fragments of papyri, including the fragments from the Wilderness of Judaea, scarcely take us back to a "wild abundance of Greek targums".

This is still a hypothetical feature, yet with some a priori element of plausibility. If with Kahle one places the beginning of the canonization of the LXX in the year 100 A.D., and considers it due to Christian initiative, it is rather annoying that we are so completely lacking evidence of the previous Greek targums.[4] It is even more difficult that the

---

[1] *Theol. Zeitschr.* 5 (1949), p. 16–17.

[2] *ibm.*, p. 14–16, and now in *Philo's Bible* (1950), especially, p. 114 ff. — KAHLE, *Die hebräischen Handschriften aus der Höhle* (1951), p. 37, remarks that Rahlfs never succeeded in identifying this recension in Genesis.

[3] *Josephus, the Man and the Historian* (1929), p. 85, cf. A. MEZ, *Die Bibel des Josephus* (1895).

[4] BAUMSTARK, *op. cit.*, p. 99 f.: "(... die) Mannigfaltigkeit auch der griechischen

common synoptic stratum is so poor in variants from the LXX. The N.T. text has not preserved any significant variants which would have been the case if the LXX was a later occurrence. This is the more so since the quotations in the N.T. possessed an authority of their own, even superior to that of the O.T.

Many times we have drawn attention to the character of the quotations common to the Synoptics. The variants within the LXX particularly have relevance to these quotations (4 10, 11 10, 15 4, 8, 19 5, 22 24, 32, 37, 39, 26 31, 27 46). In the cases where we dare to assume the integrity of cod. A etc., these N.T. readings may be witnesses to a Palestinian LXX which gave these quotations their Greek form.

The same is the case in certain of the formula quotations, although they could never be explained merely with the help of these variants. The LXX element in the formula quotations is thereby strengthened, a dependence which ZAHN and TORREY wanted to reduce to a minimum, but which LAGRANGE from a similar point of departure fully recognized in spite of his negative view on the readings of the LXX^A.[1] In the material peculiar to Matthew outside the formula quotations, 18 16 reproduces an example of agreement with the LXX^A and LXX^{Lucian}, cf. further the parallel in 2 Cor. 13 1.

The variants within LXX manuscripts in no way lead us to such marked differences as are offered by the formula quotations. Neither 11 10 nor 26 31 really lie within the range of these variants. Yet by far the greater part of the quotation material in the words of Jesus is formed from a LXX text and this at an original stage. In this form it was taken over by Matthew.

The Greek text which we have in the fragment from the Wilderness of Judaea goes far beyond these variants, however, and thus the line of demarcation between the LXX and later versions becomes less distinct. Even if with Barthélemy one insists that we here have a revised LXX text, it brings us to translations of a pre-Theodotion or pre-Aquila type. It assumes a striving after closer agreement with the M.T. and associated with Montgomery's more or less oral targums, it shows us the presence of other traditions of translation, whether these arose through primary collating of the Alexandrian LXX text or through use of oral or written Greek targums, which were taken up in Palestinian Greek O.T. texts.

Targumüberlieferung, von der bedauerlicherweise bislange kein einziges Papyrusfragment vor- auch nur sicher oder ausserchristlicher Herkunft aufgetaucht ist''.

[1] *Comm. Mt.*, p. cxix.

Justin was acquainted with such interpretations although his knowledge of the subject is not to be relied upon in details.[1] It looks as if he
only had secondhand acquaintance of the various interpretations via
Jewish and Christian material from school and discussion. It is clear that
the Synoptics are not dependent upon such variants, but Matthew and
to some extent John and Paul, were acquainted with them.

It is, however, a long step from this observation to the assumption that
the Greek text in Matthew's formula quotations should be evidence of
a Jewish revision, so that we might be able to find a Greek basis for all
of Matthew's quotation material.[2] It is worth noting that it is not in the
material peculiar to Matthew such a text is consistently made use of,
but only in the formula quotations. We must therefore first ask ourselves
whether the method of citing in these very quotations does not rather
follow laws of interpretation other than those followed by the rest of the
material. If so, it becomes still more obvious that the formula quotations
cannot be used as evidence of "a text" which was available to Matthew.

---

[1] See RAHLFS, *op. cit.*, p. 198, cf. SWETE, *Introduction*, p. 479 (apparently on
Dial. 71–73): "But of the four passages produced in proof of this assertion three
are mere glosses, probably of Christian origin; while the fourth, a genuine part of
the book of Jeremiah (11 19), is now found in all MSS. of the LXX", cf. *ibm.*, p. 423.
There is, however, also the correct reference to the Jewish reading νεᾶνις, Is. 7 14
(Dial. 71 3). Other relevant passages are: Dial. 43, 66–68, 84 (Is. 7 14); Dial. 52
(Gen. 49 10); Dial. 131 (Deut. 32 8); Dial. 124 (Ps. 82) and Justin's own reason for
rendering the same text (Is. 3 10) differently in different parts of his own work,
Dial. 17 2, 133 2, 137 3, cf. HOMMES, *Het Testimoniaboek*, p. 178–180 and 187–195,
who relates the quotation to the "Schulgut" of Hellenistic Judaism.

[2] Cf. SWETE, *Introduction*, p. 398, on the Matthaean formula quotations and referring to readings of pre-Theodotion type: "But our evidence does not encourage
the belief that the Evangelist used or knew another complete Greek version of the
O.T. or of any particular book." If Barthélemy is right in considering his fragments
a revision of the LXX — and he seems to be so — this statement still holds good. —
It was partly the influence of the Hebrew text on the Greek O.T. in Palestine which
led E. BÖHL to the strange hypothesis of "die palästinensische Volksbibel", an
Aramaic translation of the LXX, *Forschungen nach einer Volksbibel zur Zeit Jesu
und deren Zusammenhang mit der Septuaginta-Uebersetzung* (1873) and *Die alttestamentlichen Citate im Neuen Testament* (1878). The support for this hypothesis
was collected from the O.T. quotations of the N.T., particularly those of Matthew.
Böhl's work has a strong apologetic trend. He wants to explain why the words of
Jesus sometimes demand the LXX's interpretation of the O.T., *e.g.* in Mt.
15 8–9, see above, p. 58, cf. p. 155.

The formula quotations of Matthew and the Habakkuk Commentary from Qumran — The *pesher* manner of quoting Scripture

One of the scrolls discovered at Qumran[1] seems to have great significance for the citations in Matthew. Just as Matthew's formula quotations are expressly interpreted as fulfilled by the words or deeds of Jesus, so the Habakkuk Commentary (DSH) applies the first two chapters of Habakkuk verse by verse to the Teacher of Righteousness and the events which surround him.[2] These references are introduced by the words . . . פשרו על, "its interpretation bears on . . .", or similar expressions.[3] An explicit formula of fulfilment of the type found in

---

[1] The literature on the Dead Sea Scrolls (DSS) is increasing day by day. A survey of the initial stage of studies is found in W. BAUMGARTNER, Der palästinische Handschriftenfund, *Theol. Rundschau*, N. F. 17 (1948/49), p. 329–346 and 19 (1951), p. 97–154, cf. the continuous series Der gegenwärtige Stand der Erforschung der in Palästina gefundenen hebräischen Handschriften, *Theol. Lit. Zeit.*, beginning in 74 (1949).

[2] Was the Teacher of Righteousness the founder of the Sect or is he a messianic figure who is still to come — or is he both, as Jesus was the incarnate Messiah and yet still to come in his glory? The first alternative cannot easily be proved to be true, though it is mostly taken for granted. B. J. ROBERTS, *Bull. of J. Ryl. Libr.* 34 (1951/52) p. 366–387, cf. IDEM, *ibm.* 36 (1953/54), p. 75–96, has stated the case in a balanced way. He points to the apocalyptic character of the documents and to the tenses of the verbs which do not prove reference to something past but certainly to the future. We will return to one of the crucial passages of the whole issue, below, p. 190. Whatever the relation of the Teacher of Righteousness to history, the interpretation of DSH is influenced by actual history, *i.e.* by the situation in which the Sect claimed its faith and fought its fight. — Cf. L. ROST, Der "Lehrer der Einung" und der "Lehrer der Gerechtigkeit", *Theol. Lit. Zeit.* 78 (1953), col. 143–148. Rost considers the מורה היחיד of the Damascus Document (CDCb 9 29; col. xx, 1), the founder of the Sect as against the מורה הצדק.

[3] In the Book of Daniel פְּשַׁר is confined to dream interpretation, as is פְּתַר in Biblical Hebrew where פֵּשֶׁר occurs but once, Eccles. 8 1, related to Wisdom, cf. ROBERTS, *Bulletin* 34, p. 368. The term פשר can be considered peculiar to DSH though it occurs once in the Damascus Document (CDC 6 10; col. iv, 14). פתר is used later on in Rabbinics by the Palestinian Amorees, W. BACHER, *Die exegetische*

Matthew is missing[1], but the apocalyptic convictions of the Qumran Sect gives the term פשר a similar connotation.

DSH is usually called a commentary, but the accuracy of this description has been questioned. The realistic nature of the interpretation belongs rather to the characteristics of the *midrash*, but at the same time this tendency in DSH is so consistently and concretely carried out from the position of the Sect that it has been possible to label the whole as a political pamphlet.[2] The exegetic and hermeneutic structure, however, makes such a classification rather unnatural, and much speaks in favour of distinguishing a special type of *midrash, midrash pesher*, parallel to the *midrash halakah* and the *midrash haggadah*.[3]

The applications of DSH purport to show the true signification of Habakkuk's sayings. They are applied to what has occurred or what is imminent. However, neither DSH's Habakkuk text nor its application agree with the text we have in the M. T. In one of the Isaiah scrolls from Qumran (DSI a) we also find a number of deviations from the M. T.[4] Certain of these appear to be tendentious

---

Terminologie der jüdischen Traditionsliteratur II (1905), p. 178, cf. *ibm.*, p. 173, on the equivalence of פשר and פתר. — On the quotations in CDC, the introductory formulae and their equivalents in rabbinic terminology, see R. H. CHARLES, *Apocrypha and Pseudepigrapha* II (1913), p. 789 f. G. DALMAN, *Die Worte Jesu*[2], p. 382, on the Matthaean ἐρρέθη and τὸ ῥηθέν = :נאמר, cf. BACHER, *Die älteste Terminologie der jüdischen Schriftauslegung* (1899), p. 6.

[1] There are no exact rabbinic equivalents to the Matthean formula, though the verb קיים is used even in the passive, נתקיים, in a similar sense, BACHER, *Die älteste Terminologie*, p. 171, cf. T. W. MANSON, The Argument from Prophecy, *Journ. of Theol. St.* 46 (1945), p. 129.

[2] E. L. SUKENIK, *Megilloth Genuzoth* II (1950), p. 86, see BAUMGARTNER, *op. cit.* (1951), p. 117.

[3] So now W. H. BROWNLEE, *The Dead Sea Habakkuk Midrash and the Targum Jonathan*, a mimeographed paper, published through the services of the Duke Divinity School (1953), p. 12, in agreement with G. VERMÈS, *Cahiers Sioniens* 5 (1951). Similarly ROST, *Theol. Lit. Zeit.* 75 (1950), col. 477: ". . . was man kaum als Kommentar, sondern als Erläuterung oder Auslegung im Sinne einer Aktualisierung des Habakkuktextes verstehen muss. Vergleichbar ist etwa die Bearbeitung von Nah. 1 2–9 in Jer. 49." The special character of the *pesher* is worked out by ROBERTS, *Bulletin* 34, p. 375 f. and 386 f.; for the Jewish parallels and background see I. L. SEELIGMANN, Voraussetzungen der Midraschexegese, Supplem. to *Vetus Testamentum* (Congress Volume, 1953), p. 150–181. — Brownlee's paper was kindly made available to me by Prof. Reicke.

[4] DSIb is closer to the M. T., see BAUMGARTNER, *op. cit.* (1951), p. 122 f.

particularly in ch. 41–53, in which may be found a messianic tradition of interpretation as against that of the M. T.[1]

In DSH, however, the relation to the text we have in the M. T. is not only much freer but this freedom seems to be of an essentially different nature. DSH reveals the Sect's hermeneutic methods and how these methods influenced the Habakkuk text itself. This relation is thus expressed by HEMPEL: "Wie man sieht, sind die Abweichungen grösser als in der Jesajarolle. Der Kommentar behandelt den Text freier als die für den Gottesdienst bestimmte Handschrift." And he adds: "Für die Abweichungen des NT vom AT zu beachten".[2] Consequently we have here two different types of O. T. text, which cannot be estimated merely by current text-critical standards. The different function of the texts within the Sect constitutes an important factor in the nature of the texts in DSI and DSH. Perhaps this relation would help to throw some light on the differences in Matthew's quotation material.

The Habakkuk text in DSH.

The actual Habakkuk text in DSH contains about 50 variants to the M. T., apart from the purely orthographical. Many are scribal errors but most form such an intimate and organic part of the exposition of the text that they cannot possibly be dismissed as such. They show themselves to be either deliberate corrections or variant readings known to DSH, which supplied a basis for its interpretation. BROWNLEE has worked out this point of view in an arresting examination in which he brings out and amply illustrates DSH's hermeneutic principles from its handling of the Scriptures.[3]

In connection with Brownlee's study, together with ROST's[4] and VAN DER PLOEG's[5] remarks about the relation between DSH, the

---

[1] So D. BARTHÉLEMY, *Rev. Bibl.* 57 (1950), p. 546-549, cf. H. MICHAUD, *Positions Luthériennes, Supplément à Fraternité Evangélique*, 1953: 11, p. 42.

[2] *Zeitschr. f. d. alttest. Wissensch.* 62 (1949/50), p. 264.

[3] BROWNLEE, Biblical Interpretation among the Sectaries of the Dead Sea Scrolls, *The Bibl. Archaeol.* 14 (1951) p. 54–76. Cf. BROWNLEE's paper, mentioned above.

[4] *op. cit.*, col. 477-482. Rost takes more readings for scribal errors than *e.g.* M. BURROWS, *The Dead Sea Scrolls of St. Mark's Monastery* I (1950), p. xx, and Rost counts with dogmatic adaptation only in two cases, בריע for רי in 1 13 and חייך for חייך in 2 5, cf. below to 2 5 b. He disregards totally the relation between text and exposition.

[5] J. VAN DER PLOEG, *Bibliotheca Orientalis* 8 (1951), p. 2–4.

M. T., the LXX and other versions, we intend to give a few examples of DSH's use of the Scriptures so far as it can throw light on Matthew's method of quoting.

Firstly there are differences relating to number and suffix.

Hab. 1₁₃ (col. v, 8).

The M. T.'s הביט, the singular as in the Targum and the LXX, corresponds to DSH's הביטו, a plural which is made use of in the reading "the house Absalom and the men of their counsel" (line 10 f.).

Hab. 2₅b (col. viii, 5).

DSH's ויקבצו and ויאספו are the equivalents of the singular in the M. T., and DSH reads them as *niphal*.[1] In this way it was possible to emphasize how the wicked priest was successful to start with, as is also suggested in the exposition (line 9).

Hab. 2₆ (col. viii, 6).

DSH has מליצי ("scoffers" or "interpreters") as the subject of the plural ויומרו.[2] The M. T. has מליצה ("taunt"). DSH's text is adapted to contain a more concrete interpretation of actual events.

To this must be added differences in the suffixes; for example, in 1₁₀, where DSH has the masculine, whereas the M. T. has the feminine suffix. In 2₁b DSH has מצורי which would, however, be due to the influence of the parallel in 2₁a. In 2₁₅ DSH has the suffix for the third person, while the M. T. has it for the second, and in 2₁₈ the M. T.'s suffix is missing from DSH.

There are also more substantial variants in DSH's use of the biblical text.

Hab. 1₈ (col. iii, 6 f.).

The M. T. reads: "From afar shall they come . . ., they shall fly . . ." DSH omits "shall they come" but in the exposition this reading is taken up in lines 10 f., while the reading "they shall fly" is not explicitly made use of, but is natural in connection with the reference in the exposition to "the eagles".[3]

Hab. 1₉b (col. iii, 8 f.).

The M. T. has מגמת פניהם קדימה, "The . . . (?) of their faces is

---

[1] Rost, *op. cit.*, col 479, "Nifal-Formen, die als freiwillige Unterordnung der Völker gedeutet werden könnten, während die Singularform des M. T. dem Gottlosen die Sammlung der Völker zuschreibt".

[2] B. Reicke, *Symbol. Bibl. Upsal.* 14 (1952), p. 35, translates "scoffers". In DST (Sukenik, *op. cit.*, plate vii, 12) the word seems to mean "interpreters", parallel to דורשי, cf. below, p. 193, note 2.

[3] Cf. Brownlee, *Bibl. Arch.*, p. 62 f.

forward." DSH has מגמת פני הם קדים, "As for the (mutterings) of his face, they are the East wind."[1] The absence of the *heh-locale* can hardly be explained as a defective script, since in general DSH is more generous than the M. T. with final *-heh*. קדים is taken as a noun, and רוח which we find explicitly in the Targum, Symmachus and the Vulgate, is implied. Their readings support such an interpretation of DSH's text, as against the LXX.[2] In Hab. 1₁₁ (col. iv, 9 ff.) the M. T. reads אָשֵׁם ("sin-burdened"), the LXX ἐξιλάσεται but DSH has ישם. It should be possible to make this reading an argument in favour of Budde's emendation וְשָׁם adopted in Kittel's *Biblia Hebraica* (3rd edition)[3], but the case is complicated by the fact that we come upon אשמתם in line 11 of DSH's exposition. DUPONT–SOMMER remarks on this: "Le commentateur . . . connaissait donc les deux variantes, à la fois celle qu'il retient dans la citation et celle du TM! Il semble que, pour lui, le texte sacré soit si chargé d'inspiration divine que les deux leçons lui paraissent également fondées et valables, du fait que cette dualité donne lieu — et c'est l'essentiel — à une plus grande richesse de sens spirituels."[4]

Hab. 1₁₇ (col. vi, 8 f.).

DSH is like the LXX, the Peshitta and the Vulgate, without the M. T.'s and the Targum's interrogative form. The reading found in the M. T. looks like a dittography, but has the support of the Targum. In Hab. 1₁₇ DSH contains yet another variant which is of greater interest, namely חרבו for the M. T.'s חרמו, *i.e.* Giesebrecht's and Wellhausen's emendation. On this point no use is made of the reading חרמו in DSH's exposition. The LXX, however, agrees with the M. T. whereas cod. 86 mg informs us: Ἄλλος· ἐκκενώσει μάχαιραν αὐτοῦ[5], a reading which is even found in the Bohairic version. DSH's

---

[1] BROWNLEE, *Bibl. Arch.*, p. 63 — I. RABINOWITZ, *Journ. of Bibl. Lit.* 69 (1950), p. 35 f., was the first to discover that DSH had divided פני/הם into two words. He translates: "the abundance of my wrath are they to the East". Brownlee's translation requires that the obscure word מגמת is taken as a plural.

[2] Targ.: דמן בריח קידומא. — Symm.: ἡ πρόσοψις τοῦ προσώπου αὐτῶν ἄνεμος καύσων. — Vulg.: facies eorum sicut ventus urens. — LXX.: ἀνθεστηκότας προσώποις αὐτῶν ἐξ ἐναντίας. See S. M. STERN, *Journ. of Bibl. Lit.* 69 (1950), p. 28.

[3] So ROST, *op. cit.*, col. 479.

[4] *Rev. de l'Hist. des Rel.* 137 (1950), p. 143, cf. p. 148 f. BROWNLEE, *Bibl. Arch.*, p. 64, follows Dupont-Sommer.

[5] Cod. 86 is often a witness of the Lucianic text and the notes in its margin are

reading is supported by the Greek O. T. fragments published by
BARTHÉLEMY, where this is one of the two places in which DSH and
this Palestinian LXX text coincide.[1] רוב רִיק is good biblical Hebrew.[2]
The reading הרמו in the M. T. can be explained by the influence of
vv. 15 and 16 where the word occurs.

The Targum is strongly paraphrastic, but its version is of great
interest for vv. 15–16 in that "net" and "seine" are interpreted as
"arms" and "standards" just as in DSH.[3] In v. 17 it would seem
that the Targum read "net" (as also the Peshitta), and interpreted
it in a martial sense: "He shall surely send his armies."

Hab. 2 5 a (col. viii, 3 f.).

DSH reads הון ("riches") for the M. T.'s היין ("wine") as in the LXX
and the Targum. The Peshitta's more paraphrastic form lies closer
to DSH: ܚܙܐ ܡܢܣܒ ܡܚܠ ܠܐ ܣܒܥ, "A presumptuous and avaricious
man does not become satisfied." The DSH's reading is clearly a tendentious interpretation from the Sect's ideal of poverty, but at the
same time the O. T. Peshitta indicates that it had some support in
traditional interpretation.

Hab. 2 15 (col. xi, 3).

DSH has למען הבט על מועדיהם, while the M. T. has למען הביט
מעוריהם. Again in the exposition both readings are made use of:
"their festivals" and "their shame" (גלותו = "his denudation" [4]).

Hab. 2 16 (col. xi, 9).

Here we find the third example of the way in which DSH makes
use of the two readings, DSH הרעל, "to cause to stagger" and M. T.
ערל = "to uncover one's nakedness". The Targum follows the M. T.

often old and valuable. They use to coincide with cod. W, see ZIEGLER, ed. *Duodecim prophetae*, p. 77 f., cf. p. 104 ff.

[1] Cf. BARTHÉLEMY, *Rev. Bibl.* 60 (1953), p. 29. This is one of the 14 cases where
the fragments coincide with the Coptic versions, cf. *ibm.*, p. 27 and above, p. 177.

[2] GESENIUS-BUHL, *Wörterbuch*[17], s. v.

[3] BROWNLEE, *DSH and Targ. Jon.*, p. 3.

[4] So DUPONT-SOMMER, *op. cit.*, p. 148 f. Now also BROWNLEE, *Bibl. Arch.*, p. 67 f.,
instead of his earlier translation "to go into exile", *Bull. of the Amer. Schools of
Orient. Res.* 112 (1948), p. 15. — ROST, *op. cit.*, col. 480, concerning "festivals":
"keine diskutierbare Lesart sondern eine Verschreibung", but he does not discuss
the relation between the text and the exposition in DSH. Another interpretation
is given by VERMÈS, *Ephemer. Theol. Lovan.* 27 (1951), p. 74: מועד can be the
noun "festival", but also a participle *qal* of מעד "stumble", which gave the לבשילם,
line 8. — That understanding could lead over to the reading רעל in 2 16, see below.

while both the LXX (καρδία σαλεύθητι καὶ σείσθητι) and Aquila (καὶ καρώθητι) have read רעל, cf. Is. 51₁₇ where Aquila has καροῦν for רעל. The Peshitta and the Vulgate uphold this interpretation.

DSH's exposition is clearly conscious of the reading "to uncover his nakedness" since there stands in line 13: "for he has not circumcized the foreskin of his heart", while at the same time the reading of the text makes allusion to the immediate continuation "without having wandered along the paths of drunkenness". It can therefore scarcely be a question of a scribal error[1], although in the same verse such an error obviously occurs (מבוד for מכבוד).

The relation between DSH, the M. T. and the Versions is of great interest. In many cases DSH appears to be created *ad hoc*. What is more remarkable is that some of these readings are supported by one or more of the Versions. Such coincidences occur even in the case where adaptation to the dogma and situation of the Sect could sufficiently explain the text of DSH. The coincidences are follows[2]:

	DSH	M. T.	Targ.	LXX	Pesh.	Vulg.	
Hab. 1₉	קדים	קדימה	DSH	MT	—	DSH	Symm. = DSH.
(1₁₇ a	not inter-rogative	inter-rogative	MT	DSH	DSH	DSH)	
1₁₇ b	חרבו	חרמו	(MT)	MT	MT	MT	86 mg. Fragm. Bo. = DSH.
2₁	מצורי	מצור	DSH	MT	MT	MT	
2₅	הון	היין	MT	MT	DSH	MT	
2₆	מליצי	מליצה	(DSH)	MT	(DSH)	MT	
2₈	וישלוכה	ישלוד	MT	MT	MT	MT	Fragm. = DSH.
2₁₅	חמתו	חמתד	(no suffix)	no pronoun	no suffix	DSH	
2₁₆	הרעל	הערל	MT	DSH	DSH	(DSH)	Aq. = DSH.

Moreover, a group of Lucianic manuscripts (Ziegler's group *l II*, consisting of min. 46–86–711) has a text which is the counterpart of DSH's unique Habakkuk text in 1₁₅f.[3] The gap in col. v may be

---

[1] So ROST, *op. cit.*, col. 479, and earlier also BROWNLEE, who now, *Bibl. Arch.*, p. 68 f., follows the interpretation of DUPONT-SOMMER, *op. cit.*, p. 150, and takes it as a "double reading", cf. M. D. GOLDMAN, The Isaiah MSS of the Dead Sea Scrolls, *Australian Biblical Review* 1 (1951), p. 13, who considers DSH's text in 2₁₆ "another confirmation of scholarly ingenuity in text emendation".

[2] The material collected by VAN DER PLOEG, *op. cit.*, p. 3 f., with some additions and corrections.

[3] *ibm.*, p. 4.

filled in with the help of this reading and the slight traces of consonants in DSH agree with such a reconstruction. In the exposition,.
however, the different parts of the text are found with the word
and sentence order of the M. T. and it is hard to find any motive
for the transposition in DSH.

All this must now be much more than chance agreement. The
peculiar way in which DSH coincides both with those readings differing from the M. T. and with the M. T.'s own makes it inadequate
to say that DSH's Hebrew text was the one which is supported by
the said Versions. We must rather presume that DSH was conscious
of various possibilities, tried them out, and allowed them to enrich
its interpretation of the prophet's message, which in all its forms
was fulfilled in and through the Teacher of Righteousness.

The background of the pesher.

The way in which DSH handles the Habakkuk text presupposes
the conviction that the prophecy had received its fulfilment in the
events which occurred with the Teacher of Righteousness and the
community he gathered together and founded around himself. This
interpretation of the actual situation is said to go back to the
Teacher himself, as is apparent from vii, 1 ff. "And God commanded
(speaks to) Habakkuk to write the things that were (are) to come
upon the last generation; but the final phase of the end he did not
make (is not) known to him, but when it says that one may read
in them fluently, its meaning concerns the Teacher of Righteousness
to whom God has made known (reveals) all the mysteries of the
words of his servants the prophets . . ."[1]

---

[1] This may be considered a crucial passage as to the question whether the
Teacher of Righteousness is the founder of the Sect or not. It is partly a matter
of grammar, *viz.* how to render the perfect tense of the Hebrew. Thus ROBERTS,
Bulletin 34, p. 379, has all the verbs in the present tense and he seems to consider
it "unrelated to history". On the other hand the passage in question is that which
gives the theological authority to the bold *pesher* interpretation of the DSH itself.
The Sect must have had a founder and it is reasonable to suppose that it is to
him it owes its actual understanding of the mysteries concealed from Habakkuk
himself. It seems therefore most natural to make this passage an argument for
the existence of the Teacher as a fact in time past. Orally Prof. ENGNELL informs
me that the translation "Teacher of Righteousness" to a certain degree has a
misleading influence since מורה indicates not only his relation to teaching but
also to revelation, תורה being primarily the revealed truth of God. Thereby his
character of a heavenly figure of the final age is reinforced, but in the passage

From this conviction the Sect pursued an eager study of the Scriptures. This study was a focal point of the Sect's religious life as is shown by the regulation in the Manual of Discipline (DSD vi, 6 ff.): "And in whatever place the ten are, there shall not cease to be a man who does 'scholarly work' (דרש) in the Law day and night continually . . ." Now this statement concerns the Law, but how they occupied themselves also with the prophets — not only Habakkuk[1] — we saw in their interpretation of the quotation known from the gospels "Prepare a way for the Lord in the desert", Is. 40₃.[2] The Sect which had settled in the Wilderness of Judaea expounded it: "That is studying the Law (which) He commended through Moses so as to do according to all that was revealed time after time and according to that which the prophets revealed through His Holy Spirit" (DSD viii, 15).

In DSH we find the result of their scholarly work which was carried out according to certain principles. BROWNLEE found 13 principles implied in the DSH manner of *pesher* interpretation[3]:

1) Everything the ancient prophet wrote has a *veiled, eschatological meaning.*[4]

2) Since the ancient prophet wrote cryptically, his meaning is often to be ascertained through a *forced or abnormal construction of the biblical text.*

3) The prophet's meaning may be detected through the study of the *textual or orthographic peculiarities* in the transmitted text. Thus

---

now in question the ministries of revealer and teacher are combined and that also makes it a link between the history and the theology of the Sect. — A similar view as that of Roberts was expressed by ENGNELL, *Svenska Dagbladet* ⁵/₇ 1952, cf. *ibm.* ¹²/₃ 1954.

[1] There are fragments of a *midrash pesher* to Micah with the same characteristics as to the rendering of the biblical text and the method of exposition, J. T. MILIK, *Rev. Bibl.* 59 (1952), p. 412-418.

[2] Cf. above, p. 48.

[3] *Bibl. Arch.*, p. 60-62, cf. SWETE's classification of the deviations in Matthaean quotations, *Introduction in the O. T. in Greek*, p. 394: a) loose citation; b) the substitution of a gloss for the precise words which the writer professes to quote; c) a desire to adapt a prophetic context to the circumstances under which it was thought to have been fulfilled; d) the fusing together of passages drawn from different contexts; e) recensional variations; f) translational variations. — These types of changes receive a consistent background in the principles used in DSH.

[4] Cf. 1 Peter 1₁₀₋₁₂, and in Matthew especially 13₃₅.

the interpretation frequently turns upon the special readings of the text cited.

4) *A textual variant, i. e.* a different reading from the one cited, may also assist interpretation.

5) The application of the features of a verse may be determined by *analogous circumstance* or by

6) *Allegorical propriety.*

7) For the full meaning of the prophet, *more than one meaning* may be attached to his words.[1]

8) In some cases the original prophet so completely veiled his meaning that he can be understood only by an *equation of synonyms*, attaching to the original word a secondary meaning of its synonyms.

9) Sometimes the prophet veiled his message by writing one word instead of another, the interpreter being able to recover the prophet's meaning by a *rearrangement of the letters in a word* or by

10) *The substitution of similar letters* for one or more of the letters in the word of the biblical text.

11) Sometimes the prophet's meaning is to be derived by *the division of one word into two or more parts*, and by expounding the parts.

12) At times the original prophet concealed his message beneath abbreviation . . . (the *notarikon*).[2]

13) *Other passages of scripture* may illuminate the meaning of the original prophet.[3]

---

[1] So *e.g.* in 2 15 "festivals" and "stumblers", cf. above, *ad loc.* — In col. x, 1 ff. an application of a word in three senses may be found, BROWNLEE, *DSH and Targ. Jon.*, p. 11: "And when it says, 'The ends of (in the midst of) (to cut off) many peoples, and you forfeit your life', its meaning is that it is the house of judgment, whose judgment God will give in the midst of 'many peoples'; and afterwards He will bring it up for judgment, and in their midst He will sentence it — judging it with a fire of brimstone!" — "What is declared here is not merely that 'many peoples' are to be 'cut off' (the original meaning of the word קצית), but that also the 'house of judgment' (expounding 'for your house' of the preceding clause of 2 10) is to bear this penalty 'in the midst of many peoples' (equating קצוה to בתוך, cf. SUKENIK, *Megilloth Genuzoth* II, p. 90) and that further this doom is two-fold, in as much as קצוה may be understood as indicating a plurality of 'ends' (the plural of קצה): the first 'end' being military defeat in battle; the second, an eschatological judgment with fire of brimstone."

[2] In *DSH and Targ. Jon.*, p. 10 f., BROWNLEE withdraws this principle since accordance with the Targum gives a satisfactory explanation of the readings which looked like cases of *notarikon*.

[3] There is no example in DSH but in CDC 8 5–9 col; vi, 4–9, where Num. 21 18 is interpreted in the light of Is. 54 16, cf. BROWNLEE, *Bibl. Arch.*, p. 56.

Even if not everyone of these principles can be proved to have been at work in the Sect's study of the Scriptures they certainly point to the type of exegesis which led to the *midrash pesher*. The coincidence with different traditions of interpretation supports that view.[1] The scholarly character of the text and the Sect is put beyond doubt.[2]

The principles of interpretation which may thus be drawn from DSH's treatment of the Scriptures is not without parallels in rabbinic exegesis and the rules of exegesis such as we know them in the form given by Hillel, Ishmael or Eliezer ben Jose.[3] But they display a greater audacity than the rabbinic exegesis. There such a violation of the consonant text is extremely unusual for the Tannaitic period[4], for which reason we are justified in assuming that the Sect at Qumran actually possessed greater creative freedom, as is natural from the Sect's conscious messianic convictions.

The study of the Scriptures and the conviction of the fulfilment of the prophecies are the two pre-requisite conditions for the treatment of the text we find in DSH. It renders the text itself rather uninteresting from the point of view of textual criticism, since its form is created *ad hoc*, and it is not directly affected by the current discussion about "vulgar text" or "text copied from memory". That the Habakkuk text had existed in written form is obvious in view

---

[1] Unfortunately the most extensive study in the DSH was not available to me until this chapter was finished, *viz.* K. ELLIGER, *Studien zum Habakuk-Kommentar vom Toten Meer* (1953). As to the questions at issue in this chapter Elliger supports the view that the Habakkuk text of DSH is of little relevance for restoring the *hebraica veritas*, partly owing to its "fälschliche Glättung des Textes" (1 8, 14, 2 5a, 6a, 6b 2 15b, p. 48–58. On the other hand Elliger criticizes Brownlee's (and Dupont-Sommer's) understanding of the hermeneutic principles implied. He denies the "double interpretations" and finds DSH to be more akin to the Book of Daniel than to the methods of the rabbis, p. 132 f., 159–64; cf. ROBERTS, *Bulletin* 34, p. 368 f. It may be asked if Elliger does not overlook the affinity to the Targum and the other versions as a support for BROWNLEE's view.

[2] The term בית התורה for the Party behind the Damascus Document (CDCb 9 35, 38; col. xx, 10, 13) indicates a school as does a passage in the Hymns of the DSS (DST, SUKENIK, *op. cit.*, plate vii, 12 ff.): ". . . and hast rescued me from envy of false interpreters (מליצי) and from the congregation of expounders (הדורשי) of smooth things", BROWNLEE, *Bibl. Arch.*, p. 58 f.

[3] J. BONSIRVEN, *Exégèse rabbinique et exégèse paulinienne* (1939), p. 77–83.

[4] *ibm.*, p. 120 ff.

of what DSD says about the Sect's study of the Scriptures and of the ability to handle different traditions of interpretation. The way in which the exposition had affected the text confirms HEMPEL's statement that DSH's Habakkuk text is of an essentially different nature from DSI a, a text for cultic use. The Habakkuk text now in DSH has certainly never existed as "a text" outside the commentary. The eschatological conviction explains the remarkable "freedom" in relation to the text. When more of the significance of the words was known through the coming and the instruction of the Teacher of Righteousness than was known to the prophet himself, the prophet's message could be made more lucid. Through the scholarly study it was made possible from this conviction to choose and reject amongst the various traditions of interpretation, some of which are known to us from the Targum and the other versions.

This seems to be the explanation of the fact that DSH's interpretation sometimes follows one track and sometimes another, examples of which we can find in the O. T. versions. In this connection it is not out of the question that even Greek texts were available to these students of the Scriptures[1], but we can often assume that many of the Greek interpretations were also found in the Aramaic Targum tradition.

The double interpretations, at first so perplexing, where two readings stand parallel to one another, constitute in some respects the climax of this activity of learning in the Scriptures. To a certain extent they could be taken as instances of assonance and playing on words, but at the same time they are a sign of the conviction of the wealth and sanctity of the text. We cannot talk of variants in the ordinary meaning of the word, nor of "freedom" in the usual sense. Rather should we speak of a fidelity to the prophecy, the true meaning of which was concealed from the prophet himself.

The pesher and Matthew's formula quotations.

Here and there in the literature on DSS, there are hints as to the relevance of the scrolls for the quotations in the N. T. B. J. ROBERTS finds one of the closest parallels to the pesher type of exposition just in the N. T., where it is labelled "fulfilment of prophecy".[2] The

---

[1] Cf. ibm., p. 119.

[2] Bulletin 34, p. 370, cf. p. 374 f., 384 and ibm. 36, p. 78 f. So also SUKENIK, op. cit., p. 86, with special reference to the tendentious manner of citing. On this

apocalyptic idea of fulfilment and the actualizing of prophecy constitutes to him the link between DSH and the N. T. He is not concerned with the problem of deviations in the N. T. quotations. As we shall try to prove, these very deviations constitute the substantial similarity between those two texts, and in both texts the deviations may be considered typical for the *pesher*.

When Roberts assigns the *pesher* interpretation to apocalyptic literature in general, this could have far-reaching consequences for our study. We have found it to be a constant feature of apocalyptic style not to quote Scriptures literally.[1] The deviations both in DSH and in the N. T. from texts known to us could therefore be taken just as such free renderings, but in both cases the freedom was not merely a matter of looseness as in Mt. 24 or in many of the quotations common to Matthew and Luke, *e.g.* Mt. 7 23 ≠ Lk. 13 27. On the contrary, the rendering of the texts was the result of a detailed study of the texts proper.[2] We therefore venture to make it our hypothesis that in the formula quotations the biblical text is treated in somewhat the same manner as in the DSH quotations, while the synoptic quotations and the rest of the quotations peculiar to Matthew are taken from the Greek text common to the church and the synagogue, cf. DSIa as "cultic text". The formula quotations would thus have taken shape within the Matthaean church's study of the Scriptures, while the form of the remainder is on the whole that of the Palestinian LXX text. If this were the case, we should have further material for our theory that, from the point of view of form criticism, Matthew emanates from a school.[3] In its formula quotations

---

BROWNLEE, *Bibl. Arch.*, p. 73, comments: "the gospels, however, never depart from the simple meaning of words, unless it be in the supposed verbal play which derives Nazarene from 'branch' (נצר of Is. 11 1), if Mt. 2 23 indeed quotes Is. 11 1".

[1] See above, p. 158 f.

[2] As to the *Book of Jubilees*, of which a fragment was found in the cave, a closer study from the point of view of quotations may show that it can be considered a close parallel to DSH also in this respect, DUPONT-SOMMER, *Aperçus préliminaires sur les Manuscrits de la Mer Morte* (1950), p. 115. On the quotations in Jubilees, see CHARLES, *The Book of Jubilees* (1902), p. xxxiii–xxxix, IDEM, *Apocrypha and Pseudepigrapha* II, p. 5 f., and *Anecdota Oxoniensia*, Sem. ser. 8 (1895), p. xvii–xxv.

[3] C. H. TOY, *Quotations in the New Testament* (1884), which unfortunately was not available to me, may be relevant to this question, since it is reported to say, p. 21 "The New Testament writers handle the Old according to a Talmudic manner plus their Messianic hope".

it contains material of the *pesher* type, which was intended for the theology and teaching of the church.

To say that the conviction of fulfilment of prophecy is to be found in the N. T. as well as in DSH is almost to state a truism. The conviction that Jesus was the Messiah and that therefore the time was accomplished and the promises fulfilled was the focal point in the *kerygma* and the teaching of the church. The question is, however, to what extent the other assumption of the DSH quotations — the advanced study of the Scriptures — has its counterpart in the N. T. milieu. In part I we have seen that we do not lack indications of a school as the background to the First Gospel, and it is worth asking whether Matthew's formula quotations have not certain features in common with DSH's method of using Scripture.

When turning to the N. T., an important factor is further added, namely the translation. If in its Hebrew form the O. T. text had already become the object of what we consider an over-ambitious revision and interpretation, the translation makes possible — we could almost say demands — an adaptation to the messianic understanding and application. Thus both dependence upon and freedom from the LXX translations are quite natural, but even in the cases in which the LXX, in the form most probably known to Matthew, would have served his purpose, Matthew follows his own way to a large extent.

In Mt. 27$_9$ and the adjacent verses we came across a N. T. example of the retention and use of two parallel readings as in DSH.[1] It even appeared to adapt the verbs to subjects, which suited Matthew's new understanding of the Zechariah text. It unmistakably alludes to the parallels in Jeremiah where a field was mentioned and the יוצר was a real potter. At the same time, the passage was perhaps influenced by the LXX and other Greek interpretations.

The basis of Matthew's understanding of the text was certain historical facts known to Matthew by tradition as parts of the Messiah's career, and thus considered fulfilment of prophecy. The relation between historical facts and O. T. quotation is often regarded as an influence of the O. T. on the facts recorded, particularly in the accounts of the passion. This is surely true in such a case as Ps. 22 which in its entirety has become a liturgical text on the Passion.

---

[1] Or: two different interpretations. If אצר never was in the text, it was in the minds of the interpreters, see above, p. 125.

An increasing number of details creep into the story[1] and it is hard to distinguish between the facts which related the Psalm to the Passion and the details in the story evoked by the Psalm. In DSH, on the other hand, we have found good reason for assuming the opposite tendency. The facts have affected the Habakkuk text. In the same way the Zechariah quotation is affected by the facts, rather than that these are invented as suitable fulfilment of the prophecy. So we must start with the facts, as Matthew knew them[2], which gave new understanding to the prophecy:

a) There existed a graveyard called the Field of Blood.[3] The author of Acts 1 15ff. is more concerned with this fact and his account is an aetiological story around the name. The name is referred to and explained in another way by Matthew, but it belongs only to the periphery of his account.

b) Judas returned the money he received. In 26 15 it is said to be thirty pieces of silver, in accordance with Zech. 11 12f. The exact number could be an adaptation to the prophecy.[4]

c) It was a potter's field which was purchased with the money.

d) The Temple authorities were said not to have placed the coins in the treasury; in this way they unwittingly revealed the right meaning of the prophecy.[5] Matthew's understanding seems to have been that the interpretation יוצר (אוצר) = κορβανᾶς was true in the past, but that the genuine intention of the prophecy came to light in the handling of Judas's money.

It is possible that the introductory τότε in the quotation formula stresses this understanding.[6] In acting as they did, the Temple au-

---

[1] For the later spread of the same tendency, see W. BAUER, Das Leben Jesu im Zeitalter der neutestamentlichen Apokryphen (1909), p. 539.

[2] See McNEILE, Comm. Mt., p. 408 f.

[3] On the name Ἀκελδαμαχ = חקל דמא, Acts 1 19, see McNEILE, loc. cit.

[4] B. MURMELSTEIN, Die Gestalt Josephs in der Agada und in der Evangeliengeschichte, Angelos 4 (1932), p. 52–54, observed that 30 is the number indicated by the consonants of the name יהודה, and Jerome knew a tradition according to which Joseph too had been sold for 30 pieces of silver instead of the 20 mentioned in Gen. 37 28. Murmelstein therefore presumed that Matthew's account on Judas is influenced from Jewish haggadah concerning Joseph. — On a tradition of the 30 pieces of silver throughout the history from Joseph to Judas, see R. HOFMANN, Das Leben Jesu nach den Apocryphen (1851), p. 333.

[5] Cf. HOMMES, Het Testimoniaboek, p. 152.

[6] The introductory τότε in the formula of the quotation is found only here and in 2 17. There too, the application to the prophecy is somewhat far-fetched.

thorities fulfilled the prophecy hitherto concealed beneath the interpretations of the Jews. WELLHAUSEN wrote "Merkwürdig wie hier
die Kenntnis nicht bloss der Bibel selber, sondern auch ihrer Interpretation und Textkritik historisch fruchtbar gemacht wird".[1] Now
this is precisely what we have seen in DSH more explicitly than
anywhere else.[2] We have thereby got a forceful parallel. It implies,
however, that even for a Matthew quotation such as this we must
presume a function of the study of the Scriptures in the Matthaean
church. The second condition of the DSH *pesher* type of text must
also be supposed in the Matthaean church.

The text in Mt. 27 is not an isolated feature in the First Gospel.
As we saw in our examination of the quotation from Is. 42 1–4 in
Mt. 12 18–21, this too was a Christian translation which showed knowledge of various possible renderings. The O. T. Peshitta (ἐρίσει), the Targum (ϑήσω — ἀπαγγέλλει), Theodotion (ἰδοὺ ὁ παῖς μου — ὃν εὐδόκησεν
ἡ ψυχή μου) and the LXX (ἐπὶ τῷ ὀνόματι . . .) had left their imprint
in the N. T. text and the Hebrew text which had been given a more
concrete interpretation, suitable to the N. T. context. Over and above
what is shown in the quotation in 27 9, the LXX character here is
remarkable. It indicates that the school which has here been at work
had in view a Greek rendering of the prophecy.

Matthew's reference in 2 23 to a prophecy that Jesus should be
called ναζωραῖος was not accompanied by an explanatory translation,
as the saying about Immanuel in 1 23. It must therefore be thought
to have been intelligible to a Greek reader without such an explanation. This is reminiscent of Judges 13 5, 7, 16 17 where נזיר is rendered
in the LXX by ναζιραίον, and in cod. B by ναζίρ.[3] Even the closest
parallels in Luke (1 35) point in this direction, for its ἅγιον is one
of the LXX's translations of נזיר.[4]

---

[1] *Comm. Mt.*, p. 145.

[2] There is also a difference between the double interpretations of DSH and
that of Mt. 27. In DSH both readings were equal in value and truth. In Matthew
one of the meanings is that of times past, when the prophecy still was veiled
(κορβανᾶς), and the other (κεραμεύς) is the true understanding in the time of
fulfilment. Yet both are given in the text.

[3] So H. H. SCHAEDER, *Theol. Wörterb. z. N. T.* IV, p. 883. He renounces the
reference to נצר in Is. 11 1 as "ein lediglich für Liebhaber rabbinischer Auslegungs-
künste erratbares Wortspiel". The similarities between the formula quotations of
Matthew and DSH encourages us to think that Matthew was to some extent such
a "Liebhaber" himself.

[4] E. NESTLE, *Exp. Times* 19 (1907/08), p. 524.

In Matthew, however, the form of the adjective is ναζωραῖος which in Acts is the term for Jesus and the Christians before those in Antioch came to be called Christians. In all Semitic forms (Syriac[1], Mandaean, Aramaic) the middle radical is a ṣade. The rendering with ζ instead of the regular ς is consistent in the N. T. and does not lack parallels in the LXX.[2] A messianic prophecy, which could explain the puzzling fact that Jesus did not come from Bethlehem, the town of David, was required. In the light of DSH's interpretation we are bound to raise the question whether the reference to the messianic נצר is not more natural than that to נזיר. Matthew refers to the messianic prophecy in Is. 11₁.[3] His allusion did not, however, allow of translation and could not be checked in the Greek text, nor could it be elucidated in a single explanatory clause as in 1₂₃[4]; it had to be issued on Matthew's authority. On the other hand, the form ναζωραῖος shows that the term was known to the readers and was not merely created from the name of the town.

This may seem to modify our understanding with regard to the Greek character of Matthew's formula quotation. The speculation which we encounter demands a Semitic milieu and school tradition — as do all the other formula quotations — but it is not necessary to presume a ready Aramaic gospel in which this reference to Is. 11₁ was embodied, and which eluded the translators' capabilities. In this way the school tradition built on Semitic words could be of use even for the Greek gospel.

In 1₂₃ we found a changing of the number and person of the verb, in the LXX "thou shalt call" and in Matthew "one (they) shall call", a change which was clearly prompted by the quotation's application to Jesus. In his παρθένος Matthew follows the LXX; this interpretation is essential to the function of the quotation, but a direct dependence on the LXX was not absolutely necessary, though more natural.

---

[1] See A. BAUMSTARK, Zeitschr. d. Deutsch. Morgenl. Gesellsch. 89 (1935), p. 116, ܢܨܪܝܐ = נצר.

[2] See SCHAEDER, op. cit., p. 884.

[3] This interpretation of Is. 11₁ may have found support in Is. 49₆, M. T. נְצֻרֵי read as an adjective to נצר : נְצוּרֵי, G. H. Box in The People and the Book (ed. A. S. PEAKE), p. 440 f.

[4] Cf. 1₂₁, where the name of Jesus is interpreted but not explicitly translated, cf. above, p. 98, note 4.

Mt. 2₆ showed clear signs of an independent interpretation without agreeing with either the Targum or the O. T. Peshitta. The hermeneutic principles which came into use were distinguished by changing the sentence structure (through οὐδαμῶς — γάρ), and by actualizing and modernizing the geographical terms (γῆ Ἰούδα); this interpretation refers to persons instead of abstract items (ἡγεμόσιν). Here again the LXX might have afforded Matthew a rather suitable text, but the text's character of a revised school text explains its "freedom".

In 2₁₅, Matthew agrees with Aquila, who in this case may have taken up a Palestinian Greek interpretation known to Matthew. On the other hand Matthew diverged from the Targum and Theodotion, thereby obtaining the only reading useful to him.

In 2₁₈ we had a shortened form of the M. T. with a certain agreement with the LXX^A.

In 8₁₇ Matthew interpreted the M. T. *ad hoc*. His rendering was certainly a correct reproduction of the M. T. but it may nevertheless be regarded as an *ad hoc* interpretation since it differed from every Greek and Aramaic interpretation known to us.

Mt. 13₃₅ was a reading created for the occasion from the Hebrew text, both in its κεκρυμμένα and in its ἀπὸ καταβολῆς (κόσμου). The theology implied in the quotation as Matthew rendered it is a close parallel to DSH vii, 1 ff., where the Sect expressed its attitude to the Scriptures.

Mt. 21₅ confronted us with the question whether the two asses come from Matthew's understanding of the text or whether a tradition which related to two asses has given rise to Matthew's interpretation of the Scriptures, so that he is anxious to break up the *parallelismus membrorum* with reference to it. In breaking up the parallelism Matthew deviated from the common messianic interpretation of the Rabbis. The only reason for such a treatment of the O. T. text must be that Matthew knew a tradition, which spoke about two asses. That is why he stresses the two asses more than does the LXX in the rendering of the prophecy, which to him was fulfilled in a very exact way. The textual support for his rendering is the Hebrew ועל. A secondary reason for Matthew's form of the quotation might have been that he had pondered upon the virginity of the foal, cf. Mk. 11₂.

Thus all of Matthew's formula quotations give evidence of features of text interpretation of an actualizing nature, often closely associated with the context in the gospel. This feature justifies us in speaking of a *pesher* type in Matthew's quoting. Because of this the hope to find in these quotations an example of the Greek O. T. text which might be derived from a text known to the evangelist, is an illusion.[1] Plausible as this showed itself to be for the quotations which the Synoptics had in common, efforts in this direction with regard to the formula quotations are misdirected.

It is true that even the formula quotations may occasionally afford material of Palestinian Greek O. T. text, but as a whole they are not available for such a hypothesis. It is similarly misleading to see in them a meticulous translation of Aramaic Targums[2], though they afford readings which may be dependent upon Targums both known and unknown to us. In their type and *Sitz im Leben* they are not cultic texts of the authorized type, but are scholarly interpretations. The DSH material shows that such an interpretation did not thereby become a text without conclusiveness and authority. When we called Matthew's text targumic, this does not mean that they are" paraphrasing freely" and therefore of less relevance. The method of the Targum is here used rather in the same way in which it influenced DSH. Matthew's formula quotations seem to us therefore to be a decisive indication that we must postulate a School of Matthew.

Traces of the same scholarly treatment of the texts are not lacking outside the First Gospel.[3] It is thus remarkable that precisely those synoptic quotations which are closest to the type of the formula quotations show the same tendency, namely Mt. 3 3 and 11 10 with parallels. These quotations, in fact, afford instances of adaptation of the suffixes, changing of the sentence structure, and a more suitable choice of words for their function in the N. T. Here, however, we perceive an influence from the tradition of the Jewish synagogue which can be demonstrated more directly Thus we have good reason for assuming that the text was formed as an early testimony[4] without the conscious scholarly interpretation which we presume for Matthew's own formula quotations. In the Fourth Gospel we found

---

[1] See above, p. 182.

[2] BAUMSTARK, *op. cit.*, p. 114.

[3] Cf. the theological work, which led to the readings ζαφθανι — ὠνείδισας in the D text of Mk. 15 34, and the reading ἡ δύναμίς μου in the Gospel of Peter, above, p. 85 f.

[4] See below, p. 215.

how the evangelist and his school issued a translation of their own. To be sure they had access to both Greek and Hebrew O. T. texts. There were, however, far fewer intentional changes based on detailed interpretation of the Hebrew, and thus the elaborate stage of the *pesher* found in Matthew scarcely existed.[1]

---

[1] We find a similar influence of the interpretation in the way in which various N. T. authors quote Hab. 2 3f., as T. W. MANSON has pointed out. The development is here, however, entirely within the Greek and no influence from the M. T.'s אמונתי is to be found; the starting point is the LXX's messianic interpretation, which is further developed in Heb. 10 37f., *Journ. of Theol. St.* 46 (1945), p. 132–136. Manson points out the rabbinic legitimacy of such a manner of quoting. Cf. DODD, *According to the Scriptures*, p. 49–51, and HARDER, *Theologia Viatorum*, p. 37.

Additional note. In the March issue this year of the *Journ. of Bibl. Lit.*, p. 11–35, I. RABINOWITZ gives good reasons for the view that "Damascus" and "390 years" in the DSD refer to past (scriptural) history. Thereby the whole of the so called Damascus Document takes on a *pesher* character, cf. above, p. 183, note 3.

How did the formula quotations come into the Gospel of Matthew?

If our observations are correct, Matthew contains a number of examples of a special type of biblical interpretation, a *pesher* translation which presupposes an advanced study of the Scriptures and familiarity with the Hebrew text and with the traditions of interpretation known to us from the Versions. We have further noted a strong LXX element in the formula quotations, which indicates that they originated in Greek form and that the language in the Matthaean church was accordingly Greek. This presumption is reinforced when we see how these quotations have been fitted into the gospel.

The striking thing about such an interpretation of Matthew's formula quotations is that we should have two types of quotation side by side in the same gospel, both the liturgical type and the *pesher* type, following the classification suggested by HEMPEL.[1] The introductory formula of the quotations might here be something of a technical term which Matthew uses to distinguish the *pesher* type of quotation. For it is to be noted that those quotations which differ from all texts known to us are precisely the ones prefaced by the formula of express fulfilment.[2]

Thus the question of the gospel's composition is brought into a fresh light. According to BACON formula quotations are of the very essence of a supposed Jewish-Christian source which he calls "N" (the Nazarene Targum) and which he thinks was worked into the gospel when the compiler combined Mark and "S" (based on Q) and other sources. The compiler himself was, however, quoting the LXX.[3] On the other hand, SOLTAU thought the formula quotations were a part of a larger collection with Jewish-Christian trends (especially the Peter and Pilate legends), which was mechanically merged into a previously existing Matthew at a much later stage.[4]

---

[1] See above, p. 185.

[2] So KILPATRICK, *The Origins of the Gospel according to St. Matthew*, p. 57. — For Kilpatrick's view on confusion as to the quotations in Mt. 1 21 and 1 23, see above, p. 98 f.

[3] BACON, *Studies in Matthew*, p. 156–164.

[4] W. SOLTAU, Zur Entstehung des 1. Evangeliums, *Zeitschr. f. d. neutest. Wissensch.* 1 (1900), p. 219–248, especially p. 224, cf. IDEM, *Unsere Evangelien* (1901), p. 55 f.

Both of these views are rejected by KILPATRICK, whose analysis of the peculiar narratives gives good reason for taking them to be a product of the evangelist himself. Especially in the texts dealing with Peter, Kilpatrick shows that often the text of Matthew can only be derived from Mark, and in the longer independent passages, as in ch. 1–2, the phraseology is that of Matthew. He therefore maintains that this material should not be considered as coming from one or more sources (*e.g.* Bacon's N), but that Matthew is acquainted with a number of oral traditions which he handles freely. If some of these were written down they could not be said to constitute a literary source in the strict sense, but brief memoranda.[1]

The quotation material convinces us that Kilpatrick is right. Bacon's alleged N-source was built up around the formula quotations which are of two kinds:

a) The quotations in the Nativity Story, where the whole context seems to be constructed with the quotation as its nucleus — and as its germ from the point of view of growth.

b) The quotations added to Marcan material. These O.T. references do not give the impression of being picked up from a source which happened to contain a suitable quotation. The adapted reading ἐν ταῖς πλατείαις in Mt. 12 19 formed a link with the context, as did the reading ἐρεύξομαι κεκρυμμένα in 13 35. In 8 17, 13 35, 21 5, and to a certain extent also in 4 15f., 26 15 and 27 9, the Marcan text was the starting-point of the quotation.

This being so, Kilpatrick's views on the peculiar narratives in Matthew are strengthened. The formula quotations arose in a church using and studying the Gospel of Mark. Since the two different groups of formula quotations just mentioned have to be considered as a unit, the quotations in ch. 1–2 surrounded by their own context in no way lessen the impression that this material is not taken from a source, but is the result of the school-activity in the church of Matthew.

Kilpatrick, however, does not come to these conclusions when he deals with the formula quotations. He finds that their non-LXX form shows that Matthew "must have taken over these quotations from another source which was not so dependent" (*viz.* on the LXX).[2] Kilpatrick

---

[1] KILPATRICK, *op. cit.*, p. 37–55.

[2] *op. cit.*, p. 57. — Similarly V. H. STANTON, *The Gospels as Historical Documents* II (1909), p. 342–347, considers the formula quotations as a distinct group.

thinks this source was oral. He regards it as older by virtue of its independence of the LXX and assumes that even the introductory formula belongs to this source, since it is confined to this type of quotations.[1] As a tentative explanation of the existence of the two types of quotation existing side by side, Kilpatrick suggests a different background for the two. "It may be that quotations which derive from lectionary association keep closer to the LXX, while those which exhibit some freedom would come from the stock quotations of the sermon."[2] Here Kilpatrick combines his homiletic-liturgical view of Matthew[3] with the hypothesis of testimonies, but as we hope to prove in our next chapter, the theory of testimonies does not solve the problems of the formula quotations.

Kilpatrick's suggestion of different "Sitz im Leben" for the two types of quotation coincides with the view we have been led to accept. If we take "the stock quotations of the sermon" to be *pesher* quotations instead of older translations with retained Semitic phraseology, we can maintain, even in the quotations, the "non-source thinking" of Kilpatrick, which on other points he champions so well. The formula quotations are the fruits of the creative activity of the Matthaean church and they are indicated by the special type of introductory formula. Naturally they have been used in sermons, but this was not their first milieu, nor was preaching the activity within the church which brought them into being.

Kilpatrick makes much of the LXX character of Matthew outside the formula quotations. As we have found, this tendency is not without exception[4], which is quite natural if the church of Matthew in its school had access to the bulk of the Semitic O.T. text. The dominant use of the LXX, however, shows the authority of the LXX as the accepted edition of the O.T. in everyday church life. Kilpatrick's method of defining the non-LXX texts as belonging to a source is weakened by the evidence of the slight but obvious Semitic influence even outside the group of formula quotations.

When dealing with the character of the gospel as a whole, we claimed

---

They were taken from an originally Aramaic *Catena of fulfilments*, but Stanton emphasizes that "the source from which they were taken cannot have been a collection of Old Testament citations *and nothing more*", p. 344.

[1] *ibm.*, p. 93.

[2] *ibm.*, p. 95.

[3] Cf. above, p. 20.

[4] Cf. above, p. 147 f.

for it the nature of a handbook and a storehouse for teaching, preaching and church government. The homiletic-liturgical character was challenged. The formula quotations, worked in side by side with the other types of quotation, add emphasis to this evaluation of the First Gospel. If our observations and our interpretation of these quotations and of the manner in which they came into the Gospel are found to be right, they constitute an almost conclusive argument for "The School of St. Matthew".

Did Matthew make use of Testimonies?

Again and again during the course of our inquiry we have used the term "testimonies" without explaining what we meant by it. We intentionally delayed offering a detailed treatment of the question of testimonies, however. The conception of testimonies as the basis of the N.T.'s quotations from the O.T. actually appears seductive in our study. It offers an easy explanation of the quotations with differing forms, and it is often referred to without any consideration of its limitations. To me DODD's position seems illuminating as to the character of the question. He says he had taken a positive attitude to the idea of testimonies until he devoted a more thorough study to the question, when he was forced to reject this explanation.[1]

In modern research, the conception of testimonies is principally connected with the name of RENDEL HARRIS.[2] He started from the systematized collections of O.T. quotations which we find, for example, in Cyprian's Testimonia, Tertullian's Adversus Judaeos, and the work of the same title ascribed to Gregory of Nyssa. Harris pointed out the agreements between these works and the earlier writings, so rich in quotations: Irenaeus's Epideixis, Justin's First Apology and his Dialogue, the Epistle of Barnabas[3], the Second Epistle of Clement, etc. Harris attempts to trace these quotations to a stage behind the N.T. writings. To Harris *The Book of Testimonies* is the first known treatise on Christian theology.[4] It consists of quotations from the O.T. furnished with headings showing whence they had been taken and what they serve to elucidate and prove.[5]

---

[1] DODD, *According to the Scriptures* (1952), p. 26.

[2] *Testimonies* I–II (1916–1920).

[3] Cf. H. WINDISCH, *Comm. Barn.*, p. 408 ff.: testimonies are one of the main sources of the Epistle of Barnabas; and DIBELIUS, *Theol. Rundschau*, N.F. 3 (1931), p. 228.

[4] *Testimonies* I, Introduction.

[5] Most of the patristic material to which Harris referred was previously collected and treated by A. VON UNGERN-STERNBERG, *Der traditionelle alttestamentliche Schriftbeweis "de Christo" und "de Evangelio" in der alten Kirche bis zur Zeit Eusebs von Caesarea* (1913). He found "zwischen Justin, Irenäus und Tertullian wohl ein

So far as the N.T. is concerned, such a Book of Testimonies might explain 1) the composite quotations, 2) the ascription to wrong authors, 3) the readings which differ from the editions known to us — especially if these differences remain constant in the testimony tradition. The assumption might be sustained if the mutual order of the quotations appears to be constant within the testimony literature.[1]

To this should be added that the testimonies of this type might fit well into the picture of early Christian preaching. This was built upon O.T. material, principally of messianic type. The reference to the Scriptures (κατὰ τὰς γραφάς, 1 Cor. 15 3, 4) belonged to the *kerygma*. That such *dicta probantia* were collected together at such an early stage is rendered the more likely if one considers the poverty of the congregations and the travelling conditions of the missionaries. In this connection one readily thinks of the remark in 2 Tim. 4 13: ... τὰ βιβλία, μάλιστα τὰς μεμβράνας.

Possibly it is such a collection of testimonies which we have from the 4th century in Papyrus Ryland Gk. 460 and Papyrus Osloensis 11.[2] The text, which is LXX with minor differences of an internal Greek nature, lacks the references to authors and theological subjects assumed by Harris.

The conception of testimonies as the background to the N.T.'s quotations had been put forward before Harris. The first in modern times who made this assumption appears to have been HATCH. To him the testimonies were an explanation of the composite quotations from the LXX. In his exposition he confines himself to only one text in the N.T., the composite of quotations in Rom. 3 10–18.[3]

Verwandtschafts- aber kein Abhängigkeitsverhältnis" and therefore he assumes "einen nicht festgeprägten Traditionsstoff, welchen es charakterisieren würde, dass bei einer beträchtlichen Stabilität des Inhaltes die Form flüssig, variabel wäre" (p. 138 f.). BOUSSET, *Jüdisch-Christlicher Schulbetrieb in Alexandria und Rom* (1915), p. 308: "In den διδασκαλεῖα der altchristlichen διδάσκαλοι wurde dieser Schriftbeweis ausgebildet."

[1] This point was emphasized by HARRIS and also by BOUSSET, *op. cit.*, p. 304, against von Ungern-Sternberg.

[2] The latter was published by G. RUDBERG in *Videnskapsselskapets Forhandlinger*, Kristiania (Oslo) 1923:2 (with a photograph) and later by S. EITREM–L. AMUNDSEN in *Papyri Osloenses* II (1931), p. 10 f. It was labelled "for liturgical usages". Both papyri were published together by C. H. ROBERTS in *Bull. of J. Ryl. Libr.* 20 (1936), p. 237–244 (with a photograph of pap. Ryl. Gk. 460). Roberts discovered that they were parts of one leaf and took it as a fragment of a testimony book. — For a Latin collection of testimonies, combined merely by "*et*", see VON DOBSCHÜTZ, *Journ. of Theol. St.* 16 (1914/15), p. 1–27.

[3] *Essays in Biblical Greek* (1889), p. 203 and 209–211.

Burkitt gave the hypothesis of testimonies quite a different function. He wanted to explain the special form of the quotations in the material peculiar to Matthew by saying that Matthew might have made use of testimonies with more marked Semitic traces along with the LXX.[1]

Harris did not link the theory of testimonies with any special type of quotation and he makes no distinction between the various groups of citations. Nevertheless, his interest is centred around Matthew and he maintains that the observation of Papias about how Matthew collected τὰ λόγια alluded precisely to the Book of Testimonies, τὰ λόγια being used at this time only of O.T. oracles.[2] Papias's commentary in five books might then refer to this collection of testimonies, which was divided into five parts, as Matthew later became divided. Moreover, it is characteristic of Harris that he understands these testimonies as a writing "Against the Jews"[3], a conception which is connected with the fact that Harris takes as his starting point the later collections of testimonies which obviously have such a character.

In *Testimonies*, Part II, Harris is somewhat more cautious as to the

---

[1] *The Gospel History and its Transmission* (1907), p. 124–28.

[2] So also Burkitt, *ibm.*, p. 127, and earlier the anonymously published book *The Oracles ascribed to Matthew by Papias of Hierapolis* (1894) by John Burslem Gregory. The same line is followed by T. H. Bindley, Papias and the Matthaean Oracles, *Church Quarterly Rev.* 84 (1917), p. 31–43, E. C. Selwyn, *The Oracles of the New Testament* (1912), and by B. P. W. Stather Hunt, *Primitive Gospel Sources* (1951), p. 182–193 and 319–322. — J. Donovan, *The Logia in Ancient and Recent Literature* (1924) followed Gregory in taking λόγια to mean "Holy Writ" but used the argument in the opposite direction to establish the proof for an early canonicity of the First Gospel (τὰ λόγια = the Gospel). To Bacon, *Studies in Matthew*, p. 443–451, and T. W. Manson, *Bull. of J. Ryl. Libr.* 29 (1945/46), p. 392–428, the term λόγια refers to the words of Jesus, according to Bacon particularly to those composed in the five discourses of Matthew, see above, p. 24 ff.

[3] Thereby Harris (and V. Burch) are forced to assume that the quotations now in Matthew had originally another setting and function, *e.g.* 3₃, 11₁₀, 2₁₅, *op. cit.* II, p. 65, and I, p. 126 (cf. Burkitt, *op. cit.*, p. 127): The quotations now related to John the Baptist concerned Jesus in the Book of Testimonies. The testimony now in Mt. 2₁₅ had the form "When Israel was a child I loved him; and out of Egypt I called my son", and it was used to prove that Christ was called Israel. — In *Justin*, Dial. 123, cf. 100, Is. 42₁ is adduced to prove that Christ was called Jacob and Israel, an argument which requires the text of the LXX instead of the Matthaean form in 12₁₈₋₂₀, see above p. 110. There is apparently a gulf between the LXX type of testimonies and the "testimonies" of Matthew. — The main difference between Harris and Stather Hunt in his recent work is that the Book of Testimonies is now taken out of its narrow apologetic setting and given a more general character with three types of testimonies: Messianic, Legal and Apocalyptic.

connection of Papias's commentary with a Matthaean book of testimonies in five parts.[1] He and his colleague BURCH, who worked out the
chapter on the synoptic material, make no distinction within Matthew's
quotations, however.[2] MOFFATT, who is actually well disposed to the idea
of testimonies, points out that two types of testimonies must be presumed in Matthew: the LXX type (which HATCH counted) and that
coloured by Semitic wordings (which was BURKITT's assumption).[3] The
conception of a homogeneous Book of Testimonies is thereby rendered
less likely. Accordingly most later scholars who make use of the idea of
testimonies do not speak about a single Book of Testimonies.[4]

Another difficulty with Harris's reasoning is the influence from the
N.T. in the O.T. quotations occurring in Christian literature in post-
apostolic times.[5] The problem may be elucidated by Justin's rendering
of the Zechariah prophecy which we have in 21 5.[6] In his turn, Justin has
influenced Irenaeus, for example, and the testimony literature shows

---

[1] Cf. DODD's remark on the attitude of Harris towards his own ideas in later
years, *According to the Scriptures*, p. 25.

[2] To be sure, BURCH, in HARRIS, *Testimonies* II, p. 58, excises certain quotations with Semitic imprint 16 27, 18 16, 19 4, 7, 26. They are said to show the Hebrew
quality of the teaching and person of Jesus and to be without relevance for the
Book of Testimonies. The distinction is supported by a reference to literary sources,
but seems to be rather arbitrary.

[3] *Introduction to the Literature of the N.T.* (1918³), p. 258: "The dual nature of the
citations remains, however, upon any hypothesis, and it is a watermark of compilation", cf. *ibm.*, p. 23–25.

[4] e.g. A. LUKYN WILLIAMS, *Adversus Judaeos* (1935), p. 3–13, especially p. 7.
M. SIMON, *Verus Israel* (1948), p. 186, and even STATHER HUNT, *op. cit.*, p. 14.

[5] The relevant material can now be studied in MASSAUX, *Influence de l'Évangile de saint Matthieu.* — J. L. KOOLE, *De Overname van Het Oude Testament door
de Christelijke Kerk* (1938), p. 16–51, gives a list of O. T. quotations by the Early
Fathers.

[6] See above, p. 119 f. — I cannot find FINDLAY's reasons for saying (in *Amicitiae
Corolla*, p. 65) about the quotation from Zech. 11 in *Irenaeus*, Epideixis 81 — as in
Mt 27 9 ascribed to Jeremiah: "The context proves that Irenaeus is not quoting
Matthew, but the Book of Testimonies". The evidence given in HARRIS, *op. cit.* I,
p. 58 f. and 68 f. is a definite statement ("evidently not from the Gospel"). Harris
says that Irenaeus means to quote the prophet, not the gospel. Such an intention
is of little interest even to Harris who thinks that he actually quotes the Book of
Testimonies. The quotation is not used by Justin. The peculiar wording "... whom
they bought from the children of Israel" is not paralleled in any O.T. text not even
the Armenian, so Prof. Wikander informs me.

mutual dependence which rules out any conclusive argument for a tradition of testimonies independent of the N.T.[1]

Harris's interest was especially bound up with Matthew, not only by reason of his hypothesis on the relevance of Papias's statement to the Book of Testimonies. Already the wealth of citations in the First Gospel made such a hypothesis probable, and especially in ch. 1–2 it was clear that the text had been spun around the quotation and consequently this appeared primary to its context. It may therefore be justifiable to concentrate our study on the significance of the hypothesis of testimonies for the quotations in Matthew. The most obvious thing to do first is to examine the cases where the same quotation stands both in Matthew (with or without parallels in the Synoptics) and in other N.T. writings.[2]

The final words in Mt. 15₉ are found also in Col. 2₂₂, but there they are more in agreement with the LXX's word order.[3]

The quotation from Deut. 19₁₅ was included in the context relating to church discipline in Mt. 18₁₆ and in 1 Tim. 5₁₉, while it is used in a figurative sense with regard to Paul's third visit to Corinth in 2 Cor. 13₁. In all these cases it was abbreviated in the same manner though this did not result in word for word agreement. We have understood the quotation as a sort of *verbum Christi*, used as a regulation for church discipline.[4] It was precisely with such a function that we found *verba Christi* in Paul, as in 1 Cor. 7 and 14.[5]

Mt. 22₄₄ has had great significance for the Christian interpretation of the O.T. This quotation from Ps. 110, when used in Acts 2₃₄f. and Heb. 1₁₃, was treated with the same method of interpretation as in the gospels, *viz.* a *deductio ad absurdum*: It is shown that the words of the psalm had no significance if they did not point to Jesus the Messiah. But as to the form, the passages in Luke, Acts and Hebrews did not retain the peculiar ὑποκάτω which was found in Matthew and Mark, as would have been the case if the quotation was taken from a Book of Testimonies.[6]

---

[1] So N. J. HOMMES, *Het Testimoniaboek* (an extensive summary by A. KRAEMER is found in *Philologische Wochenschrift* 58, 1938, col. 73–83) p. 43. So also T. H. BINDLEY, *Journ. of Theol. St.* 22 (1920/21), p. 279–282, CH. GUIGNEBERT, *Rev. de l'Hist. des Rel.* 81 (1920), p. 58–69, F. R. M. HITCHCOCK, *Journ. of Theol. St.* 9 (1907/08), p. 285, and J. A. ROBINSON in his edition of *St Irenaeus, The Demonstration of the Apostolic Preaching* (1920), p. 6–23.

[2] The catechetical quotations Lev. 19₁₈ (Mt. 5₄₃, 19₁₉, 22₃₉, Rom. 13₉, Gal. 5₁₄) and Deut. 5₁₆ (Mt. 15₄, 19₁₉, Ef. 6₃) are hardly relevant to our question.

[3] See above, p. 56 ff.   [4] See above, p. 139.

[5] See above, p. 16.   [6] See above, p. 78.

A passage which is of vital importance for Harris's reasoning is the "stone quotation" in Mt. 21 42 ≠ Mk. 12 10–11 ≠ Lk. 20 17–18 with its parallels in 1 Peter 2 6 ff. (and Rom. 9 33).[1] Matthew's part of the quotation is word for the word the LXX text, as also the parallel in 1 Peter, while the Matthaean part of the citation is lacking in Romans. We found reason to interpret this not only as an O.T. quotation, but also as a *verbum Christi* and consider it a nucleus for the later formation of the testimony.[2]

On three points we have found quotations common to Matthew and John, Mt. 3 3 ≠ Jn. 1 23; Mt. 13 14–15 ≠ Jn. 12 40 [3]; Mt. 21 5 ≠ Jn. 12 15; Mt. 21 9 ≠ Jn. 12 13; but in none of these cases was there any agreement which gave us cause to suppose a common source in the nature of testimonies.[4]

This, however, seems to have been the case in the extremely complex quotations in Mt. 24 30 ≠ Rev. 1 7 (≠ Jn. 19 37): Zech. 12 10, 12, 14 and Dan. 7 13 a; cf. Mk. 13 26 ≠ Lk. 21 27; Mt. 26 64 ≠ Mk. 14 62.

Mt. 24 30

καὶ τότε φανήσεται τὸ σημεῖον τοῦ υἱοῦ τοῦ ἀνθρώπου ἐν οὐρανῷ, καὶ τότε κόψονται πᾶσαι αἱ φυλαὶ τῆς γῆς καὶ ὄψονται τὸν υἱὸν τοῦ ἀνθρώπου ἐρχόμενον ἐπὶ τῶν νεφελῶν τοῦ οὐρανοῦ μετὰ δυνάμεως καὶ δόξης πολλῆς.

ἐν οὐρανῷ] τοῦ ἐν οὐρανοῖς D.

Rev. 1 7

ἰδοὺ ἔρχεται μετὰ τῶν νεφελῶν, καὶ ὄψεται αὐτὸν πᾶς ὀφθαλμὸς καὶ οἵτινες αὐτὸν ἐξεκέντησαν, καὶ κόψονται ἐπ᾽ αὐτὸν πᾶσαι αἱ φυλαὶ τῆς γῆς.

ὄψεται] ὄψονται ℵ 1 al.

Jn. 19 37

ὄψονται εἰς ὃν ἐξεκέντησαν.

Zech. 12 10, 12, 14 LXX[B]

καὶ ἐκχεῶ ἐπὶ τὸν οἶκον Δαυὶδ καὶ ἐπὶ τοὺς κατοικοῦντας Ἰερουσαλὴμ

M.T.

ושפכתי על בית דויד ועל יושב ירושלם

---

[1] HARRIS, *op. cit.* I, p. 26–32 and (V. BURCH) II, p. 66, cf. DODD, *op. cit.*, p. 26: "indeed striking, but . . . almost the only one of its kind".

[2] See above, p. 69.

[3] On the coincidence of the purely LXX text of Matthew and Acts, 28 26 f., see above, p. 130 f.

[4] See above, p. 52, 120 and 64 ff.

πνεῦμα χάριτος καὶ οἰκτιρμοῦ· καὶ
ἐπιβλέψονται πρὸς μὲ ἀνθ' ὧν κατ-
ωρχήσαντο, καὶ κόψονται ἐπ' αὐτὸν
κοπετὸν ὡς ἐπ' ἀγαπητῷ, καὶ ὀδυνη-
θήσονται ὀδύνην ὡς ἐπὶ τῷ πρωτοτόκῳ . . . ¹²καὶ κόψεται ἡ γῆ κατὰ
φυλὰς φυλάς . . . ¹⁴πᾶσαι αἱ ὑπολε-
λιμμέναι φυλαί . . .

רוח חן ותחנונים והביטו אלי את
אשר דקרו וספדו עליו כמספד על
היחיד יהמר עליו כהמר על הבכור:

וספדה הארץ משפחות משפחות . . .

כל המשפחות הנשארות . . .

ἀνθ' ὧν κατωρχ.] εἰς ὃν ἐξεκέντησαν Lucian Theod.¹ — ἐπ' αὐτὸν] αὐτὸν
Aq. Symm. Theod.

Dan. 713a LXX	Theodotion	M. T.
ἐθεώρουν ἐν ὁράματι τῆς νυκτός, καὶ ἰδοὺ ἐπὶ τῶν νεφελῶν τοῦ οὐρανοῦ ὡς υἱὸς ἀνθρώπου ἤρχετο.	ἐθεώρουν ἐν ὁράματι τῆς νυκτός, καὶ ἰδοὺ μετὰ τῶν νεφελῶν τοῦ οὐρανοῦ ὡς υἱὸς ἀνθρώπου ἐρχόμε- νος.	חזה הוית בחזוי ליליא וארו עם ענני שמיא כבר אנש אתה הוא

μετὰ] ἐπὶ Q.
ἐρχόμενος] add. ἦν A.

It is not with regard to the exact wording that there is agreement.
Apart from the expression πᾶσαι αἱ φυλαὶ τῆς γῆς and the plural κόψονται
dependent upon it, there is not one word alike. Moreover we are bound
to consider the frequently stated freedom of apocalyptic literature. If
it is true that Revelation does not contain a single literal quotation, it
would be surprising if there suddenly appeared here a word for word
agreement with a testimony. The same freedom must be attributed to

---

¹ This is the reading of Theodotion according to the Syrohexapla but according
to cod. 86 mg. he read ὃν ἐξεκέντησαν. RAHLFS, *Zeitschr. f. d. neutest. Wissensch.*
20 (1921), p. 184 f., takes the latter as the genuine reading of Theodotion. To him
Lucian's text does not support that of the Syrohexapla since it seems to have been
influenced by the N.T., cf. *Justin*, 1 Apol. 52, Dial. 148, 647 and Å. V. STRÖM,
Vetekornet (1944), p. 317 f. — The LXX read רקרי for the M.T.'s דקרו but Aquila
and Symmachus use the verb ἐκκεντεῖν though they have different prepositions.
Rahlfs denies any influence from "Theodotion" on the N.T. and explains the coincidence as a common dependence upon the Hebrew, *ibm.*, p. 189 f., cf. above,
p. 179. — An exhaustive survey and classification of the variants is found in
A. DEISSMANN, *Die Septuaginta-Papyri und andere altchristl. Texte der Heidelb.*
Papyrus-Samml. (1905), p. 66—71.

the quotation in its Matthaean form, where it occurs in the apocalypse of the gospel. The variants μετά (Mk. 14 62, Rev., Th.), ἐπί (Mt., LXX, Th.Q), ἐν (Mk. 13 26, Lk.) are thus not conclusive.[1]

In Revelation (but not in Matthew) there is a quotation from Zech. 12 10, which is found also in Jn. 19 37. This is the text almost immediately preceding the saying about the tribes of the earth in Zechariah (v. 12). This speaks against the conception of testimonies and for a direct study of the O.T. — in this case according to pre-Theodotion tradition. It is observations of this type which lead Dodd to assume a N.T. dependence on certain chapters *in toto* instead of disconnected quotations.[2]

However, the combination of Zech. 12 and Dan. 7 makes it necessary for us to assume that very combination to be a common matter, either understood as a *verbum Christi* or as belonging to the church's basic teaching in Christology.[3] It is somewhat hazardous, however, to transform this rather loose agreement so far as the words are concerned, into the basis for a hypothesis of a collection of testimonies or even of a Book of Testimonies.[4]

There is another approach, more akin to Harris's own, by which it is possible to test whether Harris's hypothesis of testimonies can be applied to Matthew. Even so, the result is just as negative. In the *Festschrift* to Harris FINDLAY has undertaken such an investigation[5] and has thereby

---

[1] Against T. W. MANSON, *Bull. of J. Ryl. Libr.* 34 (1951/52), p. 316 and 319, cf. LOHMEYER, *Comm. Rev.* (1953²), p. 12: the LXX's ἐπί is a rationalized rendering of the M.T. — There is yet another variant in *Justin*, 1 Apol. 5 19: ἐπάνω, while Dial. 31 3 has a pure Theodotion text in longer O.T. context (Dan. 7 9–28).

[2] DODD, *op. cit.*, p. 64 f., and p. 67. — On the other hand it is certainly most surprising that Zech. 12 10 b is not also made use of (καὶ κόψονται . . . ἐπ' ἀγαπητῷ . . . ἐπὶ τῷ πρωτοτόκῳ), a text most suitable to Christian interpretation. It is hardly plausible to assume an implied continuation of the quotation in a passage like that of Revelation. There was however a similar case in Mt. 21 5, see above p. 119. — LOHMEYER, *loc. cit.*, emphasizes the hymnic character of the passage in Revelation and that makes it less useful as an example of a testimony.

[3] *Verba Christi* of this type have been important as can be seen in Paul's reference to "the word of the Lord" in 1 Thess. 4 15 ff.

[4] CHARLES, *Comm. Rev.* I, p. lxvii: "There is, of course, the possibility that our author was using a collection of *Testimonia*. But this explanation could not be used in the case of the passages wherein our author's text shows numerous and very close affinities to Theodotion." Charles thinks Revelation here depends on Matthew though the author of Revelation is as usual more faithful to the Hebrew text, p. lxvi, cf. lxviii, lxxxi and p. 17. G. H. Box, in *The People and the Book*, p. 442, is more in favour of "a collection of *Testimonia*".

[5] J. A. FINDLAY, The First Gospel and the Book of Testimonies, in *Amicitiae Corolla*, p. 57–71.

found that the subsequent collections of testimonies do not follow Matthew's model either in order or language. He finds that both Justin and Cyprian prefer the LXX form of words and the quotations peculiar to Matthew are on the whole not much used in this type of literature. He concludes that "the First Evangelist is not in the main Testimony-stream".[1] The supposition of Burkitt which led Harris to link his Book of Testimonies so closely with Matthew has been brought to a dead end. The formula quotations, which so often tempt commentators to say 'probably from a collection of testimonies", are not open to such a theory. The case reverts to the theory of HATCH who reckoned with testimonies in LXX Greek. *His* intention was to explain the composite quotations; there are, however, very few of them in Matthew or the other synoptic gospels.

We have found no means of deciding whether Mk. 1 2 is an interpolation from Matthew–Luke or whether the combination of the two פנה-quotations in Mk. 1 2–3 is genuine. If it is, it brings up the question of a Semitic background for this combination.[2] It is remarkable, however, that it is just in these two quotations from Malachi and Isaiah common to the synoptic gospels that we find traces of formula quotations both in function and form. At the same time both are concerned with John the Baptist. Could it be that these quotations were taken over from the disciples of John the Baptist in the form used by them? Obviously, they do not demand such an explanation, though it is rather a tempting one. If this is the case, the principles of dealing with the Scriptures in these circles would be akin to that of the Sect of Qumran. Now, we were in the happy position of finding the quotation from Is. 40 3 in the Manual of Discipline from Qumran[3], and a comparison of the two forms of this prophecy shows how the N.T. form relies on the LXX and transforms the prophecy to mention the "voice in the wilderness", that is, John the Baptist. While differing from the Qumran interpretation, this change would, however, be quite suitable for a proof-text in the groups gathered around John the Baptist. If this is the case, we are bound to assume an acquaintance with the LXX in these groups.[4]

---

[1] *op. cit.*, p. 69.

[2] Cf. MOFFATT, *op. cit.*, p. 24, on Mk. 1 2–3 as an Aramaic testimony.

[3] See above, p. 48 and 191.

[4] Cf. above, p. 194 and the Alexandrian Jew Apollos who was a "Johannite", Acts 18 25. — B. REICKE, *Religion och Bibel* 11 (1952), p. 13 f., draws the line between John the Baptist and the Sect of Qumran. He refers to the Isaiah quotation, though not considering the different interpretation in the Sect and in the gospel.

216

There are more simple alternatives than the testimony hypothesis to
explain the feature of composite quotations. We only have to glance at
one of the *midrashim* to find a storehouse of quotations brought together
by means of association. Sometimes they combine texts which have one
term in common. There is an example of this in 2 Cor. 9 10 where all the
three quotations in their Hebrew form have some bearing on "rain",
though they do not use the same Hebrew word: Is. 55 10, Deut. 28 11 f.,
Hos. 10 12.[1] The well-known O.T. foundations of Paul's doctrine on faith,
viz. Gen. 15 6 and Hab. 2 4 are to be read, separated by a few lines, in the
Mekilta to Ex. 14 30.[2] In these cases a literal dependence is not necessary
to the explanation, but the *midrashim* testify the habit of bringing quotations together, often combined merely by a ותוב, the Greek πάλιν.[3]

There is also a more elaborate method of bringing together three quotations of similar content, one from the Law, one from the Prophets and
one from the Writings. The method was called: "to string (pearls)", חרז.[4]
In the Pauline epistles we find parallels to these phenomena, but there
are none in the gospels.[5]

There is, however, a phenomenon in the gospels which looks as if it
could be explained by the theory or testimonies. We saw, for instance
in Lk. 4 18 or in Mt. 11 10, how different texts had been intermingled, or
at least, how a quotation was affected by the influence of other texts.
The testimony idea might explain how these were preserved in the tradition without being corrected or conformed to authorized O.T. texts, but
it would not explain how the N.T. form came into being. It is rather in

---

[1] VOLLMER, *Die Alttestamentlichen Citate bei Paulus*, p. 41 f., took it as an example of Jewish stock-quotation on a Hebrew basis, but by stressing the different
Hebrew terms used O. MICHEL, *Paulus und seine Bibel*, p. 43, and HOMMES, *op. cit.*,
p. 349, criticized his view. In this connection HOMMES considers Mk. 1 2–3 to be a
better argument for the case of combined quotations primary to the N.T. He assumes a pre-Christian group of quotations on "preparing the way", a group which
quite naturally came under the heading of Isaiah, the main source of this idea, *ibm.*,
p. 174 f.

[2] See Box, *op. cit.*, p. 450 f., cf. J. J. WETSTEIN's reference to ExR. 23, *Novum
Testamentum Graecum* II, p. 22 (ad Rom. 1 17).

[3] See MICHEL, *op. cit.*, p. 72.

[4] VOLLMER, *op. cit.*, p. 37, MICHEL, *op. cit.*, p. 83, and in table-form *ibm.*, p. 12 f.
HOMMES has made the most thorough investigation in this matter, *op. cit.*, p. 324–
354. For the Jewish material he makes use mainly of W. BACHER, *Die Proömien der
alten jüdischen Homilie* (1913).

[5] A typical example is found in Rom. 15 10–12. In Rom. 10 6–9 this rabbinic
method throws light upon the text, see MICHEL, *op. cit.*, p. 84 f.

the *haftaroth* tradition we get a hint as to how this came about. Lk. 4 18 can scarcely be fully explained in this way, either, but it might be Luke's creation in accordance with the *haftaroth* practice of the synagogue.[1] We know Luke as a man with classical licence of freedom where quotations are concerned. In Mt. 11 10 the *haftaroth* gave a better explanation of how the Torah-seder had influenced a passage from Isaiah.[2]

The methods of the synagogue in dealing with the texts of the O.T., both in liturgical reading and in teaching, account for most of the features Harris wanted to explain by his Book of Testimonies.[3] This is not to say that the primitive church did not know and use testimonies, oral or even written, but so far as Matthew is concerned, these testimonies are not responsible for the form of the quotations, least of all for that of the formula quotations. Of course, the formula quotations could be called testimonies, but when dealing with them, we come face to face with the process of creating testimonies[4], and a very special type of testimonies. There are no signs of use or abuse of such set forms of O.T. sayings primary to Matthew. When taking over the material of Mark and Q, in two or three cases Matthew accepts quotations which belonged to Christian tradition, and which were coined in accordance with Jewish practice. There were reasons to believe that these quotations had existed as isolated testimonies primary to their context. In Mt. 26 31 we found such reasons. Yet the quotation belonged to the passion story and the difference between that part and the rest of the gospels must be kept in mind. In Mt. 3 3 and 11 10 the quotations were adapted to the interpretation of the place God had designed for John the Baptist in sacred history, which was now advancing towards its consummation.

This feature of adaptation they have in common with the *pesher* quotations of Matthew, without sharing the elaborate character which we found in the products of "The School of St. Matthew".

---

[1] See above, p. 96.

[2] See above, p. 50.

[3] The false ascriptions to authors must partly be due to the faulty memory of the evangelist, cf. above, p. 123. They are common in the post-apostolic period as well, often without any possible relation to testimonies — Harris thought that the wrong ascriptions were due to the mixing up of the headings taken from the Book of Testimonies. Yet in *Testimonies* I, p. 59, he admits that this would not solve one of the two cases of false ascription in Matthew (27 9).

[4] Cf. DODD, *op. cit.*, p. 126: "The composition of 'testimony-books' was the result, not the presupposition, of the work of early Christian biblical scholars".

Bibliography

TEXTS

Biblia hebraica, ed. R. KITTEL. (3rd ed. by P. KAHLE–A. ALT–O. EISSFELDT) Stuttgart 1937.

Die Weisheit des Jesus Sirach Hebräisch und Deutsch, ed. R. SMEND. Berlin 1906.

Papyrus Nash, see below, S. A. COOK; on the Murabaat phylactery, see F. M. CROSS.

Targum Onkelos, ed. A. BERLINER, I: Text; II: Noten, Einleitung und Register. Berlin 1884.

Pseudo-Jonathan and Fragment Targums to the Pentateuch, in B. WALTON, SS. *Biblia Polyglotta* IV. London 1657.

Prophetae chaldaice, ed. P. DE LAGARDE. Leipzig 1872.

The Targum of Isaiah, ed. and transl. J. F. STENNING. Oxford 1949.

Hagiographa chaldaice, ed. P. DE LAGARDE. Leipzig 1873.

The Old Testament in Greek according to the Septuagint I–III, ed. H. B. SWETE. 2nd ed. Cambridge 1895–1899.

The Old Testament in Greek, ed. A. E. BROOKE–N. MCLEAN– (in II and III) H. ST. J. THACKERAY, I: The Octateuch; II: The Later Historical Books; III: 1: Esther, Judith, Tobit. Cambridge 1906–1940.

Septuaginta. Vetus Testamentum Graecum auctoritate Societatis Litterarum Gottingensis editum:

I. Genesis, ed. A. RAHLFS. Stuttgart 1926.

IX: 1. Maccabaeorum liber I, ed. W. KAPPLER. Göttingen 1936.

X. Psalmi cum Odis, ed. A. RAHLFS. Göttingen 1931.

XIII. Duodecim prophetae, ed. J. ZIEGLER. Göttingen 1943.

XIV. Isaias, ed. J. ZIEGLER. Göttingen 1939.

Vetus Testamentum Graecum I–V, ed. R. HOLMES– (II–V) J. PARSONS. Oxford 1798–1827.

Libri Veteris Testamenti Canonici I [the "Lucianic text"[1]], ed. P. DE LAGARDE. Göttingen 1883.

The Book of Isaiah according to the Septuagint (codex Alexandrinus), ed. R. R. OTTLEY, I: Introduction and Translation with a Parallel Version from the Hebrew; II: Text and Notes. Cambridge 1904–1906.

Origenis Hexapla quae supersunt I–II, ed. F. FIELD. Oxford 1875.

Greek O. T. Papyri and Fragments, see below: ALLGEIER, BARTHÉLEMY,

---

[1] See above, p. 54, note 2.

Deissmann, Eitrem, Kenyon, C. H. Roberts, Rudberg, Sanders, Stegmüller, Vaccari and Waddell.

Greek O. T. Uncials in facsimile, see above, p. 45, note 3.

The Syriac Old and New Testament, ed. S. Lee. London 1823–1826.

The Apocrypha and Pseudepigrapha of the Old Testament in English I–II, ed. R. H. Charles. Oxford 1913.

The Ethiopic Version of the Hebrew Book of Jubilees, ed. R. H. Charles. (Anecdota Oxoniensia, Sem. Ser. 8) Oxford 1895.

The Book of Jubilees or Little Genesis, translated from the Editor's Ethiopic Text, ed. R. H. Charles. London 1902.

Die Damaskusschrift, ed. L. Rost. (Kleine Texte für Vorlesungen und Übungen 167) Berlin 1933.

Documents of Jewish Sectaries, I: Fragments of a Zadokite Work, ed. and transl. S. Schechter. Cambridge 1910.

The Dead Sea Scrolls of St. Mark's Monastery:
I. The Isaiah Manuscript and the Habakkuk Commentary, ed. M. Burrows. New Haven 1950.
II: 1. Plates and Transcription of the Manual of Discipline, ed. M. Burrows. New Haven 1951.

Megilloth Genuzoth II, ed. E. L. Sukenik. Jerusalem 1950.

Der Babylonische Talmud I–IX, ed. L. Goldschmidt. Berlin (vol. IX Haag) 1897–1935.

The Babylonian Talmud [English translation], ed. I. Epstein. London 1938–1952.

תלמוד ירושלמי, א.-ב, Berlin 5689–1928.

Le Talmud de Jérusalem I–XI [French translation], ed. M. Schwab. Paris 1871–1889.

Sukka, ed. H. Bornhäuser. (in Die Mischna ..., herausg. von Beer–Holtzmann–Krauss–Rengstorf) Berlin 1935.

Mishnah Megillah, ed. and transl. J. Rabbinowitz. Oxford 1931.

Tosephta, ed. M. S. Zuckermandel. Pasewalk 1880.

Midrash Rabba, translated into English with Notes, Glossary and Indices, ed. H. Freedman–M. Simon, I–IX: Texts; X: Index Volume. London 1939.

Mechilta, ed. I. H. Weiss. Wien 1865.

Mechilta, ... ins Deutsche übers. und erläutert von J. Winter–A. Wünsche. Leipzig 1909.

Pesikta, die älteste Hagada, redigiert in Palästina von Rab Kahana, ed. S. Buber. Lyck 1868.

Pesikta des Rab Kahana, nach der Buberschen Textausgabe ... ins Deutsche übertragen ..., ed. A. Wünsche. (Bibliotheca Rabbinica 11) Leipzig 1885.

Ginzā. Der Schatz oder das grosse Buch der Mandäer, übers. u. erklärt von M. Lidzbarski. (Quellen der Religionsgeschichte 13) Göttingen–Leipzig 1925.

Novum Testamentum Graece, ed. Eberhard und Erwin Nestle. 20. Aufl. Stuttgart 1950.

The New Testament in the Original Greek, ed. B. F. Westcott–F. J. A. Hort, I: Text; II: Introduction and Appendix. Cambridge–London 1881–1882.

Die Schriften des Neuen Testaments I–II, ed. H. von Soden. Berlin 1910–1913.

Novum Testamentum Graece: Euangelium secundum Marcum cum apparatu critico nouo plenissimo ..., ed. S. C. Legg. Oxford 1935.

—— Euangelium secundum Matthaeum cum apparatu critico nouo plenissimo ..., ed. S. C. Legg. Oxford 1940.

The New Testament in Syriac, ed. R. Kilgour. London 1950.

Evangelion Da-Mepharreshe, ed. F. C. Burkitt, I: Text; II: Introduction and Notes. Cambridge 1904.

The Old Syriac Gospel or Evangelion Da-Mepharreshe, being the Text of the Sinai or Syro-Antiochene Palimpsest ..., ed. Agnes Smith Lewis. London 1910.

L'Évangile de Pierre, ed. L. Vaganay. (Études bibliques) Paris 1930.

Fragments of Unknown Gospels, see below: Dodd and Wessely.

Die apostolischen Väter I, ed. Funck–Bihlmeyer. (Samml. ausgewählter kirchen- und dogmengeschichtl. Quellenschr. 2. Reihe 1:1) Tübingen 1924.

The Apostolic Fathers I–II, ed. and transl. K. Lake. (The Loeb Classical Library) London-Cambridge, Mass., 1912–1913.

Ignatius Antiochenus & Polycarpus Sanctus, Lettres, ed. Th. Camelot. (Sources chrétiennes 10) 2ème éd. Paris 1951.

Patrologiae Cursus Completus, ed. J. P. Migne: Series Patrum Graecorum. Paris 1857–1866.

—— Series Patrum Latinorum. Paris 1844–1866.

Justin, Apologies, ed. L. Pautigny. (Textes et Documents pour l'Étude historique du Christianisme) Paris 1904.

—— Dialogue avec Tryphon I–II, ed. G. Archambault. (Textes et Documents ...) Paris 1909.

Des heiligen Irenäus Schrift zum Erweise der Apostolischen Verkündigung [Armenian version and German translation], ed. Karapet Ter-Mekerttschian–Erwand Ter-Minassiantz. (Texte u. Untersuch. z. Gesch. d. altchristl. Lit., 3. Reihe 1:1) Leipzig 1907.

St Irenaeus, The Demonstration of the Apostolic Preaching, transl. J. A. Robinson. (Translations of Christian Literature. Ser. IV: Oriental Texts) London 1920.

The Homily on the Passion by Melito, Bishop of Sardis, with some Fragments of the Apocryphal Ezekiel, ed. and transl. C. Bonner. (Studies and Documents 12) London–Philadelphia 1940.

The Apostolic Tradition of Hippolytus, transl. B. S. Easton. Cambridge 1934.

Origenis Matthäuserklärung I–III, ed. E. Klostermann. (Die Griech. Christl. Schriftsteller, herausg. v. d. Kirchenväter-Commission d. preuss. Akad. d. Wissensch.: Origenes X–XII) Leipzig 1935–1941.

Cyprianus, Testimonia (Ad Quirinum), ed. W. HARTEL. (Corpus Script. Ecclesiast. Latin. 3, p. 33–184) Wien 1868.

Porphyrius, "Gegen die Christen", 15 Bücher. Zeugnisse, Fragmente und Referate, ed. A. VON HARNACK. (Abhandl. der königl. preuss. Akad. der Wissensch., Phil.-Hist. Kl. 1, 1916) Berlin 1916.

Eusebius, Die Kirchengeschichte I–III, ed. E. SCHWARTZ. (Die Griech. Christl. Schriftsteller ...: Eusebius II: 1–3) Leipzig 1903–1909.

Hieronymus, De viris inlustribus, ed. W. HERDING. (Bibliotheca ... Teubneriana) Leipzig 1879.

LITERATURE

ABRAHAMS, I., Rabbinic Aids to Exegesis, in *Cambridge Biblical Essays*, ed. H. B. SWETE, p. 159–192. London 1909.

AICHER, G., *Das Alte Testament in der Mischna*. (Biblische Studien 11:4) Freiburg i. Br. 1906.

ALBRIGHT, W. F., A Biblical Fragment from the Maccabean Age. The Nash Papyrus, *Journ. of Bibl. Lit.* 56 (1937), p. 145–176.

ALLEN, W. C., *A Critical and Exegetical Commentary on the Gospel according to S. Matthew*. (Intern. Critic. Comm.) Edinburgh 1907.

ALLGEIER, A., Dt. 25, 1–3 im Manchester-Papyrus (PRG 458), *Biblica* 19 (1938), p. 1–18.

ANGER, R., *Ratio qua loci Veteris Testamenti in evangelio Matthaei laudantur, quid valeat ad illustrandum hujus evangelii originem*, I–III. Leipziger Universitäts-Programme 1861 and 1862.

APTOWITZER, V., *Das Schriftwort in der rabbinischen Literatur* I–II. (Sitzungsber. Akad. d. Wissensch. Wien, Phil.-Hist. Kl. 153:6; 160:7) Wien, 1906 and 1908.

ARVEDSON, T., *Das Mysterium Christi*. Eine Studie zu Mt. 11, 25–30. Diss. Uppsala. (Acta Semin. Neotest. Upsal. 7) Uppsala 1937.

AUDET, J.-P., A Hebrew-Aramaic List of Books of the Old Testament in Greek Transcription, *Journ. of Theol. St.*, New Ser. 1 (1950), p. 135–154.

—— Affinités littéraires et doctrinales du "Manuel de discipline", *Rev. Bibl.* 59 (1952), p. 219–238; 60 (1953), p. 41–82.

BACHER, W., *Die exegetische Terminologie der jüdischen Traditionsliteratur* I–II. (Vol. I = *Die älteste Terminologie der jüdischen Schriftauslegung*) Leipzig 1899–1905.

—— *Die Proömien der alten jüdischen Homilie*. (Beitr. z. Wissensch. v. A. T. 12) Leipzig 1913.

BACON, B. W., The "Five Books" of Matthew against the Jews, *The Expositor* 8th Ser. 15 (1918), p. 56–66.

—— *Studies in Matthew*. New York 1930.

BARDY, G., Pour l'histoire de l'École d'Alexandrie, *Vivre et Penser* 2 (1942), p. 80–109.

BARNES, W. E., On the influence of the Septuagint on the Peshitta, *Journ. of Theol. St.* 2 (1900/01), p. 186–197.

BARTHÉLEMY, D., Le grand rouleau d'Isaïe trouvé près de la Mer Morte, *Rev. Bibl.* 57 (1950), p. 530–549.

—— Redécouverte d'un chaînon manquant de l'Histoire de la Septante, *Rev. Bibl.* 60 (1953), p. 18–29.

BAUER, W., *Das Leben Jesu im Zeitalter der neutestamentlichen Apokryphen.* Tübingen 1909.

—— *Der Wortgottesdienst der ältesten Christen.* (Samml. gemeinverständl. Vorträge und Schriften aus dem Gebiet der Theol. und Religionsgesch. 148) Tübingen 1930.

—— *Griechisch-Deutsches Wörterbuch zu den Schriften des Neuen Testaments und der übrigen urchristlichen Literatur.* 4. Aufl. Berlin 1952.

BAUERNFEIND, O., art. νικάω κτλ., *Theol. Wörterb. z. N. T.* IV, p. 941–945.

BAUMGARTNER, W., Der palästinische Handschriftenfund, *Theol. Rundschau,* N. F. 17 (1948/49), p. 329–346; 19 (1951), p. 97–154.

BAUMSTARK, A., *Geschichte der syrischen Literatur.* Bonn 1922.

—— Pěšīṭtā und palästinensisches Targum, *Bibl. Zeitschr.* 19 (1931), p. 257–270.

—— Neue orientalistische Probleme biblischer Textgeschichte, *Zeitschr. d. Deutsch. Morgenl. Gesellsch.* 89 (1935), p. 89–118.

BENOIT, P., Une cruche avec inscription biblique: II. L'inscription, *Rev. Bibl.* 56 (1949) p. 437–442.

—— *L'Évangile selon Saint Matthieu.* (La Sainte Bible trad. en français sous la direction de l'École Biblique de Jérusalem) Paris 1950.

BERTRAM, G., Zur Septuaginta-Forschung, *Theol. Rundschau,* N.F. 3 (1931), p. 283–296; 5 (1933), p. 173–186; 10 (1938), p. 69–80 and 133–159.

BINDLEY, T. H., Papias and the Matthaean Oracles, *Church Quarterly Rev.* 84 (1917), p. 31–43.

—— Review art. on R. Harris, Testimonies II, *Journ. of Theol. St.* 22 (1921), p. 279–282.

BIRKELAND, H., *Språk og religion hos jøder og arabere.* Oslo 1949.

BIRT, TH., *Die Buchrolle in der Kunst.* Leipzig 1907.

BLACK, M., The Problem of the Old Testament Quotations in the Gospels, *Journ. of the Manchester Egyptian and Oriental Society* 23 (1942), p. 4.

—— *An Aramaic Approach to the Gospels and Acts.* Oxford 1946.

—— Aramaic Studies and the New Testament: The Unpublished Work of the Late A. J. Wensinck of Leyden, *Journ. of Theol. St.* 49 (1949), p. 157–165.

BLANK, SH. A., The Death of Zechariah in Rabbinic Literature, *Hebr. Union Coll. Ann.* 12/13 (1937/38), p. 327–346.

BLASS, F.–DEBRUNNER, A., *Grammatik des neutestamentlichen Griechisch.* 7. Aufl. Göttingen 1943.

BLAU, L., *Studien zum althebräischen Buchwesen und zur biblischen Litteraturgeschichte.* (Studien zum althebräischen Buchwesen und zur biblischen Litteratur- u. Textgeschichte I) Strassburg 1902.

BLEEK, F., *Beiträge zur Evangelien-Kritik.* Berlin 1846.

BÖHL, E., *Forschungen nach einer Volksbibel zur Zeit Jesu und deren Zusammenhang mit der Septuaginta-Uebersetzung.* Wien 1873.

Böhl, E., *Die alttestamentlichen Citate im Neuen Testament*. Wien 1878.

Bohren, R., *Das Problem der Kirchenzucht im Neuen Testament*. Zürich 1952.

Bonner, C., A Supplementary Note on the Opening of Melito's Homily, *Harv. Theol. Rev.* 36 (1943), p. 317–319.

Bonsirven, J., *Le Judaisme Palestinien au Temps de Jésus-Christ* I–II. (Bibliothèque de Théologie Historique) Paris 1934–1935.

—— *Exégèse rabbinique et exégèse paulinienne*. (Bibliothèque de Théologie Historique) Paris 1939.

—— *Le Divorce dans le Nouveau Testament*. Tournai 1948.

Bornhäuser, K., *Zeiten und Stunden in der Leidens- und Auferstehungsgeschichte*. (Beitr. z. Förder. Christl. Theol. 26:4, p. 5–62) Gütersloh 1921.

Bousset, W., *Die Evangeliencitate Justins des Märtyrers*. Göttingen 1891.

—— *Jüdisch-Christlicher Schulbetrieb in Alexandria und Rom*. (Forsch. z. Rel. u. Lit. d. A. u. N. T:s, N. F. 6) Göttingen 1915.

Box, G. H., The Value and Significance of the Old Testament in Relation to the New, in *The People and the Book*, ed. A. S. Peake, p. 433–467. Oxford 1925.

Brandon, S. G. F., *The Fall of Jerusalem and the Christian Church*. London 1951.

Brederek, E., *Konkordanz zum Targum Onkelos*. (Zeitschr. f. d. alttest. Wissensch., Beih. 9) Giessen 1906.

Brownlee, W. H., The Jerusalem Habakkuk Scroll, *Bull of the Amer. Schools of Orient. Res.* 112 (December, 1948), p. 8–18.

—— *The Dead Sea Manual of Discipline*. Translation and Notes. (Bull. of the Amer. Schools of Orient. Res., Suppl. Studies 10–12) New Haven 1951.

—— Biblical Interpretation among the Sectaries of the Dead Sea Scrolls, *The Biblical Archaeologist* 14 (1951), p. 54–76.

—— *The Dead Sea Habakkuk Midrash and the Targum Jonathan*. A mimeographed paper published through the services of the Duke Divinity School. Durham, N.C. 1953.

Büchsel, F., art. κρίνω κτλ., *Theol. Wörterb. z. N. T.* III, p. 920–955.

Bultmann, R., *Die Geschichte der synoptischen Tradition*. (Forsch. z. Rel. u. Lit. d. A. u. N. T:s, N. F. 12) 1. Aufl. Göttingen 1921; 2. Aufl. 1931.

Burch, V., Testimonies in the Synoptic Gospels, in R. Harris, *Testimonies* II, p. 58–70, Cambridge 1920.

Burkitt, F. C., *The Gospel History and its Transmission*. 2nd ed. Edinburgh 1907.

—— W and Θ: Studies in the Western Text of St. Mark: Hosanna, *Journ. of Theol. St.* 17 (1915/16), p. 139–152.

Burrows, E., *The Oracles of Jacob and Balaam*. (The Bellarmine Ser. 3) London 1939.

Butler, B. C., *The Originality of St. Matthew*. A Critique of the Two-Document Hypothesis. Cambridge 1951.

Carlson (Svenæus), S., *Aggadastoff i Nya Testamentets skrifter*. Diss. Uppsala. Lund 1920.

224

CARRINGTON, PH., *The Primitive Christian Catechism*. A Study in the Epistles. Cambridge 1940.

—— *The Primitive Christian Calendar*, I: Introduction & Text. Cambridge 1952.

CASEY, R. P., Some Remarks on Formgeschichtliche Methode, in *Quantulacumque*. Studies Presented to K. LAKE, p. 109–116. London 1937.

CERFAUX, L., Citations scripturaires et tradition textuelle dans le Livre des Actes, in *Aux sources de la tradition chrétienne*, Mélanges offerts à M. GOGUEL. (Bibliotèque Théologique), p. 43–51. Neuchâtel–Paris 1950.

CHARLES, R. H., *A Critical and Exegetical Commentary on The Revelation of St. John* I–II. (Intern. Critic. Comm.) Edinburgh 1920.

CHASE, F. H., *The Syro-Latin Text of the Gospels*. London 1895.

CHASLES, R., *L'Ancien Testament dans le Nouveau*. Tableaux synoptiques des faits et citations de l'Ancien Testament dans le Nouveau. Paris 1937.[1]

CLARK, K. W., The Gentile Bias in Matthew, *Journ. of Bibl. Lit.* 66 (1947), p. 165–172.

CLARKE, W. K. L., The Use of the Septuagint in Acts, in *The Beginnings of Christianity*, Part I, ed. F. JACKSON–K. LAKE, vol. II, p. 64–105. London 1922.

CLEMEN, A., *Der Gebrauch des Alten Testamentes in den neutestamentlichen Schriften*. Gütersloh 1895.

COOK, S. A., A Pre-Massoretic Biblical Papyrus, *Proceedings of the Society of Biblical Archaeology* 25 (1903), p. 34–56 + plate i-iii.

CREDNER, K. A., *Beiträge zur Einleitung in die biblischen Schriften*, II: Das alttestamentliche Urevangelium. Halle 1838.

CROSS, F. M. JR., The Manuscripts of the Dead Sea Caves, *The Biblical Archaeologist* 17 (1954), p. 2–21.

CULLMANN, O., *Urchristentum und Gottesdienst*. (Abhandl. z. Theol. d. A. u. N. T:s 3) 2. Aufl. Zürich 1950.

—— *Petrus. Jünger, Apostel, Märtyrer*. Zürich 1952.

DALMAN, G. H. (Gustavus Arminius Marx), *Traditio Rabbinorum Veterrima de Librorum Veteris Testamenti Ordine Atque Origene* ... Leipzig 1884.

—— *Die Worte Jesu* I. 2. Aufl. Leipzig 1930.

DAUBE, D., Participle and Imperative in 1 Peter. Appended note in E. G. SELWYN, *The First Epistle of St. Peter*, p. 467–488. London 1947.

—— Rabbinic Methods of Interpretation and Hellenistic Rhetoric, *Hebr. Union Coll. Ann.* 22 (1949), p. 239–264.

DEISSMANN, A., *Die Septuaginta-Papyri und andere altchristliche Texte der Heidelberger Papyrus-Sammlung*. (Veröffentl. aus der Heidelb. Papyrus-Sammlung 1) Heidelberg 1905.

DELLING, G., *Der Gottesdienst im Neuen Testament*. Göttingen 1952.

DIBELIUS, M., *Die urchristliche Überlieferung von Johannes dem Täufer*. (Forsch. z. Rel. u. Lit. d. A. u. N. T:s 15) Göttingen 1911.

---

[1] Not available.

DIBELIUS, M., Herodes und Pilatus, *Zeitschr. f. d. neutest. Wissensch.* 16 (1915), p. 113–126.

—— *Die Formgeschichte des Evangeliums.* 1. Aufl. Tübingen 1919; 2. Aufl. 1933.

—— Die alttestamentlichen Motive in der Leidensgeschichte des Petrus- und des Johannes-Evangeliums, *Zeitschr. f. d. alttest. Wissensch.*, Beih. 33 (1918), p. 125–150. — Reprinted in IDEM, *Botschaft und Geschichte* 1 (1952), p. 221–247.

—— Zur Formgeschichte des Neuen Testaments (ausserhalb der Evangelien), *Theol. Rundschau,* N. F. 3 (1931), p. 207–242.

—— *Die Reden der Apostelgeschichte und die antike Geschichtsschreibung.* (Sitzungsber. Akad. Heidelberg, Phil.-Hist. Kl. 1949/50: 1) — Reprinted in IDEM, *Aufsätze zur Apostelgeschichte.* (Forsch. z. Rel. u. Lit. d. A. u. N. T:s, N. F. 42) Göttingen 1951.

DIETTRICH, G., *Ein Apparatus criticus zur Pešitto zum Propheten Jesaia.* (Zeitschr. f. d. alttest. Wissensch., Beih. 8) Giessen 1905.

DITTMAR, W., *Vetus Testamentum in Novo.* Göttingen 1903.

DOBSCHÜTZ, E. VON, A Collection of Old Latin Bible Quotations, *Journ. of Theol. St.* 16 (1914/15), p. 1–27.

—— Matthäus als Rabbi und Katechet, *Zeitschr. f. d. neutest. Wissensch.* 27 (1928), p. 338–348.

DODD, C. H., A New Gospel, *Bull. of J. Ryl. Libr.* 20 (1936), p. 56–92. — Reprinted in IDEM, *New Testament Studies,* p. 12–52. Manchester 1953.

—— *The Apostolic Preaching and its Developments.* New ed. London 1944.

—— *Gospel and Law.* The Relation of Faith and Ethics in Early Christianity. (Bampton Lectures in America 3) Cambridge 1951.

—— *According to the Scriptures.* London 1952.

DÖRRIE, H., Zur Geschichte des Septuaginta im Jahrhundert Konstantins, *Zeitschr. f. d. Neutest. Wissensch.* 39 (1940), p. 57–110.

DONOVAN, J., *The Logia in Ancient and Recent Literature.* Cambridge 1924.

DRIVER, S. R.–GRAY, G. B., *A Critical and Exegetical Commentary on The Book of Job.* (Intern. Critic. Comm.) Edinburgh 1921.

DUENSING, H., *Christlich-palästinisch-aramäische Texte und Fragmente nebst einer Abhandlung über den Wert der palästinischen Septuaginta.* Göttingen 1906.

DUGMORE, C. W., *The Influence of the Synagogue upon the Divine Office.* London 1945.

DUPONT, J., L'utilisation apologétique de l'Ancien Testament dans les discours des Actes. *Ephemer. Theol. Lovan.* 29 (1953), p. 289–327.

DUPONT-SOMMER, A., *Aperçus préliminaires sur les manuscrits de la Mer Morte.* (L'Orient Ancien Illustré 4) Paris 1950.

—— Le "Commentaire d'Habacuc" découvert près de la Mer Morte. *Rev. de l'Hist. des Rel.* 137 (1950), p. 129–171.

EASTON, B. S., The First Evangelic Tradition, *Journ. of Bibl. Lit.* 50 (1931), p. 148–155.

226

EBRARD, J. H. A., *Wissenschaftliche Kritik der evangelischen Geschichte*. 1. Aufl. Frankfurt a. M. 1842; 3. Aufl. 1868.

EDERSHEIM, A., *The Life and Times of Jesus the Messiah* I–II. 2nd ed. London 1884.

EDLUND, C., *Das Auge der Einfalt*. Eine Untersuchung zu Matth. 6, 22–23 und Luk. 11, 34–35. Diss. Uppsala. (Acta Semin. Neotest. Upsal. 19) Uppsala 1952.

EITREM, S.–AMUNDSEN, L., *Papyri Osloenses* II. Oslo 1931.

ELBOGEN, I., *Der jüdische Gottesdienst in seiner geschichtlichen Entwicklung*. (Schriften herausg. v. d. Gesellsch. z. Förder. d. Wissensch. d. Judentums: Grundriss der Gesamtwissenschaft des Judentums) Leipzig 1913.

ELLIGER, K., *Studien zum Habakuk-Kommentar vom Toten Meer*. (Beitr. z. historischen Theol. 15) Tübingen 1953.

ENGNELL, I., Döda havs-rullarna, Gamla testamentet och kristendomen, *Svenska Dagbladet* 5/7 1952.

—— Debatten kring Dödahavsrullarna, *Svenska Dagbladet* 12/3 1954.

ENSLIN, M. S., The Five Books of Matthew: Bacon on the Gospel of Matthew, *Harv. Theol. Rev.* 24 (1931), p. 67–97.

EPPEL, R., *Le Piétisme juif dans les Testaments des douzes Patriarches*. Diss. Strasbourg. (Études d'histoire et de philos. rel. 22) Strasbourg 1930.

EULER, K. F., *Die Verkündigung vom leidenden Gottesknecht aus Jes. 53 in der griechischen Bibel*. (Beitr. z. Wissensch. v. A. u. N. T., 4. Folge 14) Stuttgart-Berlin 1934.

EYNDE, D. VAN DEN, *Les Normes de l'Enseignement Chrétien dans la littérature patristique des trois premiers siècles*. (Univers. Cathol. Lovan. Diss. Theol. II: 25) Gembloux-Paris 1933.

FARRER, A., *A Study in St. Mark*. London 1951.

FEIGEL, F. K., *Der Einfluss des Weissagungsbeweises und anderer Motive auf die Leidensgeschichte*. Tübingen 1910.

FILSON, F. V., The Christian Teacher in the First Century, *Journ. of Bibl. Lit.* 60 (1941), p. 317–328.

—— The Septuagint and the New Testament, *The Biblical Archaeologist* 9 (1946), p. 34–42.

FINDLAY, J. A., The Book of Testimonies and the Structure of the First Gospel, *The Expositor*, 8th Ser. 20 (1920), p. 388–400.

—— The First Gospel and the Book of Testimonies, in *Amicitiae Corolla*, A Volume of Essays presented to J. R. HARRIS (ed. H. S. Wood), p. 57–71. London 1933.

FRANKE, A. H., *Das alte Testament bei Johannes*. Göttingen 1885.

FRIDRICHSEN, A., *Johannesevangeliet*. Stockholm 1939.

—— Epilog, *Svensk Exegetisk Årsbok* 13 (1948), p. 116–123.

—— *Markusevangeliet*. Stockholm 1952.

GESENIUS, W.–BUHL, F., *Hebräisches und aramäisches Handwörterbuch über das Alte Testament*. 17. Auflage. Leipzig 1921.

GESENIUS, W.–KAUTZSCH, E., *Hebräische Grammatik*. 28. Aufl. Leipzig 1909.

GILBERT, G. H., *Jesus and His Bible*. New York 1926.

GLAUE, P., *Die Vorlesung heiliger Schriften im Gottesdienste*, I: Bis zur Entstehung der altkatholischen Kirche. Berlin 1907.

GOLDMAN, M. D., The Isaiah MSS of the Dead Sea Scrolls, *Australian Biblical Review* 1 (1951), p. 1–22.

GOPPELT, L., *Typos*. Die typologische Deutung des Alten Testaments im Neuen. (Beitr. z. Förder. christl. Theol., 2. Reihe 43) Gütersloh 1939.

GORDIS, R., Quotations as a Literary Usage in Biblical, Oriental and Rabbinic Literature, *Hebr. Union Coll. Ann.* 22 (1949), p. 157–219.

GORDON, C. H., 'Almah in Isaiah 7:14, *Journ. of Bible and Rel.* 21 (1953), p. 106.

[GREGORY, J. BURSLEM], *The Oracles ascribed to Matthew by Papias of Hierapolis*. (Published anonymously) London 1894.[1]

GROBEL, K., *Formgeschichte und Synoptische Quellenanalyse*. (Forsch. z. Rel. u. Lit. d. A. u. N. T:s, N. F. 35) Göttingen 1937.

GÜNTHER, E., ΜΑΡΤΥΣ. Die Geschichte eines Wortes. Gütersloh 1941.

GUIGNEBERT, CH., Review art. on R. Harris, Testimonies I, *Rev. de l'Hist. des Rel.* 81 (1920), p. 58–69.

HÄNEL, J., *Der Schriftbegriff Jesu*. (Beitr. z. Förder. christl. Theol. 24:5–6) Gütersloh 1919.

HAEFELI, L., Die Peschitta des Alten Testamentes. (Alttest. Abhandl. 11:1) Münster i. W. 1927.

HAERING, TH., Das Alte Testament im Neuen, *Zeitschr. f. d. neutest. Wissensch.* 17 (1916), p. 213–227.

HAMMER, H., *Traktat vom Samaritaner-Messias*. Bonn 1913.[1]

HARDER, G., Die Septuagintazitate des Hebräerbriefs, in *Theologia Viatorum*, p. 33–52. München 1939.

HAREIDE, B., Undervisninga i Palestina på Jesu tid, *Tidsskrift for Teologi og Kirke* 20 (1949), p. 77–93.

HARNACK, A. (VON), *Die Quellen der sogenannten apostolischen Kirchenordnung nebst einer Untersuchung über den Ursprung des Lectorats und der anderen niederen Weihen* (Texte u. Untersuch. z. Gesch. d. altchristl. Lit. 2:5) Leipzig 1886.

—— Probleme im Texte der Leidensgeschichte Jesu, *Sitzungsber. Akad. Berlin* 1901:1, p. 251–266 (= Arbeiten zur Kirchengeschichte 19, 1931, p. 86–104).

—— *Über den privaten Gebrauch der heiligen Schriften in der alten Kirche*. (Beitr. z. Einl. in d. N. T. 5) Leipzig 1912.

—— Die Bezeichnung Jesu als "Knecht Gottes" und ihre Geschichte in der alten Kirche, *Sitzungsber. Akad. Berlin*, Phil.-Hist. Kl. 1926, p. 212–238.

HARRIS, J. RENDEL, *Testimonies* I–II (with the assistance of V. BURCH). Cambridge 1916–1920.

—— Traces of Targumism in the New Testament, *Expository Times* 32 (1920/21), p. 373–376.

---

[1] Not available.

228

HART, J. H. A., The Scribes of the Nazarenes. *The Expositor*, 7th Ser. 1 (1906), p. 193–209; 2 (1906), p. 64–88.

HARTMANN, A. TH., *Die enge Verbindung des Alten Testaments mit dem Neuen*. Hamburg 1831.

HASENZAHL, W., *Die Gottverlassenheit des Christus nach dem Kreuzeswort bei Matthäus und Markus und das christologische Verständnis des griechischen Psalters*. (Beitr. z. Förder. christl. Theol. 39:1) Gütersloh 1937.

HATCH, E., *Essays in Biblical Greek*. Oxford 1889.

HAUCK, F., *Das Evangelium des Lukas*. (Theol. Handkomm. z. N. T. 3) Leipzig 1934.

HAUPT, E., *Zur Würdigung der alttestamentlichen Citationen im Evangelium Matthaei*. Treptow 1870.[1]

—— *Die alttestamentlichen Citate der vier Evangelien*. Colberg 1871.[1]

HAWKINS, J. C., *Horae Synopticae*. 2nd ed. Oxford 1909.

HEDLEY, P. L., The Göttingen Investigation and Edition of the Septuagint, *Harv. Theol. Rev.* 26 (1933), p. 57–72.

HEITMÜLLER, W., Zur Johannes-Tradition, *Zeitschr. f. d. neutest. Wissensch.* 15 (1914), p. 189–209.

HEMPEL, J., Chronik, *Zeitschr. f. d. alttest. Wissensch.* 62 (1949/50), p. 246–272.

HITCHCOCK, F. R. M., The Apostolic Preaching of Irenaeus, *Journ. of Theol. St.* 9 (1907/08), p. 284–289.

HOFMANN, R., *Das Leben Jesu nach den Apokryphen*. Leipzig 1851.

HOH, J., Der christliche γραμματεύς (Mt. 13,52). *Bibl. Zeitschr.* 17 (1925/26), p. 256–269.

HOLMES, B. T., Luke's Description of John Mark, *Journ. of Bibl. Lit.* 54 (1935), p. 63–72.

HOMMES, N. J., *Het Testimoniaboek*. Amsterdam 1935.

HÜHN, E., *Die alttestamentlichen Citate und Reminiscenzen im Neuen Testamente*. (= Die messianischen Weissagungen des israelitisch-jüdischen Volkes bis zu den Targumim, II) Tübingen 1900.

HUNT, P. B. W. STATHER, *Primitive Gospel Sources*. London 1951.

JASTROW, M., *A Dictionary of the Targumim, the Talmud Babli and Yerushalmi, and the Midrashic Literature*. New York–Berlin 1926.

JENTSCH, W., *Urchristliches Erziehungsdenken* (Beitr. z. Förder. christl. Theol. 45:3) Gütersloh 1951.

JEREMIAS, JOACH., *Jerusalem zur Zeit Jesu* I–II B. Göttingen 1923–1937.

—— 'Αμνὸς τοῦ θεοῦ — παῖς θεοῦ, *Zeitschr. f. d. neutest. Wissensch.* 34 (1935), p. 115–123.

—— *Die Gleichnisse Jesu*. (Abhandl. z. Theol. d. A. u. N. T:s 11) Zürich 1947.

—— art. 'Ηλ(ε)ίας, *Theol. Wörterb. z. N. T.* II, p. 930–943.

—— art. 'Ιωνᾶς, *Theol. Wörterb. z. N. T.* III, p. 410–413.

—— art. παῖς θεοῦ, *Theol. Wörterb. z. N. T.* V, p. 653–713.

JOHNSON, SHERMAN E., The Biblical Quotations in Matthew, *Harv. Theol. Rev.* 36 (1943), p. 135–153.

JÜLICHER, A., *Die Gleichnisreden Jesu* I–II. 2. Aufl. Tübingen 1910.

---

[1] Not available.

KAHLE, P., Untersuchungen zur Geschichte des Pentateuktextes, *Theol. Stud. u. Krit.* 88 (1915), p. 399–439.

—— *Masoreten des Westens* II. (Beitr. z. Wissensch. v. A. u. N. T., 3. Folge 14–15), Gütersloh 1930.

—— *The Cairo Geniza.* The Schweich Lectures of the British Academy 1941. London 1947.

—— *Die hebräischen Handschriften aus der Höhle.* Stuttgart 1951.

—— Der gegenwärtige Stand der Erforschung der in Palästina neu gefundenen hebräischen Handschriften: 27. Die im August 1952 entdeckte Lederrolle mit dem griechischen Text der kleinen Propheten und das Problem der Septuaginta, *Theol. Lit. Zeit.* 79 (1954), col. 81–94.

KATZ, P., The Early Christians' Use of Codices instead of Rolls, *Journ. of Theol. St.* 46 (1945), p. 63–65.

—— Das Problem des Urtextes der Septuaginta, *Theol. Zeitschr.* 5 (1949), p. 1–24.

—— *Philo's Bible.* Cambridge 1950.

KAUTZSCH, A. F., *De Veteris Testamenti locis a Paulo Apostolo allegatis.* Leipzig 1869.

KENNARD, J. S. JR., "Hosanna" and the Purpose of Jesus, *Journ. of Bibl. Lit.* 67 (1948), p. 171–176.

KENYON, F. G., *Recent Developments in the Textual Criticism of the Greek Bible.* The Schweich Lectures of the British Academy 1932. London 1933.

—— *The Chester Beatty Biblical Papyri*, Fasc. 5: Numbers and Deuteronomy. London 1935.

—— *Our Bible and the Ancient Manuscripts.* 4th ed. London 1939.

—— *Books and Readers in Ancient Greece and Rome.* 2nd ed. Oxford 1951.

KILPATRICK, G. D., *The Origins of the Gospel according to St. Matthew.* Oxford 1946.

KLAUSNER, J., *Von Jesus zu Paulus.* Jerusalem 1950.

KLEIN, G., *Der älteste christliche Katechismus und die jüdische Propaganda-Literatur.* Berlin 1909.

KLEVINGHAUS, J., *Die Theologische Stellung der Apostolischen Väter zur alttestamentlichen Offenbarung.* (Beitr. z. Förder. christl. Theol. 44:1) Gütersloh 1948.

KLIJN, A. F. J., *A Survey of the Researches into the Western Text of the Gospels and Acts.* Diss. Utrecht. Utrecht 1949.

KLOSTERMANN, E., *Das Matthäusevangelium.* (Handb. z. N. T. 4) 2. Aufl. Tübingen 1927.

KNOX, W. L., Some Hellenistic Elements in Primitive Christianity. The Schweich Lectures of the British Academy 1942. London 1944.

KOOLE, J. L., *De Overname van het Oude Testament door de Christelijke Kerk.* Diss. Amsterdam. Hilversum 1938.

KRAEMER A., Review art. on N. J. Hommes, Het Testimoniaboek, *Philologische Wochenschrift* 58 (1938), col. 73–83.

KRAUSS, S., *Synagogale Altertümer.* Berlin–Wien 1922.

KRAUSS, S., Die Instruktion Jesu an die Apostel, *Angelos* 1 (1925), p. 96–102.

KÜMMEL, W. G., Jesus und der jüdische Traditionsgedanke, *Zeitschr. f. d. neutest. Wissensch.* 33 (1934), p. 105–130.

LACHEMAN, E. R., Apropos of Isaiah 7:14, *Journ. of Bible and Rel.* 22 (1954), p. 43.

LAGARDE, P. DE, *Anmerkungen zur griechischen übersetzung der Proverbien.* Göttingen 1863.[1]

—— *Mittheilungen* (I). Göttingen 1884.

LAGRANGE, M.-J., *Évangile selon Saint Matthieu.* (Études bibliques) 3ème éd. Paris 1927.

—— Évangile selon Saint Marc. (Études bibliques) 4ème éd. Paris 1929.

LEIPOLDT, J., *Die urchristliche Taufe im Lichte der Religionsgeschichte.* Leipzig 1928.

LEVY, J., *Chaldäisches Wörterbuch über die Targumim* I–II. 3. Aufl. Leipzig 1881.

—— *Wörterbuch über die Talmudim und Midraschim* I–IV. 2. Aufl. Berlin–Wien 1924.

LEWIS, AGNES SMITH, *Light on the Four Gospels from the Sinai Palimpsest.* London 1913.

LIEBERMAN, S., *Greek in Jewish Palestine.* New York 5702-1942.

—— *Hellenism in Jewish Palestine.* (Texts and Studies of the Jewish Theol. Sem. of America 18) New York 5711-1950.

LIGHTFOOT, R. H., *Locality and Doctrine in the Gospels.* London 1938.

LÖVESTAM, E., *Äktenskapet i Nya Testamentet.* Diss. Lund. Lund 1950.

LOHMEYER, E., *Das Evangelium des Markus.* (Krit.-exeget. Komm. ü.d. N.T. I:2, 10. Aufl.) Göttingen 1937.

—— Die Offenbarung des Johannes. (Handb. z. N. T. 16) 2. Aufl. Tübingen 1953.

McCOWN, C. C., Codex and Roll in the New Testament, *Harv. Theol. Rev.* 34 (1941), p. 219–250.

McNEILE, A. H., Our Lord's Use of the Old Testament, in *Cambridge Biblical Essays,* ed. H. B. SWETE, p. 217–250. London 1909.

—— *The Gospel according to St. Matthew.* London 1915.

MANN, J., *The Bible as Read and Preached in the Old Synagogue,* I: The Palestinian Triennial Cycle: Genesis and Exodus. Cincinnati 1940.

MANSON, T. W., *The Teaching of Jesus.* 2nd ed. Cambridge 1935.

—— The Argument from Prophecy, *Journ. of Theol. St.* 46 (1945), p. 129–136.

—— The Life of Jesus: A Survey of the Available Material: (4) The Gospel according to St. Matthew, *Bull. of J. Ryl. Libr.* 29 (1945/46), p. 392–428.

—— Review art. on E. G. Selwyn, The First Epistle of St. Peter, *Journ. of Theol. St.* 47 (1946), p. 218–227.

—— The Cairo Geniza, *Dominican Studies* 2 (1949), p. 183–192.

---

[1] Not available.

MANSON, T. W., The Old Testament in the Teaching of Jesus, *Bull. of J. Ryl. Libr.* 34 (1951/52), p. 312–332.

MANSON, W., *The Epistle to the Hebrews.* The Baird Lecture 1949. London 1951.

MARGOLIOUTH, D. S., The Visit to the Tomb, *Expository Times* 38 (1926/27), p. 278–280.

MASSAUX, É., *Influence de l'Évangile de saint Matthieu sur la littérature chrétienne avant saint Irénée.* (Univers. Cathol. Lovan. Diss. Theol. II:42) Louvain-Gembloux 1950.

MASSEBIEAU, E., *Examen des citations de l'Ancien Testament dans l'Évangile selon saint Mathieu.* Paris 1885.[1]

MAURER, F. J. V. D., *Commentarius grammaticus criticus in Vetus Testamentum II.* Leipzig 1838.

MAYBAUM, S., *Die ältesten Phasen in der Entwicklung der jüdischen Predigt.* (Bericht über die Lehranstalt für die Wissenschaft des Judentums in Berlin 19) Berlin 1901.

MERX, A., *Das Evangelium Matthaeus nach der syrischen im Sinaikloster gefundenen Palimpsesthandschrift.* (= IDEM, Die vier kanonischen Evangelien nach ihrem ältesten bekannten Texte 2:1) Berlin 1902.

METZGER, B. M., The Formulas introducing Quotations of Scripture in the New Testament and the Mishnah, *Journ. of Bibl. Lit.* 70 (1951), p. 297–307.

MEZ, A., *Die Bibel des Josephus untersucht für Buch v-vii der Archäologia.* Basel 1895.[1]

MICHAELIS, W., art. ὁδός κτλ., *Theol. Wörterb. z. N. T.* V, p. 42–118.

MICHAUD, H., Les manuscrits hébreux découverts près de la Mer Morte mirage ou réalité?, *Positions Luthériennes*, Suppl. à *Fraternité Evangelique* 1953:11, p. 26–44.

MICHEL, O., *Paulus und seine Bibel.* (Beitr. z. Förder. christl. Theol., 2. Reihe 18) Gütersloh 1929.

—— art. ὄνος, ὀνάριον, *Theol. Wörterb. z. N. T.* V, p. 283–287.

MILIK, J.-T., Fragments d'un Midrash de Michée dans les Manuscrits de Qumran. *Rev. Bibl.* 59 (1952), p. 412–418.

MITCHELL, H. G., *A Critical and Exegetical Commentary on Haggai and Zechariah.* (Intern. Critic. Comm.) Edinburgh 1912.

MOE, OLAF, *Paulus und die evangelische Geschichte.* Leipzig 1912.

—— Fra skole til kirke, *Tidsskrift for Teologi og Kirke* 19 (1948), p. 93–98. (= IDEM, *Kirken i aposteltiden*, p. 11–17. Oslo 1951.)

MOE, OSKAR, *Die Apostellehre und der Dekalog im Unterrichte der alten Kirche.* Gütersloh 1896.

MOFFATT, J., *An Introduction to the Literature of the New Testament.* (International Theological Library). 3rd. ed. Edinburgh 1918.

MONTGOMERY, J. A., The Hexaplaric Strata in the Greek Texts of Daniel. *Journ. of Bibl. Lit.* 44 (1925), p. 289–302.

---

[1] Not available.

MONTGOMERY, J. A., *A Critical and Exegetical Commentary on The Book of Daniel*. (Intern. Critic. Comm.) Edinburgh 1927.

—— Review art. on C. H. Roberts, Two Biblical Papyri in the John Rylands Library, Manchester, *Journ. of Bibl. Lit.* 55 (1936), p. 309–311.

MOORE, G. F., *Judaism in the First Centuries of the Christian Era, the Age of the Tannaim* I–III. Cambridge, Mass. 1927–1930.

MOULE, C. F. D., The Use of Parables and Sayings as Illustrative Material in Early Christian Catechesis, *Journ. of Theol. St.*, New Ser. 3 (1952), p. 75–79.

MUNCK, J., *Untersuchungen über Klemens von Alexandria*. Diss. Copenhagen. (Forsch. z. Kirchen- und Geistesgeschichte 2) Stuttgart 1933.

—— Discours d'adieu dans le Nouveau Testament et dans la littérature biblique, in *Aux sources de la tradition chrétienne*, Mélanges offerts à M. GOGUEL. (Bibliothèque Théologique), p. 155–170. Neuchâtel–Paris 1950.

MURMELSTEIN, B., Die Gestalt Josefs in der Agada und die Evangeliengeschichte. *Angelos* 4, (1932), p. 51–55.

NESTLE, E., Die Fünfteilung im Werk des Papias und im ersten Evangelium, *Zeitschr. f. d. neutest. Wissensch.* 1 (1900), p. 249–254.

—— Über Zacharias in Matth. 23, *Zeitschr. f. d. neutest. Wissensch.* 6 (1905), p. 198–200.

—— He shall be called a Nazarene, *Expository Times* 19 (1907/08), p. 523–524.

—— Matthew xii, 19 — Isaiah xlii, 2, *Expository Times* 20 (1908/09), p. 92–93.

NORDEN, E., *Agnostos Theos*. Berlin 1913.

NYBERG, H. S., Smärtornas man, *Svensk Exegetisk Årsbok* 7 (1942), p. 5–82.

OEPKE, A., *Die Missionspredigt des Apostels Paulus*. (Missionswissenschaftliche Forschungen 2) Leipzig 1920.

ORLINSKY, H. M., On the Present State of Proto-Septuagint Studies, *Journ. of the Amer. Orient. Society* 61 (1941), p. 81–91.

—— The Septuagint — its Use in Textual Criticism, *The Biblical Archaeologist* 9 (1946), p. 21–34.

—— Current Progress and Problems in Septuagint Research, in *The Study of the Bible Today and Tomorrow*, ed. H. R. WILLOUGHBY, p. 144–161. Chicago 1947.

PAYNE SMITH, R., *Thesaurus Syriacus* I–II. Oxford 1879–1901. (Suppl., ed. J. P. MARGOLIOUTH. Oxford 1927.)

PEDERSEN, J., *Israel* I/II (2nd ed.) –III/IV. Copenhagen 1934. — Eng. ed. Copenhagen–London 1926–1940.

PETERSON, E., *Zeuge der Wahrheit*. Leipzig 1937. — Reprinted in IDEM, *Theologische Traktate*, p. 165–224. München 1951.

PLOEG, J. VAN DER, Le Rouleau d'Habacuc de la grotte de 'Ain Fešḫa, *Bibliotheca Orientalis* 8 (1951), p. 2–11.

PLOOIJ, D., The Baptism of Jesus, in *Amicitiae Corolla*, A Volume of Essays presented to J. R. HARRIS (ed. H. G. Wood), p. 239–252. London 1933.

PORTER, J. R., Review art. on C. H. Dodd, According to the Scriptures, *Church Quarterly Rev.* 154 (1953), p. 228–230.

PUUKKO, A. F., Paulus und das Judentum, *Studia Orientalis* (Societas Orientalis Fennica) 2 (1928), p. 1–87.

RABINOWITZ, I., The Second and Third Columns of the Habakkuk Interpretation-Scroll, *Journ. of Bibl. Lit.* 69 (1950), p. 31–49.

—— A Reconsideration of "Damascus" and "390 Years" in the "Damascus" ("Zadokite") Fragments, *Journ. of Bibl. Lit.* 73 (1954), p. 11–35.

RAHLFS, A., *Septuaginta-Studien 2.* Göttingen 1907.

—— Über Theodotion-Lesarten im Neuen Testament und Aquila-Lesarten bei Justin, *Zeitschr. f. d. neutest. Wissensch.* 20 (1921), p. 182–199.

RAHMANI, IGNACE EPHREM II, *Les liturgies orientales et occidentales.* Beyrouth 1929.

REICKE, B., Mika 7 såsom "messiansk" text, med säskild hänsyn till Matt. 10: 35 f. och Luk. 12: 53, *Svensk Exegetisk Årsbok* 12 (1947), p. 279–302.

—— Den primära israelsmissionen och hednamissionen enligt synoptikerna, *Svensk Teologisk Kvartalskrift* 26 (1950), p. 77–100.

—— *Handskrifterna från Qumran (eller 'Ain Feschcha)* I–III. (Symbol. Bibl. Upsal. 14) Uppsala 1952.

—— Nytt ljus över Johannes Döparens förkunnelse, *Religion och Bibel* 11 (1952), p. 5–18.

—— A Synopsis of Early Christian Preaching, in *The Root of the Vine.* Essays in Biblical Theology by A. FRIDRICHSEN *et al.*, p. 128–160. Westminster 1953.

RENGSTORF, K. H., art. διδάσκειν κτλ., *Theol. Wörterb. z. N. T.* II, p. 138–168.

RESCH, A., *Aussercanonische Paralleltexte zu den Evangelien*, I.–III. Theil (1.–5. Heft). (Texte u. Untersuch. z. Gesch. d. altchristl. Lit. 10: 1–5) Leipzig 1893–1897.

RIESENFELD, H., *Jésus transfiguré.* Diss. Uppsala. (Acta Semin. Neotest. Upsal. 16) Lund 1947.

ROBERTS, B. J., *The Old Testament Text and Versions.* Cardiff 1951.

—— Some Observations on the Damascus Document and the Dead Sea Scrolls, *Bull. of J. Ryl. Libr.* 34 (1951/52), p. 366–387.

—— The Dead Sea Scrolls and the Old Testament Scriptures, *Bull. of J. Ryl. Libr.* 36 (1953/54), p. 75–96.

ROBERTS, C. H., *Two Biblical Papyri in the John Rylands Library.* Manchester 1936. (= *Bull. of J. Ryl. Libr.* 20 (1936), p. 219–244.)

—— The Christian Book and the Greek Papyri, *Journ. of Theol. St.* 50 (1949), p. 155–168.

ROBINSON, W., Historical Survey of the Church's Treatment of New Converts with Reference to Pre- and Post-Baptismal Instruction, *Journ. of Theol. St.* 42 (1941), p. 42–53.

ROSENTHAL, F., *Die aramaistische Forschung.* Leiden 1939.

234

ROST, L., *Die Vorstufen von Kirche und Synagoge im Alten Testament*. (Beitr. z. Wissensch. v. A u. N. T., 4. Folge 24) Stuttgart 1938.

—— Der gegenwärtige Stand der Erforschung der in Palästina neu gefundenen hebräischen Handschriften: 12. Bemerkungen zum neuen Habakkuktext, *Theol. Lit. Zeit.* 75 (1950), col. 477–482. — 24. Der "Lehrer der Einung" und der "Lehrer der Gerechtigkeit", *ibm.* 78 (1953), col. 143–148.

RUDBERG, G., *Septuaginta-Fragmente unter den Papyri Osloenses*. (Forhandlinger i Videnskapsselskapet i Kristiania [Oslo] 1923:2) Kristiania 1923.

SAHLIN, H., *Der Messias und das Gottesvolk*. Diss. Uppsala. (Acta Semin. Neotest. Upsal. 12) Uppsala 1945.

SANDAY, W., The Conditions under which the Gospels were written, in their Bearing upon some Difficulties of the Synoptic Problem, in *Oxford Studies in the Synoptic Problem*, ed. W. SANDAY, p. 1–26. Oxford 1911.

SANDERS, H. A.–SCHMIDT, C., (ed.), *The Minor Prophets in the Freer Collection and the Berlin Fragment of Genesis*. (Univ. of Michigan Studies, Humanistic Ser. 21) New York 1927.

SCHAEDER, H. H., art. Ναζαρηνός, Ναζωραῖος, *Theol. Wörterb. z. N.T.* IV, p. 878–884.

SCHLATTER, A., *Das Alte Testament in der johanneischen Apokalypse*. (Beitr. z. Förder. christl. Theol. 16:6) Gütersloh 1912.

—— *Der Evangelist Matthäus*. Stuttgart 1929.

—— *Die Kirche des Matthäus*. (Beitr. z. Förder. christl. Theol. 33:1) Gütersloh 1929.

SCHLIER, H., Zur Mandäerfrage, *Theol. Rundschau*, N. F. 5 (1933), p. 1–34 and 69–92.

SCHNEIDER, C., art. κακολογέω, *Theol. Wörterb. z. N. T.* III, p. 469 f.

SCHOEPS, H. J., *Die jüdischen Prophetenmorde*. (Symbol. Bibl. Upsal. 2) Uppsala 1943. — Reprinted in IDEM, *Aus frühchristlicher Zeit*, p. 126–143. Tübingen 1950.

—— *Theologie und Geschichte des Judenchristentums*. Tübingen 1949.

SCHÜRER, E., *Geschichte des jüdischen Volkes*. I, 3. Aufl. Leipzig 1901; II–III, 4. Aufl. 1907–1909.

SEEBERG, A., *Der Katechismus der Urchristenheit*. Leipzig 1903.

—— *Das Evangelium Christi*. Leipzig 1905.

—— *Die beiden Wege und das Aposteldekret*. Leipzig 1906.

—— *Die Didache des Judentums und der Urchristenheit*. Leipzig 1908.

SEELIGMANN, J. L. (I. L.), Problemen en Perspectieven in het moderne Septuaginta-Onderzoek, in *Jaarber. van het Vooraziatisch-Egyptisch Gezelschap "Ex Oriente Lux"* 7 (1940), p. 359–390e.

—— *The Septuagint Version of Isaiah*. (Mededelingen en Verhandelingen van het Vooraziatisch-Egyptisch Genootschap "Ex Oriente Lux" 9) Leiden 1948.

—— Voraussetzungen der Midraschexegese, in *Vetus Testamentum*, Suppl. 1 (Congress Volume Copenhagen 1953), p. 150–181. Leiden 1953.

SEIDELIN, P., Das Jonaszeichen, *Studia Theologica* 5 (1951), p. 119–131.

SELLIN, E., *Das Zwölfprophetenbuch* I–II. (Komm. z. A. T. 12:1–2) 2. und 3. Aufl. Leipzig 1929–1930.

SELWYN, E. C., *The Oracles in the New Testament*. London 1912.[1]

SELWYN, E. G., *The First Epistle of St. Peter*. 2nd ed. London 1947.

SHERRILL, L. J., *The Rise of Christian Education*. New York 1944.

SIDERSKY, D., Un passage hébreu dans le Nouveau Testament, *Journal Asiatique*, 11ème Sér. 3 (1914), p. 232–233.

—— Les citations de l'Ancien Testament dans les Évangiles, in *Actes du congrès intern. d'hist. des rel. 1923*, II (1925), p. 256–260.

SIMON, M., *Verus Israel*. Étude sur les relations entre chrétiens et juifs dans l'empire romain (135–425). (Bibliotèque des Écoles Françaises d'Athènes et de Rome 166) Paris 1948.

SMITS, C., *Oud-Testamentische Citaten in het Nieuwe Testament*, I: Synoptische Evangeliën. (Collect. Francisc. Neerlandica 8:1) 's-Hertogenbosch 1952.

SOLTAU, W., Zur Entstehung des 1. Evangeliums, *Zeitschr. f. d. neutest. Wissensch.* 1 (1900), p. 219–248.

—— *Unsere Evangelien, ihre Quellen und ihr Quellenwert*. Leipzig 1901.

SPARKS, H. F. D., St. Matthew's References to Jeremiah, *Journ. of Theol. St.*, New Ser. 1 (1950), p. 155–156.

SPERBER, A., האוונגליון ותרגום השבעים לתנ״ד, *Tarbiz* 6 (1934/35), p. 1–29.

—— New Testament and Septuagint, *Journ. of Bibl.Lit.* 59 (1940), p. 193–293.

SPICQ, C., *L'Épitre aux Hebreux* I–II. (Études Bibliques) Paris 1952–1953.

STAERK, W., Die alttestamentlichen Citate bei den Schriftstellern des Neuen Testaments, *Zeitschr. f. wissenschaftl. Theol.* 35 (1892), p. 464–485; 36:1 (1893), p. 70–98; 38 (1895), p. 218–230; 40 (1897), p. 211–268.

STANTON, V. H., *The Gospels as Historical Documents*, I: The Early Use of the Gospels; II: The Synoptic Gospels. Cambridge 1903–1909.

STAUFFER, E., *Die Theologie des Neuen Testaments*. 4. Aufl. Gütersloh 1948.

STEGMÜLLER, O. (ed.), *Berliner Septuagintafragmente*. (Berliner Klassikertexte aus den Staatlichen Museen zu Berlin 8) Berlin 1939.

STENDAHL, K., Martyr. Ordet och saken, *Svensk Teologisk Kvartalskrift* 27 (1951), p. 28–44.

—— Kerygma und Kerygmatisch, *Theol. Lit. Zeit.* 77 (1952), col. 715–720.

STERN, S. M., Notes on the New Manuscript Find, *Journ. of Bibl. Lit.* 69 (1950), p. 19–30.

STRACK, H. L.–BILLERBECK, P., *Kommentar zum Neuen Testament aus Talmud und Midrasch* I–IV:2. München 1922–1928.

STRATHMANN, H., art μάρτυς κτλ., *Theol. Wörterb. z. N. T.* IV, p. 477–520.

STREETER, B. H., *The Four Gospels*. A Study in Origins. London 1924.

STRÖM, Å. V., *Vetekornet*. Diss. Uppsala. (Acta Semin. Neotest. Upsal. 11) Stockholm 1944.

STUMMER, F., *Einführung in die lateinische Bibel*. Paderborn 1928.

SWETE, H. B., *The Gospel according to St. Mark*. London 1898.

—— *An Introduction to the Old Testament in Greek*. Cambridge 1900.

---

[1] Not available.

TASKER, R. V. G., *The Old Testament in the New Testament*. London 1946.

TAYLOR, R. O. P., *The Groundwork of the Gospels*. Oxford 1946.

TAYLOR, V., *The Formation of the Gospel Tradition*. London 1933.

—— *The Names of Jesus*. London 1953.

THACKERAY, H. ST. J., Review art. on R. R. Ottley, The Book of Isaiah to the Septuagint (Codex Alexandrinus), *Journ. of Theol. St.* 10 (1908/09), p. 299–304.

—— *The Septuagint and Jewish Worship*. The Schweich Lectures of the British Academy 1920. 2nd ed. London 1923.

—— *Josephus. The Man and the Historian*. (The Hilda Stich Stroock Lectures at the Jewish Institute of Religion 2) New York 1929.

THOLUCK, F. A. G., *Das Alte Testament im Neuen Testament*. 1. Aufl. Hamburg 1836; 3. Aufl. 1849.

TORREY, CH. C., The Foundry of the Second Temple at Jerusalem, *Journ. of Bibl. Lit.* 55 (1936), p. 247–260.

—— The Biblical Quotations in Matthew, in IDEM, *Documents of the Primitive Church*, p. 41–90. New York–London 1941.

—— *The Lives of the Prophets*. (Journ. of Bibl. Lit., Monogr. Ser. 1) Philadelphia 1946.

—— The Aramaic Period of the Nascent Christian Church, *Zeitschr. f. d. neutest. Wissensch.* 44 (1952/53), p. 205–223.

TORREY, CH. C.–EISSFELDT, O., Ein griechisch transkribiertes hebräisch-aramäisches Alten Testaments aus dem 1. Jahrhundert n. Chr., *Theol. Lit. Zeit.* 77 (1952), col. 249–254.

TOY, C. H., *Quotations in the New Testament*. New York 1884.[1]

TURNER, C. H., ὁ υἱός μου ὁ ἀγαπητός, *Journ. of Theol. St.* 27 (1926), p. 113–129.

TURPIE, D. M., *The Old Testament in the New*. London–Leipzig 1868.[1]

—— *The New Testament View of the Old*. London 1872.[1]

UNGERN-STERNBERG, A. VON, *Der traditionelle alttestamentliche Schriftbeweis "de Christo" und "de Evangelio" in der alten Kirche bis zur Zeit Eusebs von Caesarea*. Halle 1913.

VACCARI, A., Fragmentum Biblicum Saeculi II ante Christum, *Biblica* 17 (1936), p, 501–504.

VAGANAY, L., La question synoptique, *Ephemer. Theol. Lovan.* 28 (1952), p. 238–256.

—— Le schématisme du discours communautaire à la lumière de la critique des sources, *Rev. Bibl.* 60 (1953), p. 203–244.

VENARD, L., art. Citations de l'Ancien Testament dans le Nouveau Testament, *Dictionnaire de la Bible*, Suppl. II (1934), col. 23–51.

VERMÈS, G., La Communauté de la Nouvelle Alliance d'après ses écrits récemment découverts, *Ephemer. Theol. Lovan.* 27 (1951), p. 70–80.

—— Le Commentaire d'Habacuc et le Nouveau Testament, *Cahiers Sioniens* 5 (1951), p. 337–349.[1]

---

[1] Not available.

VIELLIARD, R., Codices et Volumina dans les Bibliotèques juives et chrétiennes. Notes d'iconographie, *Rivista di Archaeologia Cristiana* 17 (1940), p. 143–148.

VIS, A., *The Messianic Psalm Quotations in the New Testament.* Amsterdam 1936.

VISCHER, W., *Das Christuszeugnis des Alten Testaments*, I: Das Gesetz. 7. Aufl. Zürich 1946; II: Die Propheten. 1942.

—— *Die evangelische Gemeindeordnung.* Matthäus 16, 13–20, 28. Zürich 1946.

VÖGTLE, A., *Die Tugend- und Lasterkataloge im Neuen Testament.* (Neutestamentl. Abhandl. 16:4–5) Münster i. W. 1936.

VOGEL, F., Zu Luk. 1,4, *Neue Kirchl. Zeitschr.* 44 (1933), p. 203–205.

VOLLMER, H., *Die Alttestamentlichen Citate bei Paulus.* Freiburg i. B.–Leipzig 1895.

WADDELL, W. G., The Tetragrammaton in the LXX, *Journ. of Theol. St.* 45 (1944), p. 158–161.

WEISS, B., Der Gebrauch des Artikels bei den Gottesnamen, *Theol. Stud. u. Krit.* 84 (1911), p. 319–392 and 503–538.

WELLHAUSEN, J., *Das Evangelium Matthaei*, Berlin 1904.

WEIDEL, K., Studien über den Einfluss des Weissagungsbeweises auf die evangelische Geschichte, *Theol. Stud. u. Krit.* 83 (1910), p. 83–109, 163–195.

WENDEL, C., *Die Griechisch-römische Buchbeschreibung verglichen mit der des Vorderen Orients.* (Hallische Monographien 3) Halle 1949.

WERNER, E., "Hosanna" in the Gospels, *Journ. of Bibl. Lit.* 65 (1946), p. 97–122.

WESSELY, CH., *Les plus anciens monuments du christianisme écrits sur papyrus.* Textes grecs édités, traduits et annotés. (Patrologia Orientalis 4:2) Paris 1908.

WETSTEIN, J. J., *Novum Testamentum Graecum* ... nec non commentario pleniore ex scriptoribus veteribus hebraeis, graecis et latinis historiam et vim verborum illustrante ... I–II. Amsterdam 1751–1752.

WIKENHAUSER, A., *Einleitung in das Neue Testament.* Freiburg i. Br. 1953.

WIKGREN, A., The Targums and the New Testament. *Journ. of Rel.* 24 (1944), p. 89–95.

WILLIAMS, A. LUKYN, *Adversus Judaeous.* Cambridge 1935.

WINDISCH, H., *Der Barnabasbrief.* (Handb. z. N.T., Ergänzungs-Band: Die Apostolischen Väter 3) Tübingen 1920.

WOLFF, H. W., *Jesaja 53 im Urchristentum.* Diss. Halle. Bethel bei Bielefeld 1942.

WOODS, F. H., art. Quotations, *Dictionary of the Bible*, ed. J. HASTINGS, IV (1902), p. 184–188.

ZAHN, TH., *Einleitung in das Neue Testament* I–II. 1st ed. Leipzig 1897–1899, 3rd ed. 1906–1907.

—— *Das Evangelium des Matthäus.* (Komm. z. N.T. 1) 2. Aufl. Leipzig 1905.

238

ZIEGLER, J., *Untersuchungen zur Septuaginta des Buches Isaias.* (Alttesta-
mentl. Abhandl. 12:3) Münster i. W. 1934.
ZIMMERMAN, F., The Last Words of Jesus, *Journ. of Bibl. Lit.* 66 (1947),
p. 465–466.
ZUNTZ, G., On the Opening Sentence of Melito's Paschal Homily, *Harv. Theol.
Rev.* 36 (1943), p. 299–315.

Index of authors

Index of passages